AF529411

POVERTY, GLOBALISATION AND HUMAN DEVELOPMENT

POVERTY, GLOBALISATION AND HUMAN DEVELOPMENT

Edited by
V.B. JUGALE, Ph.D.
Professor & Head, Department of Economics
Shivaji University
Kolhapur - 416 004 (India)

SERIALS PUBLICATIONS
NEW DELHI

First Published - 2005

ISBN: 81-86771-57-3

Published by

Head Office

SERIALS PUBLICATIONS
4, B.S.S. Hall, Khyber Pass Market
Civil Lines, Delhi-110054 (India)
Phone : 23245225
Fax : 91-11-23272135
E-mail: serials@satyam.net.in

Branch Office

4830/24, Prahlad Street, Ansari Road
Darya Ganj, New Delhi-110002 (India)

CONTENTS

Preface ix

PART-I
ECONOMIC REFORMS, DEVELOPMENT AND GLOBALISATION

1. Post-WTO Era: State Activism, Economic Opportunities and Chhallenges 1
   D. K. Nauriyal
2. The Economic Development Landscape Generated by Statistical- Spatial Domain Analysis 54
   Masudul Alam Choudhury & Mohammad Shahadat Hossain
3. Economic Reforms, Inequality and Poverty in Ghana 71
   John V. Mensah & Isaac K. Acheampongb
4. Consumer Interest Under WTO 105
   Geetanjali R Urankar
5. Capital Flows in ASEAN Countries 115
   Gautam Murthy
6. Indian Economy, Globalisation and World Economic Reforms 126
   Geetanjali Sharma & Sandeepa Malhotra
7. Impact of Globalisation on Indian Economy 134
   M. Raja Sekhara Babu
8. India's Foreign Trade with SAARC in the Globalisation ERA: Facts and Possibilities 142
9. Global Property Rights in Genetic Resources: An Econonomic Assessment 164
   *Clem Tisdell**

PART-II
AGRICULTURE, INDUSTRIAL RELATIONS AND TECHNOLOGY

10. Role of Bangladesh Small Industries and Commerce Bank in Promoting Small Scale Enterprises : A Critical Assessment 179
Md. Saiful Islam, Mihir Kumar Das & Md. Khairuzzaman

11. Technology Transfer in International Joint Ventures 202
Ruchi Sharma & T.V.S.Ramamohan Rao

12. The Impact of Agricultural Finance on Agricultural Output in Nigeria 220
Muftau A . Ijaiya & Gafar T. Ijaiya

13. WTO and Indian Agriculture: Issues and Concerns 232
K. Dasarathararamaiah

14. Globalisation: Is it Driving Industrial Relations in Reverse Gear? 255
P. Subba Rao

PART - III
EDUCATION AND WOMEN IN DEVELOPMENT

15. Education and Unemployment in Kerala: Challenges Ahead 273
Dolly Sunny

16. Women in Development: A Case Study on Selected Rural Areas of Bangladesh 287
Saiful Islam & Nourin Shabnam

17. Intra-household Resource Allocation and Bargaining Power of the Women Using Micro-credit in Bangladesh 301
Shahnaz Taranuum Abdullah & Munir Hassan

18. Estimating the Impact of Gender Inequality in Education on the Well-being of Women in Nigeria 346
Gafar T. Ijaiya & I. O. Balogun

19. Education and Health in Kerala 361
P. Arunachalam

20. Women Health Care Burdens and Ill-Being in sub-saharan Africa: Evidence from a Cross-Country Analysis 395
Gafar T. Ijaiya

PART-IV
POVERTY, CHILD LABOUR AND HUMAN DEVELOPMENT

21. World Failing Poverty Pledges: Towards the Millennium Development Goals 413

22. Poverty and Human Developemnt: A Status Report of Andhra Pradesh 431
T. Prabhakar Reddy

23. Poverty and Girl Child Labour: A Study in Brick Kilns 451
Siddhartha Sarkar

24. Eradication of Worst Forms of Child Labour in Hazardous Working Environment: A Case of *Bidi* Factories in Bangladesh 463
M. Zulfiquar Ali Islam & A.H.M. Zehadul Karim

25. Socio-economic Disparity in North-Eastern Regions of India: Prospective Challenges and Opportunities 480
D. Rudra Prakash Pradhan

PREFACE

The structural adjustment programmes are basically the reforms programmes, designed for the socialist and mixed economies. The stablization polices are the policy programmes designed to bring the short term economic balances. The SAP programmes paved the way to liberlisation and globalization for widening the market economies. With the expansion of globalisation programmes, the poverty issues became debatable. The studies reflect mixed reactions about the issue. However, the quality of human development activities along with globalisation processes has preceded the global efforts towards the favourabilities. The individual rationality, in fact, is improving with the introduction of competition in the markets. The market economies normally prefer to have a competition and the transitorv economies, the challenges of the globalisation have been converted into opportunities with proper policy and reforms initiatives essential for maintaining the competition and liberlisation in the system.

The book has been conveniently classified into four broad issues of the globalisation, poverty and human development. The first issue deals with the general reforms and development aspects. The challenges and opportunities of the post WTO era have been discussed with empirical evidences by Nauriyal. The statistical-spatial domain analysis has been made by M.A. Choudhury and M.S. Hussain for accounting the development. Mensah and Acheampongb have studied the Ghana economy in respect of reforms vis-à-vis inequality and poverty in the country. Similar type of study has been carried out by M. Raj Sekhar Babu and Gitanjali Sharma and Sandeep Malhotra in respect of the India's experience during the post reforms period. The consumer's interest generated out of globalisation has been exemplified by Geetanjali R. Urankar. Goutam Murthy and R.P. Pradhan have concentrated their efforts to examine the pros and cons of capital flow in ASEAN countries and India's foreign trade with SAARC countries respectively. Clem Tisdell's study is devoted to intellectual property rights in genetic resources.

The second section of the book deals with the core issues in agriculture, industrial relations and the technological aspects. A critical assessment of a bank in developing the SSIs in Bangladesh has made by Md. Saiful Islam, M.K. Das and Md. Khairuzzaman. The issues of technology transfer in international joint ventures have been discussed by Ruchi Sharma and T.V.S. Ramamohan Rao. The impact of finance and WTO on agricultural practices of Nigeria and India respectively has been exposed by Muftau A. Ijaiya and Gafar T. Ijaiya and K. Dasaratharamaiah, whereas, the issues pertaining to the industrial relations have been discussed by P. Subba Rao.

Part three is devoted to education and women development. The challenges of educated unemployment in Kerala state has been earmarked by Dolly Sunny. The role of rural women in development of Bangladesh rural economy has been discussed by Saiful Islam and Naurin Shabnam. The intra-household resource allocation and bargaining power of Bangladeshi women through micro-credit is the empirical study exhibited by Shahnaz Taranuum Abdullah and Munir Hassan. An effort to measure the impact of gender inequality in education especially on the well-being of the women in Nigeria has been exposed by Gafar T. Ijaiya and I.O. Balogun. Education and health in Kerala and Sub-Saharan Africa has been correlated with reference to the general issues and to that of ill-being and health care burden respectively by P. Arunchalam and Gafar T. Ijaiya.

The last section of the book encounters the issues related to poverty, child care and human development. T. Prabhakar Reddy has discussed the normal relationship between poverty and human development, whereas the relations between poverty and girl child has been discussed by Siddhartha

Sarkar. The hazardous working environment in *bidi* factories and the efforts to eradicate the worst forms of child labour in Bangladesh has been made by M. Zulfiquar Ali Islam and A.H.M. Zehadul Karim. The issues pertaining to the regional disparities in India have been thoroughly discussed by D. Rudra Prakash Pradhan.

The diversified and scattered sub-themes as discussed above are some of the examples of the main theme. There may be further more areas of exposition to discuss the relations with specific country studies. The areas covered in the book will definitely guide to understand the gamut of the subject matter. Of course, the reader's responses to the areas so far discussed in the book will be judicious for continuing the job of publication. The Chief Editor is very gracefully acknowledges the support rendered by S.K. Jha and his team of Serials' family.

Place: Kolhapur
Date: 25th May 2005

Dr. V.B. Jugale
Professor and Head and Dean (SS)

PART-I

ECONOMIC REFORMS, DEVELOPMENT AND GLOBALISATION

1

POST-WTO ERA: STATE ACTIVISM, ECONOMIC OPPORTUNITIES AND CHALLENGES

*D. K. Nauriyal**

INTRODUCTION

The establishment of WTO on January 1, 1995 can be considered as a landmark event in the contemporary economic history, which ceases to be history because of its significant implications for the current and more for future economic scenario. It has closest links to the expectations, ambitions, environment and with almost anything that can affect life on this planet. To some, it signals the onset of a new era of economic prosperity, substantial enhancement in the mutual understanding built up through better interaction made possible by the removal of barriers on the free movement of capital and labour. To some others, it is a new instrument to gain free access to their markets while maintaining barriers to their own markets through newly designed blockades in the form of environmental concerns, sanitary and phyto-sanitary measures. Notwithstanding the fears and mutual suspicion, the common understanding, however, is that if the principles- Trade Without Discrimination, Transparency in Regulations,

* Professor of Economics, Department of Humanities & Social Sciences, Indian Institute of Technology Roorkee, Roorkee. E-Mail : dknarfhs@iitr.ernet.in

Progressive Liberalisation Through Negotiations and Protection Through Tariff Rather than Import Quotas or other types of restrictions enunciated by WTO-are implemented without any bias, they would forge a new era of global economic integration, prosperity and as an offshoot of these the world peace. It may be further realised that the world is changing faster than we realize. Rapid strides in technology, transportation, and communication systems have allowed thoughts, people, goods and services to travel thousands of miles in seconds or hours. This stimulates business flows and development and inventions. The nations not catching up with the rest would have to pay a formidable price in the form of isolation, deprivation, and almost non-existent negotiating leverage vis-a-vis other nations. However, it would be pertinent to put a word of caution here. And it is that the Globalisation is not an end itself rather a means to achieve prosperity, better efficiency and even level playing in the national/ international trade.

GLOBALISATION: WHY THE ONLY CHOICE?

In fact, globalisation of the last decade has not been the result of a blind faith in markets imposed from above but of the utter exhaustion of any alternative vision. In contrast to the failed policies of centrally command and mixed economies, certain countries such as, four East Asian tigers viz., Hong Kong, Singapore, Taiwan, and South Korea have accomplished a remarkable standard of living today, equivalent to that of industrialized nations, with per-capita incomes in Hong Kong and Singapore rivaling those of the wealthiest nations of western Europe, North America and Japan. The picture, in retrospect, appears to be presenting sharp contrast. For instance, while around 97% of the inventions and innovations came from the relatively free economies, the closed economies and mixed economies were/are in the perpetual race for catching up with the west in terms of technology, standard of living and political clout. It appears that the major difference was caused by the fact that while the closed economies have completely suppressed the private entrepreneurial initiatives/

drives, be it the invention and innovation or the entrepreneurial venture, mixed economies never gave them a respectable role as important agents of economic change. This is evident from the wave of nationalization in late sixties and early seventies in many such economies including India. The governments in today's developed countries, on the other hand, not only encouraged private initiatives but also provided all kind of support and acted as facilitator and promoters of such activities. Thus the basic difference was caused by their pro-competition approach as compared to closed and mixed economies. It is because of this pro-competitive bias of the relatively free trade policies that saw substantial gains accruing to those who opened their economies earlier such as Chile, China, Poland, Uganda, Botswana, and Mauritius. This further implies that trade has affected a qualitatively large and robust positive change in the pace of development, and as a corollary, on the incomes. This is evident from the fact that all the nations having promoted competition and following free trade policies are the most developed nations today. A list of countries shown in Annexure–I amply highlight this reality. The well-proved relative success of openness as a policy, compared with protectionism, had spurred a global movement toward unilateral trade liberalization prompting the sixty LDCs since the mid-1980s to lower their barriers to trade without seeking any reciprocity. Such countries are now among the high income developing countries as is evident from Annexure - II. The argument that globalisation is much more about the prosperity rather than deprivation is, therefore, supported not only by economic theory but by decades of hard-earned experience, as well. Researches also confirm a strong link between openness and economic growth. A study of 117 countries has concluded that open economies grew much faster than closed economies. It was found that the developing countries that maintained open economies throughout the 1970s and 80s grew at an average annual rate of 4.5 per cent, compared to an average growth rate of 0.7 per cent for closed economies. As a result, the open developing economies tended to converge toward the slower-growing rich economies, while relatively closed economies did not converge [*Sachs and Warner 1995*]. A more recent study corroborated the above findings. The study reported that trade exerts "a qualitatively large and robust E positive effect on income." In this study of 150 countries, it was concluded that increasing the ratio of trade to gross domestic product by one percentage point raises income per person by between 0.5 and 2 per cent [*Frankel and Romer 1999*]. The Organization for Economic Cooperation and Development (OECD), in its assessment concluded that nations relatively open to trade grew on an average twice as fast as those relatively closed to trade [*OECD 1998*]. These historical evidences establish, beyond doubt, that the regions where poverty and inequality have been the most visible and intransigent for decades such as, Latin America, sub-Saharan Africa, and the Indian subcontinent are the ones which, by and large, followed the policies of autarky. A 1998 study, sponsored by the WTO, has found that global trade and investment flows have actually become less concentrated in the last two decades when adjusted for the growth in world trade. Moreover, authors have found that the concentration of trade and financial flows has fallen among countries that have more rapidly liberalized, whereas it has increased among those that have integrated more slowly. "We argue this shows that marginalisation of individual countries from world markets can be mostly explained by inward-looking domestic policies," they concluded, "and, therefore, that marginalisation is not inherent to the globalisation process [*Low et al 1998*]. The trade statistics highlight that there has been rise in the export as a percentage of GDP in case of countries that have shunned autarky especially after 1990, although the range varies from 0.4 per cent to 16 per cent. [*WTO 2000; Simao Davi Silber, 2000*]. While productivity and efficiency are expected to remain at the core of new world economy the greatest beneficiaries of globalisation are the long-suffering consumers in those nations that had been 'protected' from global competition. Globalisation has expanded the range of choice, improved product quality, and exerted downward pressure on prices. It delivers an immediate gain to workers by raising the real value of their wages. It transfers wealth from formerly protected producers to newly liberated consumers, with the gains to consumers exceeding the loss to producers because the deadweight losses to the economy are recaptured through efficiency gains. A typical example of how consumers of 'protected' markets have lost all through these years is that of the continuation of the production of standard Ambassador car in India that is based on the Morris Oxford, a make that was in vogue in the UK four decades ago. Other ailments, which had imposed heavy costs on the economy, were production inefficiencies and technological obsolescence arising out of complacency in a market well protected from internal and external competition. In case of India strong restrictions on imports coupled with the large domestic market with virtual absence of measures to protect the interest of consumers, and license and quotas virtually promoting monopolies, firms did not have sufficient incentives to increase efficiency or accomplish international quality standards. In a way, low degree of competition in some areas and virtual absence of the same in other areas could be blamed more for promotion of internal technological obsolescence and production inefficiencies than the protection from external competition through tariff and non-tariff protective measures. Promotion of competition, therefore, needs to be at the core of policies aimed at privatisation and globalisation of the economy. This would allow exports to become an engine of growth and help the country to take advantage of the disciplining role of international markets.

The future impact of globalisation would vary from country to country and within countries depending on the approach and efficacy of the policy instruments. But efforts to resist the powerful technological and economic forces behind globalisation by appealing to protectionism are misdirected, and in the long run, counterproductive, if lessons from historical evidences and current scenario are to be learnt. One evidently most viable alternative would be to redouble the efforts at international economic cooperation and strengthen the architecture of global/regional/national institutions to promote competition and investment and prosperity for all, rather than fearing the future. This appears to be the best way to ensure that the benefits of globalisation spread to all corners of the world and to all sections of society.

There may still be many arguments against opening up of the economy that can be validated on many evident convincing grounds, yet given the extremely limited choices that the nations do have after the formation of WTO, falling in line appears to be the best option. This is truer of the nations that have not formed or joined either any custom union or free trade association or any other organisation having any semblance to the regional trading blocks. Although such a proposition is not a perfect substitute of WTO, it definitely provides some flexibility and a strong negotiating leverage, provided the market of such a block is large enough to promote efficiencies and the economies are not of overwhelmingly overlapping nature. Notwithstanding, before examining the challenges and opportunities thrown by strong globalisation movement, it would be pertinent to examine some of the arguments against globalisation, especially in the context of India.

When we focus on India with a view to examine the possible fallouts of the implementation of WTO norms from January. 1, 2005 the deadline for the removal of an overwhelming majority of restrictions on the trade by all the member nations except for the least developed countries, we need to understand the dynamics of Indian economy, in general, and various economic sectors, in particular, in the backdrop of changed scenario. Developing an understanding of the same would either help us to evolve alternatives or choose the best possible among the available options.

THE FEARS: HOW WELL PLACED THEY ARE?

The most obvious fact remains that different economic sectors, equipped with powerful political lobbies, cutting across the party line, have enjoyed an attractive domestic market without significant internal competition for long, almost for the past five decades, and have started getting a semblance to exposure forced upon by the changing domestic and global environment, only after 1990. While various pressure groups are lobbying for the causes that they espouse, the consumer is ignored in the whole debate on the contention that consumer is also engaged in some employment and when the employment avenues available to the consumers would be adversely affected by WTO norms he/she would not be in a position to exercise his/her buying power to make choice among the wide range of goods and services available in the market owing to removal of import restrictions. The argument is not out of place provided a close link between removal of trade, other restrictions and increase in the unemployment could be established. Such a contention probably is based on the assumptions as given below:

1. Cheap import of industrial and agricultural products from other countries would out-compete Indian firms and as a consequence hurt the Indian economic interests and displace a large chunk of the labour force. Similarly, allowing the foreign firms to enter the domestic market in the service sector (such as telecom, insurance and financial) would cause further damage to India. It would, however, be appropriate to scrutinise the validity of the argument contained in the assumption. The argument holds water if other countries are dumping their products/services in order to kill competition in the domestic market and there are no safeguards against such an unfair practice. It may be mentioned here that under WTO norms, a wide range of safeguards are available to impose anti-dumping duties on such imports, provided proper procedure is followed to establish the case of dumping. However, if cheap imports are not the cases of dumping (or are the byproducts of better technology) then there cannot be any valid argument to protect the domestic industries that are low in efficiency and pass on this inefficiency to consumers in the form of technologically sub-standard/obsolete yet high priced products and limited choices. Since the problem arises out of inefficiency, which itself is an offshoot of lack of competition, it must be dealt with that way and cannot be used as a valid argument for restricting imports.

Another defence is, more or less, an extension of the infant industry argument which is stretched to plead that domestic players can not compete with well-established international players and would, therefore, either stand out-competed or would be acquired by bigger firms. While it is true that international players possess superior technology, financial power, and marketing skills as compared to their Indian counterparts the fact remains that Indian companies can grow up to match the profile of these international players by acquiring skills that would help the former to compete with the latter. Here government's help in the form of proper regulations to correct for market imperfections and incomplete information, and a sound yet closely monitored financial system can help the domestic firms considerably. Another fact is that more than 80 per cent of the innovations emanate from individuals and small companies and not from the multinational corporations. In fact, most of the innovations are of incremental addition to the technology resulting in improved quality, better performance, higher productivity, higher customer satisfaction and reduced costs and such innovations are not impossible to realize as is evident from the success of Indians in the Silicon Valley. Nirma is another classical example of how an unknown, cash strapped small company can grow up at the expense of multinationals by rightly understanding needs of the consumers and employing superior marketing skills for which one need not to be educated at the Harvard Business School (HBS) or Indian Institute of Managements (IIMs). Other worth mentioning instances of innovation-driven Indian business successes that have paled even some MNCs, in their drive for growth and markets are Reliance, TVS, Dr Reddy's Labs, Ranbaxy, Infosys, TCS, Wipro, NIIT etc. In the new competitive landscape, businesses have only two choices - either try and surpass the best of their competitors or simply choose to focus on innovation and create their own benchmarks and customers and a good number of Indian concerns have demonstrated that they can match the best in the world. If we look at our neighbourhood, we have the examples of East Asian tigers that successfully nurtured their industries to match the competence of multinationals. *The third defence* of maintaining high barriers on cheaper import is that the valuation procedure of goods and services is not transparent/distorted, therefore a clear cut case of dumping can never be established even though that there may be genuine case of dumping. This argument has its genesis in the sudden upsurge in Chinese exports to India. However, since China has rejoined WTO, she will have to streamline her process of valuation of goods and services and make it totally transparent. India is not alone in this and a combined pressure would force china to fall in line. The argument, therefore, has lost its sheen due to change in circumstances. When it comes to displacement of the employed labour force due to stiff competition from the cheaper imports the argument remains that inefficiencies cannot be protected on this ground. Yet in view of the fact that the displacement of employment may inflict heavy social and political costs, there is a need to take some measures to protect the interests of the vulnerable sections, One such measure could be the development of a 'social security net' (selective state transfers for the needy) in order to ensure that such a displacement does not take people to the brink of starvation. Similarly, a system could be evolved where appropriate training is imparted to the workers to upgrade their skills and find better employment. This would ensure job surety rather than job security that is one of most important reasons for the ailing public sector. Nevertheless in view of the fact that such a crisis has prolonged in Argentina, Zimbabwe, South Africa and most of the nations of former Soviet block, there is an increasing feeling that leaving everything to the market in the name of allowing structural readjustments could be dangerous. Another valid argument in this case could be the tariff and non-tariff barriers maintained by developed countries, which is one of the major problem areas that need to be corrected through WTO.

2. The high economic strength and negotiating leverage of the developed countries on account of regional trade blocks such as, NAFTA and ECM would make WTO as a forum for gaining access to the markets of the developing countries without extending such benefits to them. Even if such provisions are extended, they are made ineffective by setting stringent norms pertaining to the environmental safety, sanitary and phyto-sanitary measures and injury to the domestic industries. The assumption appears to be convincing in view of the ground realities. Growing concern among developing countries about the predominant position enjoyed by the developed countries, especially US in the WTO negotiations has also put a serious question mark on the ability of WTO to ensure a fair and equitable treatment to developing nations. However, here available options need to be evaluated. The first option could be the joining or formation of the regional trading block where India does not stand a good chance given the prevailing politico-economic dynamics in South Asia and South East Asia. One way is to forge unity with China, world's fastest growing market in order to negotiate on favourable terms at WTO. This opportunity also appears to be slim for three reasons:
   (i) Both the economies are of overlapping nature and, therefore, competing ones,
   (ii) China, being economically and politically stronger, stands a better chance to brave this competition on her own.
   (iii) China may have no real interest to forge unity with India, being its geopolitical rival.

Given the absence of any other viable alternative the best solution lies in joining other developing countries on case-to-case basis to make efforts towards lowering the non-tariff barriers erected / to be erected by the developed countries.

3. Globalisation would favour wealthy class and as a result further raise already high disparities in the distribution of income and wealth. Historical evidences do not suggest

any close connection between globalisation and deprivation. They, in fact, suggest the other way round.

Therefore, when the world is moving in one historically proved right direction, India cannot afford to remain where she was or instead move in the opposite direction. Our opting out of WTO, in any case, would not change the rules of the game that will be followed by the entire world. It could mean on the other hand, only signing bilateral agreements with every trading partner, which in turn would surely be dictated by the balance of 'power' and other trade-offs between the two. The worth mentioning example in this regard is that of China which opted out of WTO earlier. She had a tough time while negotiating bilateral agreements with USA every year. It ended up signing much harder IPR regime with the US than even smallest of nations under WTO umbrella. The result is that China rejoined the WTO. The fact remains that the privatisation and globalisation are the stark realities facing the nation. Realising the benefits of enhanced competition through opening up of the economies, many nations formed regional trading blocks in order to move towards this direction. India went for it only when it became almost inevitable. An idea of the various trading blocks in the world can be had from the Annexure-III. It, however, does not imply that globalisation has just one model of development i.e., Washington Consensus [*Williamson 1990*]. This model, which produced fine results till the decade of 60s, started demonstrating large inadequacies and imperfections probably because the changing dynamics of economic forces were not addressed by the static classical approach. This late realisation inflicted heavy economic, social and political injuries on the developing countries opting for opening of their economies especially after 1980s. Their experiences have forced the nations as well as Bretton Woods institutions to look for alternatives.

The next section focuses on this issue in order to find the first best alternative to the existing arrangement of Washington Consensus'

POST-WASHINGTON CONSENSUS : THE STARTING POINT FOR PRIVATISATION AND GLOBALISATION

To ensure that the policies of privatisation and globalisation work well and the transition is less painful, less complex, and socio-politically less risky, it would be important to learn lessons from the failure/success of the nations that have embarked upon globalisation at different points of time. It is important because of the possibility of domestic business/manufacturing/service concerns going haywire and unemployed rank swelling up as a consequence of hasty and indiscriminate privatisation and globalisation. The social and economic costs, arising out of such actions, on such countries could simply be unacceptable and in certain cases unbearable. The situation could be most grim, where it is most likely to happen, in Sub-Saharan Africa and South Asia where 40 per cent and 46.3 % of the population respectively still live below poverty line. [*World Bank 2000*]. It may be noted that such population in the above regions constitutes 58% of the total world population below poverty line. One example how a hasty privatisation and globalisation can hit the general welfare of the workers can be seen from a recent study from CUTS (1999). It examined the impact of trade liberalization on the Indian manufacturing sector. Contrary to the fundamentals of the Washington Consensus which was reached in the early 1980s, and found that formal manufacturing sector employment in India grew faster after trade liberalization in the mid 90s (employment doubled from 3.8% to 9.4%) but wages fell. Equally disturbing is the fact that employment in India's informal manufacturing sector suffered a decline. Given that the formal sector in India accounts for only 1.3% of the work force, the decline in the informal sector far outweighed the increase in formal employment. Therefore, before embarking upon any policy measures, the pragmatic approach calls for examining whether the poor population of such a magnitude is going to be worse off as a consequence of such policy measures even in the short run. Taking a leaf from the experiences of others can also be helpful to avoid repeating the mistakes. For this purpose, there could be a good number of countries that qualify to be considered for such an analyses yet the stunning success of the regional cluster of East Asian countries known as East Asian Tigers make them one pertinent case in point. These all countries pursued free trade and liberalization with some modification in what is referred to as the Washington consensus [*Williamson 1990*]. In his well-articulated WIDER annual lecture at Helsinki, Stiglitz [*Stiglitz 1998*] points out the following fundamental reasons, which essentially are major deviation from the economic orthodoxy of 'Washington Consensus', for the fast growth of East Asian economies:

1. Pursuance of an industrial policy that aimed at narrowing down and subsequently closing the technological gap between them and the most advanced countries. [*World Bank 1993*]. This was helped by the proactive role of governments in providing universal education, with greater emphasis on science and technology education that led to their transformation from largely agrarian to industrialised economies. [*Stiglitz 1998*]. The fast pace of development in these economies is known world over. An idea of their thrust into the high-technology areas can be had from the fact that the Share of High-Technology Exports (aircraft, office and computing machinery, communications equipment, and drugs and medicines) in over all exports of manufactures from East Asian Tigers went up from 15% in 1980 to over 35% by 1996.
2. Creation and maintenance of a robust financial system to mobilise savings and allocate capital efficiently. The financial restraints imposed by these countries, leading to 'increased franchise values of banks, discouraging them from taking unwarranted risks', although imposed some economic costs, provided better functionality to the economic system. Abolition of a large number of these restraints along with government inaction just before the crisis could be largely attributed to the financial crisis in late 90s. [*Stiglitz 1998*]. It may be mentioned here that the liberalization of the Financial Sector by these countries in accordance with the Washington Consensus, opened the

flood gates of 'hot money' into the Latin American countries, South Africa, Zimbabwe, East European countries, and East Asia in mid-90. The 'flow' was high and the corresponding investment avenues were so low that the situation became practically unmanageable. Even those countries which were most religiously following the prescriptions of Washington advisors suddenly found themselves unable to determine their own policies without reference to whether the policies would attract or repel international capital. The crises in Asia's 'tiger' economies, for example, showed how developing countries that allow an inflow of foreign money into their financial markets are vulnerable to disastrous, panicky withdrawals, especially if they haven't already put a developed sound banking systems in place.

Another fine example where state's pragmatic activism has fueled spectacular economic growth is that of Japan. [*Ohno and Ohno 1998*]. A comparison of Chines and Russian approaches to privatisation and liberalisation is also a notable case in point. It may be pertinent to mention that a fall in the incomes and consumption level of Russia from its level a decade ago and remarkable rise in these parameters in China can also be ascribed to the their altogether divergent approaches. Other determinants apart, one important point is that the China enhanced the scope of domestic competition with privatization of public sector. Russia, on the other hand, went indiscriminately to privatise most of state-run enterprises without creating/strengthening the conducive institutional base and regulatory framework to facilitate competition. Experiences of Latin American countries in the 1980s, Central and Eastern Europe (CEE) in the late 90s also reveal that market-oriented reforms will be ineffective, if they lack an adequate politico-institutional foundation. All these and other cases underline one pertinent point and it is that the existence of a sound financial institutional base (as opposed to financial liberalization) and building up of government's regulatory capacity to facilitate competition to overcome asymmetric information and market imperfections, are important factors to maximize the gains from privatization and globalisation. This is what is called as post-Washington consensus or currently prevailing thinking as opposed to dated Washington consensus **[Williamson 1990].** It may be mentioned that Washington Consensus rejects state's proactive role and assigns the minimalist, non-interventionist position to the state. However, many of the gains predicted by the Washington Consensus are more of ideological rather than structural nature, as the promise of dynamic efficiency gains, cheaper goods and job creation have not materialized, more so in recent times. And this has happened with the advanced countries such as New Zealand (compound annual growth rates for 1997-2002 at 1.1%) and Sweden (compound annual growth rates for 1997-2002 at 1.3%) which can boast of skilled workforce, sophisticated capital market, access to some of the best technology in the world, a modern government and an excellent infrastructure. However, the evolution of post-Washington consensus has paved the way for more realistic viewpoint that government actions must complement that of the markets as without a pragmatic government and facilitating state institutions, free economy can not thrive, thereby leaving majority of people in already poor countries with much less resources than what they had before the onset of liberalization. The old dogmatic approach of market and the state as mutually exclusive mechanisms of resource allocation, rather than seeking for complementary, has already imposed unbearable cost on the nations and shattered the credibility of world economic institutions. The experiences have demonstrated that economic reforms in most LDCs and economies in transition have proved to be less effective or even failed without a credible commitment to development and an institutional base as its starting point. In this regard, it would also not be out of place to identify the fundamental reasons of the failure of Washington Consensus prescription as it helps to avoid repeating mistakes in future. Based upon the various experiences of a divergent set of economies, it appears that Washington Consensus has erred in following areas:

(i) Too much focussing on inflation diverted attention from other important sources of macroeconomic instability such as weak financial systems and an improper sequencing of financial liberalization. [*McKinnon 1992*].

(ii) The state minimalism neglected the need for government intervention, which results from the existence of externalities, scale economies, incomplete markets, and imperfect information.

(iii) It ignored its social and political spillovers of the prescription and hence the interdependence of the economy and the polity; i.e. the fact that economic institutions and activities are embedded in a complex fabric of social and political institutions.

(iv) It neglected the role of quality governance in the policy formulation, implementation, enforcement and sustainability. Liberalisation and globalisation are not just the matter for technical experts to get the prices right, its about fostering acceptability of the reforms and developing capabilities and capacities, political and bureaucratic, and motivation to implement and enforce appropriate policies. [*Aoki et al. 1997, Rodrik 1995, Stiglitz, 1997*].

The success of the Japanese in the late 60s and East Asian economies recently has strongly demonstrated that the development is possible, and successful development requires, or at least is enhanced by, government undertaking appropriate policies that go well beyond simply 'getting out of the way of the market.' While there remains an active debate about what are the precise lessons to be learned, and to what extent the experiences of East Asia are replicable elsewhere, there remains little doubt that government played a critical, catalytic role. Today, even the World Bank [*World Bank 1997*] concedes "that development requires an effective state, one that plays a catalytic, facilitating role, encouraging and complementing the activities of private businesses and individuals." The Bank concludes, "state-dominated development has failed. But so has stateless development (...). History has repeatedly shown that good government is not a luxury but a vital necessity" [*World Bank 1997*].

OPPORTUNITIES AVAILABLE

While WTO has created considerable apprehensions, it has created immense opportunities as well. Spotting business opportunities and timely action upon them, keeping in view the global market, would decide who would gain most and how fast from the globalisation. While appropriate action on the part of the nation(s), business organisations and international community may address most of the misapprehensions; the output of the globalisation would primarily be decided by the drive of the different economic actors to meet the challenges and cash upon the opportunities. In the context of India, despite all the apprehensions, Indian market remains a favourite playing field for Indian firms provided that they shed their weight fast, become consumer savvy without any further loss of time and work with smart efficiency. They are likely to remain strong, especially in those areas where after-sale service network is required to be strong and response time is much less. To the MNCs or other foreign firms, it may not be cost-effective to develop their own distribution network at least in the short run. Therefore, they may opt to leverage upon the existing network of the Indian companies through mergers/acquisitions/strategic alliances/ outsourcing. This, however, would only be a short breather since long-term survival and growth fundamentally depend upon their fast reorganisation and restructuring for providing world level product/services to consumers. If they do so, multinational players would take much more time than what they take today to establish themselves in the Indian market. Besides, a fast growing middle income group, a large domestic market and expected accelerated pace of development would ensure that the smart Indian players would have enough space to grow global. Another opportunity that might provide a viable breathing space to rework the strategies and establish themselves as world-class competitors is by focusing on the niche markets where multinationals or other foreign giants may not have much of the interest. For example, BHEL may concentrate on small and medium sized turbines market world-over instead of spending considerable energy on the market for large size turbines, although it may keep registering its presence in the market for large turbines as well. After establishing itself in these niches, it would be better placed to offer a tough fight to the big players in the large turbine markets. Another way, more specifically for the relatively lesser established players, would be to enter into strategic alliances with the leaders in technology especially in those areas where local presence of the firms would be mandatory due to the need to provide after-sale service / solutions for the product/consultancy service supplied. Some of the future opportunities for Indian business *per se* are listed below:

(i) First being the fast development of the service and technology-intensive industries. In fact, emergence of such industries and their fast increasing importance in the international trade has changed the basic perception about the comparative advantage based upon the labour productivity (Recardian concept) and resource endowment (Heckscher-Ohlin theorisation). A look at the export composition of the newly industrialised economies (NIEs) may prove to be an eye opener in this regard. For instance, the share of such industries has gone up from 15% in 1980 to 35% by 1996 in the east Asian exports. The increasing importance of technology intensity is true for almost all types of industries, particularly for pharmaceutical industry. For example, in the post-2005 era also technological component is expected to play a vital role in terms of delivering the drugs at the exact site in the human body, thus potentiating their action with the least of the adverse effects. Formulations with a new delivery system or a highly specialized system, like the multi-cell-multilayer microdialysis cell technology or timed release are highly technology intensive and would be in great demand in the near future. The revolution to this effect is expected to take place in all the industry spheres. Technological advances in computers and telecommunications have already paved the way for new information-based economies. While work on the nano technologies would be expedited, better system integration and process intensification appears to be frontrunner at the moment. Therefore, efforts must be directed towards achieving greater degree of efficiency through process intensification and product innovation.

(ii) A greater movement of capital accompanied by technology would expand opportunities for job seekers, consumers and all other stakeholders. Capital now moves with startling speed around the world. Each day over $1 trillion is traded in a global foreign exchange market that never closes. Investment is chasing opportunities irrespective of location and boundaries, as the global investors are forcing organisations to deliver value. However, the movement of capital has to be facilitated through a sound internal financial regulatory network.

(iii) Rapid and intensive technological changes shall substantially increase the demand for better-educated and better skilled workers because of the creation of new and better- paying jobs. The recent trends in regard of outsourcing of operations, which have created ripples world-wide; more so in US, is likely to continue in future as globalisation would force the firms to cut down costs. Apart from many ways of doing so, outsourcing remains one of the important alternatives. Despite all hue and cries, outsourcing has a strong economic logic and therefore, there is every probability that it would brave the opposition from various quarters. The fast emergence of call centers in India also serves as an indicator of future relocation of economic opportunities.

(iv) Intellectual property rights are now more important. The fast emerging fields such as micro-electronics, computer software, telecommunications, civil aviation, new materials, robotics and bio-technology are knowledge intensive and could be penetrated and dominated by any visionary entrepreneur and are not the prerogatives of only big corporations. It may be pertinent to note that the sources of innovations and inventions are not the big corporations, as is commonly believed, but the smaller firms and individuals. According to the Pasadena-based Patent & Licence Exchange, trading in intangible assets in the United States has risen from $15 billion in 1990 to $100 billion in 1998, with an increasing proportion of the rewards going to small firms and individuals. Several big, established 'ideas facilitators and executors' such as Microsoft, Sony, 3M and Procter and Gamble have had dry spells recently as compared to what was achieved by individuals and smaller firms. Even the innovations of big corporations may not endure for a long time, as competing products might be introduced in the market without loss of much time. For instance, what took Gillette to spent 10 years and $1 billion to develop its new Mach 3 razor; it took a British supermarket chain only about a year to produce a reasonable imitation.

(v) There is an increasing use of information technology (IT) to transact business intra-company, across the extended supply chain, technical applications and inter-company affairs. The products and services, by and large, would be IT enabled where India has a competitive advantage. The globalisation must open new vistas for Indian IT industry. It may be mentioned here that India exported $6 billion worth of software in 2002 - accounting for 13 per cent of the country's total exports. Over the past 5 years the annual growth rate for India's software exports has been 45 per cent. And there is every reason to believe that it will keep on growing. The Software Engineering Institute at Carnegie Mellon University gives its "top quality" ranking to only 32 software companies in the world of which 17 are based in India.

(vi) With the phasing out of multi-fibre arrangement (MFA) by the end of 2004, the most critical textile items would be free of quota restrictions in markets like the US, the EU and Canada. This is likely to result in approximately US$ 100 billion of additional world trade, as a result of which, world trade is likely to touch US$ 500 billion by 2005 the emerging trend is likely to be the consolidation of multiple sourcing into few key-suppliers. The basic advantages of Indian textile sector such as, easy availability of cotton-based raw materials, a well-entrenched spinning and weaving industry supplying high quality fabric, ability to quickly adjust to demand, a virtual monopoly in embellishment and a wide merchandise line may be cashed upon, provided disparities in India's textile taxation structure, high turnaround time due to the manufacturing system, and lack of facilitating infrastructure are quickly overcome. While the flawed policy of restricting garment industry to the small scale sector has been given up in 2002, domestic produces of fabrics and apparel may have to form joint consortium in order to make smart use of technology in order to realise benefits of economies of scale. Export strategies could focus on the niche markets (such as fashion markets with shorter lead-time) in developed countries to mass markets (with longevity of the products) in developing countries. In fact, the second kind of market while suiting to Indian advantage of producing for mass markets would also help to generate enough revenue to invest in developing products for highly profitable niche markets. This may also necessitate that Indian mills must graduate from fabric export to apparel exports. It may be mentioned here that currently China has assumed undisputed leadership with garments export of the staggering value of $50 billion (with a growth of over 20% per annum). It is way ahead of Mexico and India with the exports worth $12 billion and $ 4.8 billion respectively (2003 figures).

(vii) Market would become more specialised and the value addition would determine the growth. The value addition rather than the material would become more important and therefore, role of technology would assume unprecedented importance. The packaging would be as important as the product because exporters could be discriminated against owing to stringent packaging standards in the developed markets.

(viii) Huge potential for export of services like Data Processing & Software, Computer Services, Utility Management, Advertising and Promotion, Design Services, Feasibility Studies, Health care Services, Market Research & Management, Consultancy, Oil & Gas Services, Printing & Publishing Services, Educational Services, Research & Development Projects, Surveying and Technical Consultancy, Architectural Services, Legal Service, Equipment Maintenance & Repair, Engineering Services etc.

(ix) Development of 'enabling services' such as, telecommunications, insurance, accounting, and banking would grow at a phenomenal rate providing for fast communication and efficient banking and insurance services where India can capitalize upon her strengths.

(x) The possibility of industries to shift closer to the top scientific and technology centres would also create meaningful job opportunities. The trend would further gravitate towards Asia more specifically India and China. Export of R&D and manufacturing operations to India and China where skills required are available on cheaper price especially after introduction of product patent worldover appears to be a natural destination for such purposes. Earlier, the lack of proper protection law constrained MNC investment in these regions, as most of the critical information is intangible and employee specific. China has already shown that the right infrastructure, appropriate legal protection framework, cheaper labour, and right politico-economic climate are enough reasons for the MNCs to invest in the post-WTO era. The fact is that, today 18 of the world's top 20 pharmaceutical companies have set-up their manufacturing and R&D facilities in China. Novo Nordisk, Boheringer Mannheim, Merck, Aventis all have their largest R&D centers and manufacturing facilities of Asia in China. Recently, Intel Corporation has indicated its decision to set up its chip fabrication in India with the investment provision of $2 billion. It has already its chip design facilities in India with an investment of $100 million.

(xi) Many large selling drugs are going off-patent by 2006 and this would create new opportunities for Indian companies to manufacture such drugs. One recent estimate suggests that only 15 per cent of the Indian drug market will be covered by patents after 2005 and will be subjected to price premiums as a result. The remaining 85 per cent of the market will continue to be exposed to the full impact of generic competition. Besides pharmaceuticals, India does have a competitive advantage in petrochemicals, specialty chemicals, agrochemicals, consumer chemicals, and bio-chemicals. This advantage would help them to have better access to markets, which were hitherto relatively inaccessible. And thus it leaves out the opportunity for the company to cash upon its process research or marketing skills and generate profits from old molecules to fund its future research so that both i.e., competitive position and competitive preparedness could be further strengthened. The country would gain in terms of efficiency, employment and increased fiscal revenue. Other growth avenues are: domestic bulk drug market, contract manufacturing for MNCs and forward integration into prescription formulations as well as OTC products. Internationally serving as a bulk drug-sourcing base for MNCs and global generic majors, by developing patent non-infringing processes for drugs on which the patent is set to expire. Also manufacturing advanced APIs provides growth opportunity where Indian companies currently enjoy advantage due to certified facilities and well-trained staff in process engineering of drugs in comparison to China. Indian manufacturers by focusing on high growth therapeutic segments and OTC formulations phytomedicines and biopharmaceuticals can further strengthen their position. Internationally, opportunities exist for Indian companies for serving as a sourcing hub for global majors and supplying to the generic market of the developed nations. Already, some Indian players (DRL, Ranbaxy) are aggressively filing ANDAs and product dossiers with the regulatory authorities in the countries concerned. However, pre-requisites here are cost-effectiveness and possession of quality-certified facilities, which India is already having as compared to China. It is a also a myopic view that multinationals will dominate the industry, as players are emerging at all levels. However, when it comes to the general public welfare, the scenario is worrisome as is pointed out by a recent research report [*Chaudhuri et al 2003*]. The study infers that the concerns about the potentially adverse welfare effects of TRIPS (Trade Related Intellectual Property Rights), due to upward price adjustment by the patent holders in developing countries, are valid. It was further reported that a substantial fraction of the total welfare loss is attributable to the loss of variety. The switching of expenditure from a relatively expensive marketed by a multinational to the close substitutes supplied by domestic firms was found to have a limited role in containing consumer welfare loss. It concluded that the claim that adverse effects arising from the introduction of a patent in a particular market would be mitigated by the availability of close therapeutic substitutes is thus only valid if there are patent-expired substitutes available within fairly narrowly defined therapeutic categories. Although drug companies would try to tap such segments by increasing availability of the drugs by widening their distribution reach, the possibility of a health care landscape which may go beyond the reach of the poorest of the poor definitely calls for adequate safeguards.

(xii) Increase in exports would lead to a substantial rise in the wages as export industries are generally found to be paying better to the workers. A research study shows that the US exports support jobs that pay 12 to 18 per cent higher than comparable positions in non-exporting firms [*Spero 1996*]. These countries need to take export-oriented growth strategy. In this regard, textiles, ready-made garments, and agricultural products assume importance in the exports of many of these countries. Here, export credit; export credit guarantees, and insurance programmes become quite important.

To the extent the opportunities would be utilised to their advantage by the main players of Indian manufacturing and businesses, apart from overcoming the challenges indicated above and described in the proceeding section, also depend on:

(a) Their knowledge of the trade rules and the rights that these give and the obligations they impose.

(b) Their knowledge of the new opportunities, which are being constantly created by changing dynamics of economic forces.

(c) The initiative they show in bringing to the notice of their governments their problems in selling, so that governments can raise the issues at appropriate levels under WTO.

(d) The proactive role of government as regulator (as opposed to controller) and facilitator.

CHALLENGES AHEAD

As are there immense opportunities so are the challenges. Opportunities could only be materialised by shaping up for challenges, working out right strategies, implementing them within the deadlines and constantly reorienting them to accommodate evolving realities of changing economic scenario. The strategies so worked out must have reference to markets and opportunities across the world as a whole. In fact, there is no economic activity in the world that will go unaffected by WTO and its agreements. The earlier we understand this the better it is. The belief that it is something to do with industries or for people who are in international trade only, should be vigilantly guarded against for what it is an illusion. It is as important for common public, farmers, scientists, doctors, singers, and writers as is for an industry, a trader, a banker or a sundry service provider. The reality stands that the business world is moving and moving fast towards uniformity, by which norms, standards, rules, and practices are defined and enforced with respect to regions, or the world as a whole, rather than within the bounds of nation-states. In the post-WTO scenario, therefore, it is critical for the government, businesses, and other stakeholders to be fully aware of their rights and obligations to remain fully competitive. It is important for Indian entrepreneurs to understand the complex WTO regulations in this larger context. Also, competitive advantage ultimately results from an effective combination of national circumstances and company strategy. Given the fact that efficiency and productivity would remain at the core of all economic activities, only those economic entities would survive and grow that exhibit competitiveness in price and quality. Those not able to match the profile of most competitive firms would either be out of the market or acquired by other firms. Thus, mergers, acquisitions and strategic alliances would be market reality in order to stay in the market. The recent case of Idea Cellular (the Birla-Tata-AT&T cellular service giant) picking up close to 75% stake in Escotel Mobile Communications Ltd thereby making it the third largest cellular operator in the country (after Bharti and BSNL) with over 1.7 million customers is one of the cases in point. In fact, in near future, highly fragmented Indian industrial sector would consolidate and see many a mergers and acquisitions paving the way for consolidation that could survive the global competition. Overcoming the weaknesses of Indian concerns arising out of long enjoyed protection are the first and foremost challenges that must be seen in the right perspective and corrected in time. These are: weak market penetration; low quality of exportable; lack of standardisation and insubstantial nature of FDI flow. However the biggest challenge before the Indian industries is that they must come out of inertia and come in terms with the ground reality as fast as possible. Protected markets are the past and global competition is the immediate future. Those who do not understand this and act in time would become a part of history as well. Sensitivity to the changing economic scenario has always been important for the economic actors and would remain important in future. Sooner we understand it, better it is.

An elaboration of some of the challenges ahead are listed below:

(i) The growing ease and cheapness of international communications, with the Internet the leading aspect substantially improves the awareness of the consumers about the latest products, services, and technologies across the globe. This puts heavy demands on the firms to work with smart efficiency. This would become possible only through high level of transparency and good corporate governance.

(ii) Cost optimisation has become critically important

with a pressure on prices due to competition. Even after quotas are finally dismantled in 2005, manufacturers may have to deal with high tariffs and, therefore, must plan strategies to minimise the costs as far as possible. It may be pointed out that in 2005, there will not be free trade, but quota-free trade and tariffs may remain high in the importing countries. Therefore the industry must work towards efficient logistics and supply chain pipeline, with focus on just-in time inventories, shorter production turnaround time and smart outsourcing strategies that can considerably cut down distribution and procurement costs. Delivery of quality and service with cost effectiveness would provide the competitive edge to the various business players.

(iii) The reaction time of the businesses will considerably reduce and those who do not quickly shape would lose the market and jobs to others. In the face of rapid pace of rise in the competition, creativity and speedy commercial exploitation of the same may assume unprecedented importance.

(iv) There must be closer integration of the company, customers, suppliers and partners. Companies will have to deepen their relationship with customers and the focus must shift from product to service and from mass market to the personalised ones especially in case of service and technology intensive products.

(v) Increase in the investment in R & D, especially in the speciality and knowledge segments to gain competitive advantage because of compulsion to achieve global technical and quality norms. Given the trend towards 'Green Protectionism' and health-hazard proof products the latest environmental standards along with the technology backed assurance of safety and health standards, have to be built in the technologies so that such barriers could be overcome. Allocation of resources to research and education remains a matter of serious concern for

India. The US spends 2.6 per cent of GNP on research, so does Germany and Japan, which allocate 2.8 per cent of their GNP towards R & D. India spends less than per cent of GNP on research and in absolute terms it would be around 2-3 % of that of the US.

(vi) Products and markets both become important in this context.

(vii) A shift from generic products to the packaged, quasi, regular and premium brands. Creation of a credible brand image for Indian products and services would be an important task to accomplish. It may be mentioned here that despite our advantage in software development, Indian software giants are little known elsewhere which may prove to be unprofitable in the long run in view of the fact that newly emerging players may pay more attention to this neglected yet important aspect. Even among brands, value added differentiation and product mix would provide competitive teeth.

(viii) Transformation of governmental functions and a substantive improvement in the efficiency of administration, which understands and means business, facilitates and supports rather than regulate and control the business as an engine of economic and social change. The government must now focus on providing services for enterprises, and on promoting and enhancing the role of intermediary institutions in the market economy.

(ix) Higher public investment in education at all levels with emphasis on scientific and technical education where 'cost recovery' should not be the governing principle. The quality of education need to be tightly monitored so that proliferation of private educational institutions may not undermine social, economic and political objectives of the education system.

(x) The emergence of large capacities in China with focus on exporting into global market pose serious threats to India. This threat from China could be countered effectively by what Indians have to offer i.e., superior technical/ creative skills with the capacity to quickly absorb the high-end technology. The Indian products/services, therefore, have to be backed by high technology, especially software content. Some of the components of the product/service could be outsourced to the Chinese firms to take advantage of their cost-effectiveness. In fact, Bharti Teletech, the largest non-Chinese manufacturer of telecom equipments in the world, has already started doing this.

(xi) Indian manufacturers and marketers of textiles need to correct the low quality products, low productivity, little value-addition in production, non-availability of financial and technical means essential for plant and equipment to match the knowledge-based global economies, lack of competitive export finance, lack of application of sophisticated marketing tools and poor packaging facilities. India, therefore, needs to work harder than its competitors abroad, not only towards its production but also towards creating a positive image of the country as a reliable supplier.

(xii) Production efficiency alone would not help. The firms need to be market efficient as well. For instance, Indian farmers are production efficient, yet their disorganization and market inefficiency may seriously block their efforts to improve profitability by exporting to remunerative markets. This sector, in particular, urgently needs much better organisation of production and marketing activities so that farmers may take advantage of their production efficiency in future.

(xiii) The concept of competitive advantage need be understood in a dynamic context, not static one as used in the neoclassical approach. It is justifiable to select a currently non-competitive industry that is judged important for an industry's future. In such cases, the government also needs to accelerate its development using policy instruments.

Overcoming the challenges posed above is a pre-requisite to capitalise upon the tracked and acted upon opportunities. They can only be addressed if the industry realises fast that WTO regulations are *fait accompli* and, therefore the restructuring and adjustment times have to be as short as possible because only appropriate and fast reaction would help.

PROBLEM AREAS

The positive developments and enormous opportunities for enhancing the economic prosperity and reducing deprivation and destitution in the world may remain a mirage if the various problem areas involving national privatisation policies and domestic/international competitive environment are not resolved to drastically reduce the severe pains of transition. Pending the resolution of these issues, the road to free trade may be marred by sudden upsurge in unemployment (where it is already high), and further increase in poverty levels (more so in developing countries) leading to social and political chaos. At international level, there would be significant rise in mutual suspicion among developing and more advanced countries thereby leading to the adoption of tough uncompromising stands at the negotiating table which would further jeopardise the prospects of gaining important growth benefits from globalisation. Some of the problem areas are listed below:

(i) The lack of quality governance, which denote institutional incapacities of state apparatuses as the crucial constraint to successful policy reform. In fact the quality of a country's governance structure is a key determinant of its ability to pursue sustainable economic and social development. Effective governance structures are based on five key principles including credibility, accountability, participation, predictability, and transparency, which are required for the sound management of public resources, an enabling environment for the private sector and a productive partnership between the public and private sectors that does not degrade into closed circles of influence and privilege. Governance provides the overall perspective from which these principles are derived. Furthermore, effective governance needs to be seen as a dynamic process that necessitates continuous fine-tuning and adapting institutions and policy solutions to changing technological, social, economic, and political environments.

(ii) Governments in developing countries consider privatisation of the state owned enterprises as synonymous to the liberalisation and globalisation which demonstrates a serious confusion between privatisation and competition. Privatisation/ liberalisation *per se* is not an end in itself but as a means to establish competitive markets. It may be mentioned here that the Privatisation itself does not ensure increased competition as is more clearly perceptible in case of India and many other Asian/ African and Latin American countries where there is a great rush for privatising the state-owned enterprises. In such cases it is just a transfer of monopoly from the government to private hands and there could be huge returns for such monopolies as is seen from the quick resale of a former public sector entity in India to other bidders on a huge profit margin. The governments, on their part, may be more interested in privatising the public sector in their bid to reduce fiscal deficit as most of the public sector institutions may be loss making. Therefore, the idea behind the hasty privatisation, at least in India, is not so much to promote the competition as to unburden the government from providing substantial budgetary support to such concerns that may add up to the fiscal deficit. It may be further noted that privatisation at times may foster monopolies especially if a single or a handful of the companies attain the control of distribution system. The monopolies may also be perpetuated under privatisation in those areas where rapid obsolescence of technologies is order of the day e.g., computer hardware and software, civil aviation and electronics.

(iii) The approach of minimalist state is another serious problem area. In fact, state's role in appropriate regulation, social protection, and welfare need to be properly emphasised. Social Services, the fastest growing sectors in international trade, primarily comprise trade in health and education services. In many countries these are treated as public goods. With global expenditures on education and health targeted to rise above the US $2.5 trillion mark, new norms are required to protect these services from for-profit corporations. The economic side of globalisation and its social impacts are very important to developing countries. The only recognition in the WTO that the social deficit created by global trade liberalism needs to be addressed is in area of the technical barriers of trade agreement, highlight that considerable number of issues, which may not be important from the international trade point of view but are vital for the nation states for social, economical and political reasons, would go un-addressed under WTO. It is worth mentioning that different kinds of rules in trade investment agreements have limited the reforms to a few core principles in the areas of labour, health and environmental standards. Although WTO agenda will have to be limited to make it operational yet the needs of most needy among nations, if overlooked, globalisation will have little meaning to an overwhelming majority of poor nations in the World. In fact, it is difficult and impractical to create a firewall between the social and the purely commercial issues. This calls for the new policy objectives and new policy instruments for poverty reduction, improving equity and building socially inclusive societies.

(iv) Inadequate financial infrastructure and inefficient regulatory framework to allocate capital efficiently is another area that merits serious attention. Importance of financial markets which is well equipped to a good job of selecting the most productive recipients for these resources, reducing risk and increasing liquidity could not have been felt more than the present times. However, creation of such a system itself may not guarantee success without introducing a strong legal and regulatory framework that may promote 'safety and soundness', competition, protect customers and ensure that ' underserved groups have some access to capital'. [*Stiglitz 1998*]. It is a tough goal, especially in developing countries where financial institutions had been under government ownership for a long time and are painfully slow to adapt to the new situations. Yet without attaining this objective, the very basis of globalisation i.e., efficiency gains through increased competition, will collapse, inflicting heavy costs on the initiators.

(v) Similarly, an apprehension remains that the import competition and job loss are likely to be more important for most countries as compared to the benefits from strengthening the export side of the economy and new economies of scale. The past experiences strongly demonstrate that the beneficial spread effects from tariff reduction are much less for developing countries than predicted because the adjustment costs for unskilled and low income families are difficult to control and manage without strong minimum wage guarantees and other redistributive provisions.

(vi) Financing Research and Development in developing economies, which may lack resources to sustain such activities. Without government action, there would be too little investment in the development and commercialisation of the new technologies. Since development of technologies can not be viable in all the cases, the government will have to facilitate the transfer of technology. One way is to promote the tertiary education especially in the areas of science and technology. Unfortunately governments, more so in developing countries, are promoting privatisation and withdrawing from this sector, which has made the cost of receiving such education unaffordable to the poorer section that form majority in such countries.

(vii) The unaccommodating attitude of the developed nations in making trade as a level playing field is the biggest bone of contention. Despite progress in the post-war era, advanced-economy trade barriers remain substantially high against clothing, textiles, and agricultural goods the very products in which LDCs have a natural comparative advantage. A recent study by Thomas Hertel of Purdue University and Will Martin of the World Bank have found that the average tariff that rich countries impose on manufacturing goods from poor countries is four-times higher than the average tariff rich countries impose on each other's goods [*Economist 1999*]. If the principle of comparative advantage is applied to technology, industrial products and capital, there is no reason, why should it not be applied to items in which the developing countries may fair far better. The principles of trade, to be followed by all, have to be the same across the board and should not differ from one to another item. Stiglitz also insists that in the absence of social security net and sufficient reciprocity and assistance on the part of developed countries, trade liberalization conducted in the wrong way and too fast can bring further misery to the poor especially in developed countries [*Stiglitz 2001*]. The impression emanating from the numerous trade talks at various Ministerial Conference and other meetings is that in those areas where comparative advantage of developing world is found incompatible with the interests of the most powerful forces in the world economy, the trade talks are either blocked / remain inconclusive or make certain provisions that dig holes in the Shallow pockets of their economically weaker counterparts.

(viii) The disproportionate amount of subsidies and protection to the agriculture in the developed countries is another serious departure from the principles enunciated in the WTO charter. For instance, 'Organisation for Economic Cooperation and Development Countries' total support of $311 billion to domestic agriculture in 2001 dwarfs the $50 billion these countries spend annually on development assistance. Similarly, in the past 3 years, the US has provided an additional subsidy of $26 billion to its 9,00,000 farmers. The richest trading block-Organisation for Economic Cooperation and Development (OECD)-provides agricultural subsidies to the tune of $1 billion a day. Compare this with what 550 million farmers in India receive. We provide $1-billion worth of subsidies - all indirect in form of cheap fertilizer, power etc., in a year. In 1995, when WTO came into existence the European Union used to provide roughly $90-billion worth of subsidies to its 7 million farmers. Six years down the line, the subsidies rose to $114.5 billion. This also included the subsidies that were directly paid to farmers. The US plans to pay an additional $170 billion to its farmers in the next 10 years under the new Farm Bill that has been cleared by the US Congress in 2002. And if one adds to it $12 billion it provides for market intervention operations abroad the total support to agriculture becomes colossal by any standard. Unless this issue is addressed the road to free trade would become long and arduous for the developing nations.

(ix) The insistence of some developed countries to link trade with the 'Core Labour Standards' or "Social Clause" is also a matter of concern, particularly in view of the haste with which such issues are being lobbied for and pushed through by them and trade/ industrial unions and NGOs of such countries. Such steps give rise to the fear, not totally unfounded, among the 'would be' effected low wage trading partners that the real concern of these countries or pressure groups representing trade unions / workers in these countries is not to help the workers, particularly in low wage developing countries but to use such a clause to provide protection to their own industries that may run into rough weather especially after January 1, 2005 when most of the restrictions on trade would be withdrawn. Since it is difficult to establish any close link between market efficiency and social development/fundamental rights of the workers, emphasizing the need for WTO to take up such issues when they can be more competently handled by other bodies such as ILO does not appear to bear any rationale except for that such issues could, possibly, be used to maintain unfair gains by the interested members at the expense of some of the cost competitive trading partners. It may be noted that the 'Core Labour Standards' comprise: elimination of child labour exploitation, prohibition of forced labour, freedom of association, the right to organise and bargain collectively and non-discrimination in employment. This issue is likely to remain a big problem area given the power of pressure groups in the developed countries to influence their governments.

(x) The possibility of applying discriminatory sanitary and phyto-sanitary measures especially from the developing countries where enough financial and technical resources may not be available to meet the requirements of importers in the developed countries.

This may neutralise the comparative advantage of the developing countries in tropical agro-industrial products. Therefore, unless a mechanism is found to help, in particular the developing countries, by extending technical and other kinds of support, to meet the standard requirements of importers the issue would remain a matter of serious concern especially to exporters. Although the concern of the developed countries about protecting human, animal and plant lives from avoidable infections/diseases through suitable measures merit appreciation, yet the possibility of using such measures for 'protectionist' purposes cannot be ruled out.

(xi) Serious obstacles to trade remain in market access. While average bound and applied Most Favoured Nation tariffs in the developed countries are low, tariff "peaks", and escalation can constitute major impediments to poorer countries' development and industrialisation.

(xii) Green protectionism is another area that might eventually threaten the existence of WTO as such. While environmental concerns are extremely important, they cannot serve the basis for blocking the imports. (Tuna-Dolphin case of Mexico, Shrimp-Turtle cases of many countries including India).

(xiii) By December 2004 the Agreement on Textiles and Clothing (ATC) is supposed to lead to full liberalisation of textile and garment trade akin to that in other commodities. The ATC also provides, under Article 6, for the application of safeguard mechanisms for restraining products on the basis of stipulations similar to the MFA guidelines on restraints. India has been subjected to fresh restraints on three garment items after the establishment of the ATC. All the three restraints were put on woollen garments covered under men's coats, women's coats and shirts & blouses. Similar kinds of measures may further constrain the capacity of the developing nations to realise the possible gains from globalisation.

(xiv) Trade in domestically prohibited goods. Domestically prohibited goods (DPGs) are products that are either banned or have severe restrictions on their use in the country of origin, e.g. certain pesticides, cosmetics, and pharmaceuticals; however, they are freely exported to other countries. Many developed countries, where the sale of such goods is domestically prohibited, are still producing these goods and exporting them to poor countries, thus putting the health and lives of millions at risk. Ironically, the issue of DPGs was one of the first in the debate on trade and environment and has been under discussion yet still unresolved for the last two decades.

The challenges pointed above cannot be dealt with by industry alone. They require concerted efforts on the part of government and businesses both at national and international levels. Further, in the initial stage of transition, which kinds of policy measures would help is pointed out in the subsequent section.

POLICY MEASURES

Contrary to the basic philosophy of free trade where governments are supposed to leave the economic activities on the free interplay of market forces, the Government of India like governments in all other countries, must gear up to play an important role in negotiations at WTO and other forums, modify/replace the law to make them compatible with the WTO norms, make it clear to the industries that only competitiveness through efficiency, productivity and quality assurances will help them. Multi-decade long experiences have shown that successful growth depends primarily on national policies that promote macroeconomic stability along with a pragmatic and sound financial system in place, trade and investment, human capital formation, and good governance. Eventually, it is not individual policies, but sets of mutually reinforcing policy measures, which are jointly conducive to privatisation and globalisation. Moreover the domestic economic choices - promotion of cost efficiency and competitive preparedness vs. overt or covert subsidisation - that governments make will have a major impact on international patterns of trade and investment, as well as on the prosperity of individual countries. A case in point is China where the presence of tough negotiating government machinery equipped with an attractive and competitive domestic market (no one can dare to ignore) has made things move to their advantage. The Chinese government was equally cooperated by the more than willing economic sectors to improve their cost and quality efficiency to become global. All these measures were adequately supported by an appropriate legal and institutional framework.

Globalisation presents governments with four principal challenges:

- Learning from the lessons of the economies which went about privatisation on their own / on the prescription of Washington institutions and paid heavy social, economic and political costs for indiscriminately administering the recommended policy instruments.
- Creating and strengthening institutions and structures of the international economic system as the lines between domestic and international financial markets have increasingly blurred, requiring closer international cooperation in monitoring financial institutions because crisis in a country could threaten global financial stability. Therefore, there is a need to ensure a coordination between:
  (i) International and domestic policies of individual countries and a dispute settlement mechanism that is fair and objective.
  (ii) Regional economic arrangements and the overall global system in order to strengthen the multilateral trade regime.
- Identifying new issues and rules which globalisation requires us to address? For example, environmental and

core labor standards and transparency in government procurement.

- Ensuring that all segments of society benefit from globalisation.

All these issues merit serious attention of the government in India as well. Besides, it will have to address the following broader issues in order to maximise its gains from partial free trade in goods and services:

(i) Train up trade cadres and create a pool of experts for framing trade policy, negotiating, and implementing. Strengthen negotiating capacity and facilitate flow of trade information. In view of the fact that *In WTO countries get not what they deserve, but what they negotiate,* such a step becomes a necessity. Also support compliance capacity of the parties involved by providing them necessary logistics. Provision of legal support and certain safeguards against the unfair trade practices such as dumping, erection of non-tariff barriers in the garb of environment protection at least in the initial phases, would be vital in this regard. This trade cadre may also keep a strong vigil on the import of domestically prohibited goods (DPGs) that are prohibited in the country of origin but are exportable to others. Export / import of such product puts the lives of millions at risk.

(ii) Governments also need to build up appropriate administrative and technical capacity and institute rules and norms that promote fully informed decisions and actions and effectively curb the arbitrary action and corruption.

(iii) Broader dissemination of the negotiated (event-specific, issue-specific; provision-specific; regularity; mandate) provisions amongst government officials and businessmen through workshops, training, updated posting of data / information on the website (as one created by Strategic Law Group of CII) created for the purpose and circulation of made-easy bulletins is made available to all the stakeholders and not just to government officials. This would make the consultative process more intense, inclusive, and participatory. Having a world-class patent regime and administration is particularly significant in the context of India's desire to become an IT superpower and the recognized competence of the Indian engineers in software. It takes an average of 6 years to get a patent in India while the average time in the United States is about 22 months.

(iv) While in-house R&D may be affordable to bigger organisations, it would be more feasible to make extensive use of the pool of quality technical and managerial manpower available in premier institutions like Indian Institute of Technologies (IITs), Indian Institute of Science (IISc.) Bangalore, Indian Institute of Managements (IIMs) etc. Tying up with these institutions for R&D would not only be cost effective but also ensure effective tapping of the valuable human resources available in the country. Apart from infusing a strong technology focus, Industry-Research Institution-Academic linkages need to be strengthened for pursuing an aggressive R&D. This is a must, to take brilliant ideas from laboratory to commercial production in the shortest time. The industry and academia together may contribute significantly in this regard. Besides the companies must develop a system that looks for new ideas and constantly evaluate them for their commercial viability. Encouragement and incentives in order to promote such collaboration would go a long way to help the economy.

(v) Emphasize and provide appropriate incentives for technological upgradation, improvement in productivity and quality and increasing exports. While the industry can legitimately demand proper policy inputs from the government, the initiative for R&D and modernisation for improving competitiveness have to come from the industry. Fiscal incentives probably could make a difference in this regard and the loss to government coffers due to such concessions could be more than compensated for once the industry is able to reap the commercial benefits of the R & D efforts.

(vi) Instead of futile efforts to "save" the jobs of yesterday the focus should be on preparing workers to meet the rising demands of the labor market for specialized skills. The job surety rather not job security should be the watchword. Job surety for the skills would enhance and promote the kinds of skills that would be required under the new dispensation.

(vii) Enforce the protection of intellectual property, perfect the visa procedure at port of entry, fully utilise India's cultural and linguistic advantages, amplify financial market and improve the financial services and adjust foreign investment policies to new circumstances. India has also to improve its infrastructure and environment, e.g. building new highways, subways and light rails and reducing water and air pollution. It is important because it has market access implications.

(viii) It may be noted that the protection and enforcement of intellectual property rights should contribute to the promotion of technological innovation and to the transfer and dissemination of technology, which is of mutual advantage to producers and users of technological knowledge, in a manner conducive to social and economic welfare and to a balance of rights and obligations.

(ix) There is enough evidence that small and medium sized businesses may not be able to reorganize themselves to take advantage of new market prospects because they may not have access to capital, new credit lines and leading edge technology. The failure of these innovative small to medium size firms could be a big cause for alarm because it is from their ranks that Indian multinationals are expected to emerge. It is, therefore, necessary to devise tools that may facilitate their growth and enhance competitive strength.

(x) Increase in visibility, trading power and effective participation by forging a close partnership with China on certain issues in the Multilateral Trading System. None can afford to ignore these two largest markets of the world. This would also provide the developing countries a strong leverage, enabling them to negotiate from a position of strength and would prevent their increasing marginalisation as a group.

(xi) Some of the factors needed to boost textile and garment market access have been identified as: Technological upgrade, Economies of scale, Stronger fibre base, Higher crop productivity, Removal of infrastructure bottlenecks, and Reduction in the higher costs of power and other costs. Also Taxation and EXIM policy changes, Efficiency oriented labour laws, and Creation of Integrated Apparel Export Parks.

(xii) Insertion of new clause and extension of existing ' Enabling Clause' in order to facilitate and better prepare the developing economies for meeting the global companies [*Decision on Differential and More favourable Treatment, Reciprocity and Fuller Participation of Developing Countries* (commonly known as the 'Enabling Clause')]

CONCLUDING REMARKS

The role of the government would be extremely important during the transition phase, as it would require identification of issues of importance, putting them in negotiating mode and coordinating with other countries having similar interests in order to make the outcome reasonable and fair. However the real 'threat', once the WTO regime is in place, is not the one imposed by global competition, but the under-preparedness of the government/business organisations to face the challenges/competition. While the role of the government is extremely important in providing supporting services to business organisations and facilitating internal competition, business organisations themselves are going to face formidable tasks in domestic as well as export markets. For the domestic players the pressure will primarily come from intensified competition owing to abolition of quantitative restrictions, reduction of import duties to international levels, elimination of direct/indirect subsidies, tax exemptions, de-reservation of SSIs and the incentives attached to them, and rationalisation of FDI terms. For the exporters, the business organisations will be confronted with increased global competition on price and quality and innovations, much diluted domestic incentives for exports, strictly enforced patent regulations, mandatory requirements of compliance with WTO/importing countries' norms on safety, labour, environment in respect of products and production processes, integration of global supply-chains and market consolidation. For those that are in both the markets, the squeeze would be double.

The firms, therefore, must prepare a roadmap to survive and grow by devising aggressive strategies encompassing high quality consciousness, global cost-competitiveness, intense commitment to delivery and post-delivery care, high service orientation, high receptivity to learn from one's own and others' experiences and clear business/market strategy. The cost-reduction exercises, low-cost financing, downsizing, re-engineering and outsourcing, maintaining effective supply-chain and distribution management would become critical to cost controlling efforts. Continuous product development/innovation would keep the firms in the markets and help them to grow fast. Besides as the number of competitive products jostling for the customers mind-space increase, there is a need to create distinctive brands that may be associated with the reasonable price, high quality and state-of-the-art technology features. Only then, would it be possible for the firms to inculcate strong consumer preference for their brands.

For the domestic players, expanding the business context to a global frame of reference would be the next logical step.

The strength acquired in fortifying the domestic market interests needs to be scaled up to match international requirements. For this, the firm must ensure: a global reach, globally competitive cost and price structure, internationally acceptable quality standards, international brand image, organisational set-up and skills to tap international markets, and resources at internationally competitive costs to market globally.

An even bigger challenge faces the Indian corporate - that of preparing the organisation to transform to deal with the new environment. Key elements of this dimension are: Organisational restructure and attracting and retaining skills and talent. The organisations that would 'Think Global, Act Fast and Smartly' would Keep ahead and would reap the benefits of globalisation.

REFERENCES

Aoki, M.; K. Murdock, and M. Okuno-Fujiwara (1997), "Beyond the East Asian Miracle: Introducing the Market-Enhancing View", in M. Aoki, H.-K. Kim, and M. Okuno-Fujiwara (eds.) *The Role of Government in East Asian Economic Development. Comparative Institutional Analysis*, pp. 1-37.Oxford: Clarendon Press.

Chaudhuri, Shubham, Pinelopi K. Goldberg and Panle Jia, 2003, Estimating the E.ects of Global Patent Protection for Pharmaceuticals: A Case Study of Fluoroquinolones in India posted at: http://www.columbia.edu/~sc301/pharmaceutical-patents-2004-01.pdf.

Jeffrey Sachs & Andrew Warner, Economic reform and the process of global integration, *Brookings Papers on Economic Activity* 1 (1995).

Jeffrey Frankel & David Romer, Does trade cause growth? *Am. Econ. Rev.*, June 1999, 379-99.

McKinnon, R. I. (1992), *The Order of Economic Liberalization. Financial Control in the Transition to a Market Economy*. Baltimore and London: Johns Hopkins University Press.].

Ohno, K. and I. Ohno (eds) (1998) Japanese Views on Economic Development: Diverse Paths to the Market, London: Routledge.

Organization for Economic Cooperation and Development, *Open Markets Matter: The Benefits of Trade and Investment Liberalisation*, 1998, 10.

Patrick Low, Marcelo Olarreaga, & Javier Suarez, *Does globalisation cause a higher concentration of international trade and investment flows?* World Trade Organisation, Staff Working Paper ERAD–98–08, Aug. 1998, 22.

Rodrik, D. (1995), "Getting interventions right: how South Korea and Taiwan grew rich", *Economic Policy. A European Forum* 20: 55-97.

Spero, Joan E., The Challenges of Globalisation, Under Secretary of State for Economic, Business and Agricultural Affairs, at the World Economic Development Congress, Washington, DC, September 26, 1996.

Stiglitz, Joseph A. (1998), More Instruments and Broader Goals : Moving Toward the Post-Washington Consensus, WIDER Annual lectures 2, UNU World Institute for Development Economics Research, P. 3. Also available on website : *http://www.wider.unu.edu/publications/annual-lectures/annual-lecture-1998. pdf White Man's Shame,* Economist, (25 September 1999) 89.

Williamson, John, Ed. (1990), *The Political Economy of Policy Reform* . **Washington**, Institute for International Economics.

World Bank (1993), The East Asian Miracle: Economic Growth and Public Policy, A World Bank Policy Research Report, Oxford: Oxford University Press.

World Bank (1997), *World Development Report 1997 The State in a Changing World.* New York, Oxford University Press. P.iii.

Silber, Simao Davi (2000), "Globalizacao e Tendencias da Economia Brasileira." *FIA-USP.*

Stiglitz, J. E. (1997), "The Role of Government in Economic Development", *Annual World Bank Conference on Development Economics 1996*: 11-23.].

Silber, Simao Davi (2000), "Globalizacao e Tendencias da Economia Brasileira." *FIA-USP.*

Stiglitz, Joseph E. 2001 Addressing Developing Countries Priorities and Needs in the Millennium Round. *Seattie, the WTO, and the Future of the Multilateral Trading System* Sauve, Roger Porter and Pierre. Cambridge Mass, The Centre for Business and Government, Harvard University.

WTO (2000), "Trade, Income Disparity and Poverty." *WTO, Geneva*

World Bank, (2000), Global Economic Prospects and the Developing Countries 2000.

World Bank, (1993), East-Asian Miracle.

ANNEXURE-I
DEVELOPED MARKET ECONOMY COUNTRIES AND TRANSITION ECONOMIES

Developed Market Economy Countries				
Europe	*America*	*Asia*	*Oceania*	*Transition Economies*
Andorra, Austria, Belgium, Denmark, Faeroe Island, Finland, France, Germany, Gibraltar, Greece, Iceland, Ireland, Italy, Liechtenstein, Luxembourg, Malta, Monaco, Netherlands, Norway, Portugal, Spain, Sweden, Switzerland, United Kingdom of Great Britain and Northern Ireland.	Canada, United States.	Israel and Japan	Australia and New Zealand.	Albania, Belarus, Bosnia and Herzegovina, Bulgaria, Croatia, Czech Republic, Estonia, Hungary, Latvia, Lithuania, Macedonia (the former Yugoslav), Poland, Republic of Moldova, Romania, Russian Federation, Serbia and Montenegro, Slovakia, Slovenia, Ukraine

ANNEXURE-II

DISTRIBUTION OF DEVELOPING COUNTRIES/TERRITORIES BY INCOME GROUP (1995 per capita GDP)

Above US$ 4,000: High-income (46)	Between US$ 800 and US$ 4,000: Middle-income (71)	Below US$ 800: Low-income (65)
American Samoa, Anguilla, Antigua and Barbuda, Argentina, Aruba, Bahamas, Bahrain, Barbados, Bermuda, Brazil, British Virgin Islands, Brunei Darussalam, Cayman Islands, Chile, China (Taiwan Province of), China (Hong Kong SAR), Montserrat, China (Macao SAR), Cook Islands, Cyprus, French Guiana, French Polynesia, Gabon, Greenland, Guadeloupe, Guam, Kuwait, Libyan Arab Jamahiriya, Malaysia, Martinique, New Caledonia, Netherlands Antilles, Oman, Palau, Puerto Rico, Qatar, Republic of Korea, Reunion, Saint Kitts and Nevis, Saudi Arabia, Seychelles, Singapore, Trinidad and Tobago, United Arab Emirates, United States Virgin Islands, , Uruguay.	Algeria, Armenia, Belize, Bolivia, Botswana, Cape Verde, Christmas Island, Cocos (Keeling) Islands, Colombia, Congo, Costa Rica, Cuba, Djibouti, Dominica, Dominican Republic, Ecuador, Egypt, El Salvador, Federated States of Syrian Arab Republic, Falkland Islands (Malvinas), Fiji, Grenada, Guatemala, Indonesia, Iraq, Islamic Republic of Iran, Jordan, Jamaica, Johnston Island, Kazakhstan, Lebanon, Maldives, Marshall Islands, Mauritius, Mexico, Micronesia, Midway Islands, Morocco, Namibia, Nauru, Niue, Norfolk Island, Northern Mariana Islands, Pitcairn, Palestinian territory, Panama, Papua New Guinea, Paraguay, Peru, Philippines.Saint Helena, Saint Lucia, Saint Pierre and Miquelon, Saint Vincent and the Grenadines, Samoa, Solomon Islands, Suriname, South Africa, Swaziland, Thailand, Timor-Leste, Tokelau, Tonga, Tunisia, Turkey, Turkmenistan, Tuvalu, Vanuatu, Venezuela, Wake Island, Wallis and Futuna Islands.	Afghanistan, Angola, Azerbaijan, Bangladesh, Benin, Bhutan, British Indian Ocean Territory, Burkina Faso, Burundi, Cambodia, Central African Republic, Cameroon, Chad, China, Comoros, Côte d'Ivoire, Democratic People's Republic of Korea, Democratic Republic of the Congo, Equatorial Guinea, Eritrea, Ethiopia, Ghana, Guinea, Guinea-Bissau, Guyana, Gambia, Georgia, Haiti, Honduras, India, Kenya, Kiribati, Kyrgyzstan, Lao People's Democratic Republic, Lesotho, Liberia, Madagascar, Malawi, Mali, Mauritania, Mongolia, Mozambique, Myanmar, Nepal, Nicaragua, Niger, Nigeria, Pakistan, Rwanda, Sao Tome and Principe, Senegal, Sierra Leone, Somalia, Sri Lanka, Sudan, Tajikistan, Togo, Turks and Caicos Islands, Uganda, United Republic of Tanzania, Uzbekistan, Vietnam, Yemen, Zambia, Zimbabwe.

ANNEXURE-III
REGIONAL TRADING BLOCKS IN THE WORLD

Sl. No.	*AMERICA (North and South)*	*EUROPE*	*ASIA*	*AFRICA*
1.	Central American Common Market (CACM) Est.1961, Members : 5	European Union: Est. 1957, Members: 15 No. of Countries acceding to EU on May 1, 2004: 10	Association of South-East Asian Nations (ASEAN) Est. 1967, Members:10	Mano River Union (MRU) Est. 1973 Members: 3
2.	Caribbean Community (CARICOM): Est.1973, Members: 15	European Free Trade Association (EFTA) Est. 1960, Members: 3	Bangkok Agreement, Est. 1975, Members: 8	Economic Community of West African States (ECOWAS) Est. 1975M Members: 15
3.	Latin American Integration Association (LAIA) Est. 1980, Members: 12	Baltic Countries Est. 1991 Members: 3	Gulf Cooperation Council (GCC): 1981, Members:6	Economic Community of the Great Lakes Countries (CEPGL) Est. 1976, Members: 3
4.	Organisation of Eastern Caribbean States (OECS) Est. 1981, Members: 9		Economic Cooperation Organisation (ECO): Est. 1985, Memebers:10	Economic Community of Central African States (ECCAS) Est. 1983, Members: 11
5.	North American Free Trade Association (NAFTA), Est. 1992 Members: 3		South Asian Association for Regional Cooperation (SAARC), Est.1985 Members: 7	Arab Maghreb Union (UMA) Est.1989, Members: 5
6.	Free Trade Area the Americas (FTAA) Est. 1994, Members : 34		Melanesia Spearhead Group (MSG) Est. 1988, Members:4	Southern African Development Community (SADC), Est. 1992 Members: 14

Sl. No.	*AMERICA (North and South)*	*EUROPE*	*ASIA*	*AFRICA*
7.	Southern Common Market (MERCOSUR): Est. 1994, Members:4		Asia Pacific Economic Cooperation (APEC), Est. 1989, Members: 23	Common Market for Eastern and Southern Africa (COMESA), Est.1994, Members: 21
8.	Andean Group Est. 1996, Members: 5		Commonwealth of Independent States (CIS), Est. 1991, Members: 12	Economic and Monetary Community of Central Africa (CEMAC) Est. 1994, Members: 6
9.			Black Sea Economic Cooperation (BSEC): Est. 1992 M Members: 11	West African Economic and Monetary Union (UEMOA), Est. 1994, Members: 8

2

THE ECONOMIC DEVELOPMENT LANDSCAPE GENERATED BY STATISTICAL-SPATIAL DOMAIN ANALYSIS

*Masudul Alam Choudhury**
*Mohammad Shahadat Hossain***

The objective of this paper is to present a process-oriented conception of development planning in which a relational epistemological approach is used to generate possible complementarities between selected development variables. We will formalise the methodological framework of such development reasoning and establish its empirical viability by using computer simulated spatial analysis applied to statistical data. On the basis of this spatial analysis model we will develop a normative approach to policy analysis. The paper will equally also contribute to the extension of spatial computer methodology of data analysis to the social and economic domains, which presently remain outside the domain of spatial database. Thus a correspondence is generated between the statistical database and the spatial database in this kind of

* Professor of Economics, Sultan Qaboos University, Muscat, Sultanate of Oman and the University College of Cape Breton, Sydney, Nova Scotia, Canada

** Associate Professor of Computer Science, Chittagong University, Bangladesh.

extension of the spatial analysis, which is done by the Geographical Information System.

THE EXISTING STATE OF REASONING IN DEVELOPMENT PLANNING

The process approach to development planning is distinct from the mainstream understanding of development, which is studied by the neo-classical macro-growth models (Dobell & Burmeister, 1975). The literature on economic development and growth is rich in such mainstream theorizing and applications (Meier, 1995). One of the strongest consequences of such an approach is trade-off between economic and social or cultural variables. A particular example of such a massive trade-off is that of economic efficiency (growth) versus social justice (distributive equity, poverty alleviation, employment creation). Mainstream development theorizing and application treat social and cultural variables as datum (Goodman, 2003). Thus, the dynamic and endogenous effects of such variables are not methodologically embedded in the development models. In other words, such variables remain non-systemic and are simply used exogenously to the otherwise pure economic treatment of the development models and their analysis. Thus the existing methodology of development planning is reductionist in nature.

THE RELATIONAL EPISTEMOLOGICAL MODEL OF DEVELOPMENT PLANNING

Epistemology is the study of the theory of knowledge; that is of the foundational premises of a body of thought and its attenuating model and paradigm (Smith, 1992). These together with the positivistic inferences derived from the normative foundations comprise the worldview of the predominating paradigm (Choudhury, 1993). In relational epistemology such a worldview encompasses the study of scientific epistemology in the light of systems dynamics in pervasively relational or complementary orders (Thayer-Bacon, 2003; Yolles, 1998). Through such an investigation, the emerging concept of systems dynamics premised on a multi-dimensional circular causation relational epistemology arises. Thus the epistemological study of such systems dynamics is premised on the understanding and analytics of knowledge-driven evolutionary systems as a total replacement of the linear time-dependent systems.

This choice of knowledge-flows replacing time dependence of the functionalist and structural compositions of evolutionary learning systems leads into the construction of dynamic models of development planning that are richly institutional in nature and are policy induced. That is because the complex processes of learning that emerge are the result of embedded interacting and complementing sub-systems along with their entities. These interactions lead to complementary preferences and goals formulated and guided by foundational laws. Such laws can be guidance, policies and goals of learning-by-doing in development planning. This kind of normative characterization of the embedded sub-systems negates the dichotomous learning systems that are linearly structured (Holton, 1992).

Having derived them from the background of the study of relational epistemology, we then carry these substantive concepts relating to the characterization of learning systems into the area of development planning. The result is a special form of the knowledge-induced model system now used in studying problems of development planning.

The model system we derive reflects four distinct functions, goals and attributes. First, the epistemological foundations of the learning world-systems are derived within the framework of a systems perspective relating to systems unity of knowledge. Secondly, the developmental, institutional, cultural, ethical and policy preferences of complementary and co-determined decision making are made to induce the variables and parameters of the dynamic system. This is the endogenous effect between different variables (entities) of development planning. Thirdly, the mathematical model of such a complex and learning worldview in systemic unity of knowledge is formulated to address the field of relational epistemology in accordance with the real world issues and problems of development planning (Choudhury, 2004).

Fourthly, the empirical results are subjected to quantitative policy analysis to come up with policy recommendations in the light of relational epistemology of the kind we accept as our premise for studying sectoral diversification and linkages within development planning of a national economy.

By studying such complex of issues of development planning the meaning of aggregation of preferences of embedded systems is shown to rest upon micro-functional forces. The micro-functional entities are shown to characterize the building blocks of the macro-structure. The macro-structure is found to lose an independent substance of its own in the face of the micro-functional entities. Thus, the field of development planning is understood here differently from its traditional macroeconomic treatment in the literature. This is a methodological issue emanating from the premises of relational epistemology of unified world-systems. The methodology that is so derived is found to be different also from the formalism of microeconomic foundations of macroeconomics (Lucas, 1975; Phelps, 1970). Consequently, all policy issues are differently understood and formalized. Such quantitative policy issues of endogenous nature are thereby analysed differently from the methodology of mainstream economic theory that remains differentiated along macroeconomic and microeconomic lines (Thurow, 1983).

FORMALISING AN EMPIRICAL MODEL OF INTER-SECTORAL LINKAGES AS AN EXAMPLE OF RELATIONAL EPISTEMOLOGY IN INDUSTRIAL DEVELOPMENT

In applying the methodology of relational epistemology to development planning we formalize a model of knowledge-induced variables and parameters of complementary and linked learning systems in terms of their composite systemic variables (entities). In formulating such a model we first consider two interrelated sub-models.

1. First Sub-Model

Firstly, there is a circular causation system of log-linear Cobb-Douglas type functions applied to sectoral studies with several critical indicators. The sectors selected are Petroleum and Gas, Manufacturing, Construction, Utilities and the Tertiary Services (importantly finance) for the Sultanate of Oman1. These sectors are to be linked to each other through variables and policies relating to economic output (sectoral GDP), investment expenditure (Government, Private and Foreign) and total employment. Among these variables, Government total development investment expenditure including human resource development expenditure and technology choice (capital intensive vs. labour intensive) are policy variables. This system of estimated equations is based on the method of circular causation between the variables and policies of the selected sectors that are examined. Namely, these sectors are Petroleum, Manufacturing, Mining, Gas, Utilities, Gas and Finance.

2. Second Sub-model

The empirical estimates so derived, particularly for the coefficients of the multivariate and multi-equations regression model are then fed into a second model sub-system. This model sub-system is a dynamic version of a revised form of the input-output relationship. In terms of our substantive and epistemological categorization of the meaning of systems dynamics, the dynamic form of the input-output model becomes different from that used in the time-dependent sense in the literature (Oxford University Press, 1989). The knowledge-driven meaning of systems dynamics causes the data to be treated in different ways in the knowledge-induced dynamic coefficients input-output model of development planning.

Because sufficient data appropriate for computing the input-output structure are lacking, therefore, the input-output coefficients of the model are deduced from the estimated Cobb-Douglas functional forms. The estimated input-output coefficients appearing in terms of the elements of the embedded system of relations become functionally causal with socio-economic, financial and policy variables. This method of deriving dynamic parameters of the second stage model suggests that the output and investment variables carry in them composite effects of the underlying socio-economic and policy variables (Lange, 1960, 1963; Choudhury, 1994).

The quantitative results derived by our model estimations are based on both an algorithmic formulation and estimation of the models with different sets of variables and model specifications so as to determine the appropriate model selection. The embedding of the socio-economic and policy variables into the estimated coefficients of the Cobb-Douglas forms and their transference into the input-output model carries along the underlying institutional factors that affect these variables. In the case of the Sultanate of Oman, the existing and projected state of the economy and its development planning perspectives are used to develop revisions in the coefficients of the models. Comparative results are displayed in various diagrams.

Variables of the Two-Tier Model

We use statistical data on the following variables to estimate the partial elasticity coefficients of the interrelating variables of the following variables: Inter-sectoral GDP (denoted by Qi-values by i-sectors as shown below), Total Employment (E), and inter-sectoral Government Capital Expenditure (Ki). A more extensive data search by sectors is limited by lack of availability or insufficient time-series observations.

RECURSIVELY CIRCULAR CAUSATION REGRESSION EQUATIONS: SULTANATE OF OMAN, 1980-2002

Note

The SPSS program does all regression estimations. The log-linear form is used to estimate the elasticity of the dependent variables with respect to the independent variables in the circular causation regression system. Thus the estimated coefficients are the respective elasticity estimates of the dependent variable with respect to the corresponding independent variables. *All the coefficient variables are within 95 per cent confidence intervals.*

(1) Regression (Qs ⟷ Qs, E), (1980 - 1985), (1991-2000):

Legend:

Annual sectoral GDP circularly related with total employment (1980 - 1986), (1991-2000), GDP in millions of Omani Riyals; Employment in thousands.

s= (ma) manufacturing sector, (p) petroleum sector, (g) gas sector, (mi) minerals sector, (u) utility sector, (c) construction sector, (f) sector.

E= Total number of employed labor force

Log Qma= -7.017+ 1.359log Qp+ log.306 Qg+ .291 log Qmi- .328Qu
(-.970) (1.148) (.607) (2.397) (-.397)
- .171 Log Qc- .002 Log Qfin+. 401Log E
(-.675) (-.101) (.642)

R Square: .99
Durbin-Watson: 2.51

Log Qpet= 5.509+.104 log Qma-.175log Qg+.0003 log Qmi+. 503log Qu
(6.652) (1.148) (-1.358) (.067) (3.423)
+.008Log Qc-. 003 Log Qf-.004 Log E
(1.291) (-.415) (-.270)

R Square: .99
Durbin-Watson: 1.69

MATRIX SUB-MODEL

The statistical estimates of the partial elasticity coefficients of the multivariate and multi-equations regression model are fed into a second sub-model. This sub-model is a revised form of a dynamic input-output relationship between sectors. In terms of our relational epistemological categorization of sectoral interrelations, the dynamic form of the input-output model is different from the input-output model that is dynamic only in the time-dependent sense (Oxford University Press, 1989). The knowledge-driven meaning of unified systems dynamics results in the form of the dynamic input-output model of development planning formalized below.

Because sufficient data appropriate for computing the input-output structure were lacking for the Sultanate of Oman, therefore, the input-output coefficients of the model are deduced by applying the partial inter-sectoral (GDP, employment) elasticity coefficients to the net change of the corresponding variable in the contributing sector. This method of deriving dynamic parameters of the second stage sub-model also suggests that the output and investment variables carry in them composite effects of the underlying state and policy variables under the impact of learning to generate socio-economic and institutional transformation out of inter-sectoral systemic unity of knowledge (Choudhury, 2003).

INTERSECTORAL IMPACT MATRICES GENERATED BY APPLYING THE ELASTICITY COEFFICIENTS OF THE RECURSIVELY CIRCULAR CAUSATION REGRESSION EQUATIONS: SULTANATE OF OMAN SELECTED YEARS

Note

The following matrixes were calculated by using this equation: $A_{i,j} = [\% \Delta i / \% \Delta j] * \Delta j$; where $[\% \Delta i / \% \Delta j] = \varepsilon ij$

i,j = over all sectors including itself. In the latter case, $\varepsilon ii = 1$. and $A_{i,i} = \Delta i$

Example:

$A_{M,P} = \varepsilon_{P,M} * \Delta M$; means a changes in Manufacturing causing a percentage of the change in Petroleum.

All the following matrixes are interpreted by inter-sectoral circular causation effects by reading horizontally

The matrix results being computed from the elasticity coefficients and denoting important inter-sectoral linkages (or contrarily), they carry with them important simulation effects caused by policies and selective instruments. These effects ought normatively to convert a development planning without complementary linkages conveying unity of systemic knowledge, into one with inter-sectoral complementarities.

GDP (Millions O.R) with GDP x Total Labor (thousands), Oman Selected Years

1980-81	*MAN*	*PET*	*GAS*	*MIN*	*UTI*	*CON*	*FIN*	*E*
MAN	11.6	10.7536	0.3744	2.4429	-0.0126	-3.4444	-0.0145	4.2456
PET	15.7644	103.4	-2.782	0.3213	2.478	22.236	-2.3113	-6.612
GAS	3.5496	-18.095	2.6	1.8173	0.9282	7.8153	0.348	-5.7072
MIN	3.3756	0.03102	0.2652	1.7	-0.0147	0.0981	0.34539	0.2088
UTI	-3.8048	52.0102	0.5902	-3.5224	2.1	-21.7237	4.7241	23.664
CON	-1.9836	0.8272	0.4732	0.4097	-0.4074	10.9	1.9024	-9.0132
FIN	-0.0232	-0.3102	0.0052	0.4335	0.2667	5.7443	2.9	-9.0132
THR	4.6516	-0.4136	-0.6526	1.564	0.8442	12.0445	-5.6782	34.8
1991-1992								
MAN	18.6	6.4064	0.6912	0.8622	-0.03	-8.9744	-0.034	8.5156
PET	25.2774	61.6	-5.136	0.1134	5.9	57.936	-5.4196	-13.262
GAS	5.6916	-10.78	4.8	0.6414	2.21	20.3628	0.816	-11.4472
MIN	5.4126	0.01848	0.4896	0.6	-0.035	0.2556	0.80988	0.4188
UTI	-6.1008	30.9848	5.5152	-1.2432	5	-56.6012	11.0772	47.464
CON	-3.1806	0.4928	0.8736	0.1446	-0.97	28.4	4.4608	-18.0782
FIN	-0.0372	-0.1848	0.0096	0.153	0.635	14.9668	6.8	-18.0782
THR	7.4586	-0.2464	-1.2048	0.552	2.01	31.382	-13.3144	69.8
1999-2000	*MAN*	*PET*	*GAS*	*MIN*	*UTI*	*CON*	*FIN*	*E*
MAN	92.2	9.0168	2.6496	1.8681	-0.0606	-1.6116	-0.0355	3.477
PET	125.2998	86.7	-19.688	0.2457	11.918	10.404	-5.6587	-5.415
GAS	28.2132	-15.1725	18.4	1.3897	4.4642	3.6567	0.852	-4.674
MIN	26.8302	0.02601	1.8768	1.3	-0.0707	0.0459	0.84561	0.171
UTI	-30.2416	43.6101	21.1416	-2.6936	10.1	-10.1643	11.5659	19.38
CON	-15.7662	0.6936	3.3488	0.3133	-1.9594	5.1	4.6576	-7.3815
FIN	-0.1844	-0.2601	0.0368	0.3315	1.2827	2.6877	7.1	-7.3815
THR	36.9722	-0.3468	-4.6184	1.196	4.0602	5.6355	-13.9018	28.5

This part of the exercise is done by computer real-time simulation in converting negative partial elasticity coefficients into positive valued ones. The method of spatial representation of the statistical results is used by adopting the Geographical Information Software (ARCVIEW) to the domain of development planning, an innovative extension of the use of GIS. The results are shown below.

2-D AND 3-D DIAGRAMS SHOWING REAL-TIME COMPUTER SIMULATION

The algorithmic procedures used to display the interaction between the manufacturing and other sectors in two-dimensional space are explained below.

DATABASE FIELDS

The estimated value of partial elasticity coefficient between Manufacturing and other sectors are stored as Value for one of the empirical fields of a table. The same is done with respect to Petroleum and other sectors. The database field table contains three sub-fields, namely, the 'Manufacturing (Man)' and Petroleum (Pet) sectors. The empirical field 'Man' contains the value of partial elasticity coefficients between manufacturing and other sectors. The field 'Pet' contains the value of partial elasticity coefficients between Manufacturing and other sectors. The field called 'Sectors' contains eight sectors. These are Manufacturing (Ma), Petroleum (P), Gas (G), Minerals (Mi), Utility (U), Construction (C), Finance (Fin) and Employment (E). In this way, eight records are created. Each record contains a value of each of the fields of the table. The database was saved as a file in the data repository (Table 1).

Table 1
Database Table

Sectors	*Man*	*Pet*
Manufacturing	1.0000	0.1040
Petrolium	1.3590	1.0000
Gas	0.3060	-0.1750
Mineral	0.2910	0.0003
Utility	-0.3280	0.5030
Construction	-0.1710	0.0080
Finance	-2.0000	-0.0030

SPATIAL DATA STRUCTURE

A spatial analysis is used to integrate the statistical estimations in their tabular form with spatial representation of the same in graphical form. Taking this database conversion into account, graphical data can be thought of as geometric point objects generated and the information on their shape, location and attributes stored in three separate files and an explicit relationship (one-to-one) is maintained between them. In this way, a structure to store information about a point is considered. The structure represents a spatial data format, since it considers geometric, locational and attribute information of a graphical object. We call this spatial data format as a shape file. Shape file is a combination of three files mentioned above. The display of the shape file is shown in Figure 1.

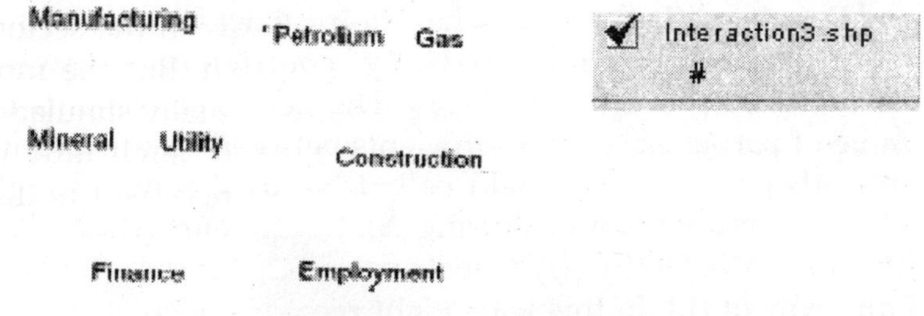

Figure 1: Point Shape File

In Figure 1, each sector is represented as a geometric point object. This facilitates a one-to-one correspondence between the records of the database and shape files. The operation of integration between tabular data and graphic data requires a common field in both of the database. A field named 'Sectors' has been created in the table associated with the point attributes of the shape file. This allows for the integration of statistical tabular data with graphical data, since both of the databases contain a common field named 'Sectors'. Finally, using this commonality the data from the database file is appended in the 'attribute file' of the graphical shape. In this way, the integration of tabular and graphical data is achieved. The resulting results representing simulation of the statistical results in spatial graphical space are shown in Figures 2-4. See further the Technical Appendix.

2-D SURFACE GENERATION

Figure 2a illustrates the interaction between Manufacturing and the other sectors. The intensity of interaction is highest in the deeply coloured region and reduces with the thinness of colour. It is important to mention that statistical data has been assigned as a value to one of the fields ('Man') of the database file and this file has been appended with one of the files of the spatial vector data structure known as shape file. In this way, statistical data has been converted into spatial domain. Figure 2 demonstrates this conversion in a graphical way. Such a transformation from statistical space to spatial domain enables a better visualisation of the interaction between the sectors, which is not possible in statistical approach. But the most important results here is the possibility of visually simulating the statistical results in real-time. Each of such moving simulated point in the spatial domain represents a policy-induced form and the use of appropriate instruments that cause better linkages between the sectors. The improving linkages move the lighter regions into deeper regions, which means that there is enhancing intersection between the regions that in the first instance of the estimated results are found to remain independent of each other. That is the partial elasticity coefficients are negative, while they are simulated in the spatial domain into positive valued ones.

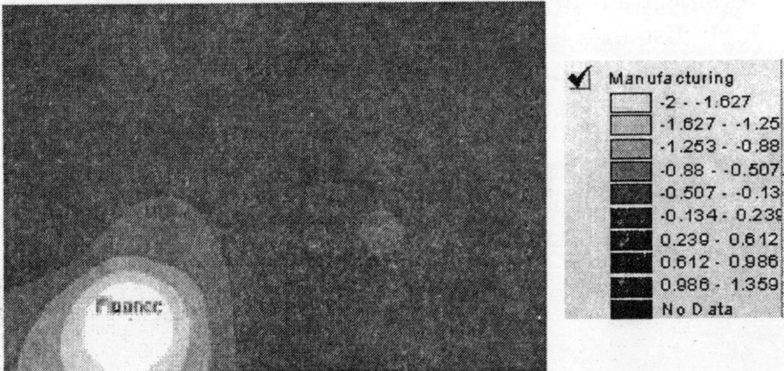

Figure 2 (a): Interaction between Manufacturing and other Sectors

3-D SURFACE GENERATION

A more realistic visual display of sectoral complementarities (linkages) conveying systemic unity of knowledge can be done in the 3-dimension representation. Figure 3 shows in this case the prevailing state of linkages (or not) between sectors.

As shown in Figure 3, a network of complex sectoral interrelationships can be shown. On the other hand, 2-D allows the linear interrelationship to be displayed [Figure 4], which is not enough to demonstrate the presence or absence of linkages or trade-offs between the sectoral output and employment (likewise capital expenditure). Figure 4 simply approximates the log-linear form that we have estimated in the statistical space.

In Figure 3 elevation means the sectoral complementarities as signs of linkages and diversification while trough means sectoral trade-off as sign of absence in linkage and diversification. In this way, various points of elevation and trough visualise the nature of the topography, which can be termed as development landscape originated through a series of spatial analysis starting from shape file.

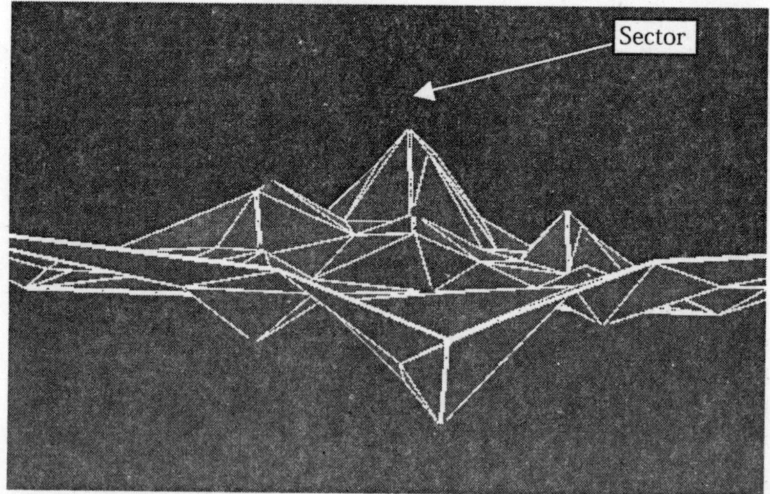

Figure 3: 3-Dimensional Graphical Display of Inter-Sectoral Relations (GDP)

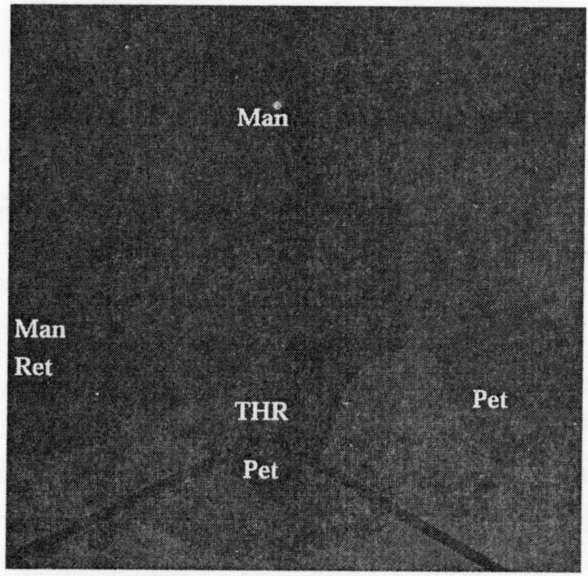

Figure 4: Linear Sectoral Relationship Displayed in 2-D space

POLICY IMPACT IN CONVERTING NEGATIVE PARTIAL ELASTICITY COEFFICIENTS INTO POSITIVE VALUES BY REAL-TIME VISUAL COMPUTER SIMULATION

It can be shown by actual real-time simulation using Figure 4 that this figure contains a pervasive field of different values of the partial elasticity coefficients in respect to different sectoral interrelationships in Gross Domestic Product and total employment. Only two of these possibilities, namely those shown by the lines in Figure 4, and which are approximated by our statistically estimated log-linear forms for Manufacturing and Petroleum inter-sectoral relationships in GDP and total employment, has been analysed in the estimated regression results. But normative policy perspectives in the light of pervasive complementarities and linkages between sectoral GDP and total employment need the negative partial elasticity coefficients to be converted into positive values. This is realized in Figure 4 by real-time simulation of a given negative partial elasticity coefficient into a positive form. This means that the lighter regions are made deeper by bringing their graphs into intersection with the deeper regions.

Movements of the partial elasticity coefficients of this kind represent important policy issues. The conversion of such negative values into positive ones implies sectoral linkages and complementarities in GDP and total employment. Hence improved human resource development, appropriate choice of technological change in concert with human resource development and employment development together with distributive policies of job-creation and sustainability of the sectoral linkages are some of the policy areas that are implied by the value transformation.

CONCLUSION

We end up this paper by pointing out that relational epistemology model of pervasive complementarities between industrial sectors is a powerful positive and normative model of development planning. While relational epistemology is a deeply philosophical conception involving economic and social issues in the development perspective, it is also a pragmatic and rigorously empirical one with extensive normative policy implications. We have shown these perspectives of the relational epistemology model by means of empirical quantification in both the statistical and spatial dimensions of real-time simulation. The results are impressive for guiding policy in cases where there are negative partial elasticity coefficients between sectoral GDP and total employment. The same model can be extended to broader contexts of development planning in inter-sectoral, national, regional and global perspectives.

TECHNICAL APPENDIX

An object with indefinite boundary is represented as a raster in spatial data model while with definite boundary as geometric object. The structure of a raster data model constitutes an array of equally sized cells. These cells are assigned numeric/attribute values and arranged in rows and column. A raster data model also consists of a number of files similar to the *Shape file*. The shape file (which is a vector data) is converted into raster data format and the value of its cells is obtained by interpolating the data of the field 'Man' associated with the attribute table of attribute file. An appropriate colour schema is used to display the raster data as a layer of raster theme as shown in Figure 2.

From a review of Figure 1 (which display the spatial data in vector format) it can be seen that it only displays eight geometric point objects and each object is associated with only one elasticity coefficient data. These point objects have been converted as cell objects in the raster data format. It is important to mention here that in converting data from vector to raster not only eight cells have been generated. Rather, a series of arrays of cells surrounding each of the eight cells have been generated to form a rectangular surface as shown in Figure 2. The additional cells have their values through the interpolation of the data of the field 'Man' associated with attribute table of the of attribute file. This file is one of the three files of the shape file as mentioned earlier and the field 'Man' contains the data of partial elasticity coefficient. Therefore, the additional cells contain another round of estimated data of partial elasticity coefficient. Hence, the entire cell values of the rectangular surface represent a range of partial elasticity coefficient. These cell values can be retrieved using 'identify' function. As we move over the rectangular surface by the cursor the function allows the visualisation of each of the cell values. This also allows the visualisation of the cell value, which is estimated in statistical space between two sectors, for example, manufacturing and finance.

REFERENCES

Choudhury, M.A. (1993), *Unicity Precept and the Socio-Scientific Order*, Lanham, Maryland: University Press of America.

Choudhury, M.A. (2003), *Dynamic Analysis of Trade and Development in the Islamic World: Selected Case Studies*, Bangladesh Institute of Islamic Thought.

Choudhury, M.A. (2004), "Learning systems", *Kybernetes: International Journal of Systems and Cybernetics,* 31:1.

Dobell, R. & E. Burmeister, (1975), *Mathematical Theory of Economic Growth, New York:* Macmillan Co. Ltd.

Goodman, A. (2003), Now What? *Developing Our Future, Understanding Our Place in the Unfolding Universe,* New York: Peter Lang.

Holton, R.J. (1992), "Defining the Economy: a Historical, Multi-dimensional Approach", *in his Economy and Society.* London, Eng: Routledge, pp. 7-22.

Lange, O. (1960), "The Output-Investment Ratio and Input-Output Analysis", *Econometrica, xxviii,* April, pp. 310-24.

Lange, O. (1963), *Introduction to Econometrics,* New York: The Macmillan Company, pp. 202-59.

Lucas, R.E. Jr. (1975), "An Equilibrium Model of the Business Cycle", *Journal of Political Economy,* Vol. 83, pp. 1113-44.

Oxford University Press (1989), *Frontiers of Input-Output Analysis, New York, N.Y.*

Phelps, E.S. (1970), "The new microeconomics in employment and inflation theory", in Phelps, E.S. *Microeconomic Foundations of Employment and Inflation Theory,* New York, NY: W.W. Norton, pp. 1-27.

Smith, T.S. (1992), "Dynamics of strong interactions", in his Strong Interactions, Chicago, ILL: The University of Chicago Press, pp. 67-104.

Thayer-Bacon, B. (2003), "Why '(e)pistemology?" *in her Relational (e)pistemologies.* New York: Peter Lang, pp. 14-48.

Thurow, L. (1983), *Dangerous Currents, the State of Economics,* New York, NY: Random House.

Meier, G.M. (1995), "Dualistic development", in his Leading Issues in Economic Development, New York: Oxford University Press, 113- 160.

Yolles, M. (1998), "A cybernetic exploration of methodological complementarism", Kybernetes:*International Journal of Systems and Cybernetics,* Vol. 27, No. 5, pp. 527-42.

3

ECONOMIC REFORMS, INEQUALITY AND POVERTY IN GHANA

John V. Mensah and Isaac K. Acheampongh***

INTRODUCTION

About one-third of the world's six billion population are afflicted by poverty of which 300 million poor people live in sub-Saharan Africa (UNDP, 2003). Although governments have made attempts at reducing poverty, significant gains have not yet been achieved. Recognising the magnitude of the problem, the United Nations (UN) put in place Millennium Development Goals in 2000. The first goal of eradicating extreme poverty and hunger was to halve the proportion of people whose incomes fall below $1.00 per day by 2015. Among the public policies recommended for eradicating poverty and creating wealth is the expansion of poor people's access to land, credit, skills and economic assets (UNDP, 2003). Reducing poverty involves promoting industrial growth, good governance, equity, efficiency and investment in public goods.

In the early 1980s, most developing countries including Ghana adopted economic reforms (stabilisation and structural

* Research Fellow, Centre for Development Studies, P.O. Box 01, University of Cape Coast, Cape Coast, Ghana.

** Senior Lecturer, Department of Economics, University of Cape Coast, Cape Coast, Ghana.

adjustment policies) following a protracted period of economic decline. The rationale behind these policies was to remove economic distortions and change the incentive structure in favour of production with the view of putting these economies on sustainable growth and development path.

Prior to the inception of the economic reforms, Ghana operated a distorted economic regime that was characterised by price controls; rent seeking, quantitative restrictions and anti-export bias. These policies, in no doubt, affected the income distribution and poverty during that period. The policy shift introduced in 1983 was bound to change the pattern of income distribution and poverty because gainers and losers accompanied adjustment programmes as revealed by political economy issues. For example, the retrenchment associated with economic reforms weakened the financial and bargaining power of organised labour in achieving improvements in their living standards. A major plank of the economic reforms was trade and financial liberalisation, which could cause many hardships for the poor but could also open up opportunities if domestic political and economic institutions and policies were encouraging.

The question is which people actually benefited from the economic reforms and who were the losers? Secondly, one would be curious to know how these policies have impacted on the poorer segments of the society since adjustment programmes do not make significant provisions for the vulnerable groups in society. Even though Ghana put in place the Programme of Action to Mitigate the Social Costs of Adjustment (PAMSCAD) at a latter stage to cater for the vulnerable groups, the programme did not go far enough (Republic of Ghana, 1986).

Poverty reduction among Ghanaians has continued to be the focus of government development policy. Attempts made by the government of Ghana to reduce poverty include:

- PAMSCAD in 1986;
- Human Development Strategy for Ghana in 1991;
- The National Development Policy Framework in 1994 (Vision 2020);

- The First Medium Term Development Plan (1996-2000);
- The Interim Poverty Reduction Strategy, 2001
- Ghana Poverty Reduction Strategy (GPRS) 2001-2007.

Having opted to take advantage of the Heavily Indebted Poor Countries (HIPC) Initiative in 2001, government of Ghana finalised the GPRS as one of the conditions for accessing debt relief, which aimed at supplementing government efforts at poverty reduction. The GPRS is, among other things, to improve the living conditions of the poor by implementing programmes that will increase access to basic needs of life, and develop strong human resource base to enable the poor identify and take advantage of economic opportunities. The target is to reduce the incidence of national poverty from 39 per cent to 32 per cent, extreme poverty from 27 per cent to 21 per cent and poverty among food crop farmers from 59 per cent to 46 per cent by 2004 (Republic of Ghana, 2003).

The experiences of the Newly Industrialising countries (NIC) comprising South Korea, Taiwan, Hong Kong and Singapore, show that countries that pursue economic liberalisation policies tend to achieve rapid economic growth, export growth, and provide opportunities that lead to marked improvement in income distribution and poverty reduction (World Bank, 1993 : 37). However, some researchers hold the view that the Stabilisation and Structural adjustment reforms advocated by the IMF and the World Bank have worsened inequality and poverty in many Latin American countries and transitional economies of Eastern Europe (Handa and King, 1997)[1].

Some critics call the structural adjustment programme 'neoclassical counter-revolution' because the mix of policies advocated to achieve macroeconomic stability, increased efficiency, and enhanced economic growth does not amount to a model but an ultra laissez-faire development ideology (Todaro, 1989; Afful, 2002). The IMF and World Bank and their associates point to the success of the East Asian Newly Industrialised Countries as proof that structural adjustment policies work. However, some writers on the East Asian countries have repeatedly attributed the success to selective interventions by their governments in the product and factor markets, protecting selected activities for prolonged periods, encouraging and subsidising exporters and investing heavily in education and research (Afful, 2002).

In Ghana, studies that were conducted in the latter part of the 1980s on income distribution and poverty profile showed that income distribution and poverty had not worsened under the ERP (Baffoe, 1992; Roe et al., 1992). It is important to note that these studies might have captured the very short run effects of the ERP. Most of the ERP policies were likely to impact on income distribution and poverty in the medium term. Thus, the outcome of studies done earlier on may differ significantly from later developments in the country. It is generally believed that if an economy is able to generate and sustain economic growth, there will be a trickle down effect where jobs and economic opportunities in the form of investment, employment and income exist for the vast majority of the people. However, it appears that there has not been any significant trickle down effect emanating from the economic growth that was achieved so far. An in-depth study on income distribution and poverty is therefore required to fill the gap in knowledge.

There is the general feeling that the economic reforms have worsened income distribution and poverty in Ghana. As such there are concerns about widespread and absolute poverty, growing unemployment and underemployment, wide disparity in income distribution and low standard of living for the vast majority of the people. However, there have not been rigorous attempts at unravelling inequality and poverty inter-temporally. This paper therefore attempts to analyse inequality and poverty in Ghana during (1983-1992) and after (1993-2000) the economic reforms both spatially and inter-temporally.

The paper is outlined in six sections. The second section focuses on theoretical issues relating to the economic reforms, inequality and poverty, sources and measures of inequality and poverty. Section three reviews the empirical literature on inequality and poverty. Sections four and five discuss research methodology and results, respectively. The last section deals with conclusions of the paper.

THEORETICAL ISSUES

This section deals with economic reforms and the concepts of inequality and poverty.

Economic Reforms and Their Distribution Consequences

Economic reforms consist of stabilisation and structural adjustment policies. Stabilisation policies are intended to manage reductions in expenditure to bring about an orderly adjustment of domestic demand to the level of external resources available to the country. They are meant to reduce inflation, balance of payments deficit and fiscal deficit at minimum cost in terms of unemployment and without jeopardising growth. They are normally recommended as a solution to the internal and external gaps of the economies of developing countries (Quarcoo, 1989)[2]. Thus, stabilisation policies are implemented to address the problems associated with external shock and balance of payments difficulties. An external imbalance in an economy is perceived to imply a mismatch between aggregate demand and supply for tradable goods, imbalance in government budgetary account (mainly budget deficits) and accelerated inflationary spiral.

Stabilisation programme often includes fiscal consolidation, monetary contraction, exchange rate adjustment and income policies. The target is external balance, based on the availability of external financing including debt service. Stabilisation policies aim at reducing absorption or expenditure and raise output in order to resolve the imbalance in the external sector and bring about the anticipated growth. They cover fiscal and monetary policies. The real exchange rate may be devalued as part of the adjustment process. In economies characterised by high inflation, apart from expenditure reduction and output expansion and real devaluation issues, there is the need to break the dynamics of inflation, especially through fiscal correction. Fiscal policies involve contraction in government spending or increases in taxes or both in order to reduce the budget deficit. Contractionary monetary policy involves reduction in money supply through raising the reserve ratio, raising central bank discount rate and maintaining credit ceiling. Stabilisation policies that tend to concentrate solely on demand management alone often run into difficulties[3].

In view of this, structural adjustment policies are recommended by the World Bank to complement stabilisation policies to ensure that aggregate demand does not exceed any given level of aggregate supply and to promote faster economic growth (Belassa et al., 1982). Structural policies give a boost to the supply-side by releasing market forces and institutional changes that re-orient the economy over the medium term to achieve growth and greater efficiency (Thomas et al., 1991; Mosley et al, 1991).

Researchers define structural adjustment programme (SAP) differently. Corbo and Fischer (1995: 2846) state that :

> *"Structural adjustment is a process of market oriented reform in policies and institutions, with the goals of restoring a sustainable balance of payments, reducing inflation, and creating the conditions for sustainable growth in per capita income".*

Thomas et al. (1991: 11) defines SAP as:

> *"Changes in relative prices and institutions designed to make the economy more efficient, more flexible, and better able to use resources and so to engineer sustainable long-term growth and structural adjustment policies as those aimed at improving an economy's efficiency and its long-term growth".*

Stabilisation and Structural Adjustment Programmes include macroeconomic adjustment, which may produce large changes in income distribution and poverty through several channels. Firstly, demand management policies tend to bring into balance the mismatch between real income and aggregate demand. Reduction in aggregate demand may affect real wages and consumption of workers in both formal and informal sectors of the economy, which may have adverse consequences on the poor and the vulnerable groups.

Secondly, structural adjustment policy may have positive or negative distribution consequences on the poor and the vulnerable as changes in relative prices have differential effects on various sectors of the economy. Thirdly, trade liberalisation changes the price vector faced by economic agents and may lead to reductions in wages and employment and make highly protected industries less competitive. Fourthly, public sector reforms may reduce employment in overstaffed public sectors of the economy, freeing scarce resources for the deployment of other sectors of the economy that may generate employment and incomes for the people, especially the unemployed. Fifthly, it could weaken the bargaining and financial power of trade unions when a large portion of their membership is retrenched (Agbesinyale, 2000).

Advocates of trade liberalisation point to the large decline in poverty in China, India and Indonesia in the recent decades of internal economic integration. Chen and Ravallion (2004) have estimated that between 1981 and 2001, the percentage of rural people living below an international poverty line of $1.08 per day (at 1983 purchasing power parity) declined from 79 per cent to 27 per cent in China, 63 per cent to 42 per cent in India, and 55 per cent to 11 per cent in Indonesia. But no one has yet convincingly demonstrated that this decline is mainly due to globalisation (trade liberalisation). Internal factors like expansion in infrastructure, land reforms and spread of Green Revolution in agriculture and relaxation of restrictions on rural-urban migration could be responsible for the change.

Chen and Ravallion (2004) have also estimated that between 1981 and 2001, the percentage of poor people (living below $1.08 per day) in SSA increased from 42 per cent to 46 per cent. But this may have little to do with trade liberalisation and more to do with unstable or failed political regimes, wars and civil conflicts, which scared off many foreign investors and traders. There is some marked variation between regions, with generally rising poverty incidence in both Latin America and Africa, and generally falling incidence in Asia (Chen et al, 1994).

Concepts of Poverty and Inequality

Poverty and inequality are interrelated but two different concepts that need to be clarified. Poverty is pronounced deprivation which encompasses a wide range of issues including hunger, lack of shelter and clothing, and inadequate access to health care, education and policymaking (UNDP, 1990). It is recognised as a complex, multi-dimensional and dynamic phenomenon. It is widely viewed as encompassing both income and non-income dimensions of deprivation. The income dimension implies low levels of income or consumption that are socially unacceptable. The non-income dimension can be categorised into three main facets: social, participatory and vulnerability. The social facet refers to lack of health care, education, good drinking water, and decent housing and healthy sanitation. The participatory facet includes lack of voice and political rights. People who lack the ability to participate in decisions that affect their lives directly may consider this as a sense of hopelessness and a fundamental characteristic of poverty. The vulnerability facet considers the situation where the poor are most often exposed to environmental hazards and environment-related conflict, and are least capable of coping when they occur.

According to UN (1995), poverty has various manifestations including lack of income and productive resources sufficient to ensure sustainable livelihoods, hunger, malnutrition, ill health, limited or lack of access to education and other basic services, increased morbidity and mortality from illness, homelessness and inadequate housing, unsafe environment and social discrimination. It is also characterised by a lack of participation in decision-making and in civil, social and cultural life.

The most important difference between poverty and inequality is that the former is a prescriptive concept while the latter is a descriptive concept. Poverty means going short materially, socially and emotionally while inequality is simply a state of affairs, and whether it is acceptable or not is a matter of opinion. Opinions differ about whether and how much inequality is acceptable or desirable (Alcock, 1993).

Inequality is a matter of relative income/consumption while the concept of poverty focuses on the low absolute income received or consumption attained by certain households. An objective definition of poverty is hard to formulate. Calculations of the minimum income/consumption necessary for physical survival indicate that one can subsist on very little if one chooses. Efforts to link poverty to its specific manifestations- starvation, severe malnutrition, illiteracy, substandard clothing and housing- are also inconclusive. Poverty is not just a matter of absolute income/consumption but also relative income/consumption. In some terms, the poor are those who must live below what most people in a particular time and place regard as the minimum acceptable standard. Thus, different standards apply in different places. Psychologically, the poor are those who feel deprived of whatever is enjoyed by other members of the society of which they consider themselves to be a part.

Researchers who focus on the measurement of poverty existing in a country usually begin by drawing a poverty line. Ideally, this line is defined in terms of household income/ consumption per capita. Households with per capita income /consumption below the poverty line are defined as poor while those with income per capita/ consumption above the poverty line are considered not poor. The simplest and most common measure of poverty is the percentage of all households that are poor. A better measure, however, would also take account of the extent to which the incomes of the poor fall below the poverty line. A reduction in poverty would then be measured through a fall in the percentage of poor households in the total number of households and also through increases in the absolute incomes of the poor (Gillis et al, 1996).

Sources of Inequality and Poverty

Equality simply means that everyone gets the same income or owns the same wealth. This never occurs in practice but the concept provides an objective standard against which any actual distribution can be judged. The sources of inequality and poverty arises from:

(i) Unemployment

(ii) Differences in resource ownership

(iii) Differences in the price obtained for these resources.

(iv) Re-distribution policies relating to these resources that affect either income or purchasing power.

Economists have attempted to explain the pattern of income distribution and poverty. Theoretically, three paradigms attempt to explain income distribution and poverty in terms of exploitation, productivity and appropriation (Samuels and Kelsey, 1991). The classical economists explained inequality in terms of separate social classes owing particular factors of production, notably landlords and workers. Modern distribution theory, as developed by Marshall (1920), is based on the marginal productivity of the factors of production. Factor prices and employment levels therefore determine incomes. The Appropriation theory, on the other hand, attempts to explain income distribution in terms of the actual factors that are actually at work such as policy effects, land ownership and employment.

Traditionally, the analysis of income distribution and equity has been looked at from the functional distribution of income. This perspective looks at income inequality from the viewpoint of factors of production, especially labour and capital. Individuals are classified into workers and capitalists, with the vulnerable group being workers. Since this approach to the analysis of income distribution and equity issues does not reflect much on how the household or the individual is worse off, most researchers tend to look at income inequity from the perspective of interpersonal distribution of income or consumption. Owing to differences in factor ownership and imperfections in factor pricing, incomes tend not to be equitably distributed.

Apart from the theoretical issues raised above, the United Nations (1995) recognises that poverty has various causes with both national and international origins. It is inseparably linked to lack of control over resources including land, skills, knowledge, capital and social connections. Without the resources, people are easily neglected by policy makers and have limited access to institutions, markets, employment and public services. Therefore, poverty eradication cannot be accomplished through anti-poverty programmes alone. It also requires democratic participation in the changes in economic structures to:

- ensure access to all resources, opportunities and public services;
- undertake policies geared towards more equitable distribution of wealth and income;
- provide social protection for those who cannot support themselves; and
- assist people confronted by unexpected catastrophe whether individual or collective, natural, social or technological.

EMPIRICAL LITERATURE ON POVERTY AND INEQUALITY

Historically, national poverty and inequality analyses in Ghana have been based on national expenditure surveys conducted by the Central Bureau of Statistics now Ghana Statistical Service. Analyses of such data have focused on the distribution of income and income inequality (Assefa, 1980: 53-61). Assefa (1980) reports that the lowest quintile received 11.5 per cent of total earnings in 1956 as against 7.1 per cent in 1975. The highest quintile, on the other hand, received 36.6 per cent of total earnings in 1956 as compared to 45.6 per cent in 1975. Using 1974/75 household survey in Ghana, Assefa (1980) and Ewusi (1984) observed that the rural sector was slightly worse off than the national profile of income distribution. The lower 20 per cent of the rural sector received 6 per cent of income as against the national lower 20 per cent that received an average of 7.1 per cent while the upper 20 per cent of the rural sector received slightly more (45.5 per cent) than the national upper 20 per cent average (45 per cent).

According to Ewusi (1984), income distribution within the rural sector appeared slightly better than that of the urban sector. In the urban sector, the lowest decile received 1.5 per cent of income as compared with 1.8 per cent of income received by the lowest decile of the rural sector. In 1974/75, the computed values of Gini coefficient for the nation, the rural sector and the urban sector were 0.3664, 0.3762 and 0.4024 respectively. As a rule of thumb, a Gini coefficient of less than 0.5 depicts a low income inequality while that of greater than 0.5 shows high inequality in income distribution.

Based on the 1962/63 and 1974/75 expenditure surveys, Assefa (1980) noted that, the urban sector with only 33 per cent of the total population accounted for 45 per cent of total national expenditure in 1974/75. Both per capita rural and urban expenditures in real terms declined over the period: 1961-1975. The fall was more with the average rural income resulting in the widening of rural-urban income gap.

After the inception of the economic reforms in Ghana, using various measures of inequality, Baffoe (1992) obtained a Gini coefficient of 0.347, Theil entropy index of 0.23 and alternative Theil entropy index of 0.24 for 1989. The outcome of these inequality measures indicate that Ghana had a more equitable income distribution than other African countries such as Benin, Côte d'Ivoire and Chad, with Gini coefficient of 0.4675, 0.435 and 0.3687 respectively. The study also revealed that inequality was more pronounced in the rural sector than in the semi-urban and urban sectors of the economy. Baffoe (1992) observed that despite the fact that income was fairly distributed, a considerable number of Ghanaians lived below the poverty line, ranging from 62 per cent to 20 per cent depending on the poverty line assumed. The Ghana Living Standards Survey showed that the average standard of living in Ghana fell by 5 per cent between 1987 and 1989 but increased sharply by 15 per cent between 1989 and 1992.

On the international scene, some research works have been done on the impact of adjustment policies on income distribution and poverty. Berry (1996) demonstrated that adjustment programmes in Argentina, Chile, Colombia, The Dominican Republic, Ecuador, Mexico and Uruguay have impacted adversely on income distribution and poverty. Berry (1996) notes that the only exception to the foregoing negative trend is that of Costa Rica, where measures of income distribution remained unchanged throughout the economic reform period. Alarcon and McKinley (1995) also showed that in Mexico, primary income inequality became more pronounced during the reform period (1984-1992) and in the immediate post reform period.

Similarly, Riveros (1995) shows that in Chile unemployment rose and formal and informal wages fell during the adjustment era. The distribution of income worsened when Chile's reforms were being implemented. In Argentina, Marshall (1995) indicates that the pattern of falling real wages and rising inequality was repeated even though the trend started well before the reforms were implemented.

A study by Cornelius and Weber (1996) on the impact of adjustment programme on Transitional Economies in Eastern Europe provided similar results as the Latin American economies featured above. Specifically, in Estonia, Lavatia and Lithuania, the economic reforms ushered the economies into successful market economies but that culminated in a significant widening of income disparities.

Handa and King (1997) provide evidence on Jamaica, where the initial reforms in the early 1980s associated with public sector retrenchment, gradual trade and price liberalisation coincided with inequality and decline in living standards. However, the second round of economic reforms which were implemented in the early 1990s were much more drastic in their orientation towards the free market, and were also associated with a sudden and sharp increase in inequality but there was a recovery in 1993. The foregoing empirical literature review shows that the economic reforms tend to perpetuate inequality in income distribution and poverty.

RESEARCH METHODOLOGY

Measurement of the direct impact of economic reforms on poverty and inequality is actually quite tricky. Apart from the scarcity of detailed household data before and after economic reforms, it is often difficult to disentangle the effects of economic reform from those of other reforms, events and shocks that affect the household poverty dynamics. Most existing attempts to measure the impact use simulations based on economic models. Ghana Statistical Service uses its household survey data [four series of Ghana Living Standards Survey (GLSS 1- 4)] for more than one period and this is very encouraging. This paper utilises the GLSS data for computation and analysis of the various measures of inequality and poverty: Gini Coefficient, Theil Entropy Index, and Foster, Greer and Thorbecke Index.

Measures of Inequality

Two measures of inequality used in this paper are the Gini Coefficient and Theil Entropy index.

Gini Coefficient

The Gini Coefficient is a statistic that measures the relative inequality in the distribution of income. The computation of the Gini Coefficient is based on the cumulative percentages of households and the corresponding percentages of the total income accruing to them. It must be emphasised that the Gini Coefficient is not able to tell whether the income level is high or low but it can help to induce either a decrease or an increase in income thresholds.

The Gini Coefficient (G) is statistically formulated as follows :

$$G = 1 - \sum_{i=0}^{n-1} (F_{i+1} - F_i)(H_{i+1} + H_i)$$

Where

n = number of households.

F_i = cumulative population shares corresponding to household, and

H = cumulative expenditure shares corresponding to household

The Theil Entropy Index

The Theil Entropy Measure (T) is defined as follows:

$$T = \sum_{i=1}^{n} \frac{1}{n} \bullet \frac{1}{n} \bullet \frac{Y_i}{u} \log \frac{Y_i}{u}$$

T = Theil entropy index

n = number of households

Y_i = Expenditure of household

u = mean expenditure

Both the Gini Coefficient and Theil Entropy Index range from zero (when incomes are equal) to one (when incomes are extremely unequal). Thus, each inequality measure is scaled to lie between zero (prefect equality) and one (perfect inequality). The Gini coefficient is more sensitive to measuring changes in the middle range of an expenditure distribution, while the Theil index measure is more sensitive to changes in the tails (Tsakloglou, 1993).

Measures of Poverty

There are a number of measures that are used in poverty analysis. These are the Head Count ratio, Income Gap index, Sen poverty index and Foster, Greer and Thorbecke index. The index adopted for this paper is the Foster, Greer and Thorbecke index (Foster et al. 1984) because it is decomposable across subgroups.

Foster, Greer and Thorbecke Index is given as:

$$P_2 = \frac{1}{N} \sum_{i \in n} \left[\frac{Y^* - Y_i}{Y^*} \right]^2$$

Where

(Y^*-Y_i) measures, for individual i in poverty, the gap between income and poverty line.

Y^* is the poverty line.

n is the set of all the poor.

N is the total population

Y_i is income for individual i.

RESULTS

The results focus on trend analysis of inequality, trend and spatial analysis of poverty, and basic needs approach to poverty analysis.

Trend Analysis of Inequality in Ghana

The results of inequality measures for the country as a whole and the decomposition of the inequality measures in deciles are shown in Tables 1 and 2 respectively.

The Gini coefficient and Theil T are calculated for the purpose of comparison and are shown in Table 1. The expenditure Gini Coefficient declined from 0.366 in 1974/75 to 0.347 in 1987 but increased thereafter. Both Income Gini Coefficient and Expenditure Theil T also increased from 1987 to 1999. These results suggest that inequality rose during and after the economic reforms.

Table 1
Inequalities in Consumption Expenditure and Income in Ghana.

Year	*Gini Coefficient (G)*		*Theil T*
	Expenditure	*Income*	*Expenditure*
1974/1975	0.366	NA	NA
1987	0.347	0.351	0.214
1989	0.370	0.366	0.230
1992	0.350	0.480	0440
1999	0.430	0.620	0.563

Note: NA = Not Available
(i) Gini coefficient for expenditure for 1987, 1989 and 1999 has been computed in GLSS1, GLSS2, GLSS3 and GLSS4.
(ii) Authors computed the Theil T
Source: Ewusi (1984); Ghana Statistical Service (GLSS various issues).

This degree of inequality in the country can also be appreciated if we further look at the disparity of expenditure accruing to the lowest and highest 20 per cent of the population as presented in Table 2. Over the period under review, the expenditure of the lowest 20 per cent of the population in Ghana ranged between 5.1 per cent and 7.1 per cent while that of the highest 20 per cent of the population ranged between 26.3 per cent and 45 per cent. The ratio of the top 20 per cent to lower 20 per cent increased from 3.7:1 in 1987 to 8.6:1 in 1999 indicating increasing inequality in expenditure.

Table 2
Distribution of Expenditure by Decile
(% Share of Per Capita Overtime)

Decile	*1987*	*1989*	*1992*	*1998/9*
1	2.97	3.0	2.9	1.9
2	4.16	4.1	4.4	3.2
3	5.26	5.4	5.4	4.2
4	6.28	5.5	6.3	5.3
5	7.55	7.0	7.4	6.5
6	8.56	8.5	8.5	8.0
7	10.15	10.1	9.9	10.0
8	11.5	11.5	11.9	17.0
9	15.40	14.2	15.2	12.6
10	27.98	30.8	28.1	31.3
Lower 20 per cent	6.95	7.1	7.3	5.1
Upper 20 per cent	26.25	45.0	43.9	43.9
Ratio of top 20 per cent to lower 20 per cent	3.70:1	6.30:1	6.01:1	8.60:1

Source: Ghana Statistical Service (GLSS various issues); and authors' computation.

Spatially, it is worth noting that the first lowest, second lowest, third lowest, fourth lowest and the highest 20 per cent lay zones represents the Rural Savannah, Rural Coastal, Rural Forest, Other Urban and Accra respectively. Overtime, Accra (highest 20 per cent) stood out clearly with the lowest expenditure gap, while Rural Savannah (lowest 20 per cent) emerged with the highest expenditure gap. Comparatively, the disparity in the distribution of expenditure between the Rural Savannah and Accra has widened in recent times and it is around 40:1 while that of expenditure distribution is about 9:1 (Ghana Statistical Service, 2000).

The computation of the Gini coefficient at constant prices, which is a relative measure of inequality as shown in Table 3 adjusts for inflation in order to make inter-temporal comparison valid. The Gini coefficient rose from 0.6 in 1987 to 0.7 in 1989 and dropped to 0.6 again in 1998/9. Gini coefficient of this magnitude appears to be on the high side because an economy that exhibits a moderate-income distribution should normally have a Gini coefficient ranging from 0 to 0.5. It is important to note the Gini coefficient at constant prices differs from those at current prices shown in Table 1.

Table 3
Cumulative Distribution of Household Expenditure and Gini Coefficient at constant prices

Decile	*Cumulative Percentage Share of Households*	*1987 % Expenditure*	*1987 Cumulative% Expenditure*	*1989 % Expenditure*	*1989 Cumulative% Expenditure*	*1998/9 % Expenditure*	*1998/9 Cumulative% Expenditure*
1	0.1	0.0171	0.0171	0.0141	0.0141	0.0169	0.0169
2	0.2	0.0226	0.0397	0.0183	0.0324	0.0212	0.0381
3	0.3	0.0280	0.0677	0.0223	0.0525	0.0252	0.0633
4	0.4	0.0330	0.1007	0.0264	0.0811	0.0289	0.0922
5	0.5	0.0381	0.1388	0.0309	0.112	0.0334	0.1256
6	0.6	0.0441	0.1829	0.0358	0.1478	0.0385	0.1641
7	0.7	0.0523	0.2352	0.0423	0.1901	0.0448	0.2089
8	0.8	0.0634	0.2986	0.0515	0.2416	0.0552	0.2641
9	0.9	0.0832	0.3818	0.0695	0.3111	0.0736	0.3377
10	1.0	0.0618	1.0000	0.6889	1.0000	0.6622	1.0000
Gini Coefficient			0.6		0.7		0.6

Source: Ghana Statistical Service (1995: 6)

The implications of the results are that during and after the economic reforms, the real growth rate of economy of about 5 per cent could not trickle down to the broad segments of the population as inequality was aggravated. The outcome is not be surprising given the fact that real aggregate income per capita for the period under review averaged about US $390 depicting Ghana as a low-income country. As postulated by Kuznets (1956), low-income countries tend to exhibit greater inequality in income.

Trend and Spatial Analysis of Poverty

The objective of this section is to examine the trends in poverty of Ghanaians inter-temporally and spatially based on Foster, Greer and Thorbecke poverty index using the GLSS. The analysis used the national lower and higher poverty lines for 1987/88 of ¢99,173 and ¢132,230 and that for 1991-1999 of ¢700,000 and ¢900,000, respectively.

In examining the incidence of poverty inter-temporally, Table 4 reveals that between 1987 and 1989, the incidence of poverty in Ghana increased from 22 per cent to 25 per cent based on the lower poverty line. Meanwhile, based on the higher poverty line, the incidence of poverty increased from 37 per cent to 42 per cent for the whole country.

Table 4
Incidence of Poverty (%) in Ghana-1987-88 to 1998-99

Area	*GLSS 1 1987/88*	*GLSS 2 1988/89*	*GLSS 3 1991/92*	*GLSS 4 1998/99*	*Poverty Ranking*
Accra	H: 9 L: 3	H: 22 L: 10	H: 23 L: 11	H: 4 L: 2	7
Other Coastal	H: 33 L: 19	H: 35 L: 18	NA	NA	NA
Urban Coastal	NA	NA	H: 28 L: 14	H: 24 L: 14	5
Urban Forest	NA	NA	H: 26 L: 13	H: 18 L: 11	6
Urban Savannah	NA	NA	H: 38 L: 27	H: 43 L: 27	3
Rural Coastal	H: 38 L: 23	H: 45 L: 27	H: 53 L: 33	H: 45 L: 28	2
Rural Forest	H: 38 L: 22	H: 42 L: 24	H: 62 L: 46	H: 38 L: 21	4
Rural Savannah	H: 49 L: 33	H: 55 L: 37	H: 73 L: 58	H: 70 L: 59	1
National	H: 37 L: 22	H: 42 L: 25	H: 52 L: 37	H: 40 L: 27	

Note: H = higher poverty line; L = lower poverty line; NA = not available.
Source: Ghana Statistical Service (2000): Computed from GLSS 1, 2. 3, 4.

The results of the GLSS 1 and 2 show that poverty in the rural areas is higher than the national average. A larger proportion of the poor is concentrated in the savanna area. The GLSS 3 and 4 show that the incidence of national poverty declined from 52 per cent in 1991/92 to 40 per cent in 1998/1999, given the higher poverty line of Ë900,000. However, the incidence of poverty declined from 37 per cent to 27 per cent based on the lower poverty line of Ë700,000 for the same period. The decline in the incidence of poverty was not uniform across the country but it was particularly striking in Accra. Even though poverty declined between 1992 and 1999, the depth of poverty for those who remain poor has worsened, with the depth of poverty being greater at the higher poverty line than at the lower poverty line.

From Table 4, it is evident from the ranking that the poorest area in Ghana is the rural savannah, followed by the rural coastal, urban savannah and rural forest. This clearly demonstrates that poverty is a rural phenomenon in Ghana.

Basic Needs Approach to Poverty Analysis

To assess the standard of living of the people, we analyse the basic needs of the people inter-temporally and spatially based on education, health, access to safe water and electricity. These needs have the characteristics of being public goods and conceptually difficult to measure in monetary terms. We analyse the access to these non-monetary indicators of standard of living by the very poor, poor and non-poor over the period 1987-1999.

Individuals use health facilities when they consider themselves to have been taken ill or injured. Analysis of access to housing facilities focuses on potable water, adequate toilet facility and electricity. Our analysis of education concentrates on school enrolment rate at the primary and secondary school levels, which have the capacity to increase the literacy rate. For the sake of the analysis, this paper adopts the definitions of the Ghana Statistical Service used in GLSS reports. The very poor are those who live below the lower poverty line; poor are those living below the upper poverty line; and non-poor are those living above the upper poverty line.

It important to note that any improvement in access to these basic needs could not be attributed to economic reforms alone. The reason is that over the period of economic reforms, Ghana also deepened its decentralisation and local governance processes and various NGOs, religious bodies and donors made contributions towards the provision of public basic facilities in the country, especially in the rural areas.

Access to Potable Water

The source of drinking water is an important household amenity, which impacts on health. Generally, over one-third of households in Ghana have access to potable water, defined as non-natural sources. However, access to potable water is higher in the urban areas than in the rural areas. In urban areas, a larger proportion of the people has access to potable water. At the national level, the non-poor are more likely to have access to potable water because they can afford houses that have such facilities.

Table 5 reveals that in the urban sector, the very poor and the poor have less access to potable water than the non-poor. However, in the rural sector, access to potable water by the very poor and the poor are not significantly different from the non-poor. Table 5 also shows that over the period under review, there had been considerable improvement in the access to potable water by all categories of people in both rural and urban areas.

Access to Toilet Facilities

The type of toilet used by households impinges on their standard of living. Obviously, a flush toilet is much more hygienic than the pit latrine. The KVIP toilet introduced in the 1990s represents an improvement on the pit latrine. Table 6 shows that pit latrine is the most predominant facility used by about 60 per cent of rural households and 30 per cent of urban households. It is also clear that non-poor households are more likely to use flush toilet and KVIP while households of low socio-economic status are more likely to use pit latrine or may not have a toilet facility at all. The general trend is that the

Table 5
Access to Drinking Water (Percent)

Area	*Type of Drinking source*	*GLSS1 1987-88*			*GLSS2 1988-89*			*GLSS 3 1991/92*			*GLSS 4 1998/99*		
		Very Poor	*Poor*	*Non Poor*	*Very Poor*	*Poor*	*Non Poor*	*Very Poor*	*Poor*	*Non Poor*	*Very Poor*	*Poor*	*Non Poor*
Urban	1. Inside Pipe	10.5	16.2	33.2	20.5	19.2	41	23.0	23.8	41.9	8.0	15.1	37.8
	2. Water Vendor	5.3	3.6	9.0									
	3. Neighbour/	23.7	25.2	22.3	3.0	5.4	8.7	3.4	3.4	3.7	1.0	1.7	7.3
	Private				24.2	33.8	22.5	18.9	31.3	21.0	31.4	28.6	28.9
	4. Public Stand	19.3	10.8	9.9	8.3	8.5	8.1	13.5	14.3	13.2	17.2	24.9	13.5
	5. Well	18.4	21.6	15.7	28.8	23.1	10.6	19.6	16.3	11.8	20.2	15.2	7.8
	6. Natural sources	22.8	22.5	9.9	15.2	10.0	9.2	21.6	10.9	8.5	22.2	14.4	4.8
Rural	1. Inside Pipe	0.0	0.0	1.6	0.0	0.6	2.5	1.4	1.8	3.7	0.7	0.7	5.2
	2. Water Vendor	0.0	0.0	0.3	0.0	0.3	0.4	0.3	0.4	0.5	0.3	0.7	2.9
	3. Neighbour/ Private	1.1	1.5	1.9	2.3	3.4	6.2	1.5	2.7	3.0	1.7	3.0	7.6
	4. Public Stand	5.1	4.5	5.8	2.7	3.7	3.3	5.0	8.5	11.1	7.1	13.7	12.4
	5. Well	27.2	22.7	20.1	28.9	24.7	26.8	38.7	34.4	37.0	28.8	23.1	10.6
	6. Natural sources	66.7	71.4	70.3	62.3	66.0	60.4	53.0	52.1	44.8	34.6	37.8	35.3

Source: Ghana Statistical Service (various issues of GLSS)

Table 6
Access to Toilet Facilities

Area	*Type of Toilet*	GLSS 1 *1987-88* *Very Poor*	*Poor*	*Non Poor*	GLSS2 *1988-89* *Very Poor*	*Poor*	*Non Poor*	GLSS 3 *1991/92* *Very Poor*	*Poor*	*Non Poor*	GLSS 4 *1998/99* *Very Poor*	*Poor*	*Non Poor*
Urban	1. Flush Toilet	0.9	3.6	16.1	3.0	5.4	17.8	0.7	9.5	20	0.4	2.8	17.5
	2. Pit Latrine	39.5	36.9	33.6	46.2	50.4	33.4	37.8	32.7	28.3	26.2	18.5	17.4
	3. Pan Latrine	32.5	38.7	28.5	20.5	17.8	25.4	20.9	26.5	25.2	4.5	7.2	13.7
	4. KVIP	-	-	-	-	-	-	10.1	15.6	12.5	48.2	53.2	49.4
	5. Other	27.2	20.7	21.8	30.3	26.4	2.3	26.4	15.6	13.9	20.8	18.3	7.0
Rural	1. Flush Toilet	0.3	0.4	1.0	0.0	0.0	1.5	0.5	1.1	2.2	0.5	0.3	2.3
	2. Pit Latrine	61.3	68.4	65.4	57.3	65.7	66.3	58.8	65.7	61.6	34.1	53.7	48.6
	3. Pan Latrine	3.0	3.7	6.7	2.5	4.6	6.7	2.8	3.1	5.4	1.5	4.8	4.0
	4. KVIP	-	-	-	-	-	-	2.5	4.3	4.4	10.4	16.7	24.7
	5. Other	35.5	27.5	26.8	40.2	29.6	28.5	35.4	25.3	26.7	58.5	24.1	23.3

Source: Ghana Statistical Service (various issues of GLSS)

proportions of households that use flush toilet have not changed significantly over time while the use of pan latrine is being phased out. The proportion of households without toilet facilities rarely changed over time.

It is striking to note that households that had access to flush and KVIP toilets increased significantly between 1990 to 1999 in both urban and rural areas. The predominant use of adequate toilet facilities is reflected in the increase use of KVIP in both rural and urban areas. The proportion of rural households with access to flush and KVIP toilets is less than half of the households with comparable standard of living in urban areas.

Access to Health Services

A healthy population is a big asset to a nation in terms of productive capacity. Table 7 shows access to health services. Until 1991/92, the data available combined rural and urban access to health services. In both rural and urban areas, the majority of Ghanaians did not contact doctors and this cuts across the very poor, poor and non-poor. It is clear from Table 7 that the very poor and the poor had less access to a medical officer than the non-poor did. As compared with 1988/89, Ghanaians were less likely to consult well-qualified health personnel in the 1990s. The decline in percentage access to doctors in the 1990s could be related to the massive exodus of doctors to developed countries for greener pastures as well as rising cost of health services associated with the "cash and carry" policy. Indeed, many people find it difficult in terms of affordability to access orthodox health services.

Access to Electricity

Electricity provides power to communities for socio-economic development. A large number of people in the country use electricity for lighting. In 1980s, the majority (more than 90 per cent) of the people in rural areas were deprived of electricity. In the 1990s, the proportion of rural population getting access to electricity improved due to the government's rural electrification programme but the non-poor had better

Table 7
Access to Health Services

Area	*Health Personnel*	*GLSS1 1987-88 Both Urban & Rural*			*GLSS2 1988-89 Both Urban & Rural*			*GLSS 3 1991/92*			*GLSS 4 1998/99*		
		Very Poor	*Poor*	*Non Poor*	*Very Poor*	*Poor*	*Non Poor*	*Very Poor*	*Poor*	*Non Poor*	*Very Poor*	*Poor*	*Non Poor*
Urban	1. Doctor	44.3	51.0	55.7	37.7	40.9	51.7	34.9	22.3	41.4	21.1	15.8	37.2
	2. Nurse	9.7	11.8	11.3	20.0	17.0	14.0	6.2	1.4	3.4	7.7	10.5	4.8
	3. Medical Assistant	32.7	24.4	21.8	26.6	27.8	25.6	8.9	13.7	4.4	4.1	6.4	3.1
	4. Pharmacist	2.5	7.3	3.5	3.4	4.4	2.4	1.4	2.2	3.8	3.0	0.9	6.9
	5. Other	10.7	5.6	7.7	12.3	9.9	6.3	2.1	5.8	6.6	6.2	7.5	4.0
	6. No Consultation	-	-	-	-	-	-	46.6	54.7	40.5	57.8	59.0	44.1
Rural	1. Doctor							13.5	17.2	23.2	7.4	12.6	17.8
	2. Nurse							7.5	8.3	10.1	7.6	12.2	8.9
	3. Medical Assistant							9.9	8.0	8.5	12.3	8.5	7.9
	4. Pharmacist							1.4	3.0	4.8	0.9	0.8	1.4
	5. Other							6.9	8.5	4.3	6.8	4.0	6.9
	6. No consultation							60.9	55.0	49.1	65.0	62.0	57.1

Source: Ghana Statistical Service (various issues of GLSS)

access than poor and very poor. Table 8 shows that the proportion of households in urban areas having access to electricity was more than three times of their rural counterparts.

Access to Education

Education enhances the human resource development of a country for effective and efficient productive services. The fundamentals of education are primary and secondary schools. This does not imply that the tertiary levels are not equally important. The issue is that the majority of people are more likely to meet their basic needs with the primary and secondary education. Table 9 and 10 reveal that the enrolment rates in both primary and secondary schools improved considerably between 1988 and 1999. The increase in net enrolment rates at the secondary level was much higher for girls than for boys but the rates for girls still remained below that for boys.

The foregoing analysis shows that over time the standard of living of Ghanaians in terms of basic needs have not improved significantly with the very poor and poor having less access to the basic needs than the non-poor. There has been some improvement with respect to the proportion of households obtaining their drinking water from safe sources, using improved toilet facilities and having access to electricity and schools. These changes have been observed in all income groups and areas of the country, though in many cases the gains have not been equally distributed with the richer groups benefiting the more. Thus, the very poor and poor benefited less relative to the non-poor.

CONCLUSIONS

The purpose of this paper was to analyse inequality and poverty in Ghana during, after and beyond the economic reforms that were implemented in the early 1980s. Based on the Gini Coefficient and Theil Entropy Index, the analyses showed that income/expenditure inequality worsened during and after the economic reforms. Using Forster, Greer and Thorbecke Poverty Index, the analyses revealed that poverty

Table 8
Access to Electricity

Area	*GLSS1 1987-88*			*GLSS2 1988-89*			*GLSS3 1991/92*			*GLSS4 1998/99*		
	Very Poor	*Poor*	*Non Poor*	*Very Poor*	*Poor*	*Non Poor*	*Very Poor*	*Poor*	*Non Poor*	*Very Poor*	*Poor*	*Non Poor*
Urban	32.5	53.2	66.2	42.4	55.4	68.2	48.0	57.1	72.7	34.2	48.3	84.6
Rural	2.2	1.5	7.0	1.6	3.4	8.9	4.3	7.9	12.2	5.8	14.8	27.5

Source: Ghana Statistical Service (various issues of GLSS)

Table 9
Net Enrolment in Primary schools

Area	*Sex*	*GLSS1 1987/88*			*GLSS2 1988/89*			*Area*	*GLSS3 1991/92*			*GLSS4 1998/99*		
		Very Poor	*Poor*	*Non Poor*	*Very Poor*	*Poor*	*Non Poor*		*Very Poor*	*Poor*	*Non Poor*	*Very Poor*	*Poor*	*Non Poor*
Accra	Male	80.0	71.4	66.7	80.0	91.7	94.0	Accra	82.4	90.0	93.3	77.0	100	94.3
	Female	50.0	40.0	68.2	64.7	85.0	79.7		85.7	68.8	90.7	44.5	100	87.3
Other	Male	76.1	83.9	76.2	87.0	68.8	82.1	Urban	75.0	79.3	89.9	80.0	86.0	89.2
Urban	Female	60.0	70.0	66.0	76.3	58.9	66.0	Coastal	84.4	65.0	85.3	82.8	85.5	89.7
Rural	Male	61.2	48.4	40.0	70.3	65.0	80.6	Urban	88.1	76.9	92.9	86.6	100	96.1
Coastal	Female	50.9	40.9	42.0	57.1	70.3	61.3	Forest	59.3	71.1	89.5	90.1	100	87.7
Rural	Male	72.4	66.2	78.2	77.7	75.8	79.1	Urban	76.3	76.9	85.0	91.5	100	95.2
Forest	Female	53.3	61.0	65.0	67.7	70.9	72.7	Savannah	35.0	100	73.6	87.2	100	89.7
Rural	Male	46.2	61.2	50.3	37.6	46.6	53.7	Rural	71.7	85.7	85.7	75.2	76.3	94.0
Savannah	Female	27.4	48.1	52.6	24.8	54.7	59.0	Coastal	63.5	64.5	80.4	75.7	85.6	90.0
								Rural	82.6	83.0	89.1	86.9	89.6	93.5
								Forest	77.6	85.5	87.4	78.2	89.7	92.1
								Rural	47.1	53.8	60.9	65.1	81.3	62.7
								Savannah	43.0	46.8	51.3	57.9	69.3	64.4
All	Male	63.9	67.7	66.3	64.2	66.8	78.0	All	68.2	76.2	85.7	75.1	86.7	90.6
	Female	47.4	58.4	60.8	56.0	65.4	67.5		62.4	68.9	81.1	69.6	85.9	87.2

Source: Ghana Statistical Service (various issues of GLSS)

Table 10
Net Enrolment in Secondary Schools

Area	*Sex*	*GLSS 1 1987/88*			*GLSS 2 1988/89*			*Area*	*GLSS 3 1991/92*			*GLSS 4 1998/99*		
		Very Poor	*Poor*	*Non Poor*	*Very Poor*	*Poor*	*Non Poor*		*Very Poor*	*Poor*	*Non Poor*	*Very Poor*	*Poor*	*Non Poor*
Accra	Male	33.3	0.0	41.5	55.6	35.7	61.4	Accra	63.0	47.2	54.5	36.8	58.1	61.3
	Female	66.7	0.0	40.2	21.1	44.4	33.6		30.4	42.1	38.6	35.1	36.3	54.4
Other	Male	37.1	36.8	46.1	39.4	27.8	41.6	Urban	40.6	57.7	57.1	42.8	62.6	54.0
Urban	Female	23.7	28.6	37.1	25.4	23.6	26.6	Coastal	37.0	47.8	43.8	41.0	18.0	50.4
Rural	Male	24.6	25.0	24.5	34.5	27.9	36.4	Urban	48.6	31.6	51.1	35.4	49.1	52.5
Coastal	Female	14.0	18.5	9.4	18.0	19.2	28.8	Forest	23.5	28.6	44.2	44.5	46.0	43.6
Rural	Male	45.0	41.9	46.3	45.1	44.9	44.0	Urban	22.5	42.9	28.4	55.8	45.4	44.2
Forest	Female	26.9	37.1	30.8	37.9	27.8	36.9	Savannah	22.2	53.8	38.3	26.5	66.3	43.5
Rural	Male	26.5	25.9	29.7	17.0	32.2	26.9	Rural	34.3	51.5	45.0	34.5	44.3	43.3
Savannah	Female	15.2	26.3	10.0	8.2	15.7	15.7	Coastal	22.5	41.2	28.7	32.1	28.1	39.5
								Rural	43.9	41.4	45.6	35.0	47.3	45.7
								Forest	36.2	31.0	36.4	30.8	38.4	43.5
								Rural	23.6	29.5	30.6	21.9	31.5	30.2
								Savannah	19.7	25.9	25.3	18.8	31.9	23.4
All	Male	34.5	33.6	39.6	33.7	34.5	41.5	All	35.6	42.1	46.3	30.5	45.6	48.4
	Female	21.4	29.1	27.7	22.0	24.6	29.5		27.6	34.8	37.6	27.5	37.6	44.0

Source: Ghana Statistical Service (various issues of GLSS)

also worsened during the economic reform period but there was the tendency for poverty to decline after and beyond the reform period. Poverty was more widespread in the rural sector than in the urban sector. The results are consistent with the general perception and related literature that economic reform programme impacts negatively on income distribution and poverty in developing countries.

A by-product of the poverty analyses focussed on the relationship between poverty and basic needs. The results indicate that generally access to basic needs by the poor, the very poor and the non-poor improved marginally during and after the economic reforms. Meanwhile, recognition must also be given to the positive effects of internal policies such as decentralisation policy, local governance and poverty reduction strategy as well as contributions of NGOs and donor community towards development. Even though various governments have made attempts to minimise inequality and poverty in Ghana, the desired results have not been achieved.

The policy implications of the results are that the current Ghana Poverty Reduction Programme (GPRP) needs to be intensified and strengthened to have the desired impact. Poverty alleviation requires a restructuring of existing budget priorities and a better and more accountable political and administrative framework. An effective system of monitoring and evaluation needs to be put in place to ensure the sustainability of the GPRP. Furthermore, government should give priority attention to rural development, provision of adequate infrastructure, business development services, human capital development and laudable policies and effective institutions to enhance the productive capacity of the economy so that the unemployed workforce could secure jobs and earn income.

NOTES

1. The empirical evidence shows that adjustment programme in Argentina, Chile, Columbia, The Dominican Republic, Ecuador, Mexico, and Uruguay have all produced evidence of higher inequality. In Mexico the distribution of primary income became

substantially more unequal during the period 1984–1992, and especially in the immediate post reform perform period after 1984. In Chile unemployment roles and formal and informal wages firms. Distribution, using both Gini and the poorest 40 per cent share markedly worsened during the 1970s when Chile's reforms were being implemented. In the transitional economies of Eastern Europe the evidence of the distributional effects of the economic reforms synchronises with that of Latin America. In Estonia, Latvia and Lithuania while the stabilisation and reforms programmes have been successful income differentials have widened significantly. The only country that is an exception the above picture is Costa Rica where income distribution remained the same throughout the economic reform (Handa and King, 1997 page 196).

2. According to Quarcoo (1989) the external gap manifests itself primarily in chronic deficits on trade and current account as exemplified by the overvaluation of the local currency and debt crisis. On the other hand, internal gap is manifested as chronic government budget deficits and savings and investment gaps depicting the inadequacy of domestic savings to meet domestic investment.

3. Kirkpatrick and Onis (1983) have demonstrated that the orthodox Stabilisation measures of the traditional demand management supplemented with supply management recommendations are unlikely to lead to sustainable development because of the limitations of the theoretical model underlying the adjustment process in the context of less developed economies. The structural characteristics of the less developed economies differ significantly from the advanced economies on which the traditional demand management theory has been modelled.

REFERENCES

Agbesinyale, P. (ed.) (2000), *Democratic Workers' Participation for Economic and Social Development: The Case of Case*, Ghana Trades Union Congress, Accra.

Afful, K.N. (2002), 'Technology: the missing link in Ghana's development efforts', *The Oguaa Journal of Social Science*, Vol. 3: 1-30.

Alcock, P. (1993), *Understanding Poverty*, Macmillan Press Ltd, London.

Alarcon, D. and Mckinley, T. (1995), 'Widening Wage Dispersion under Structural Adjustment in Mexico', *FOCAL Discussion Paper*, No. 4, Centre for International Studies, University of Toronto, Toronto.

Assefa, B. (1980), *Poverty, Inequality and Stagnation: The Ghanaian Experience*, ILO, Geneva.

Baffoe, J. K. (1992), 'Income Distribution and Poverty Profile in Ghana 1987-88', *African Development Review*, Vol. 4, No. 1: 1-29.

Belassa, B. and Associates (1982), *Development strategies in Semi-Industrial Economies*, John Hopkins University Press, Baltimore.

Berry, A. (1996), 'The Macroeconomic context for policies, projects and programmes to promote social development and combat poverty in Latin America and the Caribbean', *Working Paper*, No1, UNDP, New York.

Chen, S., Datt, G. and Ravallion, M. (1994), 'Is poverty increasing in the Developing World?' *World Bank Review of Income and Wealth Series 40*, No. 4.

Chen, S. and Ravallion, M. (2004), 'How have the World's poorest fared since the early 1980's, *World Bank Research Observer*, 19(2): 141-170.

Corbo, V. and Fischer, S. (1995), 'Structural Adjustment, Stabilisation and Policy Reform: Domestic and International Finance', in T. N. Srinivasan and J. Behrman (eds.) *Handbook of Development Economics*, Vol. IIIB, Elsevier, New York.

Cornelius, P.K. and Weber, B.S. (1996), 'Economic transformation and income distribution: Some evidence from the Baltic Countries', *Staff Papers*, 43 (3), 587-604.

Ewusi, K., (1984), 'The Dimensions and Characteristics of Rural Poverty in Ghana', *Technical Publication*, No 42, ISSER, Legon.

Foster, J., Greer, J. and Thorbecke E. (1984), 'A Class of Decomposable Poverty Measures' *Econometrica* 52: 761-766.

Ghana Statistical Service (2000), *Poverty Trends in Ghana in the 1990's*, Ghana Statistical Service, Accra.

Ghana Statistical Service (1995), *The Pattern of Poverty in Ghana 1988-1992: A case study based on the Ghana Living Standards Survey*, Commercial Associates Ltd., Accra.

Ghana Statistical Service (1995), *The Pattern of Poverty in Ghana 1988-1992*, Commercial Associates Ltd., Accra.

Gillis, M., Perkins, D.H., Roemer, M. and Snodgrass, D.R. (1996), *Economics of Development*, W.W. Norton & Company, New York.

Handa, S. and King D. (1997), 'Structural Adjustment Policies, Income Distribution and Poverty: A Review of the Jamaican Experience', *World Development*, Vol.25, No.6: 915-930.

Marshall, A. (1920), *Principles of Economics*, Macmillan Company Ltd, London.

Marshall, A. (1995), 'The labour market and income distribution in Argentina', *FOCAL Discussion Paper*, FC 1995-1, Centre for International Studies, University of Toronto, Toronto.

Mosley, P., Harrigan, J., and Toye, J. (eds) (1991), *Aid and Power, The World Bank and Policy Based Lending*, Volumes 1 & 2, Mackeys: Kent.

Quarcoo, P.K. (1983), 'Structural Adjustment Programmes in Sub-Saharan Africa: Evolution of Approaches, *African Development Review*, Vol.1, No.1: 1-15.

Republic of Ghana (1983), *Economic Recovery Programme 1984-1986*, Vol. 1 & 2, Ghana Publishing Corporation Accra.

Republic of Ghana (1986), *Programme of Action to Mitigate the Social Costs of Adjustment*, Ghana Publishing Corporation, Accra.

Republic of Ghana (1995), *Ghana Vision 2020: The First Step 1996-2000 Co-ordinated Programme of Economic and Social Development*, Ghana Publishing Corporation Accra.

Republic of Ghana (2003), *Ghana Poverty Reduction Strategy 2003-2005: An Agenda for Growth and Prosperity*, Ghana Publishing Corporation, Accra.

Riveros, L.A. (1995), 'Chile's Structural Adjustment: Relevant policy lessons for Latin America', *FOCAL Discussion Paper*, No. 1995-9, Centre for International Studies, University of Toronto, Toronto.

Rodrik, D. (1995), 'Trade and Industrial Policy Reform', in T. N. Srinivasan, and J. Behrman (eds) *Handbook of Development Economics*, Vol. IIIB, Elsever, New York.

Roe, A., Schneider, H. and Pyatt, G. (1992), *Adjustment and Equity in Ghana*, OECD, Paris.

Samuels, W. J. and Kelsey, T. W. (1991), 'Some fundamental considerations on the positive theory of income distribution', in W. L. M. Adriaansen and J. T. J. M. van der Linden (eds.) *Post Keynesian Thought in Perspective*, Wolters Noordhoff, Groningen: 119-138.

Thomas, V., Nash, J. and Associates (1991), *Best Practices in Trade Policy Reform*, Oxford University Press, Oxford.

Todaro, M. (1989), *Economic Development in the Third World*, Longman Group Ltd, London.

Tsakloglou, P. (1993), 'Aspects of income inequality in Greece: Measurement, Decomposition and inter-temporal change', *Journal of Development Economics*, Vol. 40, pp. 53-74.

United Nations (1995), "The Copenhagen Declaration and Programme of Action World Summit for Social Development: 6-12 March 1995", United Nations: New York.

United Nations Development Programme (2003), *The Human Development Report*, Oxford University Press, New York.

United Nations Development Programme (1990), *Human Development Report*, Oxford University Press, New York.

World Bank (1993), *The East Asian Miracle*, Oxford University Press, New York.

4

CONSUMER INTEREST UNDER WTO

*Geetanjali R Urankar**

The World Trade Organisation (WTO) is a single institutional framework, which has tried to expand international trade among its member countries by liberalizing trade in goods, services, investments of physical and financial assets, services etc. The purpose behind this is that all the member countries should enjoy the real gains arising out of a freer international trade. For trade facilitation, WTO has framed various rules and various Agreements with respect to agriculture, industry, foreign direct investment, intellectual property rights, environmental standards etc which its member countries are expected to follow.

Most of the WTO Agreements contain provisions for the recognition and safeguard of developing countries' interests. Developing countries however, are of the view that these provisions have been largely ineffectual. Concerns have also been raised that initiatives by DCs are lacking, to facilitate the active participation of developing countries in the relevant standard setting organizations. Thus a growing threat felt by developing members countries of WTO is that as trade is getting liberalized especially in agricultural and food products,

* GVM'S College of Commerce and Economics, Currently, Ph.d Research Fellow of UGC at Economics Deptt. Goa University-Talei gao Plateau, Goa University.

attention of the developed countries is now focused on quality, safety and environmental standards of the exports from developing countries under the Sanitary and Phyto Sanitary standards and other such standards which are being used rather misused by them as an Non tariff barrier (NTB).

The present paper aims at

1. Bringing to light the meaning of SPS measures as measures used by Developed Countries for protecting their consumer welfare.
2. Examining the implications of SPS for Indian Agricultural and other exports.
3. Finding out Whether MNC subsidiaries of DCs operating in the soft drink and bottled water segments in India sell products that are safe to consumers health.
4. High lighting some suggestions of the JPC on Safety norms for soft drinks

Let us see what does SPS Agreement which contain SPS measures mean SPS Agreement is between an importing country and an exporting country where importing country agrees not to use SPS measures to artificially block food and other relevant exports from the exporting country.

SPS measures are applied by an importing country to the stop or ban exports from a country if it threatens

- its human or animal life from risks of additives, toxins, contaminants or disease causing organisms in their food.
- its human life from plant-or animal-carried diseases;
- its animal or plant life from pests, diseases or disease-causing organisms;
- or creates a damage to a country from the entry, or spread of pests.

The SPS agreement confirms the right of nations to establish and use these measures to protect consumers, livestock, wildlife and plants, including important food crops. SPS only deals with food and agriculture sector. It uses the CODEX Commision's rules for taking decisions on safety measures.Codex is an inter governmental body set up under the joint sponsorship of FAO and WHO.

SPS-THE IMPLICATIONS FOR DEVELOPING COUNTRIES LIKE INDIA

Today SPS measures dealing with food related health and safety concerns have multiplied in developed contries. These measures DCs claim are used by them, to protect their own consumer interests . But there have been many instances where they have been used as a restrictive trade measure to block the exports of developing countries Also SPS agreements have some discriminatory provisions favouring DCs.

The SPS Agreement contains 14 articles and Annexure A, B andC (WTO 1994; 1995) and some of these have provisions that can adversely affect trade interests of India. The sectors that are getting adversely affected by SPS and other related measures are some of India's vibrant export - oriented sectors such as agricultural products, marine exports, leather and leather products textiles and chemicals.

India's share of agricultural exports in her total exports was 30 per cent in 1990-91 and this has declined to 22 per cent in 2001-02. This is mainly due to the SPS related problems Indian agricultural exports are facing from its major trading partners agriculture.

Table 1
Top 10 Indian Agricultural Trade Partners (2001)

Importing countries	*Value of imports (US $ million)*	*Share in total Indian agricultural exports(per cent)*
EU	1865.03	22.23
USA	1051.69	12.54
Japan	770.52	9.18
Bangladesh	468.03	5.58
UAE	458.83	5.47
UK	425.85	5.08
Saudi Arebia	391.9	4.67
Hongkong	342.08	4.08
Russia	317.74	3.79
Italy	314.93	3.75

Source: India Trade Version 2.0.

Agricultural products from India are under strict supervision especially in E.U., where all imported food products are liable for inspection at the first point of entry for compliance with food laws pertaining to the country of entry. Regulations in E.U are also with respect to the labeling of packaging materials used in imported products. In the case of products like peanuts and milk E.U has introduced a high level of protection by reducing the maximum level of presence of a chemical, called aflatoxin. Although specific measures have been taken to help out producers and exporters in various countries under UNDP projects to produce aflatoxin free peanuts the costs are very high. The level of protection proposed by EU is much higher than that provided under WTO's Codex guidelines.

India cannot export its milk output to EU due to the lack of mechanized practices in the diary sector and for not maintaining high hygiene standards. Recently under the fear of foot and mouth disease found in cattle, EU did not approve Indian export of fresh and frozen meat to the EU though India was certified by Codex as free from that disease.

EU imposed a ban on Indian fishery products in August 1997 mainly shrimps and squid, when it found hygiene and sanitary standards not satisfactory in several fish processing units. Shrimp exports from India fetch foreign exchange of Rs. 4,000 crore annually out of the total seafood exports of Rs. 6,000 crore The environment related NTBs faced by the Indian seafood Industry are largely related to the Minimum residual level (MRL) for pesticides and antibiotics in the produce .But various antibiotics and chemicals without any given limit are totally banned. Inspite of the fact that many fish processing units in India are fully complying with hygiene and sanitary requirements they are not allowed to export to EU. Industry sources maintained that the ban had resulted in the loss of a season calculated, in the region of Rs 4-5 billion worth of foreign exchange. (DFID 2000.) Many Indian industries in fishing exports were required to upgrade their facilities which entailed a huge expenditure and a number of units closed down their factories for a long duration to enable them to upgrade their facilities with heavy investments. Currently only 90 out of 404 plants in India are approved for fishery exports to the EU.

The Restrictions some countries are imposing on fruits and vegetables do not even have valid scientific reasons.

Spain recently detained chilli consignments from India for aflatoxin present in chillies. Italy and Germany have detained Indian spices consignment on the ground that it contains pesticide residues. These countries failed to convince Indian exporters on the changes they had made on their existing regulations on microbial contaminations and contaminations due to pesticide residues This is a blatant denial of facilities offered under Article 7 of the SPS regulation and causing not only difficulties for India in its regular exports but also leading to loss of opportunities elsewhere.

Japan has under its food sanitation law prohibited the import of many Citrus fruits and also flowers from India without justification. For instance Indian flower exporters are facing many NTBs when exporting to Japan. In recent years Japan has objected to Indian flowers on the grounds that they contain certain insects, which are already found abundantly in Japan. Also there is a lot of time, 5 to 9 hours taken by the Japanese airport authorities in clearing Indian flower consignments with the result that Indian flowers lose their freshness and fetch lower prices in the Japanese flower markets.

Similarly in the case of Textiles, Indian Exporters are facing the adverse effects of SPS. Textile exports account for 55 per cent of India's export earnings. This is also a net foreign exchange earner as the import content in textiles is very less compared with other major export products. It provides employment to 15 million people. Around 40 per cent of India's textiles are exported to the EU, but the Stringent environmental conditions in DCs have adverse consequences for India's export performance. The use of certain dye stuffs which countries like India use, have been totally banned in the International markets and viable substitutes have been explored but switching over to them for Indian textile mills entails investments of over U.S $ 13 million.

Export from leather sector today accounts for about 43 per cent of India's total exports. The export performance of the leather sector has improved considerably during the past decade. On the environmental standards, the leather industry faces problems both, on the domestic as well as the external front. Restrictions on the use of certain chemical dyestuffs and several other mandatory regulations in major export markets pose problems to the leather sector. Though Indian industrial units in leather operations are trying to adhere to new environment friendly methods it is very costly for them. Hence it is said that Indian leather exports may face a price problem in the future.

DCs like EU, Japan, USA are interested in protecting their consumers welfare, but in the name of consumer welfare misusing the protection and environment measures to block food and agriculture related exports of developing countries without stating any scientific reasons in many cases amounts to the use of SPS as a NTB rather than as a genuine measure of health and safety protection Back home, many of the MNC subsidiaries of DCs especially operating in the soft drink and bottled water segments in India have turned a blind eye to the safety and health of the consumers in India.

SOFT DRINK INDUSTRY

Two Multinational Companies Atlanta headquartered Coca Cola Company and New York based PepsiCo control the cold drink market in India. Their market share is a fiercely contested secret. It was way back in 1990s that the carbonated drinks market in the U.S. and Western Europe was saturated. Companies therefore turned to new ones like the Middle East and Asia. Pepsi Company entered the liberalized Indian market in 1991. Two years later, Coca Cola reentered. Slowly Coca Cola bought Parle Beverages and its brands Thums Up, Limca and Gold Spot and in 1999 it acquired Cadbury's brands Crush, Canada dry and Sport Cola. Pepsi on its part took over Mumbai based Duke range of soft drinks. By March 2001 Govt. estimates that 6540 million cold drink bottles were sold annually in the country. In other words with over a billion Indians each Indian would be drinking roughly 6 bottles of soft drinks each year. After capturing the urban markets the Cola giants are now busy wooing the rural markets.

These soft drink MNCs claim that they follow international quality standards for their products .Then how is it that it was found that the soft drinks contain pestiside residues in them, in quantities that are unfit for human consumption? Total pesticides in all Pepsi Co brands on an average was 0.0180 mg /1.36 times higher than EEC limit for pestisides (0.0005 mg/l). Total pesticides in all Coca Cola brands were 0.0150 mg/l, 30 times more than the same EEC limit.

These are the findings of one of research institutes, Centre for Science and Environment (CSE) released in its report on pesticide residues in 12 major cold drink brands sold in and around Delhi. CSE had pointed out that regulations for pesticide levels in soft drinks are weak in the country. Since the norms that regulate manufacture of cold drinks in India are a meaningless maze, these companies cannot be told to follow the norms. Neither the Prevention of Food Adulteration Act 1954 nor the Fruit Products Order explicitly deals with the this subject since water is not included as yet in the definition of food. The study also pointed out the fact that India has no standards to define 'clean' or potable water. The Joint Parlimentary Committee has affirmed the findings of the CSE on the presence of pesticide residues in aerated water. To cross check the CSE procured a sample each of Coca Cola and Pepsi from the U.S. The bottles were analysed for the same pesticides using the same methodology and equipment, but nothing was found. This confirms the fact that MNCs are lax when it comes to maintaining the standards in developing countries.

Thus the cold drink market is virtually unregulated. Strangely it is also exempted from the provisions of industrial licensing. It gets a one time license to operate and it has to only get a NOC from the local govt, from the state pollution control board and a water analysis report from a public health laboratory. That's it. There is no environment impact assessment or sitting regulations for the industry. Most of these soft drink units use ground water but its use of this unpriced groundwater is also not regulated.

Forget pesticides. Standards for other substances like lead or arsenic arealso above the guidelines for drinking water issued by the Ministry of Urban Development. Soft drinks have been allowed 50 times higher arsenic and lead contents than in bottled drinking water. Thus rules being lax and not binding a company would rush to set a shop in India.

BOTTLED DRINKING WATER

Bottled drinking water is no safer than the soft drinks we consume. Between July and December 2002 the CSE analysed 17 different brands of Packaged Drinking Water (PDW) and Packaged Natural Mineral Water (PNMW) in and around Delhi, Haryana and Uttar Pradesh and found Pesticide residues of the deadliest kinds in al the tested 34 samples The total pesticides were found to be 36.4 times higher than stipulated EEC levels. On checking the quality of the water being used by the manufacturers as their raw material, it was found there was no regulation that bottled drinking water industries must be located in clean zones . Currently Manufacturing plants are located in the dirty industrial estates and pesticide–drenched fields. Most of these Companies use bore wells to pump-out water from the ground at depths ranging from 24 meters to 152 meters below the ground. The plants also draw large amounts of ground water-10000 to 30000 litres per hour. The raw ground water samples also revealed the presence of deadly pesticides.

Though there are strict procedures and tests by Bureau of Indian Standards (BIS), which bottled manufacturers have to fulfill in case of both PDW and PNMW, the parameters for pesticide residues is an ambiguous phrase that does not specify what is the limit at which a pesticide residue qualifies as detectable or below. So the CSE study used EU norms when the above described results were found. EU norms lay down norms, maximum admissible concentration for pesticides for individual as well as well as for total pesticides. This way the test produced definite results.

WHAT TYPE OF STANDARDS?

So far as the bottled drinking water industry is concerned there are a lot of checks. Any businessman who wants to manufacture bottled water has to pass through a licensing procedure. His/Her infrastructure facilities have to be adequate to get a license. There must be in-House testing laboratories to conduct on-site tests to check the contents of the water which is going to be sold etc. After getting the license to produce bottled drinking water BIS inspectors go to the plant twice a year, to check if the product is conforming to the standards. According to industry sources this costs the manufacturer Rs 4000 per visit. Clearly no analysis is done for pesticides and other toxins which would be far more costly to do.

BIS conducts a product certification course that enables manufacturers to use the Std Mark the ISI MARK, under the BIS Act 1986. From 29 March 2001 it is mandatory for all manufacturers of bottled drinking water to meet the required Stds for physical, chemical toxic as also radioactive residues.

It is sad but true that though scientifically tested samples by the CSE found pesticide residues in bottled drinking water, these companies are certified to carry on. The Ministry of Health and Family Welfare states that these Companies are mostly producing Bottled water with pesticides below detectable limits—an ambiguous term without specifying what is that limit.

HOW TO STOP THIS?

The Report of the recent Joint Parlimentary Committee on pesticide residues in and safety standards for soft drinks, fruit juices and other beverages is out. It agrees with the CSE's test finding's on the presence of pesticide residues in soft drinks. More importantly it has made path- breaking suggestions on food safety, water security and public health in India. The JPC made the following suggestions

1. Water should come under the definition of Food and drinking water standards should be made legally

enforceable and Municipalities should be made accountable for not supplying clean water.

2. Instead of the 8 Ministries dealing with the multiple laws and regulations concerning food safety standards there should be one Modern Integrated Food Law and a single Independent Authority to implement it.
3. A health based pesticide policy.
4. To check adulteration in the food items the Govt should not hesitate to take the help of NGOs

All these suggestions will have significance only if the above recommendations are speedily implemented by the new govt which comes to power.

BIBLIOGRAGHY

1. Down To Earth Vol. 12, No. 19 February 29 2004.
2. Down To Earth Vol. 12, No. February 15, 2003.
3. Down to Earth Vol. 12, No. 6, August 15 2003.
4. Sachin Chaturvedi et al (Jan 4 2003) WTO AND product related Environment Related Standards. EPW Vol. xxxviii (1).
5. Anand Kumar (Nov. 8 2003) WTO Agreement on SPS. EPW Vol. xxxviii (45).

5

CAPITAL FLOWS IN THE ASEAN COUNTRIES

*Gautam Murthy**

BACKGROUND

Regional co-operation and the formation of RTAs (Regional Trading Arrangements) are gaining increasing importance for both political and economic reasons. The economic or market factors for the formation of RTAs include opening out to new markets, attracting Foreign Direct Investment (FDI), and benefits from economies of scale. The political factors include greater diplomatic cohesion, counterbalancing other RTAs, commitment to internal reform, and greater synergetic networking of nations. There has been enormous proliferation of RTAs since 1995,with their scope and geographical reach expanding. Apart from removing tariffs on intra-bloc trade in goods, the newer arrangements tend to have deeper coverage.

Developing countries in Asia made a number of attempts at regional co-operation in the 1970s,beginning with the Asian Clearing Union of 1974 and U.N ESCAP's "Bangkok Agreement"of 1975.However they failed to take-off because of limited coverage of membership, as well as in identifying products for tariff reduction. ASEAN (Association of South East Asian Nations) founded in 1967,is the most successful and

* Faculty of the Centre for Indian Ocean Studies, Osmania University, Hyderabad.

dynamic cooperative forum, not only in Asia and for developing countries, but is also a trendsetter for all RTAs.The founding members of ASEAN were Indonesia, Malaysia, the Phillipines, Singapore and Thailand.Brunei joined in 1984.Vietnam became a member in 1995, followed by Laos and Myanmar in 1997. With Cambodia becoming a member in 1999, the ASEAN now includes all the ten countries of Southeast Asia.

When ASEAN was formed it sought not only to enhance co-operation, but also have a harmonised approach to issues of foreign policy and national security. The ASEAN member-states also take a coordinated and unified approach to security issues. Further, the ARF (ASEAN Regional Forum) discussing security issues, has enabled relatively smaller and less powerful ASEAN member states to engage China in the presence of powers like the United States on their territorial disputes in the South China Sea, where China has used its superior naval strength to assert its perceived territorial claims.

The first-ever India-ASEAN Summit held in Phnom Penh, Cambodia, in 2002, sets the stage for India to move purposefully in developing a broad economic and strategic partnership with the dynamic countries of South East Asia.In pursuance of India's" Look East" policy, the dialogue has moved from a limited sectoral partnership (1992) to full dialogue partnership (1995) and membership of ARF in 1996,culminating in the Summit.

India's economic potential and geo-strategic importance in Southeast Asia in the post-cold war world is today recognised as an important aspect of international economic diplomacy.

India, needs to have a clearer "Focus" and even "Vision" with regard to its ties with the ASEAN.There is much scope for further expanding and deepening our cooperative agenda, synergising the economies of India and ASEAN and exploring new avenues for diplomatic complementarities.

SAARC continues to remain moribund because of ego clashes in the region. However, India has successful bilateral free trade agreements with Nepal and Sri Lanka.That a Free

Trade Area in South Asia remains a non-starter is not entirely the fault of Pakistan-India too has been reluctant to make the larger concessions that will make a more effective South Asia grouping. It is hoped that as India pursues and gives concrete shape to a free trade zone with ASEAN, other regional initiatives will also be reactivated, so that the Indian economy develops a multi layered set of net-works in the larger Asian and Indian Ocean regions.

The decision taken during the Fourth ASEAN Summit in 1992 to establish the ASEAN Free Trade Area (AFTA) by the year 2008 is an ambitious step for regional economic integration. The main mechanism for the implementation of AFTA is the Common Effective Preferential Tariff (CEPT). The CEPT is an agreed effective tariff, which is preferential to ASEAN member-states, and is to be applied to goods identified for inclusion under the CEPT scheme originating from member-states. AFTA has been complemented with other initiatives to facilitate movement of capital. These are the AICO (ASEAN Industrial Cooperation Organization) and the AIA (ASEAN Investment Area).

THE ASIAN ECONOMIC CRISIS

The Asian financial and economic crisis affected many countries of the ASEAN. This first came to world attention in mid-1997, as the Thai baht rapidly lost value against the US $. The interconnections among Asian economies led to its rapid spread to Indonesia, Malaysia, the Philippines, the Republic of Korea and Hong Kong.Many other countries In the region, such as Vietnam, Japan, Australia and Singapore, were also adversely affected.

Indonesia was worst affected by this economic crisis. According to the ADB, the GDP of Indonesia was estimated to have contracted by 13.2 per cent in 1998. In 1999, however, the country's GDP increased by 0.9 per cent, in 2000 by 4.8 per cent and in 2001 by 3.3 per cent. By 1999, the region's economies all began to recover. In 2000, ADB estimates placed Singapore and Malaysia at growth rates of 9.9 per cent and 8.5 per cent respectively, while the economy of Thailand expanded by

4.2 per cent and that of the Philippines by 3.9 per cent. In 2001, however, owing to the global economic downturn (particularly in the electronics sector), Singapore's GDP contracted by 2 per cent.

The predatory role played by currency speculators, and the extent of damage inflicted throughout the ASEAN region via the contagion effect, aggravated the financial crisis. There is certainly need to subject currency trading to some sort of surveillance, transparency, accountability and discipline, as the value of currencies traded far exceeds that of trade in goods and services across the globe. Heavy industries, including automotive and iron and steel were inefficient and under heavy protection. Unsound banking practices and poor corporate governance also contributed significantly to the financial turmoil. Massive outflow of capital in the form of "reverse investments" to finance long-term projects, with no prospects of early harvests exacerbated BOP problems.

The unpredictable nature of the crisis is certainly a cause for concern. In particular, the self-fulfilling nature of financial market expectations, chain reactions and herd behaviour tend to cause massive capital movements in a manner that is remotely connected to the fundamentals. All these have made high-flying ASEAN economies particularly vulnerable. While the crisis was clearly triggered by external forces, poor governance at home must share the blame to the extent that it has contributed to the vulnerability of these economies to external shocks. Sound prudential and banking norms, less crony-capitalism, and good corporate governance have put the ASEAN economies on the recovery track.

INTERNATIONAL TRADE, FINANCIAL FLOWS AND THE LDCS

The slowdown of the U.S. economy has affected the growth performance of many LDCs, through a sharp reduction in their export earnings. Overall, GDP growth in the LDCs (excluding China) fell from close to 5 per cent in 2000, to little more than 1 per cent in 2001, mainly due to a sharp deceleration in most of Latin America and Asia. China was less affected, maintaining a growth rate above 7 per cent. Elsewhere in Asia, only the Indian economy maintained the rate of the preceding year; in Latin America the Exception was Ecuador.Growth performance in Africa remained unchanged in 2001,but was again insufficient to achieve per capita income growth for the region as a whole.

In international capital markets, there has been an increase in risk premiums and less willingness by investors to lend to LDCs at a time when their external financing needs to meet rising current-account deficits have been growing. Even before the introduction, following 9/11,of more stringent and transparent reporting on financial transactions to fight illicit financial flows, capital flows to emerging markets in 2001 were forecast to fall to levels not since the early 1990s.This decline has been accompanied by considerably higher borrowing costs for several countries and the exclusion of others from international capital markets.

Thus, LDCs did not benefit from inflows of capital seeking alternative destinations or higher returns as the prospects for profits in financial markets in industrial countries deteriorated. Furthermore, the lower incomes due to the slowdown in exports and falling petroleum prices reduced fiscal receipts for many developing countries, and by cutting expenditures to keep their budgets in balance they further aggravated the downturn in economic activity. Finally, substantial declines in inflation rates and, indeed, the absolute levels of consumer prices, in a large number of developed and developing economies, such as Argentina, China, Japan, Korea and Singapore, in conditions of excess production capicity and excess supplies, have tended to limit corporate profitability and have reduced the likelihood of a return to high investment rates. Although declining inflation paved the way for a more aggressive anti-cyclical policy, most developing economies had little scope for autonomous action because of balance-of-payments constraints. However, some Asian countries loosened their fiscal stance and continued to pursue interest rate reductions designed to support domestic spending. Consequently, their cyclical growth performance was markedly better at the end of 2001 than the rest of the world.

TRADE FLOWS AND BALANCES

The slowdown of global growth during 2001 was accompanied by an even more marked deceleration of growth in international trade. This slowdown affected almost all-major regions. The economic impact of these declines was reinforced by downward pressure on export prices, leading to a pronounced deterioration, by an estimated 3 per cent, in the terms of trade of LDCs in 2001. In Asia, the worst affected was the information technology (IT) sector, involving products such as semiconductors and consumer electronics. Despite the increasing optimism that the downturn in the developed economies outside Japan would be refersed in early 2002, growth in the volume of world trade is expected to recover to only about 2 per cent in 2002 from 1 per cent for 2001.Developing countries are particularly vulnerable to this sharp slowdown in the growth of world trade. With the value of exports falling more rapidly than that of imports, the current-account surplus attained in 2000 by developing countries as a whole almost disappeared in 2001.

In Asia, where recovery after the 1997 financial crisis was driven by exports, owing to the rapid expansion of investment in the IT sector, the fall in U.S. demand led to stagnation in export growth, rapid deterioration of current-account positions and declining growth rates in early 2001 in all countries except India and China.

FINANCIAL MARKETS AND CAPITAL FLOWS

Capital flows to developing countries in 2001 remained at low levels, prolonging the downward trend that has persisted since the 1997 Asian financial crisis. In 2001, Latin America was the largest recipient of inflows; despite a substantial decline in flows to Argentina. Other regions, with the exception of the Middle Eastern countries and Turkey, also received positive inflows.

The interest rate reduction in the early 1990s followed a decade of historically high rates in the U.S.and it induced many investors to shift their investments to emerging foreign markets in order to maintain high returns. The attraction of these investments was supported by the rapid rates of economic expansion in Asia and the apparent success of adjustment policies in Argentina and Mexico in the early 1990s, and in Brazil in 1994. Liberalization of financial markets in these countries also increased their attractiveness as investment alternatives.

As a result of increased global economic integration and the greater role of external trade in the economies of LDCs, the downturn in the United States has had a more rapid negative impact on their growth and export performance than in the past.

In many Asian countries recovering from the 1997 crisis, large external surpluses have been a source of increased deposits with international banks. Since 1998 repayments to banks by borrowers in all LDCs have exceeded new loans to them, and the total exposure of BIS (Bank for International Settlements)-reporting banks to such economies is now more than $200 billion lower than in 1997. Net repayments to BIS-reporting banks by borrowers in East and South Asia and in oil-exporting countries in West Asia have been accompanied by a large build-up of deposits by the two regions, which reflects substantial current-account surpluses; they have thus been a substantial net source of funds to the international banking system.

Financing for developing countries in the form of export credits also declined in 2001. Most of the decrease of $ 6.1 billion was due to borrowers in Africa and Eastern Europe.This is shown in Table-1.

RECENT ECONOMIC PERFORMANCE OF THE ASEAN COUNTRIES

Key factors in the recovery path for all Southeast Asian countries were a resumption of domestic demand and consumption, rebuilding of the banking sectors to levels where financial intermediation can recommence, and the restructuring of private sector debt. With a need to restructure the corporate sectors, expunge bad debt, liberalise business regimes, strengthen institutions, and put in place better regulatory bodies, rapid growth took a secondary place. Healthy import demand from the United States has assisted their export growth performance, buoyed by the relative depreciation in the value of regional currencies against the U.S. dollar. In terms of potential domestic investment, local firms in Southeast Asia have been aided by the recent easing of interest rates in most countries across the region.

Table 1
Estimates of Net Capital Flows to Developing and Transitioneconomies, 1998-2002 (Billions of $). Estimates of IMF

Type of flow/region	*1998*	*1999*	*2000*	*2001*	*2002*
Total	69.6	59.6	8.9	20.1	59.8
Net direct investment	155.4	153.4	146.2	162.4	142.6
Net portfolio investment	-4.2	31.0	-4.3	-13.0	13.7
Other net flows	-81.6	-124.8	-133.0	-129.4	-96.6
AFRICA	10.0	11.9	7.0	9.5	10.0
Net direct investment	6.9	9.0	7.2	21.4	11.0
Net portfolio investment	3.7	8.7	-1.8	-6.3	4.2
Other net flows	-0.7	-5.8	1.6	-5.8	-5.2
ASIA	-53.4	-7.6	-12.2	1.4	-3.1
Net direct investment	59.9	51.9	46.8	43.7	41.7
Net portfolio investment	-15.3	13.8	3.7	-4.7	3.8
Other net flows	-89.4	-74.4	-66.4	-46.0	-50.1
MIDDLE EAST AND EUROPE	11.8	-1.1	-22.4	-29.2	-0.7
Net direct investment	6.3	5.4	7.2	6.5	8.4
Net portfolio investment	-13.2	-4.2	-15.1	-9.6	-5.2
Other net flows	18.6	-2.3	-14.6	-26.1	-3.8
WESTERN HEMISPHERE	71.7	43.6	37.9	38.8	39.5
Net direct investment	60.7	63.8	62.5	64.1	50.0
Net portfolio investment	16.5	9.8	4.6	4.0	7.6
Other net flows	-5.5	-30.0	-29.2	-29.3	-18.0
TRANSITION ECONOMIES	21.0	13.8	2.2	7.6	15.0
Net direct investment	21.6	23.4	22.5	26.7	31.5
Net portfolio investment	4.0	2.8	4.3	3.6	3.5
Other net flows	-4.6	-12.4	-24.7	-22.7	-20.0

Source: IMF, World Economic Outlook (December 2001).

The Asian crisis has highlighted the need for most Southeast Asian policy-makers not to neglect their agricultural sectors, even when making concerted bids to develop their industrial and service sectors. Previously regarded as a sunset industry at best, the agricultural sector held up well during the,regional economic downturn, and did much to cushion the social and economic impact of the financial crisis in some countries. Within the ASEAN-6 countries, the agricultural sector accounts for roughly 45 per cent of total employment in Indonesia, the Philippines, and Thailand.and just 20 per cent in Malaysia. The figure is much higher for the transitional countries of Southeast Asia. With so many people still deriving their income from the agricultural sector in most Southeast Asian countries, policy makers now appear more cognisant of the need to support the development of this sector. On the road to modernity, allocating finite resources to IT clusters or rural areas should not become a zero-sum game.

The Macro-Economic Performance for the ASEAN-5 is given in Table-2 below.

Table 2
Macro-Economic Performance of the ASEAN-5

GDP GROWTH	*1997*	*1998*	*1999*	*2000*	*2001*
Indonesia	4.7	-13.2	-0.2	2.5	6.0
Malaysia	7.5	-7.5	4.0	4.5	5.0
Philippines	5.2	-0.5	3.0	4.5	4.8
Singapore	7.8	0.7	6.5	6.0	6.0
Thailand	-1.3	-9.4	4.5	5.0	6.0
CURRENT ACCOUNT (as % of GDP)					
Indonesia	-1.4	4.2	6.9	5.7	5.2
Malaysia	-5.3	12.9	13.6	6.2	3.5
Philippines	-5.3	2.0	2.5	1.3	0.3
Singapore	15.4	18.2	14.5	13.6	14.9
Thailand	-2.1	12.7	8.3	5.0	3.3
GROSS EXTERNAL DEBT (as % of GDP)	**1998**	**1999**	**2000**	**2001**	
Indonesia	150.9	81.9	54.2	44.3	
Malaysia	59.2	72.0	58.0	50.4	
Philippines	74.3	70.3	73.5	75.5	
Singapore	-	-	-	-	
Thailand	76.8	58.3	51.9	46.9	

Source: Asian Development Bank, 2002.

The Asian Crisis has impacted the transitional countries of Southeast Asia harder than most had initially anticipated, and their economic reform programmes are in low gear as the leaderships debate how best to proceed. A coherent post-crisis recovery policy has yet to emerge from Indochina and Myanmar, leading us to believe that the transitional countries of Southeast Asia will lag the rest of the region in regaining full economic growth momentum. Recent sharp declines in foreign investment inflows and export earnings have placed added strains on these already weakened economies, and their fragile foreign exchange reserves in particular. A return to command economy policies is not a viable option, but the luster of market economies has also been tarnished, leaving doubts about the right policy-framework.

Vietnam's economy will need to counter the perils posed by a burdensome state sector, severe domestic debt problems and bank fragility, possible foreign exchange shortages, and rising urban unemployment levels from increasing migration of rural dwellers to cities.

Table-3
Financial flows in the ASEAN Countries

Country	*Net Private Capital flows ($ millions) 1990–1998*	*FDI ($ millions) 1990–1998*	*Portfolio investment flows (Equity) ($ millions) 1990–1998*	*Bank and trade-related lending ($ millions) 1990–1998*
Indonesia	3,2353,759	1,093356	312250	1,8043,512
Malaysia	7698,295	2,3335,000	293592	6173,017
Myanmar	153153	16170	00	-8-83
Philippines	6392,587	5301,713	0454	-286269
Singapore	–	5,5757,218	–	–
Thailand	4,3997,825	2,4446,941	4492,341	1,593826
Vietnam	16832	161,200	00	0-368

Source: World Development Indicators, UN.

Table 4
Fdi Flows in Asean Countries, 1987-2001 (US$ Million)

Countries	*1987-92*	*1993*	*1994*	*1995*	*1996*	*1997*	*1998*	*2001*
Brunei	1	14	6	13	11	5	4	244
Cambodia	-	54	69	151	294	204	140	113
Indonesia	999	2004	2109	4345	6194	4673	-356	-3277
Laos	4	36	59	88	128	86	45	24
Malaysia	2387	5006	4342	4178	5078	5106	3727	554
Myanmar	96	149	91	115	38	124	40	123
Philippines	518	1238	1591	1478	1517	1222	1713	1792
Singapore	3674	4686	8550	7206	7884	9710	7218	8609
Thailand	1656	1805	1364	2068	2336	3733	6969	3759
Vietnam	2060	1002	1500	2000	2500	2950	1000	1300

Source: Asean Fdi Data Base, Asean Secretariat, Jakarta, 2002.

From Tables 3 and 4, it is clear that the ASEAN region is one of the most attractive investment locations in the developing world, and attracted a disproportionately large amount of FDI, particularly after 1985.This reorientation of the ASEAN economic cooperation is consistent with the national policies of the member countries i.e., economic development through market-based growth and greater participation of the private sector. The adoption of more outward oriented industrialisation strategies based on international trade and greater FDI is now being pursued in all the ASEAN members including previously inward-looking countries like the LCMV (Laos, Cambodia, Myanmar and Vietnam) countries. The impact of these large inflows of FDI into Indonesia, Malaysia and Thailand was impressive. Growth rates began to soar as these countries began to industrialise rapidly. The major investor countries in ASEAN were Japan, EU and US.The ASEAN nations like Malaysia and Indonesia faced disinvestments because of the financial crisis, but investments are now picking up.

6

INDIAN ECONOMY, GLOBALISATION AND WORLD ECONOMIC REFORMS

*Geetanjali Sharma & Sandeepa Malhotra**

There seems to be a general consensus among policy planners in developing countries that greater integration with the global economy will greatly enhance the well being and the standard of living of developing countries. During the past decade world's market economies have become integrated like never before. International trade (exports plus imports) as a share of gross domestic product has reached very high levels even in developing countries. "The share of trade (exports plus imports) in the GDP of developing countries has risen rapidly from about 33 per cent in the mid 1990's to 43 per cent today and could exceed 50 per cent in the next decade."[1]

"In June of 1991 India was running a current account deficit of around $10 billion. Reserves were down to two weeks of imports, despite and IMF loan of $1.8 billion in January 1991, and despite damaging import cuts. Her credibility was very low and commercial borrowing was impossible. Inflation was running at an annual rate of 13 percent and an inflow of foreign currency from non-resident Indians had been reversed."[2]

The situation was desperate and called for desperate measure. The goal of the Indian government was (1) to stabilize

* School of Studies in Economics, Jiwaji University, Gwalior.

the economy in the short tun (reducing inflation and improving the balance of payments; and (2) to fundamentally restructure the economy in the long run to enable India to obtain a higher growth rate. Both these short and long term objectives required the adoption of a series of policy initiatives that would allow more efficient allocation of resources. It called for removal of all quantitative restrictions on imports, unifying and reducing the average tariff rates, reducing import subsidy, opening up the financial sector to attract foreign investment, reform the domestic banking sector and reduce budget deficit.

Globalisation implies the degree to which a particular economy is integrated with the rest of the world. There are 3 aspects of the globalisation process namely; (i) Trade in Goods, (ii) Trade in Services and (iii) Trade in Finance.[3] While the above exchanges between nations are important, we shall only concentrate on merchandise trade only. The present study fills the void in the existing literature by considering trade explicitly and focuses upon the relationship between economic growth and trade.

Globalisation implies a regime of perfectly competitive markets with no entry or exit barrier. The globalisation of financial markets means gains for private capital, which can now flow around the world in search of the highest returns. Capital crosses border more easily than labour and despite the best efforts of national governments to control it.[4] Globalisation and outward orientation is gaining ground in both the developed and the developing countries. The growth in the flow of foreign direct investment has been possible only because investment policies in western countries have changed to allow higher foreign investment, including portfolio investment. Developing countries need to take advantage, and not fight shy, of this unprecedented international mobility of capital.

Foreign investment is coming to developing countries to exploit their cost and locational advantages in surviving and prospering in the global marketplace in the age of hyper-competition. Its attitude is defensive not aggressive, and what it is looking for above all is stability and predictability. It wants to feel welcomed and not threatened. To successfully participate in the world economy, India needs to build strategic alliances.

Capital holders are, first and foremost, looking for good returns, and they are deeply concerned with risk. The key attractions for them are : (i) good infrastructure, (ii) a reliable and skilled work force, (iii) guarantees of their right to repatriate both income and capital, (iv) social and political stability, (v) a tradition of prudent fiscal management decisions of both multinationals and portfolio investors than special deals. FDI flows now respond rapidly to new profit opportunities, shifting production to places where wages are low relative to potential productivity. It is important for countries to attract capital on the basis of sound economic fundamentals, rather than through protection of domestic markets, which multinationals are only too happy to exploit.

Should we care about the pace of Globalisation simply because the gains and benefits are so far reaching in every corner of the world. While traditional theory has emphasised rather narrowly defined, efficiency-related gains from trade, there is now a large body of literature that expands sources of gains from Trade and increased Globalisation. The new expanded notion about trade, develops and insight for the new forms of specialisation and innovation. These include benefits related to innovation, new product development, specialisation in production, and growth that can be brought forward from deeper integration of the Global Economy.[5] This Global approach is a wider and open form of traditional Comparative Cost Advantage Theory of trade. This approach brings economies with more opportunities in various ways for cost, benefit and gains from trade. 'Globalisation is a motivation force for the nations to develop themselves on such a faster pace that creates more gainful environment in the world scenario for each economy. For developing and transition economies, especially for India, gloabally-oriented regimes provide access to new markets and new technologies. Among low-income countries open economies have grown much faster, exhibiting a pattern of convergence of OECD income levels.[6]

The greater trade growth over output growth throughout much of the past years, together with the revolution of other elements of global integration, suggests a certain natural momentum. Does this mean that global integration is irreversible? In seeking an answer, it is helpful to recall the three fundamental factors identified as the force behind post-war global integration. These are, development in government policies, innovation in Transports and Communication, and evolving strategies for Firms and Individual Investors. The later two factors impart a natural momentum to global integration. If governments everywhere were permanently committed of complete 'Laissez-Faire'[7] in domestic and international policies, supported where necessary by strong anti-trust laws, the first of the three fundamental factors would automatically drop out of the picture. In this case there would be every reason to believe that global integration would progress under its natural momentum.

But of course, a laissez-faire is not the dominant approach to economic policy, least of all in the area of international trade. Government policies with respect to international trade and capital flows can, however imperfectly, either speed up or slow down or, indeed, reverse progress on global integration. Experience also suggests that the presence of legally binding "international constraints" on government policy-making can play an important role in bringing about national policies that nourish integration.

National trade policies, formulated in absence of any international constraints, has played a major role in converting a recession into the Great Depression. Between 1929 and 1932, world merchandise trade declined by 25 per cent in volume and 40 per cent in value. By 1936 the volume of world industrial production had recovered to ten per cent above the 1929 level, but the volume of world trade fell 15 per cent below its 1929 level. This was a policy induced decline in global integration. Out of this experience, came the conviction that the best basis and perhaps the only basis for establishing and maintaining a liberal world trade order would be a system of international legal constraints on national trade policies, based on the MFN principle.

Throughout much of the post-war period the multilateral trading system was rightly seen as a bulwark against a return to the trade chaos of the 1930s. Today, the threat that would be posed by a loss of credibility of the multilateral rules and discipline would not be a return to the 1930s. Global integration has progressed to the point where disintegration on that scale is nearly unthinkable. If commercial relations reached the stage of trade warfare that characterised the 1930s, it would be warfare not between countries, but between blocs held together by their own free-trade treaties and a desire to protect the degree of integration achieved within the bloc. Many so called trade agreements. They are economic integration agreements intended to guarantee the global rights of global corporations to move both commodities and investments wherever they wish free from public interference and accountability. GATT is best described as a Bill of Rights for Global Corporations.

This suggests two courses of action to pursue in-tandem. One involves an examination of ways to ensure that current and future free trade areas and customs unions remain outward-oriented, complementing rather than competing with multilateral trading system. The other action involves a broader effort to protect and extend the credibility of the new rules and disciplines agreed to in the new Uruguay Round. But agreeing to strengthen multilateral rules and disciplines is only the beginning. A willingness to abide by those rules and disciplines, and to adopt them too.

As traditional trade barriers have gone down, and as global integration and interdependence have increased, many policies that were formerly considered domestic have become trade-related policies. Already evident in the Tokyo Round (domestic subsidies, technical barriers and government procurement) and the Uruguay Round (services, protection of intellectual property and sanitary and phyto-sanitary regulations) this process is continuing in such traditionally domestic areas such as financial services and tele communication (both central to the globalisation process), environment protection policies and investment policies, to name only a few.

Progress in dealing with these and other issues at a multilateral level will have a significant impact on the future pace of global integration, both directly and through its impact on the credibility of the multilateral system in influencing the broad spectrum of national trade policies.[8]

To sustain the process of globalisation in the long run, a major break-through in the export-market is considered essential. The issue thus boils down to one crucial question : will the country by able to achieve the needed break-through in the export market? This realisation has prompted policy-makers in this country to place export-oriented manufacturing in the centre-stage of our promotional efforts. The gradual policy-shift since the mid-1960s towards 'outward-looking industrialisation' and the decision in this context to set up the Santacruz Electronics Export Processing Zone (SEEPZ) near Mumbai exclusively to boost electronics exports were based upon the premise that India, like many other LDCs, enjoyed considerable 'comparative advantage' through her possession of cheap labour in abundance and it was possible for the country, through an appropriate mix of promotional and incentive schemes, to capitalise this advantage for attracting transitional corporations (TNCs) to this country to undertake export oriented manufacturing. Our analysis of the actual experience of SEEPZ shows: the assumption, as noted above, was rather simplistic; it failed to take into account the various exogenous factors that have vital bearing on the growth of country's export of manufactures. The analysis also shows that, in the foreseeable future possibilities of a major break-through in the export market will continually undermined by the following major trends discernible at the global level:

(i) deceleration of the growth rate of world market and resurgence of protectionism among the countries in the OECD block[9],

(ii) growing competition among the late-coming LDCs (to the process of globalisation) not only for a global market share but also for a slice of the incremental TNC-investment in the third world; and

(iii) The erosion of LDCs' 'comparative advantage' (following the declining labour-intensity of manufacture) and the gradual disappearance of the motivation of TNCs to use LDC sites as their export platforms.

All these, however, do not mean that the future of export oriented manufacturing is absolutely bleak. The recent trend of SEEPZ exports shows that, for a select range of product categories at least (for example, computer software), some scope for pushing up exports will always remain; through, the total volume of such exports measured as per cent of GNP might not be sufficient to fulfil the export-requirement of a globalisation plan.

It is also to be noted in this connection that the skill requirement of production for many of these 'new items'[10] is substantially different from what we used to think so long as the normal skill requirement of export oriented manufacture. For instance, generation of computer software (which is being projected as one of the most 'potential areas in terms of export capability[11]) demands recruitment of skilled professionals in large numbers. Thus, availability of cheap labour of any description can no longer be seen as the prime source of comparative advantage of LDCs; ability of these countries to generate and supply skilled labour, particularly technological and managerial personnel, at cheaper rates has become more important. The implication of this shift at source of 'comparative advantage' of LDCs needs to be clearly understood in the context of the current thrust on export oriented manufacturing within the framework of India's globalisation plan.[12]

REFERENCES

Ahluwalia, M. S. (1994), Structural Adjustments and Reforms in Developing Countries, p.31.

Ahluwalia, M. S. *ibid.*, p. 55

Berry, S. K. (1992), India-Reforms of the Financial Sector, p. 67.

Emeru, R. F. (1991), The Relations of Exports and Economic Growth, p.121.

Global Trade: WTO's Assessment of Recent Trends, Report of WTO, 1995, p.99.

Global Trade: WTO's Assessment of Recent Trends, Report of WTO, 1995, *ibid.*, p.126.

Global Trade: WTO's Assessment of Recent Trends, Report of WTO, 1995, *ibid.*, p.157.

The losts of Economic Globalisation of Third World, Report of WTO, 1995, p.13.

Kumar (1995), R. India's Export Processing Zones, Oxford University Press, p.33.

The use of Free Zones as a means of expanding Exports, UNCTAD Report, 1993, p.183.

The Use of Free Zones as a means of expanding exports, *ibid.*, p.185.

Gordon (1998), M. The Global Economy, Oxford University Press, p. 44.

7

IMPACT OF GOBALISATION ON INDIAN ECONOMY

*M. Raja Sekhara Babu**

For the last 40 years after independence, the performance of the Indian economy has been dominated by a reigme of multiple controls, restrictive regulations and wide ranging state intervention. Instead of enforcing fiscal discipline, the Government restored to adopt the soft options of printing additional notes and borrowings heavily from within the country. The crisis situation built up in the Indian economy, left no choice for the government than to act fast and bring about major economic reforms, which are popularly known as structural adjustments or liberalisation or globalisation. For a long time businessmen every where believed that home markets were adequate and safe. The scenario is different now. Gobalise are perish is the slogan now-a-days.

The Indian economy needs to be totally transformed to solve its basic problems of poverty, unemployment and equality Liberalisation or globalisation of the economy is a remedy for all these ills, Therefore, India decided to participate in the process of globalisation. In this context, an attempt is made here to analyse the connotion of globalisation arguments for and against globalisation.

* M.A., L.L.M., Ph.D., Reader in Economics, V.T.J.M. & I.V.T.R. Degree College Mangalagiri-522503.

Russi Mody views globalization as a two way thing[1]. First it envisages free competition, high productivity using the state of the art of technology and second, selling in one single market place of the whole market. "Globalisation of the economy may be defined as the global dimension of the evolving world economy. In current economic literature the term globalisation is used to mean a more liberal "outward-oriented" policy which includes eliminating anti-export biases, lowering of very high import tariffs and quantitative restrictions on imports. In simple economic terms, globalisation refers to the process of integration world into one huge market. Against this brief background this paper attempts to study,

1. The impact of globalisation on foreign investments in India , and
2. The effect of globalisation on agriculture and Industry

The growth of world exports in between 1990-99 is 64 per cent, but the Indian Exports have increased to 103 per cent during the same period. In 1990 the share of India's share in world 's Commercial value is 0.55 per cent but, now it is increased to 0.8 per cent. Now the Foreign Investments to India is floating very much. After 1991 every year on an average 4 billion dollars of Foreign Investment is coming to India. In 2002-03 alone the direct foreign investment to India is 3.6 Billon Dollars and 2 Billon Dollars is indirect investment. Up to December 2004 the indirect Foreign investment came to India is 8 Billion dollars.

In order to attract foreign Investment on a large Scale the Government has taken several steps to remove the barriers and irritants which hindered the flow of Investment on a large scale. FERA and MRTP restrictions have been lifted, Foreign investment promotion board has been set up, bureaucrat hurdles have been removed and infrastructural facilities have been stepped up. The results of all these efforts are encouraging. The numbers of approvals and the amount of Foreign Investment have been increasing from year to year. This is shown in Table 1.

Table 1
Foreign Direct Investment Actual Flows Vs. Approvals

	1991	*1992*	*1993*	*1994*	*1995*	*1996*	*1997*	*1998*	*Total*
Approvals									
Rs. Crore	739	5,256	11,189	13,590	37,489	39,453	57,149	28,783	1,93,648
Us $ million	325	1,781	3,559	4,332	11,245	11,142	15,752	6,975	55,111
Actual Inflows									
Rs. Crore	351	675	1.786	3,009	6,720	8,431	12,085	9,116	42,173
Us $ million	155	233	574	958	2,100	2,383	3,330	2,230	11,963
Actual Inflows as % of Approvals (in US $ Terms)	47.7	1301	16.1	22.1	18.7	21.4	21.1	32.0	21.7

Source: Economic Survey and RBI Annual Reports, 2000-01 and 2001-02.

Foreign Direct Investment in India has grown considerably since the process reform began in 1991 through 1997, with FDI flows from approximately $ 154 million in 1991 increased every year, peaking at more than $ 3.6 billion in 1997-1998. FDI inflows declined from peak level in 1997-1998 to US $ 2.5 billion in 1998-1999. The declining trend continued in the next two years. However, inward stock grew from $ 1.8 billion in 1991 to US $ 16.4 billion by 1999 in India.

The growth in FDI investment in India was as low as around 6 per cent per annum between 1948 and 1992 while it grew at around 30 per cent for the next six years. The surge in foreign private capital stock clearly began after 1991. During 1970s, cumulative inflows of FDI was about US $ 454 million or 0.20 per cent of gross domestic investment (GDI). FDI inflows reached $ 9.8 billion during during the 1990-1997 period from just over a billion $ during the 1980s.

GLOBALISATION OF INDIAN AGRICULTURE

Agriculture today holds a third position in India's GDP, the highest proportion in the developed and developing world,

Table 2
Foreign Investment Flows by Different Cateories (India), Us $ Million

	1992-1993	*1993-1994*	*1994-1995*	*1995-1996*	*1996-1997*	*1997-1998*	*1998-1999*	*1999-2000*	*2000-2001*	*2001-2002*	*2002-2003*
A) Direct Investment	315	586	1314	2144	2821	3557	2462	2155	4029	6131	4660
RBI Automatic route	42	89	171	169	135	202	179	171	454	767	739
SIA/FIPB route	222	280	701	1249	1922	2754	1821	1410	1456	2221	919
NRI	51	217	442	715	639	241	62	84	67	35	–
Acquisition of shares $	–	–	–	11	125	360	400	490	382	881	916
B) Portfolio Investment	244	3567	3824	2748	3312	1828	-61	3026	2760	2021	979
a) FIIs	1	1665	1503	2009	1926	979	-390	2135	1847	1505	377
b) Euro equities	240	1520	2082	683	1366	645	270	768	831	477	600
c) Offshore funds & others	03	382	239	56	20	204	59	123	82	39	02
TOTAL (A+B)	559	4153	5138	4892	6133	5385	2401	5181	6789	8152	5639

Source: Reserve Bank of India Annual Reports , 1999-2000 and 2000-01,2001-02,2002-03

and without fail, it will continue to be the back bone of the economy for the years to come. Almost 70 per cent of India's population depends on agriculture but an unfortunate dichotomy is that while in terms of total output India stands in the global markets favourably, in terms of yield it is extremely low. In Rwanda the restructuring of the agricultural system has precipitated the population into object poverty and destitution.

After entering new era of globalization and economic liberalisastion, Indian agriculture stands hoisted to prominent commercial riche and foresees increased track in global markets external liberlisation which seeks to integrate the economy with global market is all set to open new vistas for agricultural exports. The opening of the economy has brought varied changes in the agricultural sector. Infact, globalsiation compelling Indian agriculture to shift its focus from being "supply driven" to "market driven". Any inability to adopt the changing need may limit farmers market and income opportunities. In that case, commericialisation of agriculture is not only necessary but also essential. Commercialisation of agriculture promises a boost both in productivity and income to farmers.

The record production of 181 MT of food grains during 1992-93 is a testimony to the resilience of Indian agriculture. Though the year year's production fell marginally short of the targeted 183 MT. It has been lauded a credible achievement by policy markers. The shortfall was due to poor rains. It is a remarkable recovery from the previous year's performance which was about 171 MT and it has bettered the previous best production of 176.4 MT in 1990-91. The Sterling performance on the farm front and the reforms have helped the boost of Rs. 7,600/- crores in 1992-93, as against the previous year's Rs.6,200 crores. The subsidies for agrilututal in developed countiers have incrised after the W.T.O. agreement. In 2001 thery are 311 US billion $. And now they stand today at $325 billion as against $276 billion before 1994.

With the initiation of NEP, the Indian agriculture is poised to enter the wonderland of global markets. It has made good strides in the past years. It has shown remarkable resilience due to concessions given to the allied segments of agriculture under the NEP. Indian farms produces have a price advantage in the international trade and India should try to cash in such advantageous environment. Some 24 developing countries with three Billion people have doubled their ratio of trade to income over the past the three decades The more gobalised developing countries have increased their percapita growth rate from 1 per cent in the 1960's, to 3 per cent in the 1970's, 4 per cent in the 1980's and 5 percent in the 1990's.Their growth rates now substantially exceed those of the rich countries.

INDUSTRY

Improvements in transportation, communications and manufacturing technology, however provided companies with a way to reduce costs by dividing production into part processes and relocating the less skilled and more labour-intensive segments in low wage areas. Jet air craft, container ships and super tankers more reliable communications through fibre optic cables facsimiles and the internet and the increased use of numerically controlled machines and robots all played a part these changes have four important consequences. First, there has been a steep decline in industrial employment in all OFCD (Orginisation for Economic Co-operation and development). Countries and this has had an adverse impact on the trade unions.

Second, the ability of firms to easily shift their production facilities overseas underscores a fundamental difference between companies and governments. Third, the weakening of government control over the economy underminded the effectiveness of trade unions and social democratic parties forged during the age of industrial capitalism. Finally, since the wider distribution of industrial production leads to a reduction of profit margins ion the manufacturing sector.

Now the question arises whether the globalisation of Indian Economy will help in achieving the desired results, i.e., higher production, higher exports, greater employment. There are some challenges which are to be faced. Firstly it is said, "globalisation is mutually beneficial when capital labour technology and goods flow between equals when the country is ready to face the world competition on equal terms, otherwise, any attempt by the ruling elite in the third world to globalise its economy can rebound adversely on the vast majority of the people".

With regard to increasing production of exports, it is for granted that it will considerably go up and will maintain increasing tempt, as producers are free from different types of restrictions and regulations. With regard to employment, increase in investment, number of production unit, inflow of foreign capital will lead to increased production and ultimately will have a high demand for human resources, but foreign investor may prefer automation as well as sophisticated machinery manufactured by their own country. It may result in making the present skilled force in our country redundant and on the other hand, they may be free to bring skilled labour of their own country. In such a situation, a significant part of earnings may go back to foreign countries in the form of dividends and profits. Now, it is clear that in the process of globalization only those can compete in material market as well as global market who can produce and deliver goods and services of high quanlity by making best use of the latest technology at competitive cost. It is based on Darwinian selection and survival of the fittest theory. Further more, globalisation leads to consumerism.

On the other hand, Globalisation will lead the developing countries to cut-throat foreign competition which will weaken their political, social and economic independence.

Multinationals might be in position to manipulate things to their advantage which will prove detrimental to the interests of the poor nations. It has further been criticised that globalization which implies consumerism of western type, has actually led to nation to a higher priority for luxury cars over mass transport and five star hotels over the low-cost indigenous housing. Moreover, in a country like India, where there is a high income inequality and huge sum of unaccounted money in the hands of a few people it is very difficult to control imports by a devaluation accompanied by import liberalisation. In the words of J.D.Sethi that Indian liberalisation is at the wrong time and from the wrong end.

In Conclusion the FDI flows to developing countries showed a sharp rise during 1990s and emerged as an important instrument of global integration since the 1980s. This reflects the growing recognition of the role of FDI in the development process. The surge in FDI flows has been facilitated to a great extent by the changes in the policy environment in many developing countries.

Our approach to WTO and agriculture is based on the conviction that the emerging world trade regime is both a challenge an opportunity for India. There is no gain saying the fact that the liberalization of world trade in agriculture has opened up new vistas of growth.

REFERENCES

Russi Mody, (1992), "Globalisation Efforts with Accent in Export" The Economic Times, April 21.

Choossudovsky, michel : (1997), Economic reforms and in developing countries, Economic and Political weekly , July 19th , p. 1786-87.

Oxfam. International; 2002.

Barnet, A . (2001), 'Revealed: How Britan's richest man takes a pound 3 million tax hand-out', The observer, May 20.

The Hindu : New waves of globalization and its economic effects.

Venkata Ramani, (1994), G. "Good years of Foodgrains", The Hindu Survey, p.5.

Thiru Venkatachari, K. (1992), "On Globalization", Economic and Social Science Review, Vol. 1, No. 2, October, pp. 67-71.

Kurien, (1993), C.T. Indian Economic Reforms in the context of Emerging Global Economy - Economic and Political Weekly, 10the April.

Malcom S. Adiseshaiah, (1992), "Globalization of the Economy" Indian Association of Social Science Institution (IASSI), Vol.II, NO.1, July-September.

Pradhan, S. (2000), Foreign Direct Investment—Risk, Return and Host Country's Strategy, Journal of Management Research, September -December, pp. 18-30.

8

INDIA'S FOREIGN TRADE WITH SAARC IN THE GLOBALIZATION ERA: FACTS AND POSSIBILITIES

INTRODUCTION

Globalization has become very fashionable and extensively used today in all over the world. It means diverse things to diverse people and has set in a path of far-reaching change that affecting everybody (ILO, 2004). It defines as a process that draws countries out of their insulation and makes them join the rest of the world in its march towards a new world order (Kapila, 2002). It is nothing but an extension of economic transactions and the association of economic activities across the political boundaries of the states (Nayyar, 2002). Globalization is treated as a total mind-set in which the entire world becomes a single market so that the corporate strategy is based on the dynamics of global business environment.

Globalization essentially means expanded free trade and investment opportunities across the world. Economists, by and large, tend to view that free trade and open investment policies are the positive forces and expect those countries pursuing these policies to benefit significantly (Ramakrishna, 2003). However, there is no doubt about that an increasingly integrated global economy presents policy makers with both opportunities and challenges. Global economic integration in all its manifestation aimed at improving allocation of resources, promoting technology transfer, enhancing market size, creating a fair competition, reducing poverty (Mathur, 2003) and finally improving the livings standard of the people. Simultaneously, economic integration has frequently been held to be responsible for growing trade imbalances, increased financial market escalations, growing economic inequalities and lack of more or less effective domestic macroeconomic policies (Shariff, 2003).

The process of global economic integration is not something new. It has been underway since the inception of the modern world system in the 16th century. However, the basic framework of global economic integration has been in place since the nineteenth century. In today's context, globalization means homogenization of prices, products, wages, rates of interest and profits to become the same all over the world. But in reality, there are several differences between globalization today and globalization in the past. First, an obvious difference is its scale. There are subsequent flows of trade and capital, as a percentage of GDP. Second, there is the speed of communications, which makes for a much higher degree of integration and has led to the enormous increase in short-term capital flows, which, unlikely long-term capital flows, were previously very limited. Short-term capital flows have played a very important role in the instability that we have seen in the last 25-30 years. Third, globalization today has to do with the use of force. There is one final way in which the process of globalization has changed, and that is related to the process of democratization. There is much more public scrutiny now of what is going on. That is why there is a stronger globalization debate today than 100 years ago. It is also viewed as a natural process of historical change and the only possible path for the future world economy, which supposedly will increase wealth and prosperity for all countries and around the globe (Stiglitz, 2002).

In India, the first phase of globalization started in the decade 1980s during the Prime Ministership of Rajiv Gandhi (Bhuimali and Sarkar, 2004). However, this phase of globalization was assumed as half-hearted and self-reversing in nature. But, globalization was an eventual in terms of policy changes in the decade 1990's and these changes have been taking place at three different levels such as global, national and sectoral level. But the first and foremost development is the globalization process at the international level. This ensures a closer integration of the countries and peoples of the world and has been brought about by enormous reduction in costs of transportation and communication. This has also been breaking down of artificial barriers to the flows of goods, services, capital, knowledge and to a lesser extent people across the borders (Wadhva, 2003).

More specifically, globalization manifests itself in three various forms such as an increase in international trade, financial flows and foreign direct investment (Loots, 2002; Nayyar, 2002; Majumder, 2003). However, the flows of trade and finance bore the testimony to radical metamorphosis in its total scope and spectrum on account of the onset of globally coined business jargon. Again, among the many changes in foreign trade are noticeable. This is because multilateral trading has gained currency under the aegis of World Trade Organization (WTO). Although, the contradictions are galore with respect to multilateralism amidst the surfacing of inter, intra and regional trade gaping, yet the hard reality is that besides the multilateral trading, regional and Free Trade Accord (FTA) have come to stay on the global economic plane. The basic philosophy and tenet behind this is to promote inter and intra regional trade among the countries and thereby, to faster economic cooperation, growth and development (Azad and Fayaz, 2004).

South Asian Association of Regional Cooperation (SAARC) is one such regional trade grouping, which consists of seven South Asian countries such as India, Pakistan, Sri Lanka, Nepal, Bhutan, Bangladesh and Maldives. They have been working together since 1985 and trying to find out their common problems in a spirit of trust, mutual understanding and cooperation based on equity, justice and shared benefits. The primary objective of this regional trading is to promote and strengthen trade among the member countries. Keeping in above view, the paper examines India's foreign trade with other SAARC countries during the globalization era.

The rest of the paper is organized into five different sections including the earlier introduction. Section II discuses the importance of foreign trade in the economy. Section III highlights the India's foreign trade in the pre- and post-globalization era. Section IV discuses India's trade with SAARC nations. In section VI, the paper concludes with some possibilities for establishing better trade with SAARC nations.

FOREIGN TRADE: THE IMPORTANCE IN THE ECONOMY

Foreign trade plays a paramount role in the economic development of the country and treats as an engine of economic growth (Robertson, 1949). It accelerates economic growth by bringing new ideas, new technologies and new tastes. That, in turn, stimulates innovation in the economy. As per the empirical investigation, it has been confirmed that there exists a positive and significant relationship between exports and economic growth and accordingly, suggested that there is export promotion, trade liberalization and outward looking strategy because of multidimensional favourable effects of exports (Afzal, 2004; Ram, 1987; Salvatore, 1983). Foreign trade is a treasure house of static and dynamic gains for the economy. It enables an economy to compliment development of industrial or agricultural structure and ensures diversified consumption for its people. It is instrumental in equalizing factor prices and results, in a more efficient allocation of resources. Foreign trade promotes capital formation and brings sectoral and external economies in the industrial activities of a country (Ram, 1987; Feder, 1983; Balassa, 1978).

It bestows a number of economies of scale and enables a country to produce those goods, which are economical, competitive and are based on rational cost proportions. It strengthens relationship (both economically and politically) with other trading countries and provides an opportunity to enter into customs union, which bring forth trade creating and trade diverting benefits. It promotes the hidden talents on entrepreneurs and thus, augments the comparative advantages in the country. Foreign trade provides access to scarce resources needed to promote economic growth such as raw materials, machinery, capital goods and intermediary producer goods that are indispensable for economic growth.

Foreign trade is supposed to ban indirect transmitter of capital often through MNCs. It improves the allocative efficiency of nations through international specialization in the production of goods and services. It provides and promotes an atmosphere of healthy competition among trading nations by checking monopolies and restrictive trade practices. Foreign trade widens the horizons of consumption possibility frontiers of the countries far in excess of domestic production constraints. There is increasing choice of the consumers in the trading regime, as different varieties for the same good (differentiated products) are available in an open economy. Foreign trade is supposed to bring growth oriented structural changes in the economy by changing the composition of GNP, employment and consumption. In fact, trade is considered as a better alternative to foreign aid, foreign direct investment and portfolio investments. This is because the latter are mostly political vulnerable (Krishnamoorthy and Reddy, 2002).

Apart from the above mentioned benefits accruing to individual countries, the world as a whole also benefits from international trade. The world production of every commodity is maximized, through international allocation of resources. There is greater international equality in real incomes, factor prices and consumption levels and consequently in welfare levels across countries of the world. The relative wage levels would increase in a labour abundant country and fall in a capital abundant country. This would equalize real wages of labour in all the trading nations. In view of these reasons, the classical and neoclassical economists considered free trade as the first best policy to promote economic growth. Over and above, foreign trade plays a multilateral role in economic growth and thus, there is urgent need for the country to boost the trade and integrating the same with rest of the world. Moreover, trade openness promotes economic growth and raising economic growth in a sustained manner reduces poverty in the economy (Mathur, 2003).

Trading between countries is not a new concept and in fact, it was traced back since the inception of human civilization. However, these relations were limited during those days because of lack of infrastructure besides host of other factors. With the passage of time, trading between and among the countries gradually developed with respect to technological advancement. In fact, after the World War II, trade volume increased by leaps and bounds and world trade witnessed an extraordinary growth. The increase in the value and volume and the diversification of world trade were mainly due to the advancement of technology, better infrastructure and indeed, by the effect of globalization. Most interestingly, developing countries were not able to derive benefits by this growth till 1972 on account of lower growth rate in their exports. As a result, the share of developing countries in world exports declined. India also felt these worldwide changes and the revolution in the sphere of technology and thus, adopted a steady policy to enhance its trade relation with the countries of the world (Khan and Fayaz, 2004). One of such policies is the effect of globalization in the decade 1990s. Accordingly, in the subsequent section, we examine India's foreign trade in the globalization regime.

INDIA'S FOREIGN TRADE: THE PRE- AND POST-GLOBALIZATION ERA

The fundamental objective of globalization in India, which was initiated in the decade 1990s, is to boost economic growth and reduce poverty. However, Indian post-globalization regime has been somewhat evolutionary and incremental in nature. There had been cases of delays and reverses, resulted stalling of reforms in India in some areas for some times. This was probably due to interplay of forces of democratic politics and coalition governments and the existence of different pressure groups with their robed interests. Despite these problems, India has been very successful in moving ahead to open up its economy to the rest of the world and preparing herself to transform through further economic reforms for emerging as a significant player in the global economy by 2020 (Wadhva, 2003). However examining the performance of Indian economy during the globalization era, we have been observed that there is mixed picture of notable failures and achievements.

On the failure sides, there is growing revenue deficits as well as fiscal deficits, declining trends of tax revenue as a percentage of GDP, sluggish human development, low social sector expenditure (Dev and Mooij, 2004-05), wide income inequalities, slow growth of agriculture, regional variation in infrastructure, jobless growth (Bhide and Kalirajan, 2004), etc. So far as achievements are concerned, there is favorable impact on macro economic stabilization policies including the devaluation of rupee and other structural reforms (Ramakrishna, 2003; Singh, 2003). There are improvements in current account balance, inflows of external finance and accretion of foreign exchange reserves, moderate rate of inflation, sectoral diversification on economic growth, high trade-GDP ratio, etc. (See in Table 1).

Over and above, the effects of globalization can be studied through stabilization and structural adjustments. Stabilization involves measures relating to control of fiscal balance, the balance of payments and external payment deficits and maintaining a low rate of inflation. On the other hand, structural adjustment aims at improving efficiency and productivity and integrating the economy with the rest of world trade and capital movements. Most importantly, it is assumed that India's trade policies have been very effective in bringing imports and exports into an equilibrium path in the long run (Upender and Aruna, 2004). Accordingly, in this section, we examine the trends of India's foreign trade in the globalization period. That is to make comparison between pre- and post- globalization era. To establish the same, we have taken the data of 22 years from 1980-81 to 2001-02 and divided the same into two parts: one part is from 1980-81 to 1990-91 and is called as pre-globalization period; second part is from 1991-92 to 2001-02 and is called as post-globalization period.

The trade under pre-globalization period is presented in Table 2. The figures reflect that total exports of the country have grown from a low of Rs. 6710.7 crores in 1980-81 to a high of Rs. 32558.0 crores in 1990-91. However, there are wide

Table 1
A Macro Economic Profile of India

Items	*1990*	*1991*	*1992*	*1993*	*1994*	*1995*	*1996*	*1997*	*1998*	*1999*	*2000*	*2001*	*2002*	*2003*	*2004*
X_1	5.6	1.3	5.10	5.9	7.30	7.30	7.80	4.80	6.50	6.10	4.40	5.60	4.40	6.0	6.3
X_2	6.76	-1.22	4.09	5.20	10.20	11.60	7.10	4.30	3.70	4.80	6.60	3.30	6.10	na	na
X_3	13.72	-12.32	9.28	5.83	22.92	11.10	-1.00	7.70	0.70	20.30	-1.40	3.00	na	na	na
X_4	26.30	22.60	23.60	23.10	26.00	26.90	24.50	24.60	22.60	25.20	24.00	23.70	23.9	24.0	25.0
X_5	23.10	22.00	21.80	22.50	24.80	25.10	23.20	23.10	21.50	24.10	23.40	24.00	24.50	24.1	25.2
X_6	-3.50	-0.34	-1.71	-0.42	-1.05	-1.65	-1.19	-1.37	-0.96	-1.05	-0.54	0.29	0.6	0.10	0.20
X_7	2.27	1.46	1.59	3.54	2.84	1.31	2.96	2.47	2.01	2.48	1.86	1.99	2.57	na	na
X_8	-0.40	1.43	0.33	3.18	1.44	-0.82	1.52	0.94	0.95	1.38	1.31	2.46	3.35	na	na
X_9	11.81	15.71	11.58	9.63	12.5	8.1	4.6	4.4	5.9	3.3	7.2	3.6	2.8	5.0	5.0

Note: X_1: GDP growth; X_2: Industrial growth; X_3: Investment growth; X_4: Investment as a percentage of GDP; X_5: Saving as a percentage of GDP; X_6: Current account balance as a percentage of GDP; X_7: Capital account balance as a percentage of GDP; and X_8: Reserves accretion as a percentage of GDP; X_9: Inflation rate in percentage.

Source: RBI, Hand Books of Statistics, 2002-03; GOI, Economic Survey, 2003; Asian Development Outlook, 2003

fluctuations in its growth rate. The growth rate of exports is negative (7.2 per cent) in the year 1985-86 and reached a high positive (36.7 per cent) in the year 1989-90. On the average, the compound growth rate of export has increased at the rate of 16.14 per cent during the entire pre-globalization period (i.e. from 1980-81 to 1990-19991). The compound growth rate of exports is also statistically significant at 1 per cent probability level and is judged through the values of s-statistics (See Table 2).

Table 2
India's Foreign Trade during the Pre-Globalization Era
(Rs. In Crores)

Year	X_1	X_2	X_3	X_4	X_5	X_6	X_7
1980-81	6710.7	–	12549.2	–	-5838.5	4.9	9.5
1981-82	7805.9	16.3	13607.6	8.4	-5801.7	4.9	8.9
1982-83	8803.4	12.8	14292.7	5.0	-5489.3	5.1	8.9
1983-84	9770.7	11.0	15831.5	10.8	-6060.8	4.9	8.2
1984-85	11744.0	20.2	17134.2	8.2	-5390.5	5.2	8.1
1985-86	10895.0	-07.2	19657.7	14.7	-8763.1	4.4	8.1
1986-87	12452.0	14.3	20095.8	2.2	-7643.8	4.1	7.7
1987-88	15674.0	25.9	22243.7	10.7	-6570.0	4.9	7.7
1988-89	20232.0	29.1	28235.2	26.9	-8003.7	5.2	8.6
1989-90	27658.0	36.7	35328.4	25.1	-7670.0	6.2	8.9
1990-91	32558.0	17.7	43192.9	22.3	-10635.0	6.2	9.4
CGR	16.14		12.42				
t-statistics	11.99		12.11				
r^2	0.94		0.94				

Note: X_1: Amount of Exports (in Rs. Crores); X_2: Change in Exports (in percentage); X_3: Amount of Imports (in Rs. Crores); X_4: Change in Imports (in Percentage); X_5: Trade Balance (in Rs. Crores); X_6: Exports as a Percentage of GDP; X_7: Imports as a Percentage of GDP; CGR: Compound Growth Rate (in Percentage); r^2: Correlation Coefficient.

Source: Hand Book of Statistics on Indian Economy, Reserve Bank of India, Mumbai

On the other side, the amount of imports has been increased from a low of Rs. 12549.2 crores in 1980-81 to a high of Rs. 43192.9 crores in 1990-91 and its fluctuation varies from a low of 2.2 per cent in 1986-1987 to a high of 26.9 per cent in

1988-89. However, the whole imports has grown at an average rate of 12.42 per cent during the entire pre-globalization period and the growth rate is also statistically significant at 1 per cent probability level. The Table 2 also reflects the trade balance of the country, which is all along negative during the pre-globalization era. This reflects that the magnitudes of import are substantially higher in contrast to the magnitude of exports. However, more interestingly, the trade balance is in declining trend in the Indian economy during the pre-globalization era (See Figure 1). It is also inspiring to mention that both exports and imports as a percentage of GDP has been gradually increasing in the Indian economy. The exports-GDP ratio was 4.9 per cent in 1980-81 and increased to 6.2 per cent in 1990-91. On the contrary, import-GDP ratio has been fluctuating at an average of 9 per cent during the pre-globalization era and substantially higher to exports-GDP ratio (See Table 2).

India's foreign trade under post-globalization period is also in increasing trend (See Table 3). The amount of exports has been increased from a low of Rs. 44041.8 crores in 1991-1992 to a high of Rs. 209018.0 crores in 2001-02 and is about five-fold increase in the past 12 years. Similarly, the amount of imports also increased from a low of Rs. 47850.8 to a high of Rs. 245199.0 crores. There is also considerable variation in the annual growth rates of export and imports. The annual percentage changes in exports varied from a low 2.7 per cent to a high of 29.9 per cent and on the contrary, the annual percentage changes in import varies between a low of 6.2 per cent to 36.4 per cent during the entire post-globalization era. However, the compound growth rate of exports and imports during the entire periods are 16.56 per cent and 17.97 per cent respectively.

There is as usual India's export and export growth, which is lagging behind that of imports during this period. As a result, trade balance is negative through out the years in the post-globalization era. However, most interestingly, the negative trade balance has also been increasing over the years both in absolute terms as well as in relation to total trade. Furthermore, the amount of exports and imports as a percentage of GDP has also been increasing in the post-globalization era. Export-GDP ratio has increased substantially from 7.3 per cent in 1991-92 to 9.8 per cent in 2001-02 and imports-GDP ratio varies from 8.3 per cent to 13.0 per cent in the entire period from 1991-92 to 2001-02.

Table 3
India's Foreign Trade during the Post-Globalization Era
(Rs. In Crores)

Year	X_1	X_2	X_3	X_4	X_5	X_6	X_7
1991-92	44041.8	–	47850.8	–	-3809.0	7.3	8.3
1992-93	53688.3	21.9	63374.5	32.4	-9686.2	7.8	10.2
1993-94	69751.4	29.9	73101.0	15.3	-3349.6	8.1	9.6
1994-95	82674.1	18.5	89970.7	23.1	-7296.6	8.1	10.9
1995-96	106353.3	28.6	122678.1	36.4	-16324.8	8.9	12.0
1996-97	118817.1	11.7	138919.7	13.2	-20102.6	8.6	12.3
1997-98	130100.6	09.5	154176.3	11.0	-24075.7	8.7	12.5
1998-99	139753.1	07.4	178331.8	15.7	-38578.7	8.3	11.5
1999-00	159561.4	14.2	215236.5	20.7	-55675.1	8.4	12.4
2000-01	203571.0	27.6	230872.7	07.3	-27301.7	9.8	13.0
2001-02	209018.0	02.7	245199.0	06.2	-36181.0	9.4	12.0
CGR	16.56		17.97				
t-statistics	17.0		18.06				
r^2	0.94		0.94				

Note: X_1: Amount of Exports (in Rs. Crores); X_2: Change in Exports (in percentage); X_3: Amount of Imports (in Rs. Crores); X_4: Change in Imports (in Percentage); X_5: Trade Balance (in Rs. Crores); X_6: Exports as a Percentage of GDP; X_7: Imports as a Percentage of GDP; CGR: Compound Growth Rate (in Percentage); r^2: Correlation Coefficient.

Source: Hand Book of Statistics on Indian Economy, Reserve Bank of India, Mumbai

INDIA'S FOREIGN TRADE WITH SAARC NATIONS

All in all, it is discernible from the above discussion that India's foreign trade has registered a wavering trend during the period of globalization. In other words, Indian globalization process has opened up more vistas for foreign trade. But, it is up to us that how we leverage our resources to derive more more-benefits from the changing economic world order. It is evident that India's trade performance in the globalization era is quite impressive. Both exports as well as imports (in rupees) have registered an encouraging trend. But, the trade deficit has also been increased simultaneously (Bhuimali and Sarkar, 2004). This is not a good sign for the economy and mostly due to growing demand for petroleum products and its inability to compete in the western markets despite the opportunities provided after the globalization of the Indian economy. Furthermore, its share in world trade has also gone down (Khan and Fayaz, 2004) and unfortunately, the trade share is very low in comparison to their many peers in Asia (Krishnamoorthy and Reddy, 2002). Accordingly, in the subsequent section, we examine India's trade with other SAARC nations in the post-globalization era and to establish the same, we have taken seven years data from 1996-97 to 2002-03.

Examining India's trade with Bangladesh, it is inferred that India's export to Bangladesh has been in increasing trend over the years during the post-globalization regime except in the year 1997-98 and 1999-2000 (See Table 4). In case of imports, there is little bit variation between $ 50.81 million to $ 80.51 million. It is lowest ($ 558.15 million) in the year 1999-00 and highest ($ 1113.95 million) in the year 2002-03. The percentage share of exports to Bangladesh is varying between 2 per cent to 3 per cent of the overall trade of India. On the contrary, the percentage share of imports to total trade of Bangladesh is about less than 0.5 per cent during the globalization era. However, the balance of trade has always in favour of India. This is because the growth of exports to Bangladesh is substantially higher in contrast to its amount of imports.

India' trade with Maldives is substantially very low. The exports to Maldives have shown positive trend from a low of $10.36 million in 1996-97 to a high of $ 31.59 million in 2002-03. But, the percentage share of exports to Maldives has always been low and is about less than 0.07 per cent in the period under reference. Similarly, India's imports from Maldives are also very negligible and vary from a low of US$ 0.05 million in 1998-99 to a high of US$ 0.40 million in 1999-00 and 2001-02

Table 4
India's Foreign Trade with Bangladesh

Items	*1996-97*	*1997-98*	*1998-99*	*1999-00*	*2000-01*	*2001-02*	*2002-03*
X_1	868.96	786.46	995.64	636.31	935.04	1002.18	1176.00
X_2	–	-9.49	26.59	-36.09	46.95	7.18	17.34
X_3	33469.94	34784.99	33218.72	36822.49	44560.29	43826.73	52719.43
X_4	–	3.93	-4.5	10.85	21.01	-1.65	20.29
X_5	2.59	2.26	3.00	1.73	2.10	2.29	2.23
X_6	62.23	50.81	62.40	78.15	80.51	59.12	62.05
X_7	–	-18.34	22.81	25.24	3.01	-26.57	4.96
X_8	39132.41	41484.49	42388.71	49738.06	50536.46	51413.29	61412.13
X_9	–	6.01	2.1	17.34	1.61	1.74	19.45
X_{10}	0.159	0.1225	0.15	0.16	0.16	0.11	0.10
X_{11}	806.63	735.63	933.24	558.15	854.54	943.06	1113.95

Note: X_1: Amount of Exports to Bangladesh (in US$ Million); X_2: Percentage of Growth of Exports to Bangladesh; X_3: India's Total Export (in US$ Million); X_4: Percentage of Growth of Total Exports of India; X_5: Percentage Share of India's Export to Bangladesh; X_6: Amount of Imports from Bangladesh (Us$ Million); X_7: Percentage of Growth of Imports to Bangladesh; X_8: India's Total Import (in US$ Million); X_9: Percentage Growth of India's Total Import; X_{10}: Percentage Share of India's Total Import from Bangladesh; and X_{11}: Trade Balance between India and Bangladesh (in US$ Million).

Source: Directorate General of Foreign Trade, Government of India, New Delhi.

(See Table 5). The percentage share of imports from Bhutan to India's total imports is considerably very negligible. However, the trade balance is always in favour of India, as the amount of exports is above than that of the amount of imports.

Coming to India's trade picture with Bhutan, it is observed that export to Bhutan shows a high volatile scenario with both highly negative and positive growth rates. The amount of exports to Bhutan is considerably low and varies from a low of US$ 1.08 million in 2000-01 to a high of US$ 39.05 million 2002-03 under the post globalization era. In contrast to the amounts of imports from Bhutan is substantially high in comparison to imports. The amount of imports is low in the year 1998-99 (is about US$ 6.13 million) and high in the year 1996-97 (is about US$ 33.37 million). The percentage share of

Table 5
India's Foreign Trade with Maldives

Items	*1996-97*	*1997-98*	*1998-99*	*1999-00*	*2000-01*	*2001-02*	*2002-03*
X_1	10.36	8.74	8.38	7.30	24.61	26.88	31.59
X_2	—	-15.72	-4.11	-12.84	237.10	9.20	17.53
X_3	33469.94	34784.99	33218.72	36822.49	44560.29	43826.73	52719.43
X_4	—	3.93	-4.5	10.85	21.01	-1.65	20.29
X_5	0.0310	0.0251	0.030	0.020	0.060	0.060	0.060
X_6	0.17	0.24	0.05	0.40	0.19	0.40	0.33
X_7	—	39.10	-79.16	671.33	-52.63	108.73	-16.00
X_8	39132.41	41484.49	42388.71	49738.06	50536.46	51413.29	61412.13
X_9	—	6.01	2.1	17.34	1.61	1.74	19.45
X_{10}	0.0004	0.0006	0.000	0.000	0.000	0.000	0.000
X_{11}	10.19	8.50	8.32	6.90	24.42	26.48	31.25

Note: All notations and source are same, as mentioned in Table 4.

exports to Bhutan is also very low and is about less that .07 per cent. On the contrary, the percentage share of imports from Bhutan reflects highly fluctuating trends and varies from 0.01 per cent to 0.09 per cent in the post-globalization era (See Table 6). The trade balance is always in the favour of Bhutan, as the amount of imports is much higher in contrast to the amount of exports. However, it is only in the year 1998-99 and 2002-03, the trade balance is in the favour of India.

Table 6
India's Foreign Trade with Bhutan

Items	*1996-97*	*1997-98*	*1998-99*	*1999-00*	*2000-01*	*2001-02*	*2002-03*
X_1	21.98	13.33	9.56	7.57	1.08	7.60	39.05
X_2	—	-39.37	-28.28	-20.78	-85.78	605.38	413.89
X_3	33469.94	34784.99	33218.72	36822.49	44560.29	43826.73	52719.43
X_4	—	3.93	-4.5	10.85	21.01	-1.65	20.29
X_5	0.065	0.038	0.030	0.020	0.000	0.020	0.070
X_6	33.37	13.44	6.13	18.01	21.09	23.92	32.15
X_7	—	-60.22	-54.38	194.00	17.08	13.42	34.41
X_8	39132.41	41484.49	42388.71	49738.06	50536.46	51413.29	61412.13
X_9	—	6.01	2.1	17.34	1.61	1.74	19.45
X_{10}	0.086	0.032	0.010	0.040	0.040	0.050	0.050
X_{11}	-11.8	-0.11	3.43	-10.44	-20.01	-16.32	6.89

Note: All notations and source are same, as mentioned in Table 4.

India's trade with Pakistan is somewhat extraordinary in comparison to other SAARC countries and mainly due to the existence of high tensions between the countries. India's exports to Pakistan have registered a wide fluctuating trend and vary from a low of $101.01 million in 2000-01 to $ 206.16 million in 2002-03. The total exports to Pakistan as a percentage of India's total trade is about 0.5 per cent. On the other side, imports from Pakistan is also showing fluctuating trend. It registered a high amount of $ 214.45 million during 1998-99 and a low amount of per cent 36.16 million during 1996-97. Indian imports accounted for less than half percent of total imports during the period under study. The trade balance is in favour of India except in the year 1998-99 (See Table 7).

Table 7
India's Foreign Trade with Pakistan

Items	*1996-97*	*1997-98*	*1998-99*	*1999-00*	*2000-01*	*2001-02*	*2002-03*
X_1	157.22	143.15	106.10	92.95	186.83	144.01	206.16
X_2	–	-8.95	-25.88	-12.40	101.01	-22.92	43.16
X_3	33469.94	34784.99	33218.72	36822.49	44560.29	43826.73	52719.43
X_4	–	3.93	-4.5	10.85	21.01	-1.65	20.29
X_5	0.35	0.33	0.32	0.25	0.42	0.33	0.39
X_6	36.16	44.45	214.45	68.21	64.03	64.76	44.85
X_7	–	22.93	382.45	-68.19	-6.14	1.14	-30.74
X_8	39132.41	41484.49	42388.71	49738.06	50536.46	51413.29	61412.13
X_9	–	6.01	2.1	17.34	1.61	1.74	19.45
X_{10}	0.924	0.1071	0.510	0.140	0.130	0.130	0.070
X_{11}	121.06	98.70	-108.35	24.73	122.81	79.25	161.31

Note: All notations and source are same, as mentioned in Table 4.

Investigating India's trade with Nepal during 1996-97 to 2002-03, we could highlight that exports to Nepal have shown a fluctuating trend and varies from a low of $ 122.41 million in 1998-99 to $ 350.36 million in 2002-03. The share of exports to Nepal is below half percent of the total exports of India during these periods. On the contrary, the amount of imports from Nepal is in increasing trends. It is of US$ 64.07 million in 1996-97 and has increased to US$ 281.76 million in 2002-03. But, unfortunately, the amount of imports as a percentage of

Indian total imports is substantially low and about less than 1 per cent. Most interestingly, the trade balance is in the favour of Nepal except few exceptions (See Table 8).

Table 8
India's Foreign Trade with Nepal

Items	*1996-97*	*1997-98*	*1998-99*	*1999-00*	*2000-01*	*2001-02*	*2002-03*
X_1	165.72	170.05	122.41	151.23	140.84	214.46	350.36
X_2	–	2.61	-28.02	23.54	-6.87	52.28	63.37
X_3	33469.94	34784.99	33218.72	36822.49	44560.29	43826.73	52719.43
X_4	–	3.93	-4.5	10.85	21.01	-1.65	20.29
X_5	0.4951	0.4889	0.370	0.410	0.320	0.490	0.660
X_6	64.07	95.16	144.85	188.63	255.08	355.94	281.76
X_7	–	48.51	52.22	30.23	35.23	39.54	-20.84
X_8	39132.41	41484.49	42388.71	49738.06	50536.46	51413.29	61412.13
X_9	–	6.01	2.1	17.34	1.61	1.74	19.45
X_{10}	0.1637	0.2294	0.340	0.380	0.500	0.690	0.460
X_{11}	101.65	74.89	-22.44	-47.40	-114.24	-141.48	6.89

Note: All notations and source are same, as mentioned in Table 4.

India's trade with Sri Lanka is always in the favour of India, as the amount of exports is substantially higher in contrast to imports in the entire period under reference (See Table 9). India's export to Sri Lanka has registered a dithering trend. It has increased from a low of $ 437.13 million in 1998-99 to a high of $ 920.98 million in 2002-03. India's export to Sri Lanka as a percentage of total trade is about less than 2 per cent in the globalization era. The low export to Sri Lanka is mainly ascribed to similarity of basket of goods and services and more or less concentration on exports to western countries rather than among the member nations. On the other side, the amount of imports from Sri Lanka is substantially low in comparison to the amount of exports. It varies from a low of US$ 30.21 in 1997-98 to a high of US$ 90.83 million in 2002-03. Interestingly, the growth rate of imports from Sri Lanka is negative in the year 1997-98. India's imports from Sri Lanka as a percentage of total trade are about less than 1 per cent through out the years.

Table 9
India's Foreign Trade with Sri Lanka

Items	1996-97	1997-98	1998-99	1999-00	2000-01	2001-02	2002-03
X_1	477.41	489.23	437.0	499.27	640.14	630.89	920.98
X_2	–	2.48	-10.65	14.22	28.22	-1.45	45.98
X_3	33469.94	34784.99	33218.72	36822.49	44560.29	43826.73	52719.43
X_4	–	3.93	-4.5	10.85	21.01	-1.65	20.29
X_5	1.4264	1.4064	1.320	1.360	1.440	1.440	1.750
X_6	42.84	30.21	37.68	44.23	45.01	67.38	90.83
X_7	–	-29.49	24.73	17.40	1.75	49.71	34.80
X_8	39132.41	41484.49	42388.71	49738.06	50536.46	51413.29	61412.13
X_9	–	6.01	2.1	17.34	1.61	1.74	19.45
X_{10}	0.1095	0.0728	0.090	0.090	0.090	0.130	0.150
X_{11}	434.57	459.02	399.45	455.04	595.14	563.51	830.16

Note: All notations and source are same, as mentioned in Table 4.

CONCLUSION AND POLICY IMPLICATIONS

Over and above, as per the preceding discussion, the paper finds that there is substantial improvement in India's foreign trade in the globalization era. Both exports and imports are in increasing trend. However, the amount of imports is much higher in comparison to exports and thus, there is trade deficit in the Indian economy. There is also diversification of foreign trade in the Indian economy in the globalization era (Bhuimali and Sarkar, 2004; Majumder, 2003). In fact, this has also been substantially taken place with other SAARC countries and mostly due to the impact of globalization and establishment of South Asian Preferential Trading Agreement (SAPTA) during the reference period.

The main objectives of SAPTA are to promote and facilitate mutual trade and economic cooperation among the member states. The measures to be taken during this period to improve the trading among SAARC nations are tariff, non-tariff and direct measures. Some adjustments also made with respect to product-by-product basis, across the broad tariff reduction sectoral basis and also depending upon the circumstances prevailing in the SAARC in particular and world in general.

However, the critics say that despite these substantial opportunities, trading among SAARC nations is about less than 4 per cent of their total volumes. This mainly attributed diverse socio-economic status of SAARC countries, the emphasis of west policy to the member countries, same basket of commodities, tension between the member nations (especially Indian and Pakistan) and the comparative advantage enjoyed by India over the rest of the SAARC nations (Azad and Fayaz, 2004).

The paper accordingly suggests that these hindrances can be set off by liberalizing regional economies further and making effective peace between neighboring countries. Besides, under the WTO agreement, SAARC countries could assign Most Favoured Nation (MFN) status to each other. They should also cut their tariff rates. By doing so, India can channalise unofficial lucrative trade normally benefits of which are being enjoyed by the unauthorized agents and smugglers. India should come forward to implement Free Trade Agreement (FTA) with the neighboring countries on bilateral basis under the umbrella of SAPTA. The setting up of FTA will enhance trade between India and its neighbours in transportation, equipments, engineering goods and IT products and also the flow of investment, which will result in economies of scale through access to larger market. Mutual trade and understanding will help in improving the status of trade, generating employment opportunities, facilitating innovations, etc. (Mathur, 2003).

Furthermore, it will better, if SAARC countries focus their attention towards trade among themselves rather than with the west and develop their own capacities. This will ultimately provide them inner strength to fight the fierce competition in the global market. The steps like abolition of quota will adversely affect most of the member nations. Thus, in order to compensate them, multilateral trade among the group should be promoted. Besides, India and Pakistan should overcome their political differences and promote trade on priority among the member nations by shouldering their responsibility as being the bigger nation of the group.

In short, India can improve her trade with SAARC in particular and world in general by giving stress on its economy at a broad level. In this context, some of the possibilities, which, we can establish here as follows:

- To fall in line with the globalization process, India has already initiated removal of quantitative restrictions, simplification and rationalization of tariffs, reduced export restrictions and liberalized the trade and payments aspects. However, in this scenario, economy requires more openness and more transparency of their policies.
- Besides the operation of globalization since 1991, tariff rates are still high in India as compared to other developing countries. Thus, to enter to FTAs with SAARC countries and Asian Countries, rate of tariff should be reduced further.
- There is need of internal economic reforms in the form of structural adjustment in a broad level to enhance the economic efficiency.
- There is need of encouraging Foreign Direct Investment (FDI). Most importantly, FDI related policies have to be rationalized to attract more FDI in export-oriented sectors of the economy. Further, to attract NRI funds, procedural simplifications have to be outlined properly.
- There is need of improving infrastructural base in the Indian economy, as it is a pace setter of economic growth and helps in integrating the economy through trade, investment and financial flows. Here, the step must be taken to encourage greater public investment as well as private investment in the infrastructural sector.
- There is need of boosting more and more bilateral and multilateral trade agreement under the regime of WTO. This is because under the WTO provisions there are enough opportunities for making Free Trade Agreements (FTA).

- Since Indian exports are more or less traditional in nature, steps should be taken by Indian corporate for making their export products more competitive by improving quality. New markets should be exploited and more commodities should be brought on the export list so that we can capture at least one percent of global trade.
- Marketing information system should also be improved so as to know the size, nature, trend of consumer demand and the degree of foreign competition.
- There is need of introduction of new cost effective technology for improvement in productivity and export competitiveness.
- WTO agreements should be exploited as leverage for growth and development rather than impediments. New destinations for exports should be explored for Indian traditional and other goods.
- There is overall need for the simplification of export procedures in the light of WTO agreement.
- The position of Balance of payments (BOP) needs to be handling carefully. This is because invisible account balance is doing well in the globalization era and is due to high demand of IT professional and remittances by NRIs.
- Last but not the least, there is need of political stability. This requires political will and simplified trade procedural formalities in accordance with WTO agreements.

To conclude, India's trade with SAARC nations is not satisfactory. Thus, there is need of better trading with SAARC nations by integrating its economy with rest of the SAARC nations. The ongoing economic integration not only focus trade as a means of strengthening international competitiveness and as an engine of economic growth. This helps in alleviating poverty, curbing imbalances, reducing inequalities, plummeting backwardness, and ensuring terrorism free society with equity and justice.

REFERENCES

Afzal, M. (2004), "Export-Economic Growth Nexus: Pakistan's Experience", *Indian Journal of Economics and Business,* Vol. 3, No. 2, pp. 315-340.

Azad, I. And Fayaz, M. (2004), "India's Trade with SAARC in Globalized Trade Regime", *Banking Finance,* Vol. 17, Vo. 8, pp. 5-12.

Balass, B. (1978), "Exports and Growth: Further Evidence", *Journal of Development Economics,* Vol. 52, No. 2, pp. 181-189.

Bhide, S.and Kalirajan, K. (2004), "Impact of Trade Liberalization on Employment in Indian Manufacturing: Evidence from the Organized Sector", *Journal of Social and Economic Development,* Vol. 6, No. 1, pp. 1-19.

Bhuimali, A. and Sarkar, B. (2004), "India's Trade Performance in the Post-liberalization Era", *Indian Journal of Social and Economic Policy,* Vol. 1, No. 1, pp. 117-125.

Dev, S. M. and Mooij, J. (2004-05), "Patterns in Social Sector Expenditure: Pre-and Post-Reform Periods", in Parikh, K. and Radhakrishna, R. (eds.), *Indian Development Report*, Oxford University Press, New Delhi, pp. 96-111.

Feder, G. (1983), "On Exports and Economic Growth", *Journal of Development Economics,* Vol. 5, No.1, pp. 59-73.

ILO (2004), "Report on World Commission on the Social Dimension of Globalization", International Labour Organization, Geneva.

Kapila, U. (2002), "Globalization and the Indian Economy", in (R. Kapila and U. Kapila, eds.) *India's Economy in the 21st Century,* New Delhi: Academic Foundation.

Khan, A. Q. and Fayaz, M. (2004), "Niche for Indian Foreign Trade in Globalizng Regime", *Banking Finance,* Vol. 17, No. 9, pp. 5-17.

Krishnamoorthy, D. and Reddy, V. V. S. (2002), "Growth and Instability in India's Foreign Trade: A Comparative Analysis of Pre and Post-Liberalization Periods", Artha Vijnana, Vol. XLIV, Nos. 3-4, pp. 349-366.

Loots, E. (2002), "Globalization, Emerging Markets and the South African Economy", *South African Journal of Economics,* Vol. 70, No. 2, March, Pretoria.

Mathur, S. K. (2003), "Trade Liberalization and the Poor: A Framework for Poverty Reduction Policies with Special Reference to Some Asian Countries Including India", *Indian Development Review,* Vol. 1, No. 2, pp. 179-230.

Majumder, B. (2003), "India's Trade-Link with The European Union: Facts and Possibilities", *Management and Change,* Vol. 7, No. 1, pp. 49-73.

Nayyar, D. (2002), Governing Globalization: Issues and Institutions. New Delhi: Oxford University Press.

Ram, R. (1987), "Exports and Economic Growth in Developing Countries: Evidence from Time Series and Cross Section Data", *Economic Development and Cultural Change,* Vol. 35, pp. 50-72.

Robertson, D. H. (1949), "The Future of International Trade", Readings in the Theory of International Trade, AEA & Co., Blankiston, p. 507.

Ramakrishna, G. (2003), "Globalization and Balance of Payments Experience of India", *Indian Development Review,* Vol. 1, No. 1, pp. 27-46.

Salvatore, D. (1983), "A Simultaneous Equations Model of Trade and Development with Dynamic Policy Simulations", Kyklos, Vol. 36, pp. 66-90.

Shariff, I. (2003), "Global Economic Integration: Prospects and Problems", *Indian Development Review,* Vol. 1, No. 2, pp. 163-178.

Singh, T. (2003), "Trade Flows, Trade Policy Regimes and Some Issues in Capital Account Liberalization in India", *International Journal of Applied Economics and Econometrics,* Vol. 11, No. 4, pp. 607-646.

Stiglitz, J. (2002), Globalization and its Discontents, Allan Lane, London: Penguin Press.

Upender, M. and Aruna, M. (2004), "Are Exports and Imports Drifting Apart from Each Other in India? An Application of Cointegration and Error Correction Modeling", *Indian Journal of Economics and Business,* Vol. 3, No. 2, pp. 397-407.

Wadhva, C. D. (2003). "Economic Reforms in India: In Retrospect and Prospect", *Man and Development,* Vol. 25, No. 3, pp. 17-62.

9

GLOBAL PROPERTY RIGHTS IN GENETIC RESOURCES: AN ECONOMIC ASSESSMENT

*Clem Tisdell**

1. INTRODUCTION

Liberal economic philosophy, involving the use of market systems and private property rights, in recent times, has come to dominate thinking about economic policy globally. As a result, there has been growing support for the global creation of (or recognition of) private property rights and communal property rights in genetic resources (Bhat, 1999; Swanson, 1997) and for these resources to be managed by market operations rather than by government regulation, as an alternative, in some cases, to global open-access to these resources.

Advocates of this policy foresee several advantages for it compared to previous policies. They consider that such an approach is likely to be more effective in conserving genetic resources, will be more efficient in the utilization of such resources, and that it will strongly encourage 'improvements' in the genetic resource base, for example, the development of new plant varieties and new breeds of livestock. In addition, some argue that this approach will promote distributive justice by ensuring that a larger share of the economic returns or rents

* School of Economics University of Queensland Brisbane 4072 Australia. Email: c.tisdell@economics.uq.edu.au.

from the use of genetic resources will flow to the guardians or developers of these.

The matter is, however, quite complex. There is a danger that such policies may be 'oversold'. In several circumstances, such policies can prove to be less supportive of the conservation of biodiversity and less efficient in managing genetic resources than claimed by their supporters because of inescapable market failures. Furthermore, in some instances, their fairness is open to question (cf. Jugale, 2001). The purpose of this essay is to provide a preliminary assessment of these matters.

This is done by first noting some changes in the nature of international policies governing economic rights in genetic resources and considering how these might be related to a classification of natural assets. Then a variety of reasons for favouring private or communal property rights in genetic resources are outlined and these are compared with reasons sometimes given in support of intellectual property rights, such as those granted by patents. The penultimate section of this essay explores how market failures may undermine (at least, in some cases) the reason given for favouring property rights in genetic material and the final section concludes.

2. GLOBAL DEVELOPMENT IN LEGAL RIGHTS IN GENETIC MATERIAL

Globally there is now much greater legal recognition of property rights in genetic resources than in the middle of the 20th century.

Developments that have extended property rights in genetic material include the UPOV (Union international pour la Protection des Obtentions Vegetales) Convention. In English, this is the International Convention for the Protection of New Plant Varieties. This convention came into effect in 1961 and provides international property legal rights in new plant varieties (involving 'improved' genetic material) to plant breeders who develop these varieties and register these with the relevant authorities. These rights are recognised in nations that are signatories to the UPOV Convention.[1]

Originally, however, this approach was rejected by developing nations. They felt that it was economically unjust to them because germplasm was taken free of charge from developing countries, 'improved' in more developed countries to produce more desirable varieties of plants, and these in turn were liable to be sold back to developing countries at high prices and without recognising the benefit obtained by the developer as a result of using the original germplasm.

"In 1986 this controversy resulted in the adoption of the International Undertaking on Plant Genetic Resources (IUPGR) in which the developing world agreed to recognise the legitimacy of the concept of plant breeders' rights in return for the creation of a reciprocal concept termed 'Farmer's Rights'...These are rights granted in recognition of the contributions of farmers toward the conservation of genetic resources for use in the plant breeding and seed industries generally" (Swanson, 1997, p.102). While this has been internationally agreed in principle, and the possibility of a body such as the FAO collecting funds for farmers and distributing these to relevant nations and for these nations to distribute these in turn to farmers has been aired, this agreement has not yet been implemented (Swanson, 1997, p.102). With international property rights in genetically modified organisms (GMOs) legally recognised, developing countries have also expressed additional concerns about lack of rents from genetically modified crops such as GM soya beans (Xie et al., 2004). In fact, GMOs can be given patent protection.

Jugale (2005) outlines legislation that has been passed in India to protect farmers' rights in genetic material. He argues that the UPOV Convention is unfavourable to less developed countries and is concerned about the Trade Related Intellectual Property Rights (TRIPs) agreement which requires all WTO members to legislate to protect new plant varieties.

In no jurisdictions are property rights granted in naturally occurring organisms. Currently, exclusive marketing rights are only granted when "it is demonstrated that human intervention has produced an organism that was not previously existing in nature" (Swanson, 1997, p.103).

However, the Convention on Biological Diversity which came into effect in the 1990s opens the way for the granting of national property rights in naturally occurring genetic resources. Swanson (1997, p.105) argues strongly in favour of the granting of property rights in naturally occurring genetic material.

He believes that bias in the legal system has undermined the conservation of natural genetic stocks. He states: "In essence, the legal system has contrived to treat the informational products of nature as 'open access'. And thus the only appropriable genetic information is that which results from human intervention. Again, such a bias actively discourages any investment in the maintenance of the stocks of natural genetic capital, instead of encouraging the development of capital stocks that are compatible with the international property rights structure" (Swanson, 1997, p.105).

Swanson (1997) is also of the view that property rights regimes and greater international trade in wildlife and their products (the products of natural genetic material) are likely to be more supportive of wildlife conservation than restrictions on such trade, as exemplified in the Convention on International Trade in Endangered Species (CITES). His attitude has been influenced by his joint study of bans on trade in ivory (Barbier et al., 1990). The Convention on Biological Diversity, in contrast and to some extent in conflict with CITES, appears to be supportive of the type of approach recommended by Swanson (1997). However, as Tisdell (in press) points out, Swanson's preferred approach is only likely to be effective in conserving some wildlife species. Globally, many economically valued species (for example, those with high non-use economic values) would disappear under such an approach unless conserved in protected areas. Unfortunately, due to market failures (missing markets or partial markets), private and communal property rights regimes combined with marketing of genetic materials and natural products does not in itself result in a socially optimal outcome.

3. CLASSIFICATION OF GENETIC MATERIAL AND RELATED PROPERTY RIGHTS

Private and communal property rights in genetic resources are in a state of flux. In general, property rights have only been firmly assigned to legal entities able to show that they have developed organisms that do not occur in nature. However, such rights have been agreed in principle for farmers who have communally or over long periods of time evolved organisms that would not have evolved without their intervention or which would not have been conserved without their intervention. Nevertheless, a similar funding mechanism has not, it seems, been considered for hunters and gatherers who may also have, in a somewhat similar manner, conserved or even to a limited extent developed genetic material. In principle, however, the Convention on Biological Diversity would make such an approach possible.

Nations are increasingly claiming global property rights in indigenous genetic material. However, these rights cannot be enforced retrospectively, but could be enforced in relation to future global use of indigenous genetic material not previously known to be useful and still contained within a country's borders.[2]

In order to envisage the type of property rights that have been or could be granted in genetic resources, it is useful to classify these resources in a systematic manner. This is done in Figure 1. As a first approximation, genetic resources or assets may be divided into those that produce organisms that occur naturally (Set A) and those that produce organisms that have not evolved naturally but are the product of human intervention in natural processes (Set B).[3] The latter (Set B) can be further subdivided into organisms that have evolved, often by co-evolution and communal activities, as a result of efforts of several generations of human beings. Designate this as set C. Farmers' rights are being sought for genetic material in this set. Set D covers new organisms that have been produced in modern times by legal entities manipulating or selecting genetic material to produce organisms that previously did not exist. A legal entity is able to obtain legal rights in such genetic material via plant variety rights or patents, for example, for GMOs, depending on the nature of the genetic change.

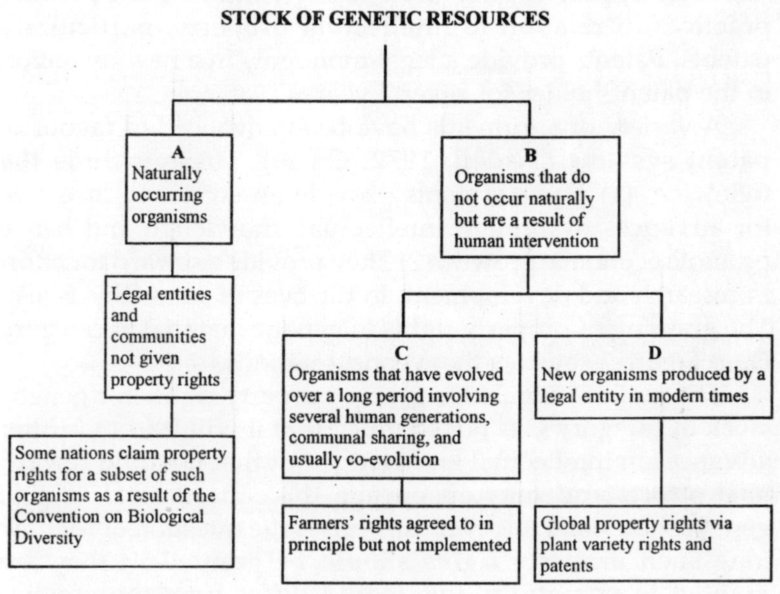

Figure 1
A classification of the stock of genetic resources and associated regimes of property rights in genetic resources

Currently, global property rights are biased in favour of set D, the areas in which more developed nations have the lead. Farmers' rights have not yet been supported effectively. Legal entities or social groups have not yet been granted legal rights in the genetic material contained in natural organisms but several nations now claim such rights, an outcome supported by the Convention on Biological Diversity. Thus, it is clear currently that property rights in genetic material are patchy and show bias in favour of Set D in Figure 1. It is therefore useful to consider why this bias may exist and the reason often given to justify property rights in genetic resources.

4. REASONS FOR GRANTING OR DENYING PROPERTY RIGHTS IN GENETIC RESOURCES

Legal views about the granting of property rights in genetic resources appear to have been strongly influenced by earlier practices in relation to intellectual property, particularly patents. Patents provide a legal monopoly in a new invention to the patent-holder for several years.

A variety of arguments have been advanced in favour of patent systems (Tisdell, 1972, Ch.20). These include the following: (1) These systems provide an economic incentive for advances in applied intellectual knowledge and hence promote economic growth; (2) They provide a reward for effort in research and development. In the eyes of some, this is just. The granting of property rights in genetic material in category D, in Figure 1 satisfies these considerations.[4]

The main rationale for giving property rights for genetic stock in category C is not so much that it will lead to further advances in intellectual knowledge but that it would reward past efforts and may encourage the conservation of this genetic material. However, this raises the question of for how long such property rights should be granted. If they are granted in perpetuity, this would differ from the practice adopted in relation to the granting of property rights in category D. These rights are only granted for a finite period of time.

In relation to the granting of property rights to local communities or national governments for genetic material in category A, the reasons cannot be that it is an economic reward for adding to intellectual capital. A possible rationale, however, is that it is an economic reward or incentive for conserving natural capital (compare Swanson, 1997). However, in many cases, payments arising as a result of such rights would constitute a rent because some or much of the pool of natural genetic resources may be conserved incidentally rather than consciously.

Thus, it is clear that different economic reasons need to be advanced to support the granting of property rights in different types of genetic resources.

Given the degree of support globally for property rights regimes and the use of markets, the question needs to be asked of how effective this approach is likely to be in conserving biodiversity and to what extent the possible economic benefits of this approach are likely to be limited by market failures. Let us consider this matter.

5. MARKET FAILURES RESTRICT SOCIAL BENEFITS FROM PROPERTY RIGHTS IN GENETIC RESOURCES

The potential for using patent systems and property rights in genetic resources to provide social benefits is limited by a number of market failures. The operation of such systems rely on those who are granted property rights being able to appropriate a significant proportion of economic benefits from the genetic resources involved.

The ability of holders of property rights in genetic material to appropriate economic benefit is likely to be greatest when use value constitutes a high proportion of the total economic value of such material, that is, when private goods are mainly produced by such material. Conversely, other things equal, the higher is non-use value as a proportion of the total economic value of genetic material, the less is the ability of economic entities to appropriate economic benefits from it. In such cases, a high public good element is present.

Thus, the property rights method in genetic material is likely to favour private goods in comparison to goods with high public good component.

Secondly, the granting of property rights in genetic material usually takes no account of any externalities generated. For example, the granting of patent rights in a GMO or property rights in a new plant variety depends merely on whether the GMO or new plant variety constitutes a novel organism. The body granting such rights does not take account of any externalities that might be generated by its use. It is usually the function of other public bodies to take account of possible adverse environmental externalities from new organisms and limit their use if necessary. Fears exist that such screening processes may prove to be inadequate and could result in new organisms being used which yield high private economic returns to business but generate significant adverse environmental externalities. For example, one such concern is that genetically engineered herbicide-resistant crops will give rise to herbicide-resistant weeds (Tisdell and Wilson, 2004).

Market transactions usually involve costs and these can be quite high in the case of property rights in genetic material (Swanson and Göschl, 2000). This limits the scope for economically using market systems for determining economic activity, and this applies to their use for using and developing genetic resources. For example, the transaction costs involved in ensuring Farmers' Rights might be so high that no economic benefit is received by farmers (see Tisdell, 2005, Ch.5). It may also be that the transaction costs involved in marketing genetic material and protecting private property rights in it favours very large corporations because economies of scale occur in transaction costs. Small firms are liable to be at a disadvantage in enforcing their property rights in genetic material. Therefore, a property right system for genetic material appears to be relatively more beneficial to big business compared to small firms, including farmers.

It is also the case that such a system can reduce biodiversity. For example, genetic items in category D involve additions to the genetic stock, that is, they involve the creation of new organisms. However, if these are commercially successful organisms, they are liable to replace or displace existing organisms. Thus, the composition of the genetic stock alters. Both natural genetic diversity and existing genetic diversity due to human intervention could conceivably be reduced. There is a risk that commercially successful new organisms, such as some GMOs, could, as a result of their consequences, reduce rather than add to biodiversity. This is the fear of some conservationists, many of whom in turn are worried that this reduction in biodiversity might threaten economic sustainability.

Even in cases where genetic property rights do not legally exist, for example, for wildlife, some economists, for example

Swanson (1997), and conservation groups (IUCN-UNEP-WWF, 1991) advocate the granting of property rights to local communities or individuals in harvested wildlife and greater international trade in this wildlife and its products. They favour the concept of conservation of wildlife by means of sustainable use. If such a strategy is successful, it will also conserve the genetic material inherent in this wildlife. Tisdell (in press) argues that while such an approach can be effective in conserving some species, it will fail to do so for many, even when they have high economic value. Once again, the property rights approach, when combined with market guidance, is shown to be subject to failures.

6. CONCLUDING COMMENTS

The new global policy approach favouring the granting of private, communal, or in some cases, national property rights in genetic resources is not likely to be as effective a policy for promoting conservation of biodiversity, overcoming failures in genetic resource use, and promoting sustainable economic growth, as its strongest advocates claim. Furthermore, this approach is limited in its capacity to ensure a just distribution of economic benefits from the conservation and development of genetic resources.

It is important to be aware of such limitations because they have institutional implications. The main implication is that it is dangerous to entrust the conservation and development of genetic resources solely to the private sector. It is necessary for the public sector to play a significant role in the stewardship of genetic resources and the development of these resources. The exact role that the public sector should play needs investigation. A step towards this, taken here, is to demonstrate that the private sector cannot be expected to husband and develop genetic resources in an ideal manner because it is bound to exhibit predictable economic biases.

ACKNOWLEDGEMENT

This research has benefited from an Australian Research Council grant for studying the economic impacts of property rights and commercial use on wildlife conservation. The usual *caveat* applies.

NOTES

1. The UPOV Convention was revised in 1972, 1978 and 1991. Its objective is to protect new varieties of plants by means of an international intellectual property rights in these. The 1991 revision allows for the granting of patent rights in new plant varieties. Jugale (in press) suggests that is very unfavourable to less developed countries.
2. Retrospective enforcement by a government of property rights in indigenous genetic material that has already been distributed internationally as a result of previous open access does not appear to be a legal possibility. Most nations now have obtained, as a result of open access, genetic material from many other nations without payment for using the genetic resources involved. For example, soya beans were introduced to the USA from Asia and maize was introduced from the Americas to most other countries of the world, including India. Similarly, the potato. The list of such introductions is in fact very long. To give an Australian example, the macadamia nut *Macadamia intergrifolia* is a native of southern Queensland. Although it is now cultivated in Australia, cultivation did not begin until 1963. Cultivation first commenced in the United States in Hawaii in the early 1900s using seed exported from Australia (Low, 1991, p.92). No payment was made for access to this Australian genetic resource. The potential commercial value of the resource would have still been uncertain in the early 1900s and Australia has probably obtained reverse economic benefits from the development of macadamia nuts as a cultivated crop in Hawaii.
3. In practice, it may be difficult to decide whether some organisms belong to set A or C. For example, the genetic composition of some wild species is altered by human activities.
4. The economic benefit from greater technical or scientific progress as a result of the patent system have to be weighed against the social economic deadweight loss resulting from the grant of a monopoly in the invention for a specified period (Tisdell, 1972, Ch.20). Greater technical or scientific progress does not in itself provide sufficient justification for patent systems, and in particular for granting patents for GMOs (Tisdell and Wilson, 2004).

REFERENCES

Barbier, E., Burgess, J., Swanson, T. and Pearce, D. (1990) *Elephants, Economics and Ivory*. Earthscan, London.

Bhal, M.G. (1999), On biodiversity access, intellectual property rights and conservation. *Ecological Economics*, **29**, 391-403.

IUCN-UNEP-WWF (1991), *Caring for the Earth: A Strategy for Sustainable Living*. IUCN, Gland, Switzerland.

Jugale, V.B. (2005), Plant variety rights in SAARC countries in global context. Ch.36 in C.A Tisdell (ed) *Globalisation and World Economic Policies*. Serials Publications, New Delhi. In press.

Low. T. (1991), *Wild Food Plants of Australia*. Angus & Robertson, Sydney.

Swanson, T. (1997), *Global Action for Biodiversity*. Earthscan, London.

Swanson, T. and Göschl, T. (2000), Property rights issues involving plant genetic resources: implications of ownership for economic efficiency. *Ecological Economics*, **32**, 75-92.

Tisdell, C.A. (1972), *Microeconomics: The Theory of Economic Allocation*. John Wiley, Sydney.

Tisdell, C.A. (2004), *Economics of Environmental Conservation, 2nd edition*. Edward Elgar, Cheltenham, UK. In press.

Tisdell, C.A. (in press) Economic incentives for global conservation of wildlife: new international policy directions. In N. Narayana, *Issues of Globalisation and World Economic Reforms*. Serials Publications, New Delhi.

Tisdell, C.A. and Wilson, C. (2004), Genetically modified (transgenic) crops and pest control economics. pp. 246-256 in C. Tisdell, *Economics and Ecology in Agriculture and Marine Production*. Edward Elgar, Cheltenham, UK.

Xie, D., Lin, Y. and Tisdell, C. (2004), Conflicts about global trade in GMOs: general issues and Chinese case studies. pp. 314-335 in C. Tisdell and R.K. Sen (eds) *Economic Globalisation*. Edward Elgar, Cheltenham, UK.

PART-II

AGRICULTURE, INDUSTRIAL RELATIONS AND TECHNOLOGY

10

ROLE OF BANGLADESH SMALL INDUSTRIES AND COMMERCE BANK IN PROMOTING SMALL SCALE ENTERPRISES: A CRITICAL ASSESSMENT

Md. Saiful Islam Mihir Kumar Das** and Md. Khairuzzaman****

INTRODUCTION

With human civilization, people have flourished their economic activities to attain better lives. In the early days they had to depend just on agriculture and even during the 1970s almost of 60 per cent country's value added accrued from agriculture sector (World Bank 2003). However, with faster growth of population and fragmentation of land, they are to opt for different non-farm activities to meet the increasing needs of growing population. Therefore, soon after independence Bangladesh adopted for massive nationalization of industry and opted for controlled development strategy, during the late seventies it moved towards the strategy of mixed economic development, and during the eighties it followed an open economic system with greater emphasis on private sector development. Thus throughout the decades of

* Associate Professor & Head Economics Discipline, Khulna University Khulna, Bangladesh, Email:*dsaif@khulna.bangla.nct*

** Economics Graduate, Khulna University.

*** Economics Discipline, Khulna University.

planned development it exerted huge efforts to manage the changing economy and achieve industrial development.

However after more than 30 years of planned development efforts, it remained one of the least developed countries among the developing ones of the world, with agriculture as a dominant sector of the economy. For example, Bangladesh with a per capita income of US$ 386 is positioned in the low human development group of HDI and the value of its index was only 0.478 in 2000 (UNDP 2003), and agriculture still remains the dominant sector of the economy where 80 percent of its total population directly depends on it (Ministry of Finance 2002). Therefore, the industrial base and share of industry in overall economic activities remained very small, e.g., 17 percent of GDP (World Bank 1998). Moreover, agriculture cannot employ the growing population, and thus a significant proportion (34%) of the population in Bangladesh live in abject poverty with low productivity (World Bank 2003). Therefore, to raise productivity of farm laborer, to employ the workless population, and to enhance the standard of living of the mass, it is urgent to promote small scale enterprises in the country.

The Small scale enterprises (SSEs) are considered to be the most important for growth and development of such a developing economy as Bangladesh, which has abundant of surplus labor. To achieve economic development, this surplus labor should be shifted to industry that calls for the development of SSEs, as the SSEs require low capital and low level of technology. Besides promotion of small industries has direct impact on balanced growth for a developing country as it forms the base of industrial structure and accelerates the process of industrialization in most of the countries in the world. The relative share of SSEs in total employment and total output seem to be about 80 per cent and 50 percent respectively in many of the Asian, African and Latin American countries (Khan, 1993). In Bangladesh, for example, SSEs provided nearly 82 per cent of industrial employment and 43 per cent of industrial output during the eighties (GOB 1990).

Thus, the contribution of SSEs in the process of economic development is paramount, and in spite of this fact, this sector is facing a number of problems mainly inadequacy of supply of capital. Therefore in 1989, the Bank of Small Industries and Commerce (BASIC) was established with a view to supply adequate capital and unhindered financial services to the SSEs. It has a statutory obligation to deploy at least 50 per cent of its advances to the SSEs and to ensure timely credit facilities to them.

Thus, BASIC bank provides a variety of services that include full fledge commercial banking services such as collection of deposit, short term trade financing, and working capital finance, and micro credit to the urban poor through linkage with NGOs. Its services are specially directed towards the promotion and development of the entrepreneurs in the small industries sector. The importance of SSEs is mainly because of labor intensity, use of indigenous raw materials and easily adaptable technology, and local skill-entrepreneurship. The present study aims to uncover the role of BASIC bank in the promotion of SSEs in the process of economic development of a country like Bangladesh.

METHODOLOGY

This study is mainly based on primary data. A detailed survey was made to collect primary data through the schedule approach with two separate questionnaires; one for the BASIC bank personnel and the second one to gather information and opinions of the clients of this institution (SSEs) as to the difficulties and problems encountered by them while seeking assistance from the BASIC bank. To uncover the views of the clients of the bank, a random sample of 41 SSEs in the southwestern region of Bangladesh namely Khulna city and its suburbs, and Jessore is carried out[2]. Data have been processed by using computer packages and appropriate statistical tools such as SSPS is applied to analyze the collected data and verify the validity of the hypotheses.

Besides, secondary data from different annual reports of the BASIC bank and unpublished official records of the bank are also used. Unpublished information has been collected from official files and records to have a comprehensive picture of the role (policies and operations) of BASIC bank in the development of the SSEs in this region.

Objectives of the Study: The main objectives of this study are as follows:

- To evaluate the role of BASIC bank in the promotion of SSEs in Khulna region,
- To identify the status in terms of problems faced by the SSEs in Khulna region,
- To suggest policy options addressing the role of BASIC bank and the SSEs.

AN OVERVIEW OF THE BASIC BANK: BACKGROUND INFORMATION

BASIC bank is as a scheduled bank and a blending of development banking and commercial banking. Bank of Small Industries and Commerce (BASIC) was established as a banking company under the Companies Act 1913. It was incorporated under this Act on the 2nd of August 1988 and lunched its operations from the 21st January 1989 with a single branch. The Bank was established as the policy makers of the country felt the urgency for a bank in the private sector for financing Small Scale Industries. The bank started as a joint venture enterprise of the BCC Foundation with 70 per cent shares and the remaining 30 per cent shares with the Bangladesh Government. However, when the BCC Foundation became nonfunctional following the closure of the BCCI, the Government of Bangladesh took over 100 per cent ownership of BASIC on 4th June 1992. Thus the bank became a state owned enterprise. In 2001, however, the official name of the bank was changed to BASIC (Bangladesh Small Industries and Commerce) Bank Limited. At present it has 26 branches operating over the major industrial hubs of the country.

ROLE OF BASIC BANK IN PROMOTION OF THE SSEs

Bangladesh, the world's highest densely populated country with 1020 people per square kilometer (World Bank 2003) widely differs in interregional development. Majority of its population (nearly 80 per cent) live in rural areas, with low level of living, and mainly rely upon farm activities. The industrial sector accounts for only 15 per cent of GDP (Ministry of Finance 2003) and the industrial base of the country is clustered around the capital city Dhaka and port city Chittagong only. Therefore there is an urgent need for variety of promotional activities such as entrepreneurial development, regional dispersion of industry and coordination of the activities among regional level financial institutions and other operational agencies, training of personnel, availability of relatively inexpensive consultancy services to entrepreneurs particularly of the SSEs. Hence the BASIC bank is targeted to fulfill this role, and as a financial intermediary it plays the following functions:

MOBILIZATION OF DEPOSITS

Deposit mobilization in Bangladesh in general remained quite small (Islam and Moniruzzaman 2000, and Khalily et. al 1987). One of the most important macro economic problems in Bangladesh is the vast gap between saving and investment. For example, gross domestic saving as the percentage GDP in 2001 was only 16.07, while that of gross investment was 23.08 per cent, led to a gap of 6.89 per cent of GDP (World Bank 2003). Therefore mobilization of deposits remained the primary function of the banking sector. Thus, as a part of banking system, the BASIC bank is to play a paramount role in mobilization of deposits, which constitutes the core of its fund generating activities. For example during 1999, the amount of fixed and saving deposit grew from Tk. 2615 million to Tk. 3727 million and from Tk. 280 million to Tk. 293 respectively. The volume of deposit mobilization in this region by the two branches of BASIC bank is summarized in table 1.

Data in table 1 capture the actual scenario of deposit mobilization by the BASIC bank in Khulna region. It shows that the growth of deposits is not promising at all. Except two years particularly 2000 and 2003 growth of deposits was either very low or negative. Thus, the surveyed data reveal that the bank failed to maintain a sustained growth in deposit mobilization during the period under study.

Table 1
Deposit Mobilization of BASIC Bank in Khulna Region (Million Tk.)

Year	*Jessore branch*	*Khulna branch*	*Total*	
1998	51.32	231.70	283.02	Growth Rate (%)
1999	63.59	209.01	272.60	-3.68
2000	67.86	271.98	339.84	24.67
2001	103.41	247.21	350.62	3.17
2002	150.90	269.24	420.14	19.83
2003	165.20	280.91*	446.11	6.18

Source: Field Survey, May, 2004. * Up to September

LOANS AND ADVANCES

The foremost role of any bank is to intermediate between the savers and borrowing investors. That is, it mobilizes savings from savers in the form of bank deposits, which it uses as bases to extend credits in the form of loans and advances to investors of various categories. However, in spite of the fact that the volume and growth of deposit mobilization by BASIC bank has been very poor (table 1), the growth of loans and advances extended by the two branches in the region to various kinds of investors marked a significant increase over the years except year 2000 (table 2) due to the bank's smooth linkage to several banking institutions to raise funds to finance development-banking activities[3].

Table 2
Loan and Advances by BASIC Bank in Khulna Region (Million Tk)

Year	*Khulna branch*	*Jessore branch*	*Total*	
1998	124.33	31.30	155.63	Growth rate (%)
1999	155.50	35.40	190.04	22.11
2000	139.13	46.20	185.33	-2.48
2001	188.89	113.30	302.19	63.06
2002	278.94	133.80	412.74	36.58
2003	372.93*	190.00	562.93	36.39

Source: Field Survey, April-May 2004, *Up to September

BASIC BANK AND SMALL INDUSTRIES DEVELOPMENT

The state of the industrial development in this region is not promising at all, and the contribution of industry in the region's

GDP is even less than 10 per cent (table 3). Moreover, of this meager contribution of industry, the share of the SSEs was only 2.43 per cent in 2000 that shows the insignificant contribution and poor status of small scale industries in Khulna area.

Table 3
Industrial Value Added in the Khulna Region (percentage)

	1992-93	*93-94*	*94-95*	*95-96*	*96-97*	*97-98*	*98-99*	*99-00*
Share of Industry in Khulna's GDP	9.27	9.37	9.61	9.64	14.03	9.69	9.19	8.69
Large Scale	97.04	97.21	97.39	97.43	97.41	97.52	97.60	97.57
Small scale	2.96	2.79	2.61	2.57	2.59	2.48	2.40	2.43

Source: BBS (2002).

Therefore promoting and financing small scale industries remained the urgent and the foremost job that shoulders on the BASIC bank in this region. The bank was mainly launched to meet the financial requirements of the SSEs, and it has a statutory obligation to extend at least 50 per cent of its total loans and advances to this sector. With this end, industrial loan to the SSEs have increased over the recent years both in terms of volume and growth rate, but remained insignificant as a percentage of total loans and advances. Thus the statutory obligation of extending at least 50 per cent of its advances to the SSEs remained simply a dream, and the sector is therefore badly affected. Data on table 4 capture these facts.

Table 4
Industrial Credit by BASIC Bank in Khulna Region (Million Taka)

Year	*Khulna branch*	*Jessore branch*	*Total*	*Growth rate (%)*	*As % of total Advances*
1998	20.51	11.90	32.41		20.83
1999	34.30	11.20	45.50	40.39	23.94
2000	46.50	12.20	58.70	29.01	31.67
2001	74.84	17.90	92.74	57.99	30.69
2002	119.73	44.00	163.73	76.55	39.67
2003	170.48	74.30	244.78	49.50	43.48

Source: Field Survey, April-May, 2004, * Up to September.

Major Findings: The major findings of this study are summarized in the following table 5.1 and 5.2.

Table 5.1
A Summary of Survey Findings

		No of SSEs	*Percentage*
Types of advances	Short term	37	90.24
	of which working	10	24.39
	capital Long term	04	9.76
Education	Undergraduate	13	31.70
	HSC	24	58.54
	SSC	4	9.76
Management Training	Yes	02	4.88
	No	39	95.12
Separate Marketing Division	Available	14	34.15
Not available		27	65.85
Research & Development	Available	11	26.83
	Not available	30	73.17

PROBLEMS OF THE SSEs

Although the SSEs are playing paramount role in the process of economic development of Bangladesh economy by providing employment to bulk of the labor forces and also significantly adding to industrial output, this sector is facing a number of problems including inadequacy of capital supply. The problems often faced by the SSEs are presented below in terms of two categories:

A. Internal Constraints

Inadequacy of Capital Supply: Capital supply to the SSEs in comparison with that to large scale enterprises historically remained quite small due to several reasons[4]. The banking sector exclusively favored the large and medium scale enterprises and neglected the small-scale industrial units in extending credits. For example during 1991-97 a total of 711.71 billion Taka was extended as industrial finance, of which almost 93 per cent was channeled to large and medium scale enterprises, while that of only 7 per cent was extended to the SSEs including the cottage industry (Islam 2003). Therefore,

BSAIC bank was lunched to look after the financial needs especially of the SSEs. However, after 15 years of operation of this bank, inadequacy of capital remained the main problem for the SSEs.

Table 5.2

A Summary of Survey Findings: Customers Perspective

Interest rate	High	26	63.41
	Moderate	06	14.63
	Low	09	21.95
Obstacle to get loan	Yes	03	7.32
	No	38	92.68
Obstacle to pay back loan	Yes	21	51.22
	No	20	48.78
Support Services	Available	02	4.88
	Not available	39	95.12
Amount of Loan	Sufficient	33	80.49
	Insufficient	08	19.51

Inadequately Trained Workforce: As the SSEs faces short supply of capital, their capital bases are quite low in comparison to those of large enterprises. Therefore, low capital base inhibit the ability to train up their workforce adequately.

Lack of Specialized Education and Management Skills: Our survey data reveal that only 31.7 percent of the entrepreneurs have only undergraduate education (Bachelor degree). None of them have any graduate education, and most of them have little educational qualification (table 5.1). Similarly data on Table 5.1 also highlights the fact that only 4.88 per cent of the entrepreneurs have management training, and rest of the 95.12 per cent of the entrepreneurs have no specialized training in industrial organization and no skill in management.

Difficulty in Separating Household Finance from Business Finance: As the entrepreneurs of the SSEs have no specialized education in industrial organizational and no skill in management, they are hardly capable enough to separate household finance from business finance.

Lack of Information Processing Ability: Lack of proper education among the entrepreneurs invariably affects the information processing ability of the SSEs. They suffer from inadequacy of data and information. They have little or no knowledge about dynamic role of entrepreneurship, little ability to analyze public policy, information, and secondary data.

Outdated Technology and Low Productivity: As the capital bases of the SSEs are quite narrow, with untrained workforce, having lack in information processing ability, they mainly opt for outdated and own techniques. These eventually affect the productivity the SSEs.

B. External Constraints

Besides the internal problems, the SSEs face many external problems which are equally important. They include low purchasing power of the customer, unstable political condition, regional/local administration that is more of an obstacle than a source of support owing to prejudice, inefficiency, and/or incompetence; limited access to raw materials and intermediate products and markets, difficulty in getting access to information e.g. technology, know-how, and markets, limited access to formal credit and financial services, and lack of adequate organizations that provide effective services.

However, in a business environment with many internal as well as external problems as discussed above, a small scale entrepreneur succeeds in his business due to efficiency, not because of his ability to conceptualize market opportunities or plan ahead in strategic terms. In contrast, large companies, which can usually afford specialist staff, the small entrepreneur is a relatively isolated individual trying to deal with day-to-day operational problems. He often operates without adequate quantitative data or other information, and follows the strategy of other successful entrepreneurs. Due to low wages, limited job security and a low status in a small-scale enterprise, he cannot easily recruit and keep qualified employees.

PROBLEM OF MARKETS AND MARKET DEVELOPMENT

Market and Marketing Environment

Markets in our country are characterized by the very limited purchasing power of the average consumers. In recent years the small firm has to contend with the shift from import controls to import liberalization. These factors bring about intense competition resulting in price cutting. A variety of laws at the national and local levels also constrict the operations of the SSEs. These laws range from price control to regulatory measures that prescribe mandatory registration and payment of fees. These factors intensify the pains and problems of the SSEs operating in this region.

Entrepreneur

An entrepreneur needs to know how to sell, how to design products, how to compute costs and how to undertake market research to run any business successfully. Data in table 5.2 captures that more than 95 per cent of the entrepreneurs had no educational background in entrepreneurship and management training. However, the entrepreneurs of the SSEs in this region gain knowledge and management skills through experience rather than education.

Marketing Organization

It is clear that market development cannot proceed without the appropriate marketing organization. The survey reveals that only 34.15 per cent of the enterprises have separate marketing division to deal with their products, and the majority (65.85 per cent) of the entrepreneurs does not have any marketing section.

Marketing Arrangements

There are instances when middlemen provide the SSEs with their input requirements but arrange to pay with their production at an agreed price. This usually results in a lower profit margin for the entrepreneurs of the SSEs. The issue arises whether government either directly or through the banking system can provide financing for working capital which would allow them to get credit and increase sales. This calls for the enhanced financing to the SSEs including the working capital finance. However, our survey revealed that the BASIC bank even failed to supply the stipulated amount of credit (at least 50 per cent of total advances) to them. Here it is to be mentioned that here the obligation is at least 50 per cent, that is, the bank is designed and therefore desired to raise its financing the SSEs even more than 50 per cent of its total advances so as to facilitate growth and development.

ASSESSMENT OF THE ROLE OF BASIC BANK: ECONOMETRIC EXERCISE

1. Amount of Loan and Employment-a linear relation

We try to test whether level of financing and volume of capital has any impact on the employment level created by the SSEs. Number of persons employed by the SSEs is recorded as employment data, while amount of credit (lac taka) taken by the SSEs from the BASIC bank is recorded as loan amount. We assume that greater the amount of loan available for financing, the greater will be the level of employment in the SSEs. This hypothesis is summarized in the following equation:

$$X = \alpha + \beta Y + U \qquad ...(1.1)$$

Here, X stands for employment level, Y for volume of loan, U for disturbance term. The letter α refers that even the firm does not borrow still it has some positive level of employment. The regression analysis produces the following results that are summarized in the table 6 below. The estimated equation is expressed in terms of equation 1.2.

$$\hat{X} = \mathbf{5.79 + 1.32}Y \qquad ...(1.2)$$

Table 6

Variable	*Estimated Coefficient*	*Standard Error*	*t-statistic*	*R-squared*	*Signi.*
β	5.79	1.23	4.72	0.46	0.00
Loan	1.32	0.26	5.01		0.00

Dependent variable: Employment — Estimated equation ⟹ Employment = 5.79 + 1.32 Loan

The estimation of above equation tells us that there is a strong and positive relation between loan and employment. The greater the volume of loan available for industrial investment, the larger will be volume of employment in the economy. However, the volume of loan extended to the SSEs by the BASIC bank has been significantly limited and the statutory obligation of extending at least 50 per cent of its advances to the SSEs remained a dream. Besides, the interest rate charged to entrepreneurs of SSEs also remained quite higher (in a range of 12 to 14 per cent). Thus of the surveyed entrepreneurs, 63.41 per cent considers this range of interest as high. Accordingly, 51.22 per cent of borrowing entrepreneurs face problems in paying back the high interest burden (Table 5.2).

2. Redistribution of Income and Source of Economic Growth

The BASIC bank works as a financial intermediary and source of economic growth through mobilization of deposits and advancing loan to the SSEs that increases the capital stock in the process of investment. The following table captures these facts.

Table 7
The Size of Deposits and Loan and Profit in Khulna Region (Million Tk)

Year	*Deposits*	*Advances*	*Industrial Credit*	*Profit*
1998	283.02	155.63	32.41	17.93
1999	272.6	190.04	45.5	16.75
2000	339.84	185.33	58.7	15.61
2001	350.62	302.19	92.74	21.88
2002	420.14	412.74	163.73	24.81
2003	446.11	562.93	244.78	26.52

Source: Field Survey, April-May, 2004

DEPOSITS AND DISBURSEMENT OF LOAN

The main task of any financial intermediary is to bridge up the financing gap by mobilizing savings from surplus units and extending credits to deficit units. Thus, BASIC bank mobilizes deposits and extends financial assistance to the industrial units in order to play a positive role in the promotion of SSEs. Here an attempt has been made to examine any possible relationship between these three variables viz.

deposits, disbursement of loan and profit. With this end, we formulate the following two separate equations to estimate possible relationships among them.

$$\text{Advance} = \alpha_0 + \alpha 1 \text{ Deposit} + U \qquad ...(2.1)$$
$$\text{Profit} = \beta_0 + \beta_1 \text{ Advance} + U \qquad ...(3.1)$$

The equations 2.1 and 3.1 have usual meaning and interpretations as the equation 1.1 have. The findings of the regression analysis are summarized in the table 8, and table 9 below. The estimated equations are of the following types.

$$\text{Advance} = -446.59 + 2.13 \text{ Deposit} \qquad ...(2.2)$$
$$\text{Profit} = 12.53 + 0.026 \text{ Advance} \qquad ...(3.2)$$

The equation 2.2 reveals that there is a positive and strong relationship between disbursement of loans and volume of deposits. Greater the volume of deposits mobilized, the larger amount of loan disbursement will take place.

Table 8

Variable	*Estimated Coefficient*	*Standard Error*	*t-statistic*	*R-squared*	*Signi.*
Constant	-446.55	145.56	-3.07	0.88	0.04
Deposit	2.13	0.41	5.22		0.01
Dependent Variable: Advances		Estimated Equation: Advances = -446.59 + 2.13 Deposit			

DISBURSEMENT OF LOAN AND TREND OF PROFIT

Profit accrues from the difference between lending rate of interest and the interest rate bank pays against deposits and is termed as interest rate spread. Thus larger the interest rate spread, the greater will be the level of profit. Given the interest rate spread, the volume of profit will depend on the amount of loan disbursement. Therefore, an attempt is made, to test whether there is any significant relationship between these two variables. Table 9 and equation 3.2 summarizes the test results that reveal that there is a strong, positive, and statistically significant relationship between these two variables.

Table 9

Variable	*Estimated Coefficient*	*Standard Error*	*t-statistic*	*R-squared*	*Signi.*
Constant	12.53	1.49	8.43	0.88	0.00
Advances	0.026	0.004	6.02		0.00
Dependent Variable: Profit			Estimated Equation: Profit = 12.53 + 0.026 Advances		

Thus, surveyed data reveal that BASIC bank appears as a successful financial intermediary in terms of deposit mobilization, loan disbursement with a view to profiteering. Data on the following table 10, further acknowledge these facts that the bank maintained a good recovery of its disbursed loans, measured in terms of low percentage of classified loans that enabled the bank as a high profit making one.

Table 10
Classified Loan as % of Total Loan

Year	*Khulna Branch*	*Jessore Branch*
1998	1.00	Not found
1999	0.46	Not found
2000	0.50	Not found
2001	0.73	0.12
2002	0.49	0.46
2003	1.16	0.31

Source: Field survey, April-May, 2004.

However it remained unsuccessful to meet its legal obligations as already mentioned. Besides, it has no commitment to meet the long term credit requirement of the industrial sector in this region. Surveyed data show that, of the loans and advances less than 10 per cent was long term; rest of the extended credit in the region was short term in nature that also includes working capital. High rate of lending rate again was the important factor that prevented many borrowers to opt for long term credit that is likely to impose greater interest burden on the entrepreneurs of the SSEs. Thus, high lending rate affected the safer borrowers adversely. That is, as the lending rate remained high, many safer borrowers dropped out of the loan market.

CRITICAL EVALUATION OF BASIC BANK'S PROMOTIONAL ROLE

BASIC bank is not a simply a commercial bank, but it is a blending with development banking. Therefore, as a specialized financial institution, the bank is expected to look after the SSEs, it was originally established for. Thus, a careful evaluation of its performance shows that it failed to address the following issues:

- Identifying the prospective entrepreneurs and motivating them.
- Identifying new areas of investment where opportunities exist and prospective entrepreneurs can enter, and thus accelerate industrialization.
- Counseling and suggesting the small entrepreneurs regarding improvements and expansion of their business.
- Providing technical and managerial advice to the entrepreneurs of the SSEs so that they can materialize the floated prospects.
- To carry market research and survey for specific products and to identify potential industrial regions.
- To conduct project supervision where necessary, and render technical and administrative facilities.
- To set up information cells and data banks relating to industrial and economic activities.
- Training of new entrepreneur, and rehabilitation management consultancy
- Creation of and strengthening institutional infrastructure, identification of industrial promotion needs of deserving segment of the industrial sector and evolving measure for their growth and development with appropriate support services.
- Support for industrial potential surveys, particularly in the 'no industry region.

LACKING OF PROVISION OF TECHNICAL ASSISTANCE AND GENERAL ADVISORY SERVICES

Our survey also reveals that available services of BASIC bank by and large go those SSEs, which are situated in urban areas and use modern mechanized techniques. The bank does not play any role regarding:

- Coordination and promotion of small and tiny industries;
- The branches at Khulna region do not facilitate the tasks of economic investigation, credit, marketing, training information, infrastructure etc. depending on the local need. As a result in one hand the efficient use of local resources has been tapped and on the other hand the further developments of small scale industries have not been accelerated.
- No special assistance is provided to encourage location of industry in backward areas. Assistance in term of low rate of interest has not been charged and other incentives include preferential treatment in the grant of industrial licenses and outright subsidy on fixed capital investment. Besides, they do not play any role regarding development of industrial estates/ areas and preliminary feasibility studies.

FAILURE TO PROVIDE LOAN ACCORDING TO MEMORANDUM STIPULATED

It is well defined that the objective of the BASIC bank is unique in blending development financing and commercial banking. The memorandum of BASIC bank stipulates that at least 50 per cent of its loanable funds shall be extended for financing small scale industries, but the survey and collected data reveal that it completely failed to comply with this stipulated legal obligation as already discussed.

LIMITED BRANCH

The SSEs are scattered throughout the country not necessarily always in urban areas. In Bangladesh nearly 75 per cent of its total population lives in rural areas. But all the branches of BASIC bank are located in the urban areas. Therefore, a major portion of the deserving SSEs is deprived from the services of the bank.

Thus we find that most of the functions performed by BASIC bank are financial in nature and not promotional as desired. If any bank is able to comply with the desired, above mentioned role and functions, it can be said to have made a reasonably good contribution towards fulfilling its role as a promotional agency. However in this process, the bank cannot be said to have made reasonable contribution in the promotion of the SSEs in Khulna region.

SUMMARY AND CONCLUSIONS

The foregoing analysis suggests that the role and importance of the SSEs in the economic development of developing economies such as Bangladesh is well recognized and inevitable. Therefore, the government of Bangladesh like other developing countries have introduced special support program to encourage the growth and development of the SSEs. This resulted in the establishment of BASIC bank to ensure timely credit to the SSEs at concessionary rates. But credit is not the only element in the myriad of factors of business environment in which the SSEs operate, and it alone cannot be expected to induce the type and level of responses desired for healthy promotion of the SSEs. Therefore government policies on pricing, agricultural development, industrial incentives and law and order situation all determine the vigor with which the small industries will develop.

The access of the SSEs to institutional credit remained limited and highly competitive even when credit programs are designed specifically for them. The BASIC bank even failed to extend its stipulated minimum amount of loan to the SSEs. The bank also failed to foster any comprehensive support services to the SSEs operating in this region. Improving their access to credit requires improvement of overall functioning of the urban financial market in general and in particular, the BASIC bank needs to adopt some of the positive features of the informal finance such as low transaction costs, limited collateral requirements, and easy procedures.

Technical assistance, both as part of the loan appraisal and supervision is an essential element in financing the SSEs. The way in which the technical assistance is provided, needs to be carefully worked out to avoid conflict and to ensure effectiveness. The cost of the assistance also needs to be clearly separated from the cost of financing. Thus we find that although the BASIC bank has a number of promotional activities to produce industrial development in the country, its contribution is not significant. The study indicates that it is yet to start working on all the facets of its scope. Thus it has played only a limited promotional role in the development of the SSEs in the region.

RECOMMENDATIONS

The foregoing analysis suggests that the SSEs generate more direct jobs per dollar of investment than do the large enterprises. They can serve as training grounds for developing technical and entrepreneurial skills and by virtue of their greater use of indigenous technological capabilities; they promote local inter-sectoral linkages and contribute to the dynamism and competitiveness of the economy. Therefore with the existing services by the BASIC bank the following issues should be addressed to achieve the targeted objectives.

Markets: There seems to be a need for some government or private organizations in terms of supplying market information, giving publicity to their products and consolidation of production either through cooperative associations of small firms.

Support Infrastructure: Support of infrastructure in terms of training, information, technical consultancy, marketing and financial assistance, as well as hard infrastructure in terms of roads, bridges, and ports should be facilitated to enhance the development of the SSEs in the region.

Law and policy: Laws and regulations at the national and local levels should be facilitative of the development of these enterprises rather than be restrictive. The taxes and other fees should be kept at a minimum to encourage the setting up and formal registration of different small scale enterprises.

Product Design: The entrepreneurs should be guided for product design by making available copies of such specifications by yielding design specialists.

Entrepreneurship Development: There is a need to set up an appropriate training program in all enterprise facets, including marketing, managing, and financing and so on. This will call for the continuous training of the entrepreneur in managerial skills and the provision of financing and other functional assistance and will facilitate firm development.

Expanded Government Assistance: In general, government efforts to extend marketing assistance should be maintained and expanded. In this respect a network of government assistance units at the lowest political level may be more relevant than one at a regional or national level.

Services by the BASIC Bank: We have already mentioned that the operation of BASIC bank is concentrated to provision of different financial services. But there are several factors, on which the success of the SSEs depends; therefore the BASIC bank should add the following services.

CONSULTANCY FEE SUBSIDY SCHEME

Consultancy fee subsidy is needed to the SSEs for consultancy to small enterprises related to agriculture, horticulture, sericulture, and pisciculture, to subsidy to new entrepreneurs to meet cost of market research, to provide marketing assistance, for consultancy on use of non-conventional sources of energy and conservation measures and to control of pollution

INTEREST SUBSIDY SCHEME

Interest subsidy is needed for self-development and self-employment of unemployed persons, for socio-economically backward section of people, for encouraging quality control measures in the small enterprises, and for encouraging the adaptation of indigenous technology.

ENTREPRENEURSHIP DEVELOPMENT SCHEME

Entrepreneurship development program should be started that requires identifying persons with entrepreneurial urge, who are confident in what they are doing or want to do. Efforts should be made to select those people likely to succeed in business ideas. The selection process of clients should reveal the applicant's background, age, and earlier working experience, the realism of his business idea, motivation, entrepreneurial attitudes, and other relevant information. Then training to the selected persons is needed so their infantile business ideas are converted into realities. The training component should cover all major areas of business.

MARKET ENCOUNTER PROGRAM

Market encounter programs aims at bringing the producers and potential customers together. The program essentially includes occasional such as monthly and quarterly sales fair for the SSEs products for high-potential producers.

ENLARGEMENT OF BRANCH OFFICES

BASIC Bank is the only financial institution aimed at the promotion of the SSEs, and unfortunately all of its branches are located in either metropolitan cities or in district headquarters. Therefore to reach its benefits to nationwide scattered SSEs, extension, and expansion of branches into urban and sub-urban areas is desired in the promotion of the SSEs.

NOTES

1. The paper is the product of a research project titled "The Role of Bangladesh Small Industries and Commerce Bank in the Promotion of Small Scale Enterprises: Problems and Prospects: A Case Study in Khulna Region", and financed by the Research Cell, Khulna University, Bangladesh. Therefore, the authors acknowledge the financial support extended by the Khulna University authority. Authors are also grateful to the staffs of the BASIC Bank Limited for extending their coordinal and all out cooperation.
2. In Bangladesh, BASIC bank has 26 branches of which two are

located in the southwestern region i.e., Khulna region, one in Khulna city and another is at Jessore.

3. For example, BASIC bank has linkages with *Kreditanstalt fur Wiederaufbau* a German bank, and Asian Development Bank, where the first one is financing for micro credit scheme and small-scale industries. Total outstanding amount of fund from the above sources in 1999 increased to Tk. 369 million from Tk. 345 million in 1998 representing a 7 per cent growth (Annual Report, 1999).
4. It is not our intention to discuss those reasons here; rather we simply want to state the comparative financial services available to the SSEs.

REFERENCES

BASIC Bank, Annual Report 1996, 1997, 1998, 1999, 2000, and 2002.

Barrow, B. (1993), *The essence of small business*, Prentice Hall International (UK) Ltd.

Chopra, C. (1888), *Managerial Business and Finance*, Deep and Deep Publications, New Delhi, India.

Gupta, R.K. (1993), *Development Banks and Industrial Development*, Deep & Deep Publications, New Delhi., India.

Islam M S (2003), Industrial Credit Allocation: The Role of Banking Sector in Bangladesh, *Business Review*, Khulna University, Vol. 3, No. 2, , July–December.

Islam, M S and Aktaruzzaman K (2001), 'The Problems of Rural Women Entrepreneurs in Bangladesh: A Case Study of Jhenaidah District', *Islamic University Studies (PART-C)*, Vol. 4: No. 1, June.

Islam M S and Moniruzzaman A.K.M. (2000), 'Domestic Saving Mobilization in Bangladesh: The Role of Scheduled Banks', *Islamic University Studies (PART-C)*, Vol. 3, No. 2, December.

Khalily M A B, Meyer R L, and Husak L J, (1987), Deposit Mobilization in Bangladesh: Implications for Rural Financial Institutions and Financial Policies, *Bangladesh Development Studies, Vol. 15, No. 4.*

Khan, A. R (1991), *Entrepreneurship Small Business and Lives of successful Entrepreneur*, Abul Printing Press, Dhaka, Bangladesh.

Khan, M. A (1992), *Entrepreneurship Development in India*, Kanishka Publishing House, New Delhi, India.

Miya, S. (1997), *Business Finance and Financial Management*, the Eagle Publication, Dhaka, Bangladesh.

Ministry of Planning (2002), Statistical Year Book of Bangladesh 2000, Bangladesh Bureau of Statistics, June.

Ministry of Finance (2001), Bangladesh Population Census Report, Bangladesh Bureau of Statistics.

Ministry of Finance (2002), Government of Bangladesh, Economic Review, June.

Ministry of Finance (2003), Government of Bangladesh, Economic Review, June.

Ministry of Planning (1990), The Fourth Five Year Plan (1990-95), June.

UNDP (2003), Human Development Report, deepening democracy in a fragmented world.

World Bank (1998), The World Development Report, Washington D.C.

World Bank (2003), *The World Development Report*, Sustainable Development in a Dynamic World: Transforming Institutions, Growth, and Quality of Life, Washington D.C.

World Bank (2003), *The World Development Indicators*, C D Version.

11

TECHNOLOGY TRANSFER IN INTERNATIONAL JOINT VENTURES

*Ruchi Sharma and T.V.S.Ramamohan Rao**

INTRODUCTION

Technological development by MNCs generally centers around resources (both physical inputs and entrepreneurial skills) available in their country and their management culture. They design machinery, procedures for installation and operation, and specifications for maintenance with this environment in perspective. MNCs expect a clearly defined level of output from given resources if such tangible (formal) knowledge is adequate to operate the technology efficiently. See, for example, Arora (1996, p.234). MNCs generally transfer the formal knowledge to foreign firms and hope that foreign firms can develop adequate informal procedures, specific to their industrial environment, to operate the technology efficiently.

However, two types of information asymmetry are intrinsic to such technology transfer. First, MNCs do not generally have adequate knowledge about the availability of appropriate resources to organize production efficiently and the size of markets in foreign countries. By way of contrast, entrepreneurs in the foreign country will be better informed about these aspects. Second, foreign firms may not have the skills or the

* Indian Institute of Technology, Kanpur.

management culture to absorb and implement the new technology efficiently. MNCs will not be in a position to ascertain this at the time of negotiating contracts. This information asymmetry makes it necessary to conceptualize a joint venture based on comparative advantage.

Joint ventures experience adverse selection due to information asymmetry inherent in such arrangements. First, the MNC may not have an adequate knowledge of the competence (skill level) and commitment of the specific foreign firm with whom they form the joint venture. This results in the expected output not being realized or an increase in the average cost of production. More pertinent to the argument is the fact that MNCs will not be in a position to ascertain this change in expected value ex ante. Hence, there will be fundamental randomness that can be reflected in the variance in output[1]. Second, MNCs do not have adequate information about the more general economic environment in which the joint venture operates (for example, the attitudes of consumers towards the new product and the foreign country government toward participation of MNCs in their production and distribution processes). This results in adverse selection irrespective of the motivation and commitment of the specific foreign firm. Such loses are more difficult to predict and are random. Hence, it would be realistic to argue that adverse selection due to environmental uncertainty manifests itself in the form of an increase in the variance of output[2].

In practice, formal knowledge about technology will not be sufficient for proper assimilation, utilization, and adaptation of new technology even if the foreign firm has the skills and commitment and the foreign country government policies are not inhibitive. For, some rules of thumb, informal adaptations to local production conditions, and other tricks of trade may be necessary for the efficient use of technology and effective marketing of the product[3]. In general, whatever may be their level of motivation and commitment, most of the foreign firms may find it difficult to assimilate such information if they are expected to acquire it through learning by doing. That is, inadequate informal knowledge may also be an environmental problem resulting in adverse selection.

The MNC chooses contract parameters (in particular, royalty rates) with these sources of adverse selection in perspective. However, the MNC generally deals with many foreign firms. Instead of discriminating between them in the choice of royalty rates it would find it more practical to set a uniform rate. Such a practice was reported in the context of franchise contracts. See. For example, Kaufmann and Lafontaine (1984). Similarly, as Chisholm (1997) noted, the royalty rates to the distributors of movies and theaters are fixed ex ante and the contract negotiation concerns the number of days over which a movie is exhibited. Such a practice implies that only those agents with a high skill level and/or low risk aversion will accept the contract. For, given such royalty rates, the ex ante rents accruing to the agent will be higher the higher his skill level. In general, such policies of the MNCs are not firm specific. They apply to all foreign firms uniformly. Environmental uncertainty persists even if some firm specific adjustments are incorporated.

Another alternative available to the MNC is to devise policies that eliminate the sources of adverse selection. In particular, assume that there is a necessity for informal knowledge. The MNC may then offer to (a) train the personnel in the foreign country in the use of technology, (b) depute specialists to provide technical assistance in establishing production, quality control, and testing, (c) provide assistance in the design and layout of the manufacturing unit, (d) assist in the adaptation of drawings and designs, and (e) transmit technical information about the improvements in product and manufacturing processes. In general, the provision of informal knowledge may be considered as one incentive mechanism to improve the skills and elicit commitment from the foreign firm. However, it can only partially reduce environmental uncertainty. For, the costs of reducing the variance further may not be commensurate with the perceived benefits. This problem is far more pertinent when it is necessary to structure firm specific transfer of informal knowledge. Hence, as in the previous situation, MNCs devise general policies towards all joint venture partners and expect more efficient firms, that can generate ex ante rents, to accept partnership in joint ventures. Once again it is pertinent to note that environmental uncertainty cannot be fully eliminated even if some firm specific fine tuning of policies is attempted.

A third alternative available to the MNC is to entice the foreign firm to share in the fixed capital investment. For instance, the MNC may offer firm specific informal knowledge only if the foreign firm agrees to pay for it. There is a possibility that this policy elicits even greater motivation from the foreign firm. A similar argument holds even in the context of more pervasive deficiencies. For, suppose the foreign firm is expected to share in the investment necessary to identify and generate technological adaptations to local raw materials. It can be expected that the foreign firm has greater motivation because it must now recover these sunk costs. The more conventional argument is that by forcing such sharing the MNC can exert greater control on the foreign firm when there is randomness.

As noted earlier, whatever may be the sources of inefficiency, and however carefully the MNC policies are chosen, there may be a problem of generating the desired motivation and commitment. In such a case the only recourse to the MNC is to offer older technologies that may not require a high degree of skill and effort from the management of the foreign firm. The nature of the technology chosen necessarily depends on whether the problem is at the firm level or it is more general to the foreign country. On the whole, it can be concluded that appropriate identification of the sources of deficiency, suitable policy measures to elicit commitment or control as the source of problems suggest, and efficient implementation of such policies will be necessary to restore efficiency of technology transfer to joint ventures.

The following details are therefore obvious. (a) The realized level of output of a joint venture is random. This may be either due to the decisions and actions of the foreign firm or intrinsic to the more general environment in the foreign country. The variance in output captures this aspect accurately.

(b) Confronted with adverse selection MNCs devise general policies that they will apply equally to all foreign firms in their joint ventures. The primary reason for this is that fine tuning policies to suit the requirements of specific firms may involve greater costs in relation to perceived marginal benefits. Further, such general policies can be expected to entice firms to enter joint ventures in the hope of obtaining ex ante rents. (c) Irrespective of the details of such policy specification there will be some residual randomness in the operation of joint ventures.

However, as of now there is inadequate information about the channels through which policies of MNCs affect the choice of contract parameters and the performance of joint ventures. The basic observation from the above reasoning is that most of the policies attempt to reduce the variance in output resulting from adverse selection. As Svejnar and Smith (1984) noted, such policies may neutralize the deficiencies due to the lack of skill and commitment of the foreign firms. One basic objective of the present study is to provide a theoretical demonstration of this result. It will also be shown that policies operating exclusively on specific firms, and hence the expected levels of output, cannot result in contract parameters that are independent of skill levels of specific firms. This differs from the general belief that policies of MNCs operate only through expected values and the randomness remains purely exogenous and determined by the environment in which the joint ventures operate.

The rest of the study is organized as follows. Section 2 outlines a basic modification of the KM model. The provision of informal knowledge will be examined in section 3. It will be shown that it neutralizes the deficiencies in firm specific skills if the provision of informal knowledge reduces the variance attributable to more general environmental problems. Section 4 considers sharing fixed costs as an alternative incentive mechanism. The control exercised through the choice of technology is the theme of section 5. The concluding section highlights some related issues (such as the possibility of moral hazard) and the necessity to develop similar results with respect to the choice of foreign country government policies.

THE ANALYTICAL FRAMEWORK

The benchmark model of the principal agent framework to study the problem under consideration is Kawasaki and McMillan (1987). However, some important modifications are necessary to address the pertinent questions.

It will be assumed that a multinational firm (an IPR and/or patent holder designated as P hereafter) entrusts production and/or distribution of a product based on his invention to a foreign firm (an agent referred to as F). Assume that an output e is planned. Corresponding to this P undertakes an investment ke^2, where k is a constant, in physical capital[4]. Therefore, it is implicitly postulated that there are diminishing returns to the use of physical assets. Further, the more efficient the technology the lower will be the capital requirements for a given output. Hence, a lower value of k indicates the transfer of superior technology[5]. Assume that P finances the entire capital and hence operates a wholly owned subsidiary. However, due to the information asymmetry with respect to production and market conditions in the foreign country, he entrusts the operational management to F. In his turn, F incurs a variable cost $e^2/2d$, where d is the skill level of F. It should also be acknowledged that P will get to know the variable cost only to the extent that F is willing to reveal it. Diminishing returns with respect to variable factors is implicit in this formulation. However, unlike Das (1998) and Desai et al (2001), complementarity between the fixed and variable factors is postulated[6].

In practice it is more realistic to assume that a low d makes the output, for a given variable cost incurred by F, random. Denote the actual output by (e+u) where u is a random variable with $E(u) = 0$, and $V(u) = \sigma^2$. The variance is assumed to be exogenous to the decision making process of P and F. That is, information asymmetry with respect to production and marketing conditions, and the vagaries of the policies of the foreign country may be the primary sources of randomness. It should also be noted that this represents the risk perception of the MNC.

After the output is produced and sold the two parties share it[7]. Let p be the share of (e+u) offered to F. Fundamentally, the assumption is that P seeks an insurance against the risk by asking F to share it with him. Consequently, the share of output accruing to P can be interpreted as an insurance effect.

In its simplest form the KM model postulates that

$$\pi_F = \text{profit of F}$$
$$= p(e+u) - e^2/2\delta$$

Let λ be the degree of risk aversion of F. The value of the contract to F can be written as

$$V_F = pe - e^2/2\delta - \lambda p^2\sigma^2$$

The KM model assumes that F chooses e, for a given p, to maximize V_F. That is, F will choose

$$e = p\delta$$

On the contrary, P has many more avenues of generating income, and thereby hedging his risk, given his diversified portfolio (of products as well as financial assets). Hence, P is postulated to be risk neutral[8]. The value of the contract to P is

$$V_P = (1-p)\, e - ke^2$$

The other essential feature of the KM model is its assumption that P chooses p so as to maximize the net value of the contract, viz.,

$$N = V_F + V_P$$
$$= e - e^2/2\delta - ke^2 - \lambda p^2\sigma^2$$

taking the participatory constraint of F into account. Hence, the optimal royalty rate is given by

$$p = \delta/(\delta + 2k\delta^2 + 2\lambda\sigma^2)$$

Note that the choice implies p = 0 if and only if $\delta = 0$ or $\lambda\sigma^2 \rightarrow \infty$. The intermediate cases, where $0 < p < 1$, are more likely in practice. The assumption that the randomness is exogenous therefore implies that the efficient contract merely adjusts p and e keeping it in perspective. The pertinent observation is that such an efficient p is not independent of δ. Clearly, the model does not incorporate any mechanisms that can neutralize the effect of information asymmetry.

INFORMAL KNOWLEDGE

Assume that the MNC transfers the latest technology. Consequently, k is exogenously given. Consider a situation wherein P feels that foreign firms will not be in a position to manage the technology efficiently unless the informal knowledge about the technology is transferred along with the formal knowledge. It then becomes necessary for P to incur some expenditure for providing the requisite informal knowledge. To examine the effect of such an expenditure on the contract parameters in the KM framework it is necessary to specify the channels of transmission. One possibility is that the requirements of informal knowledge are firm specific. Transfer of such informal knowledge increases the expected value of output for a given variable cost. Or, equivalently, the variable cost of producing a given level of output can be expected to decrease. The second possibility is that all foreign firms are in need of such informal knowledge in varying degrees. That is, the MNC providing such knowledge reduces the variance of the output. These specifications will now be considered sequentially.

Consider firm specific informal knowledge to begin with. It can be expected that such expenditures on informal knowledge will also be subject to diminishing returns. Hence, for a given level of output e, it can be assumed that P spends an amount me^2. The corresponding variable cost can be written as

$$v_F = e^2/2\delta(k+m)$$

For, the efficiency in the use of technology is a result of the use of the informal knowledge in conjunction with the formal aspects of technology transfer. Note that this specification is also consistent with the notion that there will be diminishing returns with respect to m. Clearly, the basic assumption underlying this approach is that such an expenditure cannot alter the exogenous randomness in the market conditions and the degree of risk aversion of F. Hence, it is necessary to maintain that the realized level of output is random with $V(u) = \sigma^2$. As a result, the profit of F is[9]

$$\pi_F = p(e+u) - e^2/2\delta(k+m)$$

The efficient choice of output is therefore

$$e = p\delta(k+m)$$

The net value of the contract becomes

$$N = e - e^2/2\delta(k+m) - \lambda p^2\sigma^2 - (k+m)e^2$$
$$= p\delta(k+m) - p^2\delta(k+m)/2 - \lambda p^2\sigma^2 - p^2\delta^2(k+m)^3$$

Consequently, the optimal choices of m and p are such that

$$2-p-6(k+m)^2p\delta = 0, \text{ and} \quad ...(1)$$

$$\delta(k+m)[1-p-2p\delta(k+m)^2] = 2\lambda p\sigma^2 \quad ...(2)$$

From (1) it can be inferred that

$$p = 2/[1+6\,(k+m)^2\delta] \quad ...(3)$$

Equation (2) therefore indicates that the choice of m is such that

$$\delta(k+m)[-1+2(k+m)^2\delta] = 4\lambda\sigma^2 \quad ...(4)$$

Note that, to make the analysis meaningful, it should be assumed that

$$-1 + 2(k+m)^2d > 0$$

since δ, $(k+m)$ and $\lambda\ \sigma^2$ are positive. From the viewpoint of economic theory, this indicates that ceteris paribus the MNC would be willing to deal with only those foreign firms whose skill level δ exceeds $1/2(k+m)^2$. It is also natural that the MNC would be willing to work with a lower skilled foreign firm the more it is willing to spend on the transfer of tacit knowledge.

Differentiating both sides of equation (4) partially with respect to δ it can be readily verified that

$$\partial m/\partial\delta = -\,(k+m)[-1 + 4\,(k+m)^2\delta]/\delta[-1+6(k+m)^2\delta] < 0$$

and, similarly,

$$\partial m/\partial\lambda\sigma^2 = 4/\delta[-1+6(k+m)^2\delta] > 0$$

The MNC has to incur less cost to transfer tacit knowledge to F if it is more efficient. For any given (k+m), an increase in $\lambda\sigma^2$ decreases N. To restore a higher net value of the contract the MNC is compelled to increase m and reduce the variance further.

Partially differentiating equation (3) with respect to d and $\lambda\sigma^2$ successively it can be shown that

$$\partial p/\partial\delta > 0, \text{ and } \partial p/\partial\lambda\sigma^2 < 0$$

These results are consistent with the KM formulation. However, contrary to expectations, p cannot be independent of δ[10]. That is, P cannot effectively counteract the inefficiency if its expenditure affects only the expected value of output or the variable cost.

The possibility that the transfer of tacit knowledge reduces the variance may now be examined. Assume that me^2 of expenditure by P leaves the variable cost unaltered at $e^2/2\delta$ while making $V(u) = \sigma^2/(k+m)$. Then, the value of the contract to F becomes

$$V_F = pe - e^2/2\delta - \lambda p^2\sigma^2/(k+m)$$

The efficient choice of e will now be

$$e = p\delta$$

and the net value of the contract is

$$N = p\delta - p^2\delta/2 - (k+m)p^2\delta^2 - \lambda p^2\sigma^2/(k+m)$$

The optimal choices of (k+m) and p are determined by the equations

$$\delta^2(k+m)^2 = \lambda\sigma^2, \text{ and}$$

$$p = 1/(1+4\sqrt{\lambda}\sigma)$$

Hence, the choice of m that neutralizes the effect of low skill level is

$$(k+m) = \sqrt{\lambda}\sigma/\delta$$

It will be lower the higher the skill level. However, a higher $\lambda\sigma^2$ necessitates a greater m. The most important finding is that p is now independent of δ. Clearly, an efficient choice of m neutralizes the deficiency, due to the lower skill level of the foreign firm, through its effect on the variance of output.

SHARING FIXED COSTS

It was pointed out in the previous section that the MNC may find it necessary to offer informal knowledge to F in order to neutralize the lack of skills on the part of F. However, the MNC financing the entire capital investment of the joint venture may not elicit adequate commitment from F in the use of the equipment transferred. The MNC may then insist that the foreign firm share a fraction s of ke^2 to elicit compliance. This may make F feel more committed because recovery of his share of the fixed costs will now be at stake.

Assume that the share of F has the effect of reducing the variance to σ^2/s. More pertinent to the argument will be the changes in the cost to P. The following observations are relevant. (a) The MNC may have to pay F an extra share of output by way of royalties due to the increase in his share of capital and F's bargaining power. (b) Gomes-Casseres (1989), Al-Saadon and Das (1996), and Chen and Hennert (2002, p.4) pointed out that due to information asymmetry with respect to production and marketing conditions in the foreign country the MNC has to incur proportionately higher costs as s increases. (c) The MNC has to make much greater efforts and incur greater costs to convince F to provide the commitment if abinitio the transfer of highly efficient technology enables F to capture some rents. The MNC may experience diminishing returns to its efforts to persuade F to comply. This was noted in Al-Saadon and Das (1996). (d) The costs of negotiation, management, and conflict resolution increase with the share of the foreign firm. This may arise purely due to differences in expectations, management and cultural values, and attitudes of labor. Gomes-Casseres (1989, pp.7ff; 1990, p.3) and Cai (2003, p.75) contain explicit statements to this effect. In particular, Cai observed that "joint ownership may result in considerable governance costs. When multiple parties jointly own a firm, they have to reach agreements on how to use the assets effectively. The costs (of) making collective decisions can be quite substantial, especially when these owners have diverse preferences." (e) There will be greater scrutiny of the decisions of P as s increases. This has the effect of reducing the flexibility of P with respect to transfer pricing and resource allocation across subsidiaries in different countries. The significance of such an opportunity cost was acknowledged in Gomes-Casseres (1989) and Das (1998). It will be postulated that $aske^2$

represents the total costs with the understanding that as >1. The share of F will be restricted to ske^2 of capital alone. Note that the profit for F will now be

$$\pi_F = p(e+u) - e^2/2\delta - ske^2$$

Given his risk aversion the value he attaches to π_F is

$$V_F = pe - e^2/2\delta - ske^2 - \lambda p^2\sigma^2/s$$

Observe that a risk averse F will not accept a large s because he incurs an additional cost of greater commitment to reduce production risk. Further, there is a possibility that F experiences liquidity constraints while raising the resources required for capital investments. Both these considerations suggest that F will prevail on the choice of s. Hence, he can be expected to choose s and e to maximize V_F. This results in

$$s = (\lambda/k)^{1/2} (\sigma/\delta)$$

$$e = p\delta^*, \text{ where}$$

$$\sigma^* = \beta\delta, \text{ and}$$

$$\beta = 1\text{-}2\,(\lambda k)^{1/2}\sigma$$

the net value of the contract is

$$N = e - e^2/2\delta - \alpha ske^2 - \lambda p^2\sigma^2/s$$

$$= p\delta\beta - p^2\beta^2\delta/2 - 2\beta(\lambda k)^{1/2}p^2\delta\sigma$$

P will therefore choose

$$p = 1/[1+2(\lambda k)^{1/2}\sigma]$$

The efficient choice of s so obtained is consistent with several observations in the literature. (a) Das (1998, p.139) pointed out that F would accept a higher s to counteract the effect of a low d. That is, he will signal greater commitment to P. (b) Pan and Li (2000) noted the direct relationship between s and $\lambda\sigma^2$. Even in this context, a larger λ and/or σ^2 necessitates F indicating a greater commitment to P. (c) A large market in the foreign country can be expected to provide an incentive for P to transfer more efficient technology. Along with it the MNC may seek grater security and commitment. F will therefore agree to a larger s. A larger s may also be due to the greater bargaining power of F given the IPR protection. It must however be acknowledged that an increase in s beyond a point may be a disadvantage to P because F gains control.

On the whole, it can be concluded that an efficient s, whose effect is through the variance, generally neutralizes the effect of a low d. The commitment effect induced by P, rather than the voluntary motivational changes of F postulated by the changes in expected values, appear to be more reliable.

TECHNOLOGY CHOICE

Note that the technology transferred need not be entirely exogenous in practice. Instead, as noted in section 1, the MNC may find it more risky to transfer a more recent (and hence relatively more efficient) technology. The MNC may only offer technology of an older vintage. This can be introduced in the principal agent model by making k a choice of the MNC.

The choice of technology can be expected to have one of two effects on the choice of contracts. First, many studies argue that the basic change is in the expected value of output. For, by transferring an older technology, the MNC can make sure that the extent of inefficiency is reduced. In particular, the damage that the foreign firm can inflict on the MNC will be lower. Operationally, this can be represented as a reduction in the variable cost of production for a given level of output. More efficient technologies are subject to greater adverse selection and hence greater variable costs. Clearly, an efficient choice of technology is based on the tradeoff between the fixed and variable costs. Second, it may be argued that given the technology and the operating procedures, variable costs are determined and the management of the foreign firm has very little choice. Adverse selection manifests itself only in the form of a change in variance. Specifically, the more efficient the technology the greater the possibility of adverse selection and a greater variance. The pertinent question is as follows. Which of these two mechanisms is apriori more plausible and is also consistent with empirically observed stylized facts? It was pointed out in section 1 that the variance route is more plausible on apriori grounds. For, the motivational effect, implied by expected value changes, is much less reliable compared to the control effect implied in the changes of variance.

It is immediately obvious that the analytical details are analogous to those of section 3. The only difference is that k is the pertinent choice variable with m set as zero. Hence, all the results of that section carry over ceteris paribus. Note also that a joint choice of k and m leave the results in tact.

CONCLUSION

A MNC is confronted with the possibility of adverse selection in its technology transfer. This generally depends on the level of skill of the foreign firm. The MNC then attempts to choose a technology that it can efficiently transfer. Such a choice may motivate the foreign firm to reduce its variable cost for a given level of output. However, this effect is not very reliable and cannot eliminate the deficiencies of a low skill on the choice of royalty rates. On the other hand, given the skill level and the motivations of F, the MNC may be in a position to reduce the variance inherent in the environment in which the joint venture operates. The MNC, having greater control on this effect, will find it more reliable. This will also render the efficient choice of the royalty rate to be independent of the level of skill. A similar result can also be established with respect to the sharing of capital investments between the joint venture partners.

Two other observations are in order. First, other policy choices, such as equity participation, can be adopted by the MNC. The results can be shown to be invariant though the analysis requires a major modification. They will be reported elsewhere. Second, the necessity for changes in randomness to sustain this result cannot however be taken for granted. For, there may be other channels through which the effects of policy choices can be transmitted to the choice of contract parameters and the performance of the joint venture. But, as of now, no other theoretical explanation is available.

It is often suggested that the MNC may experience moral hazard if the IPR protection of the foreign country is inadequate. For, in any form of joint venture, the foreign firm may not operate efficiently and in consonance with the expectations of the MNC. In particular, after the MNC makes the investment the foreign firm, or its workers, may reengineer the technology, create a competitive firm, and compete for the same market as the joint venture. Similarly, the government of the foreign country may change its policies with respect to profit taxation, transfer prices, and tariffs so as to drain profits of the MNC. It may also redefine the limits of equity participation or confiscate the assets altogether. Das (1998) designated this as policy moral hazard. Utilizing an analytical structure similar to the present study it can be shown that policies affecting variance of output can mitigate moral hazard effectively. This will be presented in a companion paper.

On the whole, the conceptualization of changes in randomness resulting from the policy options of the joint venture partners appears to be a promising theoretical development in understanding the nature of efficient contracts in international joint ventures.

From a strategic management perspective the results of the present study suggest the following. MNC policies directed to assessing and reducing overall environmental uncertainties, especially those related to firms in the industry and government policies, will be superior to the provision of firm specific informal knowledge.

NOTES

1. Note that this is only in an ex ante sense. There may not be much of any ex post variation in output over time for any one joint venture.
2. This variance is across different firms ex ante. Information asymmetry may therefore make an MNC choose an inefficient firm while forming a joint venture.
3. As Arora (1996, p.235) put it, "transfer of chemical technology will typically involve training the licensee in a variety of issues such as how to handle and store chemicals, how to control the production process and return it to operation after (an) unscheduled breakdown caused by (an) accident or impurities in the feedstock."
4. It will be assumed that this is the cost of using the capital equipment per unit of time to facilitate the static analysis that

follows. Note, however, that capital costs can be fully recovered only if the integrity of the joint venture can be sustained over a sufficiently long time.

5. Technological development by the MNC will not generally pay attention to the variable costs in its implementation under various production conditions. Hence, substitution between capital and variable factors will not be acknowledged explicitly.
6. It can be shown that allowing substitution between capital and variable factors does not yield royalty rates commensurate with the stylized facts if randomness is acknowledged.
7. The fixed costs are assigned to P and the variable costs are borne by F. Hence, sharing output is the only relevant contract parameter.
8. The apriori expectation would have been one of relatively greater risk aversion of P. For, the risks associated with information asymmetry make it difficult for him to recover his sunk investments. It can be easily verified that such a modification of the KM framework yields similar results. However, the basic theme of this study is that P can modify the effects of randomness through his actions. Hence, the risk will primarily impinge on F if such choices are efficient.
9. Clearly, P must be compensated for the additional expenditure. The obvious mechanism is to adjust p suitably. Some authors suggest that P will claim a fixed amount upfront for the transfer of informal knowledge. See, for example, Brickley (2002). However, a change in p is more realistic if the expenditure by P depends on the skill level of F. This approach will be adopted in the sequel.
10. The context of liquidity constraints is somewhat analogous. Postulate that P makes an apriori judgement that the randomness is due to liquidity constraints and not the shortage of tacit knowledge. Assume that F is experiencing liquidity constraints primarily because his skills and collateral are inadequate. One approach available to F is to locally obtain finances at a higher interest rate. On the other hand, P may agree to raise finances in its parent country if some saving is possible. Suppose, P incurs a n extra cost me^2 and expects F to accept the variable cost $e^2/2\delta$ as before. Or, alternatively, P may allow F to raise the requisite finances and reimburse me^2 of expenditure. The greater the value of m offered the lower the σ^2 due to the randomness created by the liquidity constraints. Hence, the optimal choice of m will be

exactly the same as before. Once again it is evident that the endogenous randomness specification compensates for the lack of skill on the part of F to raise the requisite finances. However, note that the basis for this formulation will be lost if the liquidity constraints are external to the operation of F.

REFERENCES

Al-Saadon, Y., and S.P.Das (1996), Host-Country Policy, Transfer Pricing and Ownership Distribution in International Joint Ventures: a Theoretical Analysis, *International Journal of Industrial Organization,* 14, 345-364.

Arora, A. (1996), Contracting for Tacit Knowledge: The Provision of Technical Services in Technology Licensing Contracts, *Journal of Development Economics,* 50, 233-256.

Brickley, J.A. (2002), Royalty Rates and Upfront Fees in Share Contracts: Evidence from Franchising, *Journal of Law, Economics, and Organization,* 18, 511-535.

Cai, H. (2003), A Theory of Joint Asset Ownership, Rand *Journal of Economics,* 34, 63-77.

Chen, S.F.S., and J.F. Hennert (2002), Japanese Investors' Choice of Joint Ventures Versus Wholly-Owned Subsidiaries in the U.S.: The Role of Market Barriers and Firm Capabilities, *Journal of International Business Studies,* 33, 1-18.

Chishlom, D.C. (1997), Profit-Sharing Versus Fixed-Payment Contracts: Evidence from the Motion Pictures Industry, *Journal of Law, Economics, and Organization,* 13, 169-201.

Das, S.P. (1998), On the Choice of International Joint Ventures: The Role of Policy Moral Hazard, Policy Reform, 2, 135-150.

Desai, M.A., C.F. Foley, and J.R.Hines (2001), International Joint Ventures and the Boundaries of the Firm, Available at www.stern.nyu.edu/clb/Desai 01. pdf.

Gomes-Casseres, B. (1989), Ownership Structures of Foreign Subsidiaries, *Journal of Economic Behavior and Organization,* 11, 1-25.

Gomes-Casseres, B. (1990), Firm Ownership Preferences and Host Government Restrictions: An Integrated Approach, *Journal of International Business Studies,* 25, 1-22.

Kaufmann, P.J., and F. Lafontaine (1994), Costs of Control: The Sources of Economic Rents for McDonald's Franchisees, in S.E.Masten (ed.) Case Studies in Contracting and Organization (NewYork: Oxford University Press).

Kawasaki, S., and J. McMillan (1987), The Design of Contracts: Evidence from Japanese Subcontracting, *Journal of the Japanese and International Economics,* 1, 327-349.

Pan, Y., and X. Li (2000), Joint Venture Formation of Very Large Multinational Firms, *Journal of International Business Studies,* 31, 179-189.

Svejnar, J., and S.C.Smith (1984), The Economics of Joint Ventures in Less Developed Countries, *Quarterly Journal of Economics,* 99, 149-167.

12

THE IMPACT OF AGRICULTURAL FINANCE ON AGRICULTURAL OUTPUT IN NIGERIA

Muftau A . Ijaiya and Gafar T. Ijaiya***

INTRODUCTION

Prior to the discovery of oil in the early 1960s and the oil boom of the 1970s, the importance of agriculture to the economic development of Nigeria is enormous owing to the fact that agriculture was the main source of food and employment for a sizeable number of the people. Agriculture also provides raw materials for most of the industries in the country and income for individuals and the government. For instance, in the 1960s more than 80 per cent of the rural population of Nigeria was engaged in one type of agricultural activity or the other and between 1963 and 1964 the sector contributed as much as 65 per cent of the nation's Gross Domestic Product (GDP) (Anyanwu, et.al 1997, Yesufu 1996).

But recently, these roles seems to elude the country because of neglects resulting from the discovery of oil and the oil boom of 1970s; the global economic crisis of the 1980s resulting from the deterioration in the nation's terms of trade, and the continuous decline in government finance to the sector (see Ijaiya 2000, Iwayemi 1994).

* Department of Accounting and Finance, University of Ilorin, Ilorin, Nigeria.
** Department of Economics, University of Ilorin, Ilorin, Nigeria.

The aim of this paper therefore is to examine the influence of change in government expenditure in agriculture on agricultural output over the years using a time subscript and difference-in-difference estimator.

The rest of the paper is structured as follows: a conceptual and empirical overview of the role of agriculture and agricultural finance in Nigeria are provided in section two. Section three provides the data source and methodology. Section four presents and interprets the results. Recommendations and conclusion are contained in the last section.

CONCEPTUAL AND EMPIRICAL OVERVIEW OF AGRICULTURE AND AGRICULTURAL FINANCE

Definition and Role of Agriculture to Economic Development

According to Anyanwu, et.al (1997) agriculture involves the cultivation of land, raising and rearing of animals for the purpose of production of food for man, feed for animals and raw materials for industries. It involves cropping, livestock, and forestry, fishing, processing and marketing of these agricultural products. Essentially it is composed of crop production, livestock, forestry and fishing.

In discussing the role of agriculture to economic development, Binswanger, et. al (1999) said that agriculture has both backward and forward linkages with itself and other sectors of the economy. It supplies raw materials to the agro-allied sector which enhances the provision of foods, job opportunities and income to those engaged by the sector as well to the government. Thus playing a key role in agriculture led industrialization (see also Vogel 1994 and Adelman 1984).

Anyanwu, et. al (1997) also observed that the role of agriculture in transforming both the social and economic framework of an economy through the food it provide the people and the raw materials it provide for the industrial sector. The sector is also essential for the expansion of employment opportunity which makes it possible for poverty reduction, improvement of income distribution and the speeding up industrialization and improvement of a nation's balance of payments. (see also IFPRI 1996).

The World Bank (1997) further posited that agriculture plays an important role in the overall economic development of a country, to the extent that a country that is able to achieve a 4 per cent annual growth rate in agriculture will record an improvement in technology and an increase in agricultural production is capable of reducing food import bills, which in the long run can translate to a favourable terms of trade, which in tune can be used in increasing the importation of manufactured capital goods that would possibly improve the living standard of the people.

Qureshi, et. al. (1996) reiterates that an increase in the rate of agriculture can also increase the demand for credit and as rapid increase in agriculture raises the demand for credit, farmers income will rise and the ability of farmers to self-finance themselves would in the long run improve thereby improving their well-being.

Agricultural Finance in Nigeria: The Trends and Constraints

Prior to the discovery of oil in the late 1950s and early 1960s, agriculture was the dominant sector of Nigeria economy. It consisted over 65 per cent of the country's Gross Domestic Product (GDP) and provided the bulk of the foreign exchange earnings through the export of cash crops. But with the emergence of oil as a major source of government revenue and foreign exchange earner the sector was neglected and hence led to its decline. (Ijaiya 2000, Iwayemi 1994, Ukpong and Malgwi 1991)

Having realized the declining role of agriculture to economic development, the government over the years has put in place certain policy measures and programmes with a view of increasing the contribution of agriculture to economic development. However, a peep into the Federal Government capital expenditure on agriculture as a ratio of the total Federal Government capital expenditure portrait a gloomy future for the sector's development in the country. As indicated in Table 1, from 1977 to 2002, the Federal Government capital expenditure on agriculture were low except in the following years; 1980, 1984, 1987, 1988, 1993, 1994, 1997, 1998, 1999, 2001 and 2002, because these were the years that coincides with different government agricultural development policies and programmes such as the Green Revolution in 1980, Food for all Programme in 1987, the Better Life for Rural Women Programme also in 1987, the Family Support Programme in 1993 and the National Economic Empowerment Development Strategy.

Table 1

Federal Government Capital Expenditure on Agriculture 1977-2002

Year	*Total Federal Government Expenditure (₦ Million)*[a]	*Total Capital Expenditure to the Agricultural Sector (₦ Million)*[b]
1977	7676.4	105.5
1978	5637.2	128.4
1979	8379.1	321.9
1980	10654.1	435.6
1981	6564.2	775.1
1982	7998.0	1035.1
1983	6807.3	1185.2
1984	4634.6	252.5
1985	6516.4	985.4
1986	5445.9	892.5
1987	4759.4	365.1
1988	10588.6	595.7
1989	9297.1	981.5
1990	12555.6	1758.5
1991	13085.4	551.2
1992	15975.9	763.0
1993	18600.0	1820.0
1994	31000.0	2800.1
1995	44559.0	4691.7
1996	48000.0	3892.8
1997	115690.0	6247.4
1998	185375.0	8876.6
1999	136984.0	6912.6
2000	70059.4	5761.7
2001	1018025.6	57879.0
2002	1018155.8	323664.4

Source: a and b Central Bank of Nigeria Annual Report and Statement of Account for the year 2000; and Central Bank of Nigeria Statistical Bulletin for the year 2002.

Despite these huge sums of money allocated to the sector during these years, there was little or no improvement in agricultural production because successive governments only used the policies/programmes to embezzle public funds to the total neglect of food production. Besides, agricultural policies in Nigeria are tangles of contradictions as government is simultaneously encouraging and at the same time discouraging the increase in farm production by refusing to pay farmers the true value of their crops and at the same time selling fertilizer and seeds to them at high prices.

The food pricing and exchange rate policies of government have over the years been faulty thus affecting the financing of agriculture in Nigeria. The pricing policies the government had pursued over the years have been relatively low to the world market prices and in most cases what is paid the farmers is half the world price. The continuous depreciation of the Naira and the ineffective system of subsidies for inputs have also had their toll on agricultural finance. For instance, the subsides which were aimed at helping the poor, ended up reducing the income of the farmers who are much poorer than many of the urban consumers who actually benefit from the subsides. The consequence of this is that the policies have reduced farmers incentives for production while consumption of urban dwellers have continue to increase thus making government rely on imported food dumped by industrial countries, which in turn makes farmers to abandoned their farms and migrate to the cities. (World Bank 1986).

Rapid advances in agricultural production in Nigeria are also a constraint to agricultural finance. For example, technology has vastly increased the productivity of farm labour and greatly decreases the number of farm labourers needed. This resulted in a steady decline in the cost of production and a decline in crop prices. The fall in crop price with increasing opportunities in urban areas have combined to create a strong incentive for rural-urban migration. Besides, Nigeria government has taken advantage in the reduction of food prices to increase their food import to the neglect of the agricultural sector, thus increasing the government food import bills which further impede finance to the agricultural sector (World Bank 1986).

Another constraint to agricultural finance in Nigeria is the delay in the disbursement of loans to farmers. According to Aku (1995) farmers in Nigeria are usually confronted with delays in the disbursements of loans approved by government. These loans sometimes come after the planting season and with the actual disbursement falling far short of loan needed and approved. Even when these loans are disbursed early, it does not get to the poor farmers but rather to the rich farmers who divert such loans to other activities that has no effect on agricultural production. Some of these rich farmers at times fail to pay back such loan because they cannot be penalized due to what is called "high political cost".

Farmers are also faced with natural hazards such as infestation of crops by pest and diseases, inadequate rainfall, soil erosion and retardation in the conduct of extension activities and the adoption of new improved farming techniques following the financial crisis which most Agricultural Development Projects (ADP) faced as a result of the phasing out of the World Bank loan facilities following the failure of the government to account for already disburse loans and the subsequent annulment of the 1993 general election.(CBN 1992, 1996).

DATA SOURCE AND METHODOLOGY

Data Source

Time series data for the period 1985 to 2002 on the total expenditure of the government on the agricultural sector and the total output of major agricultural commodities in Nigeria were used. The data were obtained from the Central Bank of Nigeria Annual Report and Statement of Account for the year 2000; and Central Bank of Nigeria Statistical Bulletin for the year 2002.

The Model

In specifying the model emphasis is placed on whether the

total expenditure of the government on the agricultural sector has any significant influence on the total output of major agricultural commodities in Nigeria.

Having established this link the first equation is formulated as:

$$TAOUT_t = f(TGEA_t) \quad ...(1)$$

Following Barro and Sala (1995) and Grootaert, Kanbur and Oh (1995) methods of analysis that uses a time subscript ($_t$) and first difference operator (D), we therefore model the relationship between total agricultural output and total government expenditure on agriculture as follows:

$$\Delta TAOUT_t = f(\Delta TGEA_t) \quad ...(2)$$

Equation (2) thus describes the changes in agricultural output as a function of changes in government expenditure on agriculture.

The introduction of the initial level of government expenditure on agriculture in Nigeria i.e.($TGEA_t$) into equation (2) therefore gives the following equation:

$$\Delta TAOUT_t = f(TGEA, \Delta TGEA_t) \quad ...(3)$$

The transformation of equation (3) into a linear equation then become:

$$\Delta TAOUT_t = \beta_0 + \beta_1 TGEA_t + \beta_2 \Delta TGEA_t + U \quad ...(4)$$

Where:

$TAOUT_t$ = the initial level of total agricultural output in Nigeria (in 000 tonnes).

$\Delta TAOUT_t$ = the changes in the total agricultural output in Nigeria (in 000 tonnes)

$TGEA_t$ = the initial level of total government expenditure on agriculture (in million Naira)

$\Delta TGEA_t$ = changes in the total government expenditure on agriculture (in million Naira)

β_0 = the intercept

β_1 and β_2 = the parameter estimates that stands for the speed of convergence of total government expenditure on agriculture in Nigeria, with a positive value indicating convergence of total government expenditure on agriculture towards agriculture output, while a negative value indicates a divergence.

U = the error term

To estimate the model, a multiple regression analysis is used in order to reflect the explanatory nature of the variables. To verify the validity of the model, two major evaluation criteria are used: the *a–priori* expectation criteria which is based on the signs and magnitudes of the coefficients of the variables under investigation; and (ii) statistical criteria which is based on statistical theory, which in other words is referred to as the First Order Least Square (OLS) consisting of R-square (R^2), F–statistic and t–test. The R-square (R^2) is concerned with the overall explanatory power of the regression analysis, the F-statistic is used to test the overall significance of the regression analysis and the t-test is used to test the significant contribution of the independent variables on the dependent variable (Oyeniyi 1997).

Drawn from the model the *a-priori* expectations or the expected pattern of behavior between the dependant variable $\Delta TAOUT_t$ and the independent variables $TGEA_t$ and $\Delta TGEA_t$ are: $TGEA_t > 0$, $\Delta TGEA_t > 0$. Indicating that an increase in the initial level of total government expenditure on agriculture and a positive change in the total government expenditure on agriculture are expected to increase agriculture output in Nigeria.

RESULTS AND DISCUSSION

The results of the regression analysis are presented in Table 2.

A look at the model shows that it is fairly good, since it has an R^2 of 0.66 which in other words means that 66 per cent variation in the dependent variable (Ä$TAOUT_t$) is explained by the independent variables ($TGEA_t$ and Ä$TGEA_t$), while the error term take care of the remaining 34 per cent, which are variables in the study that can not be included in the model because of their qualitative features. At 5 per cent level of significance, the F-statistic shows that the model is useful in determining the influence of government expenditure on agriculture on agricultural output in Nigeria as the computed

Table 2
Regression Results of Poverty Reduction and Economic Growth in Nigeria.

Explanatory Variable	*Co-efficient and t-values*
Intercept	111.6
(t)	(22.8)
$TGEA_t$	1.10
(t)	(5.22)
$\Delta TGEA_t$	-0. 81
(t)	(-2.15)
R^2	0. 66
F	14.1

t-values in parentheses

F- statistic which is 14.1 is greater than the tabular F-statistic (2, 17) valued at 5.85.

The estimated parameters of the variables (initial level of government expenditure on agriculture and changes in government expenditure on agriculture are positively and negatively related to agricultural output respectively. An indication that the initial level of government expenditure on agriculture induces an increase in agricultural output than the changes witnessed in government expenditure on agriculture in Nigeria. Statistically this implies that at a point estimate of 100 percent a reduction in government expenditure on agriculture would have the cumulative effect of reducing agricultural output in Nigeria by 81 per cent in the following year.

CONCLUSION AND RECOMMENDATIONS

Using a multiple regression analysis that includes the initial level of government expenditure on agriculture and the changes in government expenditure on agriculture, this paper explored the relationship between government finance on agriculture and agricultural output in Nigeria.

From the analysis, our findings indicate that the initial level of government expenditure on agriculture has helped improve agricultural output more than the changes experienced in recent times, a situation that can be improved upon if certain policy measures are put in place. The first most important measure is a vigorous improvement in the nation's tax bases and the administrative capacity of the Board of Internal Revenue to collect the taxes. This is essential given the role of tax as the number one source of government revenue. Couple to this is the government ability to provide incentives for public officials (that are in charge of revenue collection and disbursement of government funds to the various sectors) to perform better while keeping arbitrary action and corruption in check.

Increasing government spending on the agricultural sector should be complimented with stable macro economic policies (where inflation is kept under control, internal and external debt remain manageable and macroeconomic crisis that emerge are resolved quickly), protective import duties on imported food items and heavy public investment in the area of land development and management, infrastructural development, agricultural research and agro-industries. The effectiveness of all these must be enlarged by adequate delivery system of agricultural input and the marketing of agricultural output that come from the investments; and participatory co-operation of the Nigerian farmers and experts in agriculture. If all these are accomplished such investments are assumed would gradually increase and further improve the price ratios for farmers and boast government revenue and spending in not only the agricultural sector but also into other sectors of the economy that are supportive to the agricultural sector.

Financial institutions, most especially banks should be called upon to supplement government efforts at financing agriculture through the disbursement of loans at low interest rate and at appropriate time in order to avoid the diversion of such loans. For effective disbursement, the banks should create specialized units within the banks with the help of non-governmental organizations and farmers' co-operatives. The units will have to be efficient in their operations in order to overcome high transaction cost of small loans and be made to apply an effective targeting strategy that would provide loans to recognized farmers who will use it for productive purpose.

REFERENCES

Adelman, I. (1984), Beyond Export-led Growth. *World Development. Vol.* 12 No. 9:937-949.

Aku, P.S. (1995), Comparative Analysis of NACB and ACGSF Loan Disbursement to Agriculture in Nigeria: *Journal of Social and Management Studies.* Vol 2. No. : 99-108,.

Anyanwa, J.C. Oyefusi A. Oaikhenan H. and Dimowo, F.A. (1997), *The Structure of the Nigerian Economy (1960-1997).* Onitsha Joanee Educational Publisher.

Barro, A and Sala I. M., (1995), *Economic Growth.* London: McGraw-Hill Inc.

Binswanger, H. Townsend, R. and Tshibaka T. (1999), Spurring Agriculture, Land and Rural Development. *In Proceedings of the Conference on Can African Claim the 21st Century? Held in Abidjan, in July 1999.*

Central Bank of Nigeria (CBN) (1992), *Annual Report and Statement of Account for the year ended 1992.* Lagos CBN.

Central Bank of Nigeria (CBN) (1996), *Annual Report and Statement of Account for the year ended 1996.* Lagos CBN.

Central Bank of Nigeria (2002), *Statistical Bulletin.* Lagos CBN.

Grootaert, C; Kanbur, R and Oh, G. (1995), Dynamic of Poverty-Why some people Escape and others Don't: An African Case Study. *World Bank Policy Research Working Paper No. 1499.*

Ijaiya G.T. (2000), Economic Growth in Nigeria An Asymmetry of the Balanced Growth Doctrine. *In Usman A and Ijaiya G.T. (eds.) Selected Essays on the Contradictions of Economic Development Theories in Nigeria.* Ilorin: Haytee Publishing Co.

International Food Policy Research Institute (IFPRI) (1999), *Feeding the World, Preventing Poverty and Protecting the Earth: A 2020 Vision.* Washington D.C. IFPRI.

Iwayemi A. (1994), *Perspectives and Problems of Economic Development in Nigeria: 1960–1990.* Ibadan: CEAR.

Oyeniyi T.A. (1997), *Fundamental Principles of Econometrics.* Lagos: Cader Publication Ltd.

Qureshi, S., Nabi, I. and Faruquee, R. (1996), Rural Finance for Growth and Poverty Alleviation. *World Bank Policy Research Working Paper* No. 1593.

Ukpong, G. and Malgwi, U. (1991), Federal Government Policies in Respect of Agricultural Finance. *CBN Bulletin*. Lagos: 47-59.

Vogel, S.J. (1994), Structural Changes in Agriculture: Production Linkages and Agricultural Development-Led Industrialization. *Oxford Economics Papers* 46: 136-156.

World Bank (1986), Trade and Pricing Policies in World Agriculture. *World Development Report 1986*. New York: Oxford University Press.

World Bank (1997), Rural Development: From Vision to Action. *A Sector Strategy Paper*. Washington. D.C. The World Bank.

Yesufu T.M. (1996), *The Nigeria Economy Growth without Development*. Benin: Benin Social Science Series for Africa.

13

WTO AND INDIAN AGRICULTURE: ISSUES AND CONCERNS

*K. Dasarathbaramaiah**

INTRODUCTION

Agriculture is the mainstay in the development of the Indian economy. It accounts for about 26 per cent of the Gross domestic product and about two–thirds of the labour force is depending on agriculture for their employment. Agricultural exports account for 20 per cent of the India's exports. India has been a great advantage and potential in the global economic scenario. Agriculture in India has 2.4 per cent area of the world and land area consists of 2.3 per cent, which is 6th rank in the world. The arable land accounts 11.8 per cent of the world, which comprised of 23.6 per cent of the world, which is the second rank next to USA. The irrigated land of 57 million hectares, which comprised of 23.6 per cent share, stood First Rank in the world. As far as agricultural active population is concerned, it is 19.3 per cent of the world has attained 2nd rank next to China.

IMPORTANCE OF AGRICULTURAL SECTOR IN INDIA

The primary role of agriculture is to provide sufficient food and manpower to an expanding industrial economy and

* Associate Professor Department of Economics & Applied Economics, Sri Krishnadevaraya University, Anantapur-515 003, A.P., India.

tertiary economy. Hence, agricultural sector is considered as his dynamic leading sector of overall economic development in the initial stages. Development economists have come into realize that far from playing a passive, supporting role in the process of economic development, agricultural sector in particular and the rural economy in general, are the dynamic and leading sectors in any overall strategy.

At present in India, agriculture engages 65 per cent of the workforce. Agricultural development has assumed greater importance in the context of a growing economy. Higher proportion of agricultural employment coupled with lower share of agricultural output to Gross National Product, therefore, reflects relatively low levels of labour productivity compare with that in advanced countries. The liberalization policy introduced in the year 1991 has pared the way for agricultural export promotion policies. However, the export growth of agricultural sector depends on a host of internal factors like, the domestic production and distribution situation for the exportable commodities

GROWTH OF AGRICULTURAL PRODUCTION IN INDIA

Since independence the contribution of agricultural sector to GDP has been declining in India and GDP of agricultural sector has also been declining at the rate of 3.04 per cent per annum during 1981-82 to 1990. Further it has been declined to 2.9 per cent during 1991-92 to 2001-2002. Despite, the capital formation of agricultural sector has been increasing considerably, it has increased at the rate of 1.11 per cent per annum during a decade of 1981-82 to 1990-91 and it has also been increased to 2.7 per cent during 1991-92 to 2001-2002. The growth rate of major agricultural products registered the declining trend for the last 20 years. Notwithstanding all these adverse effects of productivity growth in agriculture, India has great potential to export agro products to international markets.

ECONOMIC REFORMS AND INDIAN AGRICULTURE

Two significant developments were occurred in the decade of 1990. The first development relates to initiation of economic liberalization as part of the economic reforms started in 1991. The second development concerns to the formulation of WTO. These two developments in 1990s have made a significant impact on India's agricultural trade. It was anticipated that implementation of the WTO agreements would benefit agrarian countries like India. India being an agrarian country does not have a strong service sector. As in all developing countries, the agricultural sector is a dominant one of its economy. Moreover, the developed countries market, that is EU, JAPAN and US have been major export destinations of Indian agricultural exports. In these countries, agricultural sector has always been a protected sector and agro imports were highly restricted. So, with the agricultural sector getting included into mainstream of WTO, India expected a lot in terms of market access for these products. Thus globalization of agricultural trade was further seen as a great opportunity for promoting farm exports.

India launched a process of Economic Reforms in July 1991. Besides macro economic standardization and structural reforms, these reforms are designed to integrate the domestic economy with the global economy. In the beginning, economic reforms bypassed agriculture in terms of direct reforms, except with trade liberalization and relaxation of some export controls over agricultural products. Liberalization in India had a mixed response. There are areas of success and areas of failures. But the areas of success are more than areas of failures. We are able to stabilize the economy and bring structural changes in various sectors. Despite Global recession, the Indian economy is counted as one of the best performing countries in the World.

The GDP of India has improved marginally after liberalization. The revenue deficit was 2.1 per cent as against 3.2 per cent, the primary deficit was 4.45 per cent as against 0.60 per cent, and the fiscal deficit was 7.4 per cent as against 5 per cent during 1980-90 and 1990-00 respectively. The gross domestic capital formation was 22.6 per cent and 22.9 per cent respectively during the same period. The performance of all these indicators showed better performance during the second half of the reforms period i.e., 1996-2001 as compared to the first half of the reforms period, i.e., 1991-96. The private saving ratio to GDP in the country improved from 16 per cent during 1981-90 to 22 per cent during 1991-2000. The inflation ratio was reduced from double-digit figure of 12 per cent in the early 1990's to single digit figure of 3 per cent in 2002. It has obtained substantial gains after liberalization. Thus liberalization helped Indian economy to develop the nation.

GLOBALIZATION AND AGRICULTURE IN INDIA

Globalization aims at the integration of the domestic economy with the global economy and the optimum utilization of growth potential. The process of globalization has revolutionized world agriculture. Hence, in the process of globalization, all the sectors of the economy are directed to improve the efficiency, productivity and cost competitiveness. The development and growth of each sector depends on its ability to supply quality goods at international competitive price. Globalization of agriculture mainly implies the exposure of Indian agriculture to international market forces through free exports and imports of agricultural commodities.

If the policies of globalization have created a conducive environment to the agricultural sector for its development, there should be sizeable increase in production and corresponding increase in the exports of agricultural commodities. Developing countries are becoming more influenced by the business and social culture of industrialized countries. In addition, most developing countries have undertaken their own Structural Adjustments Programmes designed to liberalise both their internal and external economies.

As India has steered its economic policies towards increased participation in the global economy, a range of political, ideological and economic parameters have been modified, while others are likely to be more drastically revised in the future. However, India's basic commitment to its constitution remains paramount, globalization will continue to be subject to the democratic process.

When the trade and GDP ratio is taken as an approximate measure for indicating the extent of globalization in general, trade of agricultural commodities and GDP ratio may be taken as a measure for indicating the extent of globalization in the agricultural sector. The agricultural trade and GDP ratio was 2.42 in 1980-81 and has come down to 1.29 in 1990-91. From 1991-92, the ratio started improving marginally and reached 2.12 in 1995-96. With fluctuations, it has reached 1.95 in 2000-01. However, the extent of overall globalization, measured as the ratio of total trade and GDP, has increased from 15.05 in 1990-91 to 22.92 in 2000-01. This clearly points out the fact that agricultural sector could not develop its position even to retain its earlier position (2.42 in 1980-81) and the industrial and manufacturing sectors have exceeded the agricultural sector in their contribution to the process of globalization. A declining share of agriculture in the process of globalization means that agricultural sector is lagging behind in development compared to other sectors of the economy.

GATT AND AGRICULTURE IN INDIA

GATT was found in 1947 with the objective of prescribing the rules for international trade. The principal purpose of GATT is to expand international trade by liberating trade so as to bring about all-round economic prosperity. The basic recommendations of GATT in relating to agriculture are [a] Non–Tariff barriers like quotas imposed by nations on foreign agricultural products will be converted into tariffs, which will be reduced by 36 per cent in case of developing nations. [b] By 1999, the term subsidies should not exceed 10 per cent of the value of the output of a product. Trade distorting support for farmers will be cut by 20 per cent over 6 years for developed countries. [c] The value of export direct subsidies will have to cut by 36 per cent and the volume by 21 per cent over the next 6 years by the developed countries. [d] Countries having a closed market for agricultural products have to import at least 3 per cent of their domestic consumption. (e) Regarding the prohibition of export subsidies, GATT agreement stipulates that countries like India with per capita income less than $1000 are exempted from the removal of such subsidies for products where their share in world trade is less than 3.25 per cent.

WORLD TRADE ORGANIZATION (WTO) AND AGRICULTURE

The new world trade organization (WTO) which replaces the GATT had came into effect from January 1, 1995 with the backing of at least 85 founding member countries, including India. The major objectives of the WTO are (a) by recognizing that their relations in the field of trade and economic endeavor should be conducted with a view to raising standards of living, (b) ensuring full employment and a large and steadily growing volume of real income and effective demand and expanding the production of trade in goods and services, (c) while allowing for the optimal use of the world's resources in accordance with the objective of sustainable development, seeking both to protect and preserve the environment and to enhance the means for doing in a manner consistent with their respective needs and concerns at different levels of economic development. All most all countries have now committed themselves to the objectives associated with their membership of the WTO. In order to meet these objectives, member countries are obliged to reform many of their existing internal economic policies and external trade policies.

WTO Agreement on Agriculture stipulated that developed countries would reduce their subsidies by 20 per cent in six years and developing countries by 13 per cent in 10 years. But as facts stand today, developed countries tried to circumvent this agreement by providing Green Box and Blue Box subsidies to support agriculture.

Green Box: A Green Box subsidy includes amount spent on Government services such as research, disease control, and infrastructure and food security. They also include payments made directly to farmers that do not stimulate production, such as certain forms of direct income support assistance to help farmers to restructure agriculture, and direct payments under environmental and regular assistance programmes. This definition is very wide and includes all types of government subsidies.

The 'Green box' covers subsidies that are expected to cause minimal or no trade distortions. In simple words, it includes direct income support for European, US and Japanese farmers, which is formally decoupled from production levels and prices. 'Green box' also includes subsidies granted in the name of environment protection and preservation, and for agricultural research and development. In reality, these subsidies are termed 'non-trade distorting' because of the ability of only the rich countries to provide for such support.

Blue Box: Blue Box subsidies are certain direct payments made to farmers where the farmers are to limit production, certain government assistance programmes to encourage agriculture and rural development in developing countries, and other support on a small scale when compared with the total value of the products supported 15 percent or less in the case of developed countries and 10 per cent or less for developing countries.

Domestic support subsidies in developing countries are not allowed to increase their negligible level of export subsidies while developed countries are allowed 64 per cent of their subsidy outlays on the base level. Consequently, agricultural imports from developed countries are available at much below the market price in the domestic economy. Earlier, Indian agricultural prices were mostly lower than international prices. But as a result of the heavy subsidization of agricultural exports by developed countries, the situation undertook a dramatic about-turn. The Indian farmers have been put to serious disadvantage.

TRIPS AND INDIAN AGRICULTURE

Trade Related Intellectual Property Rights (TRIPs) is an out come of historic Uruguay Round of Trade Negotiations during 1986. The TRIPs agreement covers the patents of plant and seed variety, micro-organism copyrights and neighboring rights, trademarks, including services marks, integrated circuits and geographical indication. Under the TRIPs Agreement, India has agreed to accept applications from January 1, 1995 onwards. The applications will be received in the "Mailbox" and will be examined only with effect from January 1, 2005. Further, India's domestic policy has undergone various changes to adjust to this new international scenario. The latest legislation in this regard is the protection of plant and farmer's rights Act, 2001, passed by the parliament of India.

The major provisions of this act are (a) breeders or farmers can claim IPR for their varieties provided that it meets the criteria of novelty, distinctness, uniformity and stability, (b) This IPR comes in the form of plant breeder's rights defined as the exclusive right to produce, sell, market, distribute, import or export the variety, (c) A farmer can save, use, exchange, share or sell his farm produce including seeds of the protected variety (d) after receiving a claim and examining the case, the authority would decide the amount of compensation that breeder must pay under this gene fund. The Act included the limitation on this right, such as the term is limited to 18 years for trees and vines and 15 years for extent varieties and all other fields. Thus, in future, India would gain by ensuring access to materials it needed to promote agricultural research and development. India could strengthen its bargaining power by negotiating multilaterally for royalty payments and transfer of technology.

TARIFFS AND SUBSIDIES

There are several provisions in the WTO agreement restricting the assistance to agricultural sector. WTO agreements specify that the value of farm subsidy allowed should not be more than 10 per cent of the value of production and input subsidies should be granted only to low income farmers. Also member countries should open up their market to the tune of 3 to 5 per cent of the total domestic consumption. If they face balance of payment crisis, they are exempted from this. Since India comes under the category of a country with BOP problem, this provision does not affect its agriculture at present. According to WTO agreement, developing countries should eliminate Quantitative Restrictions on import of both agricultural and consumer goods. But they can impose tariff on such imports to discourage the import on non-essential goods. Developing countries, suffering from Balance of Payments crisis, can use Quantitative Restrictions. At present India is maintaining Quantitative Restrictions on few agricultural and consumer goods.

Similar is the case with tariff cuts. It can be managed in such a way that there is substantial reduction in tariffs of less protected products with negligible cuts in tariff for the highly protected commodities. In the EU, for instance products like meat, milk and cream, cheese, rice, wheat floor and bran continue to carry tariffs of over 120 per cent. As a result, the potential gains to a country like India remains elusive. India, therefore, must insist on the maximum tariffs not to be more than 50 per cent on any tariff line relating to agriculture.

AGREEMENT ON AGRICULTURE (AOA)

Agriculture has hitherto remained outside the framework of GATT and the industrialized countries have been heavily subsidizing and protecting their agriculture thereby completely distorting world production and trade of Temperate Zone of agricultural foodstuffs. The Agreement on Agriculture has only in theory favoured agriculture in developing countries, but in practice, its implementation has seriously affected agriculture in developing countries.

Agreement on Agriculture (AOA) was made under GATT, 1994 to achieve greater liberalization of trade in agriculture. The main objectives of AOA are, (a) to establish a basis for initiating a process of reform of trade in agriculture, (b) to establish a fair and market-oriented agricultural trading system, (c) to provide for substantial progressive reductions in agricultural support and protection sustained over an agreed period of time, resulting in correcting and preventing restrictions and distortions in world agricultural markets, (d) to achieve specific binding commitments in market access, domestic support, export competition and (e) to provide social and differential treatment for developing countries is an integral element of the negotiations and taking into account the possible negative effects of the implementation of the reform programme on least-developed and net food-importing developing countries.

There are five major provisions of AOA, namely, (a) market access (Tariffication), (b) reduction in domestic support, (c) export competition, (d) TRIPs and (e) sanitary and phyto-sanitary provisions. The basic aim of all these provisions is to end the era of protectionism and to initiate a competitive, free and efficiency-based growth. So, the agreement was introduced to raise the volume of world trade in agricultural products. The commitments under domestic subsidy require that the members should reduce the extent of domestic support (subsidies, support prices) to the agricultural sector.

It is obvious that WTO commitments will increase access of agricultural commodities in the world market. But commitments are such that they have trade distorting effects. Such is the commitments on aggregate measures of support (AMS). At present, reduction commitments are on total AMS. This implies that a country can offer substantial domestic support to one or more commodities and yet have an overall total AMS within the commitment level. India should, therefore, press for reduction commitments on product specific AMS rather than total AMS, arguing for a ceiling of not more than 20 per cent.

Salient features of the AOA: The Agreement applied to the agricultural products, such as manitol, sorfitol, essential oils, albuminoidal substances, hides and skins, raw fur skins, raw silk, wool and animal hair, raw cotton, raw flax, raw hemp etc. A member shall not provide support in favor of domestic producers in excess of the commitment levels. A member shall not provide the listed export subsidies in respect of the specified agricultural products or groups of products in excess of the budgetary outlay and quantity commitment levels specified therein and shall not provide such subsidies in respect of any agricultural product not specified in that selection of its schedule. The Agreement on Agriculture precludes a counting from support in favor of domestic producers in excess of the levels specified in its schedule but excludes from the calculation support which does not exceed 5 per cent of the value of production of a particular product of 5 per cent of the total value of agricultural production. In developing countries, the relevant percentage is 10 per cent. The level of support provided by a country is measured in terms of Aggregate Measurement of Support (AMS). An AMS shall be calculated for each basic product receiving market price support, non-exempt direct payment or any other non-exempt support as well as support provided to the agricultural sector as a whole.

The Agreement allows governmental programmes which provide infrastructural support to agriculture or rural areas such as research, pest and disease control, inspection services, training and advisory services, marketing and promotional services, water supply, dams and drainage schemes, roads and other means of transportation. The Agreement exempts governmental expenditure relating to public stockholding for food security purposes from reduction requirements if the operation of such programme is transparent and follows officially published objective criteria.

INCENTIVES TO AGRICULTURAL SECTOR IN DEVELOPED COUNTRIES

The agricultural activities in developed countries receive a number of supports from the government. Further in these countries farming activities are undertaken as a commercial proportion through large scale farming with capital intensive and advanced technology. A review of domestic support shows that the total support to agriculture for the OEDC countries together mounted to around 361 millions of U.S. Dollars in 1999, representing 3 per cent rise over the previous year's level. The countries belonging to European Free Trade Association (EFTA) have been among the highest PSEs in the world. Another group of countries that heavily protects its agriculture is the East Asian group, comprising Japan, South Korea, Taiwan and a few other countries.

The developed countries have agreed to adopt WTO Agreement on Agriculture in principle and they make an illusion that they are implementing the agreement. An objective and comprehensive assessment reveals that they continue to extent support to the agricultural sector in several forms. It is interesting to note that high support levels to agriculture in OECD countries are not visible when one looks at their Aggregate Measure of Support (AMS) and the commitments they have undertaken to reduce that. United

States has given a subsidy of 40 billions of US Dollars to less than 10 million farmers.

INCENTIVES TO AGRICULTURAL SECTOR IN INDIA

Compared to the developed countries, the subsidies given to the agricultural sector in India are very meager and these subsidies are not inducing the farmers to undertake farming activities as business; rather they help the farmers to sustain in the agricultural sector at subsistence level. In many cases, marginal and small farmers undertake farming activities even if the return does not cover the actual cost, just to meet their domestic requirements. In several cases, Indian farmers remain net buyers of food grains only.

The estimates of domestic support to Indian agriculture have been negative in all the years. A comparative study on the subsidies to US farmer and Indian farmer reveals that the average subsidy given to a farmer in the United States comes about 12000 U.S. Dollars, whereas the subsidy given to a farmer in India worksout to a meager value of 6.3 U.S. Dollars. This comparison provides an indication and idea about the level of support and incentives given to the agricultural sector in India. Further India hardly provides any export subsidies in agriculture, except for a very small sum as freight subsidy for some horticultural products. From all available accounts, it is thus clear that India is providing no support to the farmers, rather it is trying to taxing agriculture.

AOA AND DEVELOPING COUNTRIES

The developing countries which did not apply domestic support and export subsidy measures earlier, have naturally not recorded them in their schedules; and thereby they have been debarred from applying these measures in future beyond the de minimize levels. This is highly intuition. As their farmers generally are in a disadvantaged position, compared to those in developed countries, it is only fair to lift this restriction. In the content of Article 3 of the agreement, there should be an understanding that developing countries will not be subjected to this restriction. Similarly, the developing countries that have given their schedules of reduction of domestic support and export subsidy should be allowed flexibility to enhance the levels of these measures or to lessen the pace of reduction of the levels. It will be dangerous for developing countries to depend on imported food, as their foreign exchange position is often not comfortable, and the provision of food for the population is of essential. Hence, what is needed is that developing countries should be encouraged to produce food for their domestic population. The current disciplines on import control and domestic support may hamper their efforts in this direction. The food products in developing countries should be excluded from the disciplines of import control and domestic support.

Many developing countries have a larger number of small farmers, whose farming activities will not be able to stand up to a large scale of international competition. They need protection, otherwise there will be large-scale unemployment and spread of poverty in these countries. Developing countries should have flexibility regarding import restraint and domestic subsidy for the protection of and support to household subsistence farming and small-scale family. The current provision regarding relief to the net food-importing developing countries does not contain specific and concrete action for the relief. In fact, hardly anything has been done in this regard. There is a need for some specific action to provide relief to those developing countries.

AGREEMENT ON AGRICULTURE: IMPLICATIONS TO INDIA

The WTO Agreement on agriculture primarily aims at the removal of trade distortions resulting from different levels of input subsidies, price and market support, export subsidy and other kinds of trade distorting supports. Hence, the Agreement on Agriculture directs to replace all quantitative restrictions on agricultural commodities by appropriate tariff measures. Member countries are therefore expected to go for complete Tariffication. All the restrictions on farm trade should be through tariffs only. Within the time agreed upon the tariffs should be then progressively reduced. The WTO Agreement further requires reduction in Aggregate Measure Support and export subsidies. In the area of export subsidy, WTO Agreement emphasizes the reduction of direct export subsidies to a level of 24 per cent of developing countries within a period of six years.

The developing countries, if necessary, can provide certain subsidies such as those of export marketing costs, internal and international transport and freight charges etc. There is a remarkable change after the Agreement of Agriculture in Indian food trade as evident from the mean trade indices. This is really great concern for India. During the post AOA period the production of cereals and pulses increased at the rate of 6 per cent and 12 per cent respectively. In the case of developed countries both of these decreased by 9.37 million tonnes and 2.46 million tonnes respectively during the same period. However, export of food grains from India improved in the post agreement period. Trade liberalization is a mixed bag and its impact could vary from commodity to commodity. The process of economic reforms created favorable terms of trade.

The benefits from the trade liberalization have not brought the significant results and it is evident from the structure of production of crops in different economies and the global trade in the post AOA period. Though the production of cereals increased by 110 million tonnes with almost six per cent increase during the post agreement period, the trade share in production remains 12 per cent. However, the export of food grains from India improved in the post agreement period and it is also clear from the imports that India adopted strongly outward oriented policies for economic development. Rationalizing the domestic tax structure, capitalizing the steady exports market and pushing the processing sectors are major agenda.

To understand the implications, we have to discuss the performance of India's agricultural exports under WTO regime.

PERFORMANCE OF INDIA'S AGRICULTURAL EXPORTS UNDER WTO

It was expected that under WTO, the entry of agricultural products from India in the world market would be without much restriction owing to market predictability, reduction in aggregate measures of support (AMS) and export subsidies. Undoubtedly, there are significant improvements in India's agricultural exports after the adoption of New Economic Policy in 1991. Increasing production on a sustained basis, rising exportable surplus after catering the domestic needs and quality improvement through proper processing are among the major essential conditions for export promotion of Agricultural products. Low level of out put and tough market conditions added by the policy of protectionism in disguise, adopted by the developed countries have been the leading factors for our poor performance of agricultural exports. Despite a comparatively higher growth rate in exports, the share of agricultural exports in total exports has shown a declining trend as shown in the following table.

Table I
Growth rate and percentage share of agricultural exports India

Products	*Annual Average Growth Rate* *1980-81 to 1990-91*	*1992-93 to 1999-2000*
Agriculture and Allied	3.3	8.1
Products	(24.2)	(18.3)
Manufactured Goods	10.1	10.6
	(62.0)	(76.6)
Total Exports	7.4	10.1
	(100.00)	(100.00)

Source: Govt. of India: Economic survey, 2000-2001
Note: Figures in Parentheses Indicates Percentage share of Agricultural Exports

India's exports of principal agricultural product reveals a discouraging trend. The exports of tea and coffee declined from 9 per cent and 8 per cent to 7.2 per cent and 4.3 per cent respectively during 1998-99 to2000-01 as shown in table 2. The share of exports of cereals from India increased form 16.2 per cent of the total agricultural products in 1996-97 to 24.9 per cent in 1998-99. However, its share in total agricultural exports declined from 24.9 per cent to 12.4 per cent during 1998-99 to 2000-01. The share of fruits and Vegetables to total agro products increased from 3.0 per cent to 4.1 per cent during 1996-97 to 2000-01. The export of processed fruits and juices are also increased from 0.9 per cent to 2.0 per cent during the same period. Regarding to the products of meat and preparations and marine products (allied activities) share of total agricultural exports increased from 2.9 per cent to 5.4 per cent and 16.5 per cent to 23.2 per cent during the period 1996-97 to 2000-2001 respectively. However, due to various reasons percentage of agricultural products to total exports declined from 18.2 per cent to 13.5 per cent.

Table 2
India's Exports of Principal Agricultural Products

Product	*1996-97*	*1997-98*	*1998-99*	*1999-2000*	*2000-01*
Tea	292	505	538	407	433
	(4.3)	(7.7)	(9.0)	(7.4)	(7.2)
Coffee	412	456	411	315	259
	(5.9)	(6.9)	(6.8)	(5.7)	(4.3)
Cereals	1104	910	1495	918	744
	(16.2)	(31.8)	(24.9)	(31.1)	(12.4)
Tobacco	213	288	181	229	191
	(3.1)	(4.4)	(3.0)	(4.2)	(3.2)
Spices	339	379	388	393	354
	(5.0)	(5.8)	(6.5)	(7.2)	(5.9)
Cashew	362	337	387	566	411
	(5.3)	(5.7)	(6.4)	(10.3)	(6.8)
Sesame and Niger seed	78	81	78	86	131
	(1.1)	(1.2)	(1.3)	(1.6)	(2.2)
Gaurgum meal	100	147	173	189	322
	(1.9)	(2.2)	(2.9)	(3.9)	(5.9)
Oil meals	985	924	461	370	448
	(14.4)	(14.0)	(7.7)	(6.8)	(7.5)
Fruits & Vegetables	208	204	183	208	248
	(3.0)	(3.1)	(3.1)	(3.7)	(4.1)
Processed fruits & Juices	59	73	69	113	112
	(0.9)	(1.1)	(1.1)	(2.1)	(2.0)
Meat & Preparations	200	217	183	180	322
	(2.9)	(3.3)	(3.1)	(3.3)	(5.4)
Marine products	1129	1207	1038	1180	1394
	(16.5)	(18.3)	(17.3)	(21.6)	(23.2)
Others	1359	824	422	527	815
	(19.9)	(12.5)	(7.0)	(9.6)	(13.6)
Total Agrl. Exports	6828	6594	6014	5475	6004
	(100)	(100)	(100)	(100)	(100)

Source: Govt. of India, Economic survey, 2000-2001 Page No.168.
Note: Figures in Parentheses Indicates Percentage share of Total Agricultural Exports

The Performance of agricultural exports of India has been classified into two periods Pre–Reforms period (1960-61 to 1990-91) and Post Reform period (1995-2001). During the Pre-Reforms period, agricultural exports as per cent of total exports of India declined from 44.2 per cent in 1960-61 to 19.4 per cent is 1990–91 (see table3). During the post-reforms period also the share of agricultural exports to total exports of India declined from 19.8 per cent to 13.5 per cent during 1995-96 to 2000-01. India's share in the world exports during the pre-reforms period also declined from 1.2 per cent in 1960-61 to 0.5 per cent during 1990-91. It shows that there was a significant declining trend during the pre-reforms period relating to India's exports to total world's exports. However, during the second phase, India's exports as a percentage of total world's exports increased slightly from 0.6 per cent in 1995-96 to 0.7 per cent in 2000-2001.

Table 3
Performance of Indian Exports ($ Million)

Year	*India's Agricultural Exports*	*India's Total Exports*	*World Total Exports*	*India's Agricultural Exports as % of Total Exports*	*India's total Exports as % of world total Exports*
			Pre- Reforms period		
1960-61	596	1346	113200	44.2	1.2
1970-71	644	2031	313804	31.7	0.6
1980-81	2601	8486	1997686	30.6	0.4
1990-91	3521	18143	3303563	19.4	0.5
			Post-Reforms Period		
1995-96	6320	31797	4951450	19.8	0.6
1997-98	6840	35006	5363038	18.5	0.6
1998-99	6205	33218	5075047	18.2	0.6
1999-00	5773	36822	5627000	15.2	0.6
2000-01	6246	44560	6319700	13.5	0.7

Source: Economic Survey, various issues.

Let us objectively examine the effects of India's commitments to WTO in the context of agricultural sector. The following uses and abuses are expected to accrue to India from liberalization of its foreign trade under WTO regime.

USES: The major uses of WTO Agreement on Agriculture to developing countries especially India are as follows. The reduction of export subsidies on agriculture by developed countries will make Indian agricultural exports more competitive in world markets. So, India would be in a position to increase export quantum of wheat, rice and sugar at higher prices. India can push up productivity and slash cost of production. The clubbing of product and non-product agricultural subsidies will allow much greater flexibility to provide subsidies for agricultural production. The accord provides for a subsidy level of ten per cent of the value of agricultural production which is far higher than the current level of subsidy in India.

Reduction in Tariffs by the developed countries should work to the advantage of India rather than its disadvantages. With the reduction in tariff, it should be possible to enter the markets of the developed countries as well. Naturally, they will depend on identifying those agricultural commodities in which India has a comparative advantage. The AOA is expected to give a new impetus to agricultural trade in the international market. The developing countries like India too will benefit provided the developed countries adhere to all the provisions of the Agreement. India's gains depend upon the level and type of technology used and the size of the market developed for agricultural commodities apart from the level of inflation in relation to other countries.

Due to globalization, food grains production in India will be increased and if the country maintains 4 per cent of growth rate in agricultural production, then after meeting its domestic demand, the country can export the surplus amount of food grains to the foreign countries. Another impact of globalization has been felt that it boosted the productivity of agricultural resources. Increasing potentiality of the agricultural sector as emerged from the liberalization/globalization wave has set up new trends in horticulture, floriculture and animal husbandry and has created ample opportunities and scope for employment of huge number of population. This allied sector being labor intensive can provide better solution to the unemployment problem in rural India.

Abuses: On the other hand the Agreement on Agriculture has some negative effects in India. Subsidization in India resulted in lowering the prices of agricultural products, and thus India is unable to compete on agricultural commodities. Most developed countries provide a heavy subsidy on agriculture. It is a problem to the Indian farmers with the reduction of Quantitative Restrictions. The farmers will be badly hit as developed countries are avoiding the domestic reduction commitments in one pretext or other.

Special and differential treatment is available only for least developed countries. The concessions given to the developing countries like India in terms of long transition period etc., do not recognize their qualitatively different position in the world economic structure. In each of the areas under discussion, namely market access, domestic support and export competition, the developing countries like India have been given a raw deal.

The forced opening up of the Indian market is one of the most dangerous consequences of the draft. It will be totally wrong to assume that India can be protected from those provisions on market access by taking recourse to the provision on balance of payments.

The developing countries are also supposed to grant a minimum market access of 2 per cent of domestic consumption in 1993, to be increased to 3.33 per cent by 2003. Therefore the domestic market is also going to be opened up in the case of many commodities which were not imported earlier. The denial of the right to use subsidies would prevent the government from using subsidies as an instrument to change the cropping pattern. The Agreement allows some forms of domestic support which can be used by the developed countries to continue to support their agriculture. The support systems in developed countries allow farmers to export below the cost of production and this leads for dumping in Indian Market.

FUTURE STAND OF AGRICULTURE IN INDIA

In view of WTO stipulations and the Doha declaration 2001, Indian Government has to review its policies on Agriculture, specifically relating to self sufficiency in food grains and the burden of subsidies. The agriculture development strategy should aim at increasing the value added per hectare, improving the productivity of agricultural inputs and irrigation, prevention of environmental and ecological degradation and supporting the self-help institutions of the farmers.

All the States must evince keen interest in implementing the reforms in agricultural sector. To increase the productivity in Indian Agriculture, more investment on agriculture is essential. To raise the high value crops which give high income to the farmers, encouragement of contract farming on small forms is necessary. Production and Processing of high value crops are to be separated and the value addition in processing is to be organized by the farmers' cooperatives. Minimum support price and procurement prices are to be distinguished and the continuous rise in the later is to be restricted.

In India, at present, to review and rationalization of agricultural input subsidies is to be the major concern. Subsidies are to be withdrawn progressively and the amount saved is to be used to strengthen the rural infrastructure and extension. Minimum support should be extended through crop insurance for limited important crops and all high rich crops. Full utilization of Green Box measures is necessary to enhance the ability of Indian Agriculture of drive home the gains from the Agreement on Agriculture. The domestic support to agriculture is to be qualified by Aggregate Measure of Support. It is necessary to maintain the gap between fixed external reference price and applied administered price to keep the market price support within limits. In the area of export competition, agricultural commodities receive no export subsidies in India. Hence, India has the right to ask for compensation from subsidy giving exporting countries for the potential loss of her markets. Further, India, a non-subsidiary country has to take advantage of the right to impose countervailing duty equivalent to the export subsidy by exporting nations.

The transitional period to implement the provisions of Agreement on Agriculture should be extended for another five years. Specification in the terms and conditions, structure of tariff which enhanced to India is necessary. Indian Government has to restructure the export subsidies to ensure Indian exports to be competitive in the world market. India has to study the impact of phasing out quantitative restrictions on the basis of her balance of payments problems. India has to expand its access to cost effective modern technologies particularly the agricultural technology to make a major impact on the cost of production and prices of agricultural commodities.

CONCLUSIONS

The decade of 1990s witnessed two significant developments. The first development relates to initiation of economic liberalization in the country in 1991 and the second development relates to established of WTO in 1995. In many ways India is favorably placed to take advantage of certain provision of WTO. As India has steered its economic policies towards increased participation in the global economy, a range of political, ideological and economic parameters have been modified, while others are likely to be more drastically revised in future, with the entry of WTO agreement, India expected a lot in terms of market access for those products. It is obvious that the commitments of WTO agreement will increase access of agricultural commodities are such that they have trade distortion effects.

In the changed world economic scenario it is desirable to give priority to the agricultural sector to protect the nation's economy. Thus there is a need to accept the liberalized agricultural trade. Globalization helps to reduce poverty and to raise the living standards of the rural people. Globalization of agriculture mainly implies the exposure of Indian agriculture to the international market forces through free exports and imports of agricultural commodities. The reforms suggested in agricultural programme to farmers. The scaling down of exports subsidies to form products in the developed countries should produce beneficial effects on countries like India.

Due to the WTO agreement on agriculture there will be a rise in the prices of the agricultural inputs but India's market opportunities in the exports of agricultural commodities would raise automatically. The tariffication process stipulated by WTO is gradual and it provides adequate scope for adjustment. The ceilings of tariff agreed by WTO are indeed fairly high. Hence, the government should protect the agricultural sector and formers using the upper limit of tariffs agreed by WTO and side3 by side should solve the internal problems of agricultural sector for the development of agricultural sector, a proper Mix of reform policies, tariffication and support policies should be designed by the policy makers in a developing country like India.

REFERENCES

Ahluwalia, M.S. (1996), " New Economic Policy and Agriculture: some Reflections" Indian Journal of Agricultural Economics, Vol.51,No.5.

Alagh Y.K. (2003), *Globalization and Agricultural Crisis in India,* Deep & Deep Publications, New Delhi.

Anderson, K. (2001), *Globalization, WTO and ASEAN,* Asian Economic Bulletin, Vol.18, No.1, April.

Ashok Gulati and Tim Kenlay (1999), *Trade Liberalization and Indian Agriculture,* Oxford University press, New Delhi.

Devinder Sharma (2004), *WTO and Agriculture,* Economic and political weekly, may 15.

Govt. of India: *Economic Survey,* Various issues

Gulati Ashok (2000), Indian Agriculture and WTO preparing for New Millennium, 83rd I.E.A. Conference volume.

Gupta S.P (1998), *Liberalization,* Macmillan, New Delhi.

Hanumantha Rao, Ch, (2001), "WTO and viability of Indian Agriculture", Economic and Political weekly, September 8. 2001.

Mynemi, S.R. (1996), *International Economic Law,* Pioneer Books, New Delhi.

Nagesh Kumar, (1999), *Globalisation and its Effects on Indian Economy,* Economic and political weekly, march 4,

Paramjit Nanda (1998), *Performance of Indian Exports,* Deep and Deep Publications, New Delhi.

14

GLOBALISATION: IS IT DRIVING INDUSTRIAL RELATIONS IN REVERSE GEAR?

*P. Subba Rao**

INTRODUCTION

The business across the border of the countries had been carried out since times immemorial. The post World War II period witnessed an unexpected expansion of national companies of mostly capitalistic countries into international or multinational companies. The post 1990s period has given greater fillip to international business due to globalisation of world economies along with the strides in information technology. Thus the phenomenal change in economic and technological environments brought significant changes in the business. Though the business environment comprises of social, technical, economic, political, international and natural environments, the type of economic system that a country adapts decides the major part of the environment. Most of the countries initially adapted capitalistic economic systems and later shifted to communistic/socialistic or mixed economic system/socialistic pattern of societies as a result of revolutions

* Professor of Business Administration, School of Business Administration, University of Papua New Guinea, PO Box: 320, University P.O., N.C.D., Papua New Guinea.

or demands of the masses. These types of economic systems necessitated the Governments to play the role of businessmen also as a part of discharging their responsibilities of being the custodian of the nation. This role made the Governments to use the public sector mainly as a means to achieve their objectives and control the private sector toward its ends. As such the economic environment in such countries did not allow either the domestic or foreign businesses to formulate and implement competitive strategies and to give the best to the customer. In deed businesses formulated non-competitive strategies centred on the governments' protective policies (Skaria George, 1996:28-33). Human resource management strategies in various companies in these countries-derivates of corporate strategies-were also centred on the employee protection that in turn led to the emergence of various industrial relations institutions to check and control the implementation process of employee protection (Subbarao, 2003: 130).

Governments in capitalistic economic systems, in contrast, provide free and deregulated environment to the business to operate and formulate competitive corporate as well as human resource management strategies (Human Resource Management Journal, 1997: 50). Further, globalisation provides free and deregulated environment for the business in all those countries whose economies are opened for the rest of the globe. As such business in such economies centre their strategies on customer, but not on humanness of human resources as they treat all resources equally for the purpose of winning the customer deliciousness. The deregulated environment created by the Governments and/or globalisation discourages most of the business regulative institutions or measures including industrial relations institutions, which hampers the freedom of the business to operate competitively. As such the terms and conditions of employment of human resource management are mostly determined by the market forces, as is the case with other resources. Therefore, human resource management structure and industrial relations pattern are based on the theme of the corporate strategies that, in turn, are shaped mostly by the country's economic system and/or globalisation. Thus, globalisation along with the capitalistic economic system results in insignificant role for business regulating devices including industrial relations institutions (Sundeep Khanna, 1996). Against this thesis, an attempt is made to find-out the impact of globalisation on human resource management structure and on the industrial relations pattern.

Globalisation tends to result in exchange of the cultures across the globe, location of manufacturing centres and/or various business processes in and spread of markets to various countries. Thus globalisation led to internationalisation of capital, human resources, markets, material, management and manufacturing posing sever competition to the companies of developing countries from multinational and translational companies not only in their home counties but also in various foreign countries wherever they operate (Subbarao, 2003: 114-121). This multidimensional competition made the companies to align and realign all their strategies, operations and resources including human resources around the customer and adapted customisation approach. Customisation approach to business was in fact, the earliest approach and it is coming back in a different degree (Moffat, 1990: 132-135 and Kotler, 2003: 36-37). This process has its impact on management of various resources including human resources.

Businesses' sole objective, during their early days of operation, was profit maximization through cost minimization of all inputs including labour. Then they followed commodity approach, machinery concept and factor of production approach to labour. Owners' of businesses in those days exploit the labour by following individual approach to human resource management viz., wages based on demand and supply factors and performance of individual employee etc., and maintenance of industrial relations with individual employees, but not with a group of employees. Thus the individualistic approach to HRM in those days resulted in individual based industrial relations. This approach along with the then prevailing capitalistic pattern in India led to excessive and undue exploitation of labour particularly in tea, coffee and rubber plantations and Jute and Cotton textile industries until the early 1920s. The cumulative effect of such exploitation led to the formation of first all India trade union in 1920 i.e., All India Trade Union Congress, which inspired the formation of a number of company level trade unions and other all India unions like Indian National Trade Union Congress, Centre for Indian Trade Unions and Hind Mazdoor Sabha (Subbarao, 1999: 511-515). Emergence of these trade unions along with their militant tendency and revolutionary approaches clog the labour exploitation to some extent through the establishment of industrial relations institution like Collective Bargaining, Labour Welfare Officers, Joint Consultative Committees, Standing Orders and Tripartite and Bipartite Bodies. In addition, Government started playing its role by involving itself in the industrial relations process and by enacting labour legislations. These developments changed the individualistic approach to collective approach of HRM, which in turn shifted the industrial relations from individual employee-employer relations to collective relations among employees, employer, trade unions and the Government.

India's choice of mid-way of economic system i.e., mixed economy and subsequent trend of socialistic pattern of society enabled the trade unions to protect the workers even unduly by regulating the managements and taking the advantage of the labour laws in force, resulting in absence of work culture, formation of employee negative mind set, high demands and lower contributions of the employee and the like. This was more prevalent in public sector particularly during 1960s and 1980s. These developments to a considerable extent resulted in negative performance of most of the public sector undertakings and limited performance of and low labour productivity in private sector.

At this point of time, most of the economies in the world including the erstwhile communistic counties have chosen capitalistic pattern of society/market economies in view of the limitations of communism and/or due to the conditions laid by International Monetary Fund and World Bank. This global trend along with the huge fiscal deficit and crisis in balance of payments forced the Government of India to globalise its economy in 1991 and create a favourable climate for restoration of capitalistic tendencies or markets economic situations.

Papua New Guinea (PNG) is relatively a newly born country, which got its Independence on September 16th 1975. PNG globalised her economy in 1986 along with the major world economies. Against this background, an attempt is made to know the impact of globalisation on industrial relations via human resource management in India and Papua New Guinea during the post-globalisation period.

OBJECTIVES

The objectives of this paper are:

- To examine the impact to globalisation on the industrial relations institutions and pattern in India and Papua New Guinea, and
- To identity the cause and effect relationship among globalisation, human resource management and industrial relations in these two developing countries.

METHODOLOGY

Impact of the globalisation on significant areas of industrial relations in selected public and private sector companies in India and Papua New Guinea has been studied. Companies are randomly selected representing both manufacturing and service sectors in India and Papua New Guinea. Both secondary and primary sources of information are resorted to collect necessary information for writing this paper. Structured questionnaires were canvassed electronically to selected companies and trade unions in India and personal interviews were conducted with the present and the former human resource and other executives, trade union leaders and labour historians in Papua New Guinea in order to collect necessary information. However, limited responses of the respondents and availability of less time at the disposal of the researcher have been the limitations of the study.

IMPACT OF GLOBALISATION ON SALARIES AND BENEFITS

Government of India before globalisation favoured socialistic pattern of society and consequently minimization of inequalities in the distribution of incomes and salaries. In fact, these were the trends in many countries before globalisation particularly in socialistic pattern of societies and communistic counties. But, the market economies around the globe disfavoured these trends and set a new trend for wage differentials in order to attract high skilled and talented employees (Human Capital, 1999:16). In addition, market forces determine the price for all resources, products and services including labour. Thus globalisation results in higher salaries and benefits for those employees whose skills are in greater demand and lower salaries for those employees whose skills are in abundant supply (Human Capital, 2001:18).

In addition, globalisation also set trends for adjustment of salaries based on performance. As such different employers working on the same job get different salaries based on their performance levels, as is the case with Coca-Cola India, Infosys, Satyam Computers and Wipro in India and Daltron, Datec and Global Technologies in Papua New Guinea. Thus salaries and benefits vary from employee to employee based on their performance levels and demand and supply factors in most of the private sector companies. However, public sector is an exception to this shift. Consequently individual bargaining based on demand and supply factors displaced the collective bargaining in this regard also paving the way for individualistic HRM.

SHIFTS IN HUMAN RESOURCE MANAGEMENT STRUCTURE

The preceding analysis indicates that globalisation resulted in paradigm shifts in human resource management in various sectors in varying degrees and nature. Large scale private sector which has been exposed to international competition directly and small scale private sector which exposed to domestic competition directly and global competition indirectly experienced paradigm shifts in human resource management viz., down-sizing, de-layering, virtual organizations, team design, outsourcing, de-jobbing, employee empowerment, development based performance appraisal, on-line training, employee-based training, salary based on performance and demand and supply factors, and the like which resulted in the individual employee based human resource management in case of employment, training, development, and compensation and team based human resource management as far as employee contribution to the achievement organisational strategies is concerned. These paradigm shifts invariable have their impact on industrial relations, as industrial relations are the outcome of the human resource management.

IMPACT OF GLOBALISATION ON INDUSTRIAL RELATIONS

Industrial relations deal with the relations among workers and their unions, management and their organizations and the state. As such the three important actors of industrial relations are the workers and their organizations, employers and their organizations and the government (Dunlop, John T. 1958: viii). The interactive and dynamic roles played by these crucial actors in the process of protecting the interests of workers and management in a balanced and mutually exclusive manner created a number of industrial relations institutions including collective bargaining, machinery to prevent and settle industrial disputes and participative management. Traditionally, these actors and institutions of industrial relations had been expected to maintain industrial peace and to secure unreserved cooperation and goodwill among different groups in industry with a view to drive energies and interest towards economically viable and socially desirable channels. It also aims at the development of a sense of mutual confidence, dependence and respect and at the same time encouraging them to come closer to each other for removing misunderstanding, redressing grievances, if any, in a peaceful atmosphere and with open mind and fostering industrial pursuits for mutual benefits and social progress (Subbarao: 1999: 494-495).

TRADE UNIONS

The commodity approach towards labour and machine concept of labour together with the management's exclusive concentration on their goal of profit maximization by exploiting labour resulted in the formation of trade unions to remind the management to aware of their responsibilities towards the most important and living resource of the organization i.e., human resource. Thus trade unions were emerged to protect the employees' interest.

Trade unions across the globe had been recognised as legitimate social and economic organizations of employees and have become part and parcel of industrial organizations as a vital organ of industrial relations. Trade unions aim at achieving various objectives primarily protecting the economic and social interests of employees and they have helped workers in getting higher economic gains, sometimes without enhancing contribution of employees to the organisational goals. They have also succeeded in unionising workers in small business entities.

Trade unions have undergone serious stresses, negotiated with managements and sometimes fought against employers by organising strikes and by threatening managements before they could achieve legitimate demands of workers. They adopted various strategies to safeguard workers' interests including representing the workers' issues to the management, collective bargaining, organising strikes, political pressures etc. As such, managements of most of the companies could not make unilateral decisions before globalisation that might have affected employee-employer relations directly or indirectly, positively or negatively. Further, managements were restricted in the areas when they could take decisions about human resources management independently of the trade unions as the latter became more sophisticated and professional. Thus, unions before globalisation became employer-regulating device and sought to regulate the discretion of employers at every point where their action might have affected the welfare of employees. Trade unions questioned, criticised, challenged, modified and regulated even the corporate strategic decisions particularly those affected the employees (Subbarao, 1999: 531-532).

Trade unions, thus, played a vital role in protecting employees' interest and a devil's advocate role for managerial decisions and actions, before globalisations. This is true in case of all kinds of Indian organizations (public sector, private sector and small industries) like Indian Railways, Department of Telecommunications, Tata Electrical and Locomotive Company Limited and Andhra Pradesh Lightings Limited and organizations in Papua New Guinea like Air Niugini, PNG Telekom, and the erstwhile PNG Banking Corporation. The situation of protective and welfare economics strengthen the trade unions in terms of membership, finance, organization and militant and/or political leadership and enabled them to fight against managements of various companies, some times leading to organisational dysfunctional and chaos.

Globalisation along with the deregulation of economies led to severe competition and placed the customer first by deregulating the position of employees and made the latter and their unions to realize that they are for customers but not vice-versa. This situation led to the employees to realize that they have to protect themselves and serve the customer most efficiently by means of developing their skills and positive attitude. The able employees came out of the shadow of trade unions, acquired new skills, realized their capabilities and have grown beyond the expectations of their own as well as organizations through their individualistic approaches.

The deregulation process forced the governments and political parties to withdraw their support to trade unions. As such trade unions could not protect the interest of less skilled employees from loss of jobs when organizations downsized their operations and retrenched the less able employees and finally became lean in membership, finance, organization and leadership. Even the largest employees' federations in India like All Indian Trade Union Congress and Indian National Trade Union Congress and in Papua New Guinea like Communication Workers' Union, Financial Workers Union etc. tend to reach this stage. As such, it is needless to mention the situation of regional and organisational level trade unions. Thus trade unions tend to reach the stage of decline. It can be said that the capitalistic and globalisation trends drive the trade unions in a reverse gear. The decline of trade unions in variably has its impact as the functioning of collective bargaining.

COLLECTIVE BARGAINING

Collective bargaining is a process of negotiations about the terms and conditions of employment between employer and a group of employees or one or more trade unions with a view to reaching an agreement (International Labour Organization, 1957:3). There has been evident that trade unions and management of almost all the public sector organizations and large and medium private sector organizations used to negotiate on terms and conditions of employment and arrive at agreements and consequently notify human resource management policies and strategies based on the collective agreements. Collective bargaining in Indian Railways, Indian Posts etc. has been a continuous process under the permanent negotiating machinery. Similarly, collective bargaining in private sector industries like Southern Pesticides Limited, Navabharat Ferro Alloys Limited and Nizam Sugars Limited was also a continuous process. Collective bargaining played a vital role in settling the terms and conditions of employment, before globalisation, though minor issues of individual employees who had no bearing on other employees were redressed through the grievance procedure in most of the Indian organizations. This was also the case with PNG Telekom Limited, erstwhile PNG Banking Corporation, Eda Ranu, etc. in Papua New Guinea. Thus, the collective bargaining was instituted and functioned with a certain degree of effectiveness mostly due to the fact that terms and conditions of employment were common at least for a group of employees in each company before globalisation.

The post-globalisation scenario tends to drive collective bargaining in a reverse direction as terms and conditions of employment vary from employee to employee. The decaying trend of trade unions and/or emergence of non-union organizations during the late 1980s contributed to the shift from collective bargaining to individual bargaining in private sector. Dr. Reddy's Laboratories, Ushodaya Publications Limited, Eicher Tractors Limited, Satyam Computers switched over to individual negotiation during the post-globalisation era. However, the public sector industries like Indian Railways, Bharat Heavy Plates and Vessels Limited, Visakhapatnam Steel Plant of Steel Authority of India Limited, and Hindustan Cables Limited still continue collective bargaining in principle as the terms and conditions of permanent employees are common. However, collective bargaining institutions in public sector organizations have become inactive after globalisation due to the organization's poor financial position consequent upon competition and the withdrawal of budgetary support by the Government of India. Similar trends are also observed in public sector undertakings of Papua New Guinea like Eda Ranu.

Public sector organizations took a deviation in dealing with the issues of employment and development rather than discussing in collective bargaining. The competition from domestic private sector industries and multinational companies forced them to adopt retrenchment and restructure strategies. For example, Visakhapatnam Steel Plant of Steel Authority of India Limited, Hindustan Cables Limited and Bharat Heavy Plates and Vessels Limited adopted down sizing and turnaround strategies. Consequently they retrenched redundant employees, outsourced certain employees' functions, trained and developed the partially redundant employees without negotiating most of these issues in collective bargaining. Thus management tend to take unilateral decisions in these areas without negotiating in collective bargaining meetings.

Thus collective bargaining institutions in public sector have become inactive regarding the monetary issues that could not be individualized due to the public nature of the organizations and have become unconcern with regard to the other issues. In a way, bargaining even in public sector is forced to shift to individual bargaining relating to non-monetary issues. The fundamental changes in trade unions and collective bargaining invariably bring the shifts in nature and degree of industrial disputes.

INDUSTRIAL DISPUTES

Though several measures are taken to manage human resource, satisfy the demands of employees and employer, disputes between employees and employer take place due to conflict of interest between capital and labour. The collective forms of industrial dispute like work-to-rule, strikes by all or a group of employees, lay-offs and lockouts were common before globalisation. It is not exaggeration to state that there was no issue of news paper and magazine without a report on strikes/ lock-out before 1990s, but not later. It is quite abnormal to listen to strikes and lockouts in India as well as Papua New Guinea public, private, large and small-scale sectors after globalisation. This is mostly due to the individualistic approach adopted by the business in managing their human resources. Under this approach, employee quits the job on his own, if he is dissatisfied with the terms and conditions of employment and the management terminates the services of individual employee, if it is not satisfied with employee contributions and /or discipline. This is just and a simple way of solving the employee-employer disputes and terminating their relationships. These trends have become more prevalent in various private sector organizations like Satyam Computers, Infosys, Larsen and Toubro Limited, Coca Cola India and Tata Consultancy Services Limited. However, public sector organizations like State Bank of India, Hindustan Cables Limited, and Hindustan Petrochemicals Limited introduced the voluntary retirement scheme and enabled the employees to quit the organization on their own. But, they are still unable to terminate the service of unwanted/redundant employees due to the nature of the organization. Bank of South Pacific, ANZ Bank (PNG) Limited, Telekom PNG Limited etc., terminate the services of unwanted or redundant employees. In fact Papua New Guinea organizations mostly follow the contractual employment even for the nationals. Thus, manifestation of conflicts took a reverse direction in all organizations in PNG and private sector organizations in India and a mid–way direction of docile nature in Indian public sector organization during the post-globalisation era.

PARTICIPATIVE MANAGEMENT

The next important institution of industrial relations is the worker's participation in management. The concept of workers' participation in management crystallizes the concept of industrial democracy, and indicates an attempt on the part of an employer to build his employees into a team that works towards the realization of a common objective (Kesari, 1971: 4). Some of the public sector organizations and a few private sector organization adopted different schemes of workers' participation in management like Works Committees, Shop Councils, Joint Councils and Joint Management Council before globalisation. But these councils or committees could not function efficiently even before globalisation mostly due to non-cooperation of the managements which were of the view that workers lack managerial abilities and they encroach the management and ownership of the firm as India was a socialistic pattern of society before globalisation (Papola, T.S., 1991:23).

But globalisation and economic liberalisations changed the direction of Indian and PNG economies towards market economies. Competition, consequent upon globalisation forced the managements to realize that human resource offers them a distinctive competency. As such managements to day encourage the employees to participate in decision-making, share their ideas and knowledge, disseminate the information they acquire at workplace and empower them by developing multi-skills to make decisions on their own. Globalisation led to optimum utilisation of human resources through participative management idea and contributed to the attainment of the goals of workers' participation in management which hitherto failed before Globalisation. Thus globalisation tends to drive the operation of if not the theme of workers' participation in management in reverse direction.

CONCLUSION

The analysis of impact of globalisation on human resource management structure and on industrial relations indicates that globalisation brought paradigm shifts in human resource management structure and pattern in both the countries understudy with varying degrees like de-layering, team and virtual structures, downsizing, multi-skilling de-jobbing, more weighages on attitudes, emotional intelligence and other soft skills in employee selection, outsourcing of human resource, on-line training and employee's own initiatives for self development, use of performance appraisal for employee development, compensation based on demand, supply factors and performance levels of each employee and the like. These paradigm shifts changed the traditional collective approach of human resource management to individual approach of human resource management in case of employment, development and compensation and team based structure in case of employee utilisation.

The paradigm shifts in human resource management structure brought fundamental change in industrial relations institutions and structure. The major actors of industrial relations have been either made defunct or tend to withdraw from their respective roles and consequently only employees and employer remain to play their roles in industrial relations which was similar to pre-1920s periods of Indian industrial relations scenario and the early stage of industrial relations in Papua New Guinea. Similarly the important institutions of industrial relations like Collective Bargaining, Welfare Officers, Bipartite and Tripartite bodies became irreverent and redundant as employer directly deals with individual employees based on market forces and/or employee performance levels after globalisation with minor exceptions. However, the institution of Workers' Participation in Management, which could not function efficiently before globalisation, started functioning in its idea-form efficiently after globalisation due to the competitive environment.

Therefore, it is viewed that globalisation provided free and deregulated environment to the business to operate, which in turn resulted in severe competition and formulation of competitive strategies. This competitive situation forced the companies to develop competency building-cum-low-cost centred human resource strategies. These strategies demand for getting highest human resource productivity at the lowest possible cost. The efficient implementation of new human resource management strategies demanded a non-regulative environment from the industrial relations institutions paving the way for a fundamental change in industrial relations system. Thus globalisation tends to bring significant shift in HRM i.e., from collective to individual HRM and thereby a fundamental change in Industrial relations i.e., collective relations to individual relations.

In contrast, communistic/socialistic economic systems along with closed economies made the governments to act as the custodian of the respective nation and establish welfare institutions and demanded both the public and private sector industries to formulate welfare-centred corporate level and human resource strategies. Consequently a number of industrial relations institutions came in to being and checked and controlled the implementation process of employee protection. Thus Industrial relations institutions find a significant role to play in communistic/socialistic economic systems.

Therefore, it is viewed that the communistic/socialistic economic systems (closed economies) result in protective human resource management structure and thereby collective and welfare-centred industrial relations and capitalist economic systems (global economies) result in competitive human resource management structure and thereby individual and contingency based industrial relations.

REFERENCES

Dunlop John, (1958), *Industrial Relations Systems.*

Human Capital (1999), July

Human Capital (2001), August

Human Resource Management Journal, 1997

International Labour Organization (1957), *Collective Bargaining*, Workers' Educational manual Series.

Kesari, J.P., (1971), *The System of Workers' Participation in Management*, Indian Journal of Social Work, xx (i).

Kotler Philip (2003), *Marketing Management*, Prentice Hall.

Moffat Susan (1990), *Japan's New Personalised Production*, Fortune, October 22.

Papola, T.S. (1991), *Industry and Employment: Recent Indian Experience*, ISID Foundation Day Lecture, New Delhi.

Skaria George (1996), *The New People Management*, Business To-day, January 7-21.

Subba Rao, P., (1999) *Essentials of Human Resources Management and Industrial Relations*, Himalaya Publishing House, Mumbai.

Subba Rao, P., (2003) *Personnel and Human Resources Management*, Himalaya Publishing House, Mumbai.

Sundeep Khanna (1996), *The New People Economy*, Business To-day, January 7-21.

PART-III

EDUCATION AND WOMEN IN DEVELOPMENT

15

EDUCATION AND UNEMPLOYMENT IN KERALA: CHALLENGES AHEAD

*Dolly Sunny**

INTRODUCTION

After the attainment of independence, on reorganization of the erstwhile princely states of Travancore, Cochin and the district of Malabar, Kerala state came into existence on November 1, 1956. Key indicators of the demographic profile of Kerala vis-à-vis India are given in Table 1. As can be seen, Kerala state has the dubious distinction of being the most densely populated state partly due to fact that it is a narrow strip of land and due to low death rates. At the same time its high literacy rates and education have brought it the appellation of a demographically forward state: However, Kerala's high demographic achievement has not been matched by a commensurate economic development; primarily on account of lesser employment opportunities created. This has acted as a negative factor in the development of the state (Bose, 1991).

In fact, the unemployment situation is getting precarious over a period of time. The dimension of the problem of unemployment prevailing in the state can be gauged from an

* Reader in Economics, University of Mumbai, Vidyanagari Marg, Mumbai-400098, India.

Table 1
Selected Demographic Indicators of Kerala and India 1991-2001

		1991		*2001*	
Sr. No. (1)	*Indicators* (2)	*Kerala* (3)	*India* (4)	*Kerala* (5)	*India* (6)
1.	Density of Population	747.00	267.00	819.00	324.00
2.	Literacy rate	90.59	52.11	90.92	65.38
3.	Sex rate	1040.00	929.00	1058.00	933.00
4.	Birth rate	19.00	29.00	17.09*	27.20*
5.	Death rate	5.90	9.60	6.20*	8.90*
6.	Infant Mortality Rate	21	80	12	71

Source: Government of Kerala, Economic Review 1998, State Planning Board, Thiruvananthapuram.

interstate comparison of labour force participation. The fourteenth Round National Sample Survey conducted in the year 1958-59 is considered as a reliable survey since it is based upon proper methodology regarding rural and urban unemployment in Kerala. It indicates that 3.6 per cent of the rural people and 2.2 per cent of the urban people were unemployed. In accordance with it, 3.38 per cent of the total population which is about 10 per cent of the labour force was unemployed. The 1961 census showed that 17.3 lakh people were unemployed out of the total labour force of 58.03 lakh. However, it is reported that about 19.05 per cent were underemployed (Prakash, 1989).

Based on various statistics maintained by Dept of Labour, Government of India viz. NSSO Weekly Status, Daily status and other estimates, the labour force participation rate and the rate of unemployment and underemployment in 1972-73 it can be seen that states like Kerala, Tamil Nadu, West Bengal, Andhra Pradesh, Karnataka faced severe unemployment on Weekly Status. In Kerala, Tamilnadu, West Bengal & Andhra Pradesh underemployment is also high. States like Assam, Uttar Pradesh, Rajasthan, Madhya Pradesh and Himachal Pradesh have a lot of unemployment as well as underemployment. This shows that both weekly status and daily status unemployment situation is very severe in Kerala and Tamilnadu as compared with states like Andhra Pradesh and West Bengal. Brahmananda says that "Kerala is conspicuous for the high rate of unemployment" (Robinson et al, 1983). Even National Sample Surveys of 1987-88 in terms of Usual Status and Current Daily Statues unemployment shows the rate of unemployment was the highest in Kerala (GOI, 1992). This is presented in Table 2.

Table 2
Total Job Seekers in Kerala

(No. in lakhs)

Year	*General **	*Professional & Technical*	*Total job seekers*
(1)	*(2)*	*(3)*	*(4)*
1980	15.79	0.38	16.17
1985	2.57	0.69	26.43
1986	27.05	0.79	27.84
1987	29.91	0.87	30.78
1988	29.00	0.87	29.89
1989	30.92	0.98	31.90
1990	33.20	1.05	34.25
1991	36.39	1.00	37.40
1992	37.19	1.28	38.47
1993	40.21	1.36	41.57
1994	40.39	1.30	41.69
1995	31.07	1.19	32.26
1996	31.58	1.29	32.87
1997	34.12	1.39	35.51
1998	36.09	1.44	37.53

Note: * Includes job seekers with qualification below SSLC, PDC Graduates & Post Graduates.

Source: Government of Kerala (1991, 1997), Economic Review, State Planning Board, Thiruvananthapuram. P.149 and p.13.

As per data presented in Table 2, the number of unemployed people stood at about 37.5 lakh and the proportion of educated among unemployed is increasing in the state. The ratio of unemployed persons in Kerala is around 10 per cent of that for the entire country. The population of Kerala which stood at 290.38 lakh according to 1991 census was 3.5 per cent of the total population of the country.

According to Government of Kerala (1991, 1997) the VIIIth and IXth Five Year Plans have taken creation of employment opportunities as important agenda items for reform on a priority basis in order to address the serious issues of unemployment.

Kerala has some peculiar socio-economic features which have resulted in endemically high rate of unemployment. Some of the characteristics are fast increasing population, extremely low land-man ratio, declining share of agricultural income in the national and state income, unsatisfactory rate of growth of industry, high literacy rates as well as education and state's developmental and educational policy.

DISTINGUISHING FEATURES OF THE ECONOMY

In order to understand the seriousness of the problem of unemployment, it is necessary to get an insight in the aforesaid distinguishing features of Kerala economy.

High Population Density

Kerala's population density in 1981, 1991 and 2001 was 655, 747 and 819 respectively while for India as a whole it was 254, 264 and 324 respectively as given in table 1.1. The total population of Kerala in 1981 was 254.54 lakhs which increased to 290.11 lakhs in1991 and 318.39 lakhs in 2001. The birth, death and infant mortality rates of Kerala are compared to all India level in table 1.1 as per Censuses of 1991 and 2001. When the birth rate for India as a whole was in the range of (36-27), Kerala's birth rate was in the range of (32-17).

High Proportion of Agriculture in SDP

Economic activities of the state are largely concentrated in agriculture, which has the highest proportion in the State Domestic Product (SDP). But there has been a decline in the share of income from agriculture in recent years. It decreased from 49.5 per cent in 1970-71 to 39 per cent in 1989-90 and to 30.86 percent during the mid-nineties. However it has not resulted in the diversion of the labour force to other sectors of the economy. More than half of the labour force is still dependent on this sector for livelihood and so it marginalized the size of agricultural holdings from an average of 0.73 ha to 0.33 ha (GOK, 1999). Within the state's agricultural sector, the total numbers of workers are estimated to be 114 lakh, out of which 68 lakh are employed at least for 183 days. The number of underemployed people stood at 16 lakh. This adds up to only 71 lakh standard person years employment which points towards severe unemployment. About 30 lakh people are estimated to be unemployed in the agricultural sector of the economy. A closer examination reveals that the unemployment situation in agricultural sector is related to many factors, such as decrease in size of land holdings and resultant increase in pressure on land, lack of sufficient investment of capital, decline in cropped area, decline in rainfall etc (Chacko, 1972; GOK, 1991 b and 1998).

Sluggish Growth of the Industrial Sector

Kerala's industrial growth has been lesser than that of India as a whole and this has adversely affected the development of the state. In the early sixties the per capita income of Kerala was almost equal to the national average but after two decades it came down (GOK, 1991 a).

The share of the manufacturing sector in the State Domestic Product showed an increase of only about 2 per cent in the decennial period followed by 1980 compared to the all India rate of 10 per cent (GOK, 1991a). The share of secondary sector to state domestic product continued to remain as low as 24.1 per cent in 1995-96 while it was 24.8 per cent in 1996-97 in constant prices (GOK, 1997).

Linkages

As regards high rate of unemployment prevailing in the state, there is an opinion that the expansion of education post-school withdraws people of young age group from the work force and as a result there is a decrease in work participation and high rate of unemployment of the state (Nair, 1989). While this is a debatable proposition it is nevertheless true that a disproportionate investment on education has tended to starve other productive sectors of the required investment funds. One corollary of this has been the achievement of near total literacy in the state. The state's investment on education has also resulted in lopsided economic development. Prakash (1989) argued that the improvement in the level of education among the people changed the contours of the labour force when the educated job seekers became interested only in getting white collar jobs. As noted before the liberal policy pursued by the state by providing heavy subsidy in education acts as a catalyst towards the goal of educational advancement. Further Bhagawati Committee highlighted that there is an increasing propensity by Indians to seek more education in order to improve their social status Keralites have also demonstrated a similar propensity to acquire higher education in order to climb up the social ladder.

Education Policy of the Government

The educational policy of the state focuses on development of general education. As a result a large number of schools, arts and science colleges are in operation. Graduation was made the minimum qualification for clerical posts. So when the demand for graduate degrees increased, the colleges were not able to cope up with admission to increasing number of students, and consequently the University of Kerala and the University of Calicut introduced private registration system in 1971 and 1977 respectively. It resulted in the increase in the number of private parallel colleges in Kerala. So the large numbers of pre-degree holders, graduates and post graduates have emerged in Kerala (Nair and Joseph, 1983).

The lop-sided importance given to general education in Kerala is clear from the comparison of per capita government expenditure with some other states like Maharashtra, Tamil Nadu, Karnataka, Uttar Pradesh etc. (Table 3). We get a clear picture of the excess importance given to education in Kerala when considering the fact that out of the total plan outlay, the share allotted for education is very high. For instance, the total outlay of the states VIII Five Year Plan was Rs.5460 crore, of which Rs.202.25 crore were allocated for education (GOK, 1991a).

Vocational Education

Introduction of job oriented vocational courses were neglected as a result of undue importance attached to expansion of general education. The state has not started adequate number of technical education institutions like engineering colleges and polytechnics. Some students desiring to seek technical education go out of the state, pay high donations and get admission. Even though there is an increase in demand for medical education, Kerala has not been able to give due priority for the development of various disciplines of medical education like Allopathy, Ayurveda and Homeopathy. Study done by Mathew (1995) brought out the fact that unemployment rarely exists in the case of medical graduates, and post graduate nurses, though the state has not taken initiative in opening up adequate number of medical and para medical colleges. Kerala does not have a system of vocational education to train the people to work in agricultural, livestock, fishing, dairying, poultry farming and other primary occupations. Vocational training facilities for training people to take up trade, commerce and other business occupation are also absent (Prakash, 1989).

Table 3
Per capita State Government Expenditure on Education in Selected States

	1980-81	*1985-86*	*1988-89*	*1989-90*
Kerala	85	153	199	240
Maharashtra	61	114	176	219
Tamil Nadu	50	107	145	171
Karnataka	47	92	146	167
Andhra Pradesh	43	92	127	168
West Bengal	45	89	134	155
Uttar Pradesh	32	64	99	150

The Imbalance

The state of Kerala has given disproportionate importance to popularization of general education to the detriment of other important aspects (Prakash, 1989). Both the state as well as the central Government have not given due priority to the setting up of industrial undertakings which can generate employment opportunities. So it can be concluded that even though the rapid increase in the supply of educated people can be linked with growing population, the imbalance is largely due to the inappropriate policy package adopted by the government related to education, human resources development and industry.

Special Schemes

Certain programmes were implemented by the government to solve unemployment problems of the state. These programmes included Integrated Rural Development Programme (I.R.D.P) and Jawahar Rozgar Yojana (J.R.Y) which have twin objectives of alleviation of poverty and creation of employment opportunities in the state (GOK, 1992). Nehru Rozagar Yojana was introduced in 1989-90 to create more employment opportunities in urban areas to those who are below poverty line. There is one more programme called TRYSEM, which is for training rural youth with assistance for self employment ventures (GOK, 1991a). While TRYSEM could provide wage and self employment to 16187 and 7326 youths respectively, J.R.Y could provide employment to 589.63 lakh by 1996-97 (GOK, 1997).

Employment Exchanges

In 14 districts of Kerala, employment Exchange with vocational guidance units are functioning which are meant for educated youth. A self employment guidance unit at District Employment Exchange functions at Kollam with central assistance. There are market information units which have been introduced in District Development Exchanges to collect, compile and distribute employment related information. In a state confronting the problems of educated unemployment, the role of employment exchanges would be catalytic. A cursory look at the organization and functioning of employment exchange is revealing. While vital function of an employment exchange is to provide information about vacancies and to bring the increasing number of employment seekers and employers into closer contact so as to bridge the demand supply gap, however they have not been very successful with regard to achieving their objectives (GOK,1991c).

In order to make up for the inability of the government to create employment opportunities and to provide some temporary relief to the unemployed, the Government of Kerala initiated the Unemployment Assistance Scheme in 1982. In 1982-83 there were 1.6 lakh applications for receiving unemployment doles in the state. There were 44,011 beneficiaries among whom a total of Rs. 80.22 lakh was distributed. In 1990-91, the number of beneficiaries increased to 2, 64, 134 who received a total assistance of Rs. 1934.87 lakh (GOK, 1991c). This is explained in Table -4.

Table 4

Unemployment Assistance Scheme in Kerala: 1982-83 to 1996-97

Sr. No.	*Year*	*Application received (in lakhs)*	*No. of beneficiaries*	*Amount disbursed (Rs.lakhs)*
(1)	*(2)*	*(3)*	*(4)*	*(5)*
1.	1982-83	1.61	44011	80.22
2.	1983-84	0.45	98261	649.79
3.	1984-85	1.03	136471	768.52
4.	1985-86	0.49	179146	1012.08
5.	1986-87	1.14	218446	835.00
6.	1987-88	0.93	205556	1095.65
7.	1988-89	0.65	215456	2353.77
8.	1989-90	0.81	246040	1996.36
9.	1990-91	1.18	264314	1934.87
10.	1994-95	3.11	281424	2137.00
11.	1995-96	3.16	272371	2649.00
12.	1996-97	3.38	264382	2270.00

Source: Government of Kerala (1997), Economic Review, State Planning Board, Thiruvanthapuram.

Attitude of Educated Youth

The educated youth today prefer white collar jobs especially in the public sector, to self employment in the private sector, since it does not require physical exertion. This necessitates restructuring of training programmes and streamlining of employment exchanges for achieving equilibrium between demand and supply of skills in the economy. On the basis of studies conducted in 1989 by Prakash in educated unemployment it is brought out that twenty nine per cent of the total unemployed are educated of whom majority were SSLC holders, fifty two per cent of technical certificate holders, twenty two per cent of technical diploma holders and twelve per cent of technical degree holders were found to be unemployed . According to State Planning Board 1999, the percentage of educated unemployed out of total unemployed increased to seventy six in per cent as on 31st October 1998.

Studies have shown that due to increasing number of educated unemployed the waiting period for salaried job increased especially among those with a lower level of education as there will be a crowding out effect by the highly educated applicants. The UN study on poverty, unemployment and development with reference to Kerala showed average waiting period of 33 to 36 months for the first job (Mathew, 1995). Since chances to secure higher education increased in the case of rich people, one may argue that the duration of waiting period of poor increases to 72 months for the candidates from families of comparatively lower level of income have to wait for even longer period to secure a job. Another relevant point is that the income earned after getting a salaried job is not higher than that of an unskilled person which leads to the conclusion that education is not helpful for reducing income inequalities (Prakash, 1979).

Higher Education

Unemployment among educated people is increasing at an alarming rate in Kerala. Evidently people are forced to accept jobs for which they are over-qualified; it amounts to a fall in their real earnings in relation to their educational credentials (Mathew, 1995). On the other hand, the appointment of a more qualified applicant for a lower level job leads to underemployment. Due to this when unemployment increases in Kerala people have predilections to secure more and more education (Nair and Joseph, 1983). It brings to light the existence of vicious circle of educated unemployment and higher education, which accentuates the rate of educated unemployment in Kerala.

As is clear from the above discussion, though formal education is considered as one of the fundamental ways of developing human skills, knowledge and work capacities, if it is not capable of performing this basic task, then naturally employment and development suffers. Though educated people of Kerala acquire skills and potential to contribute to the state's development process, as waiting period for the jobs increases and as they remain unemployed, their skills are in turn ruined due to its non–utilisation. Thus, unemployment causes loss of productivity in the immediate term as there are no returns on the education, and if sustained over a longer period of time, it leads to long term loss of productivity as the skills depreciate with time.

POLICY IMPLICATIONS

The above discussion revolves around the following policy-implications:

(1) Kerala has to grapple with the problem of unemployment in general and educated unemployment in particular, due to the successive governments in the State that gave all out priority to education at all levels. In the process, the goal of industrialisation remained neglected. Development strategies in the State, which are crucial for generation of employment opportunities, therefore require a paradigm shift from allocation of resources for creation of new jobs to generation of self employment including opportunities offered by the new generation information technology sector.

(2) While considering the virtual absence of self employment in the state, it can be concluded that creation of self employment has never been seriously considered as an alternative policy of development of

the state. It may be seen that in recent times, there has been a focus on setting up professional colleges with private sector participation, however the steps taken so far are not sufficient to address all the problems related to higher education as it is unable to meet the aspirations of the students. Considering the rich background of handicrafts and artisanship evident in wood carvings, brass casting, and exquisite jewellery which even today forms an important part of exports from Kerala, there is a great deal of scope for improving upon existing techniques introducing innovative methods and exploring the potential of talent in handicrafts and other artisan work. Similarly, processing of forest resources of bamboo, honey, softwood etc. could also be taken up in a big way to help people augment their incomes.

(3) Any plan for employment creation through rural economic growth in Kerala must consider the very promising opportunities for growth based on the mixed cultivation of diverse crops that require skilled crop management with financial assistance from public institutions.

(4) In Kerala new areas of skill utilisation are emerging in software development (Dolly Sunny, 2000). The Government has to tackle irritants standing in the way of software industries coming up in the State so that educated youth find employment readily on completion of the required technical courses which are available everywhere. Other technological developments taking place in the area of telecommunications, networking, Television and other multimedia also offer tremendous scope for employment in the State as also self-employment of talented persons who are, at present, dependent on opportunities in other areas. There is also a vast reservoir of talent in paramedical and health research activities particularly in traditional medicine such as

Ayurveda which is finding acceptance worldwide. So the pattern of education of Kerala is urgently required to be modified to impart adequate skills at the school level itself. Insofar as the avenues for employment are concerned, there is a strong case for an increase in the allocation of central funds in proportion to the pre-eminent position of people of Kerala origin who contributes significantly to the national income by way of deployment of their skills in enterprises both in India and abroad.

REFERENCES

Bose Ashish, (1991), Population in India 1991-Census Results And Methodology, BR Publishing Corporation Delhi.

Chacko A.J. (1972), Development of Agriculture in Kerala in PKB Nair(Ed) Development of Kerala Problems and Promises, Department of Sociology University of Kerala, Thiruvananthapuram.

Dolly Sunny (1999), Unemployment and Migration: A Case Study of Educated Unemployed Migrants, Ph.D Thesis, University of Mumbai.

Dolly Sunny (2000), Unemployment and Employment of Educated Youth in Kerala, The Indian Journal of Labour Economics Volume 43 No. 4 October-December.

Dolly Sunny (2001), An Enquiry into the Migration of Educated Women of Kerala State, Indian Journal of Social Development Volume 1, No.1 June.

Dolly Sunny (2001), Unemployment: An Analysis Of Causes And Effects The Radical Humanist Volume 65 No. 3 June.

Eapen Mridula and Mohan Chandra (1983), Data Base of Kerala Economy, Data Base for Estimates of Employment and Unemployment in Kerala, Department of Economics, Thiruvananthapuram.

Government of India (1991), National Sample Survey, New Delhi. Government of India, Census of Kerala, Various Reports.

Government of Kerala (1991), "Draft Eighth Five Year Plan, 1992-97 and Annual Plan, 1992-93", Vol. I, State Planning Board, Thiruvananthapuram.

Government of Kerala (1991b), "*Economic Review*", State Planning Board, Thiruvananthapuram

Government of Kerala (1991c), "Eighth Five Year Plan 1990-95", Report of the Steering Committee on Housing Urban Development, Labour Welfare and Social Security and Welfare, State Planning Board, Thiruvananthapuram.

Government of Kerala 1997, 1998, 1999 Economic Review State Planning Board, Thiruvananthapuram.

Nair Gopinathan, P R & Thomas Joseph (1983), "Department of Economics and Statistics, Thiruvananthpuram", Data Base of Kerala Economy, Government of Kerala, Thiruvananthapuram.

Nair Gopinathan P. R. (1986), 'Asian Migration to the Arab World: Migration from Kerala (India) (mimeo), Centre for Development Studies, Thiruvananthapuram.

Nair Gopinathan P.R. (1989), "Enhancement of Household Capacity in the Post Migration Phase: Kerala (India)", Centre for Development Studies, Thiruvananthapuram.

Prakash B.A. 1989 ''Unemployment in Kerala: An Analysis of Economic Causes", C.D.S. working paper No: 231, Thiruvananthapuram.

Rajeev P.V. (1983), Economic Development and Unemployment (Relevance of Kerala Model), Asian Publication Services, New Delhi.

Ramachandran, V.K. (1999), "On Kerala's Development Achievements", Jean Dreze & Amartya Sen (eds), A Study prepared for the World Institute for Development Economics, Research of the United Nations University, Oxford University Press, New Delhi.

16

WOMEN IN DEVELOPMENT: A CASE STUDY ON SELECTED RURAL AREAS OF BANGLADESH

Saiful Islam and Nourin Shabnam***

INTRODUCTION

Several studies[1] evidence women as the important engines of growth and development. Women have strong ability to earn, save, and invest in their families in rural economy. In rural area their largely unrecorded role in agriculture sector explains the survival of traditional subsistence community. Yet in many places, traditions, social stigma, limited mobility, and lack of voice or access to information make women the most marginal group. With the men seeking work elsewhere, women tend the fields and look after the children, the elderly, and the farm animals, fetch fuelwood and water, and prepare food for the family members. Some 80 per cent of economically active women in Sub-Saharan Africa and South Asia are in agricultural activities-largely subsistence farmers in female headed households or day laborers on larger commercial farms. These economic realities are beginning to give women more influence (World Bank 2003_a).

* Associate Professor & Head Economics Discipline Khulna University, Khulna 9208, Bangladesh.

** Economics Graduate Khulna University.

Bangladesh is agrarian economy with nearly 75 per cent of its population living in rural areas, and women constitute almost half (49.64 per cent) of its total population (World Bank 2003_b). But the majority of the economically active women remain outside the active labor force of the country as women's capabilities and needs are seldom counted in a male dominated society. Therefore, Bangladesh still remains one of the least developed countries of the world with a per capita income of US$ 386 only. For example, Bangladesh is positioned in the low human development group of HDI and the value of its index was only 0.478 in 2000 (UNDP 2003).

In recent years, some employment opportunities have been created for rural women with subsistence living in public works such as Food for Work (FFW) Program, Rural Works Program (RWP), and Test-relief Program (TRP). But these activities are quite seasonal, and very much informal, and low remunerative. Besides, women are engaged in various non-farm activities such as homestead cultivation, poultry, and livestock raring. These activities are directed both towards domestic consumption and toward generation of income to supplement family expenditure and to generate saving.

Thus it calls for the exploitation of the potential ability and skills of half of the population (women) to empower them to be the engines of growth especially of rural economy. Therefore, it is indispensable that women must participate in different types of income generating activities, to increase their income, to come out of poverty, and to get better standard of living to face the challenges of rural development. This study aims at to uncover various income generating activities undertaken by rural women, to find out the constraints for women's participation in income generating activities in rural areas, and to recommend appropriate steps addressing women's participation and rural development.

MATERIALS AND METHODS

This study is based on primary data, which is collected through face to face interview. A survey has been carried out in three selected rural areas namely Shiromoni, Nichkhamar, and

Mohammadnagar of Khulna district in the southwestern region of Bangladesh. A random sample of 60 respondents (20 respondents from each area) has been selected, and relevant data are collected. Statistical package such as SPSS is applied to analyze the collected data and compute the objective functions. Gini Coefficients are calculated to present the real picture of rural workingwomen. Besides, secondary data sources such as books, journals, and articles have also been reviewed to make this study fruitful.

OBJECTIVE FUNCTIONS

Empirical evidence shows that women have important impetus for growth and development of an economy as already mentioned. They have strong ability to save and invest in their families and thereby to contribute in the development especially of the rural economy. When involvement of women in income generating activities increases, economic development takes place. Therefore, we assume that economic development is a function of the involvement of women in income-generating activities, and all factors that may effect the economic development are exogenous, and women have free access in income-generating activities. Thus, we identify two variables 'participation of women in income generating-activities' and 'economic development' and try to assess the impact of income generated by workingwomen on economic development through following econometric model.

$$Y_i = b_0 + b_1X_i + e_i \quad ...(1)$$

Where Y_i is household expenditure, which is a proxy for economic development. If the rural area experiences economic development, the standard of living of rural people will increase, and increased amount of household expenditure will reflect higher level of economic development. The variable X is the monetary income generated by the self-dependant workingwomen and is a proxy for income-generating activities in selected rural areas. Thus the equation 1, measures the impact of income-generating activities on the economic development of selected rural areas of Bangladesh. Besides, we also test the following model to assess how the income generated by the rural women accelerate small savings, and thereby contribute in economic development.

$$Y_t = \beta_0 + \beta_1 X_t + e_t \quad ...(2)$$

where Y_t is household saving, and X_t is household income.

RESULTS AND DISCUSSIONS

Socioeconomic Status of Rural Women: Socio-economic status of rural women is very much important as it reflects their standard of living. Here, we analyze the socio-economic status under the following heads:

Demographic Background and Age Distribution of Workingwomen

In the selected three rural areas namely Shiromoni, Nichkhamar, and Mohammadnagar number of population are 2750, 3300, and 2150 respectively totaling 8200, of which 49.80 percent are women (BBS 2001). Thus the ratios of men to women in the study are similar to that of national figure. Data in table 1 captures the age distribution of workingwomen in the study area.

Table 01
Age Distribution of Workingwomen

Age Group	*Frequency*	*Percentage*
15-30	13	21.67
30-45	32	53.33
45+	15	25.00

Source: Field Survey, June 2004

It is witnessed that most of the workingwomen are of mid age ranging 30-45 years. The older section of women constitute one fourth, and the younger section constitute the least percentage of self dependant workingwomen. As the life expectancy at birth for female is only 51 years, data in table 1 reveal that majority of the workingwomen in the study area are middle aged, while the younger section of women are taking less challenges towards economic uplift.

Educational Qualification and Occupational Pattern

Education directly affects the productivity, and greatly influences the income generating activities. The women who are comparatively educated can be involved in good professions. The overall percentages of women who can write her name in black and white in Shiromoni, Nichkhamar, and Mohammadnagar area are 47 per cent, 40 per cent, and 52 per cent respectively *(BBS 2001)*. The educational statuses of women involved in income generating activities to change their fates in the selected areas are summarized in table 2.

Table 02
Educational Qualification of Workingwomen

Educational Status	*Frequency*	*Percentage*
Illiterate	14	23.33
Able to Sign	7	11.67
Primary	8	13.33
Secondary	15	25.00
Higher Secondary	6	10.00
Graduation	6	10.00
Post Graduation[2]	4	6.67
Total	60	100

Source: Field Survey, June 2004

Data in table 02 reveal that nearly 24 per cent rural workingwomen can neither read nor write, and 11.67 per cent are only able to sign. Among the total respondents, 13.33 per cent have very little education, 25 per cent have only secondary level of education, and 10 per cent have higher secondary level of education. Thus the survey shows that lack of education is an important factor, which hinders the productivity of rural workingwomen.

Similarly, the data in table 03 disclose that the occupational pattern of workingwomen in the rural areas. The survey reveals that the majority of the working women are engaged in tertiary sector which engrosses teaching, banking, trade, and servicing, followed by primary sector, and then the secondary sector.

Table 03
Types of Works Undertaken by Women
Percentile Involvement of Women in Different Sectors

Tertiary (%)		*Secondary (%)*		*Primary (%)*	
Teacher	15.00	Handicrafts women	6.67	Poultry Farming	8.33
Banker	10.00	Seamstress	11.67	Dairy Farming	10.00
Trade	10.00			Kitchen Gardening	3.33
Maid Servant	8.33			Goat Farming	8.33
Day Labor	8.33				
Total	51.66		18.34		29.99

Source: Field Survey, June 2004

The study finds that the women with sufficient education are involved in the good profession such as teaching and banking. Within teaching 8.33 per cent are primary school teachers, 3.33 per cent are secondary school teacher, and 3.33 per cent are college teachers, and among the bankers 3.33 per cent are management trainee officer, 5 per cent are trainee assistant officer, and 1.67 per cent are probationary officer, whereas the educational level of traders, poultry farmers and day laborers is very poor.

CONTRIBUTION OF WORKINGWOMEN IN RURAL ECONOMY

The workingwomen mostly belong to poor families engaged in various income-generating activities to supplement their family income to support the survivals of households, otherwise income stemming from other members of their families are not sufficient for subsistence living. The amount of income accruing to rural women varies in size due to occupational diversity. Table 04 provides a picture of the average income of different categories of women engaged in income-generating activities in rural economy, and confirms that the bankers' monthly income is the highest while that of maidservant is the lowest. The bankers' are not only earning highest income but also contributing the highest share (62.76 percent) in family income, followed by teachers contributing 49.56 percent of family income. Data in table 04 reveal that all categories of women have significant contribution and are augmenting their family income.

Table 04
Average Monthly Contribution (in Tk.) of the Respondents towards Household Income, Consumption and Saving

Profession	*Respondent's Income* [a]	*Family's Income* [b]	*Contribution to Expenditure* [c]	*Saving* [d]
Teacher	3466.67	6994.44	3081.48	385.19
	(25.50)	(49.56)	(88.89)	(11.11)
Banker	6333.33	10091.67	5277.77	1055.56
	(46.59)	(62.76)	(83.33)	(16.67)
Seamstress	842.86	2111.43	722.46	120.40
	(6.20)	(39.92)	(85.72)	(14.28)
Maid Servant	290.00	1420.00	272.00	18.00
	(2.13)	(20.42)	(93.79)	(6.21)
Day Labor	720.00	1736.00	695.00	25.00
	(5.30)	(41.47)	(96.53)	(3.47)
Handicraftswomen	337.50	1550.00	263.12	74.38
	(2.48)	(21.77)	(77.96)	(22.04)
Poultry Farmer	510.00	1410.00	494.63	15.37
	(3.75)	(36.17)	(96.99)	(3.01)
Dairy Farmer	466.67	1508.33	441.00	25.67
	(3.43)	(30.94)	(94.50)	(5.50)
Others[3]	626.92	1638.46	614.86	12.06
	(4.61)	(38.26)	(98.08)	(1.92)

Source: Field Survey, June 2004

(a) Figures in parentheses indicate share in total income of workingwomen
(b) Figures in parentheses indicate respondent's contribution in family income
(c) Figures in parentheses indicate percentage of respondent's income spent on family utilities
(d) Figures in parentheses indicate percentage of respondent's income saved.

The respondents' augmented incomes are mainly utilized to finance daily expenditure of various types to ensure the survival of their family members, and therefore, they have a great deal of contribution to the daily consumption expenditure of their households. All workingwomen irrespective of their profession greatly contribute to meet the daily expenditure of various types such as expenditure on food, cloth, fuel, health, education, transport, and recreation. For example, a teacher spends 88.89 per cent of her earned income to finance family's monthly expenses, and rest of the amount she saves to generate fund for future. Similarly a maidservant also spends 93.79 per cent of her income she earns, and the rest of the amount she saves for future.

Thus rural working women contributing in three ways, (a) augmenting income for family, and thereby raising the per capita income, (b) financing the various family expenditure, and thereby raising the standard of living, and lastly (c) accelerating the saving culture in rural economy.

PROBLEMS FACED BY WORKINGWOMEN

Most of the surveyed workingwomen raised their voice about a number of problems they face while participating in various income-generating activities. Here is an attempt to uncover those problems in the following manner:

Family Problem: Most of the workingwomen are housewives. It is a growing concern for them that they cannot devote sufficient time for the maintenance of their household activities. Thus, a significant portion of working women (38 per cent) suffer from mismanagement of their own household activities, as they are to spend most of their times outside their homes to generate income for their families.

Social Attitude to Workingwomen: The social scene of the selected villages presents a picture of rural family life in which the norms of a traditional society are reshaping themselves under extremes pressure. However, according to 61.67 per cent women, family and social attitudes have changed from negative to positive towards them when they have started to earn money. On the other hand, 18 per cent of them said that their neighbors see their activities as negative due to their superstitious beliefs. Their neighbors have faith in that to go outside the home means to break the religious law of Islam. Again, 20 per cent are to stomach the disturbance of local people during moving along roads.

Professional Problems: The workingwomen face various professional problems amongst unsatisfactory working environment is the main. Majority of the respondents (54 per cent) complained that they work in such a situation, where there is no set rule regarding working hours. Therefore they are to work for longer hours without any additional wage. Further they are paid lower wage in comparison to men. For example, in case of day labor, a man gets Tk.100-120, whereas a woman gets only Tk.70-90, although the woman offers same level of labor. The workingwomen are also facing other problems such as lack of capital and lack of skill. These phenomena are made clear in Table 05.

Table 05
Professional Problems of Workingwomen Women

Lack of Capital	*Lack of Training*	*Unsatisfactory Working Environment*	*No Problem*
59.00 %	81.67 %	53.33 %	20.00 %

Source: Field Survey, June 2004

Problem of Training: Training is an important factor to increase skill and thereby the scope for income-generating activities of rural workingwomen. Amongst the workingwomen, 48.33 per cent work in secondary and primary sectors, but only 1.66 per cent of handicraftswomen and 5 per cent of poultry farmers have necessary training related to their works from various NGOs such as BRAC, ASA, and CARE. Again, 5 per cent of seamstresses have got training from Youth Development Center (YDC), 6.67 per cent of primary school teachers have taken training from Primary Training Institute (PTI). But 81.67 per cent of workingwomen have no training related to their jobs at all.

Most of the NGOs (except BRAC, ASA, and CARE) are supplying capital to rural women but have no specific training program necessary to use such capital with competency. Further the NGOs who offer only short-term training are very limited in number. Thus, the NGOs are offering low or no training and providing capital at usurious lending rate and thus making their own financial structure stronger, but paying no or little attention to the betterment of rural women for whom they are set up.

Credit Problem: Lack of credit is serious problem for those rural women, who are mainly engaged in primary and secondary sector. Most of the rural women are very poor, they have no capability to finance their activities from own sources. Therefore, they depend on borrowed money. But they have no access to scheduled banks, as they require collateral and complicated loan processing, what most of the rural women cannot afford. Besides, these banks are mainly located in urban areas. Therefore, very often they borrow from the nearby NGOs and the Grameen Bank operating mainly in the rural areas, and supplying micro credit to the rural women without any collateral. The rural workingwomen have easy access to these institutions, and 41 per cent of respondents who need financing borrow from these institutions.

By contrast, the majority of the workingwomen (59 per cent) are not excited to take this opportunity, as these institutions charge unbelievably high rate of interest on their credits, and the determination of interest rate on their credits remained very much unclear. Almost all NGOs including Grameen Bank operating in the study area employ very critical way of lending and recovery that make the determination of interest rate very complicated. Islam and Aktaruzzaman (2001) in a very similar study estimated the simple rate of interest of the loan of such NGOs and micro credit institutions as 38 per cent per annum. Their further detailed analysis showed that the actual interest rate on loans from micro credit institutions stands to be 100.61 per cent per annum, which is unbelievably higher.

Unequal Distribution of Income: The data on rural workingwomen reveal that there is an unequal distribution of income, and there exists clear income disparities even among the rural families. Data on table 06 capture these facts.

Numerical values of Gini coefficient also show the income disparities among the women. If there is perfect equality, the Gini coefficient will be zero. If there is perfect inequality, the Gini coefficient will be one. Thus the data clarify that at the lower level of income, the Gini coefficient tends to be one, which explains the existence of greater income inequalities.

Table 06
Income Distribution of Rural Workingwomen

% of Women	*Share of Income (%.)*	*Cumulative Share (%)*	*Gini Coefficient*
Lowest 20 %	2.32	2.32	0.99
Second 20 %	4.53	6.85	0.96
Next 20 %	8.63	15.48	0.86
Fourth 20 %	19.05	34.53	0.60
Highest 20 %	65.47	100	

Source: Field Survey, June 2004

ESTIMATION OF OBJECTIVE FUNCTIONS

We have estimated the objective functions by applying SPSS program, which produces the following results that are summarized in the table 07, and 08.

The analysis shows that the estimated equation 1 has a very high explanatory power and the regression line is a 'good fit' to the surveyed cross section data. Besides, the value of Durbin-Watson statistic also acknowledges the fact that the model is correctly specified. Thus, we conclude that there is a strong and significant relationship between income-generating activities of self-dependant rural women and rural development.

Table 07
Coefficient

	Unstandardized coefficients		*t*	*Sig.*
	B	*Std. Error*		
Constant	951.583	152.333	6.247	0.00
Women's Income	1.238	0.06	20.631	0.00

Estimated Model 1: $Y_i = 951.583 + 1.238\ X_i$

Model Summary

r	R Square	Adjusted R Square	Std. Error of the Estimate	Durbin Watson
0.938	0.88	0.878	922.2	2.121

Predictors: Constant, Women's Income
Dependent Variable: Household Expend

Therefore, when the degree of involvement of women in income-generating activities increases, their income level will rise up; this will help to improve their overall standard of living. Eventually this will push up economic development.

Table 08
Coefficient

	Unstandardized coefficients		*t*	*Sig.*
	B	*Std. Error*		
Constant	-97.18	73.31	-1.33	0.19
Income	0.23	0.03	7.867	0.00

Estimated Model 2: $Y_t = 0.23\ X_t$

Model Summary

r	R Square	Adjusted R Square	Std. Error of the Estimate	Durbin-Watson
0.72	0.52	0.51	443.80	1.44

Predictors: Constant, Household Income.
Dependent Variable: Saving.

The result estimation of equation 2 is summarized in table 08. It shows that, there is a significantly strong relationship between the earning and saving behavior of the rural women. The statistical data analysis supports to conclude that the rural workingwomen save almost 23 percent of their monthly income on average, which is much more than national average, 16.20 per cent of GDP (World Bank 2003_b). Thus the study also proves that the rural workingwomen have a higher propensity to save, and thereby can have more direct role in the capital formation of the country, and accelerate the process of economic development.

CONCLUSION AND RECOMMENDATION

The foregoing analysis reveals that the rural working women have a great deal of potentials which are yet to be properly exploited. They are taking challenges by undertaking various income-generating activities. However, various socioeconomic problems come across to their efforts, and in spite of those obstacles, the contribution of rural workingwomen to their family income, expenditure, and saving is remarkably significant in fostering development in the rural economy. Thus efforts are needed to accelerate and promote the participation of rural women in the development process of the economy. Therefore, it is urgent to ensure greater participation of rural women in the income-generating activities, and with this end we suggest the following steps:

In rural area non-farm agricultural activities such as poultry farming, dairy farming, goat farming, and batik; and agro-based industries should be promoted to foster income for women including rural people. Since lack of capital remains one of the major problems in the rural economy, undertaking such farm will be realistic as they require low level of capital.

Provision of credit facilities on easy terms should be made available. In this regard, the activities of various micro finance institutions should be monitored and controlled. With this end, transparent financial rules should be established to prohibit usurious lending practices and determine the highest ceiling of lending rate of interest.

Sufficient training facilities should be promoted to create and upgrade the skills of rural women and to facilitate their participation in non farm activities through Youth Development Center, and NGOs.

Women should be treated equally and rational wage payment irrespective of gender must be ensured. Proper working environment for women and rules should be ensured. To ensure the participation of women in development, above all, social motivation is a prerequisite to bring gradual and positive change in the traditional views and outlooks how men dominated society evaluates women, who constitute nearly half of total population of the country.

NOTES

1. Such studies include Ostram & Gardner, 1993, and Baland & Platteau, 1996.
2. The respondents having Masters Degree are considered as postgraduate.
3. Others include trader, goat farmer and kitchen gardener.

REFERENCES

Baland J M, and Platteau J P. (1996), *Halting Degradation of Natural Resources*. Food and Agriculture Organization of the United Nations, Oxford: Clarendon Press.

Bangladesh Bureau of Statistics (2001), Bangladesh Population Census Report.

Islam, M S and Aktaruzzaman K. (2001), 'The Problems of Rural Women Entrepreneurs in Bangladesh: A Case Study of Jhenaidah District', *Islamic University Studies (PART-C)*, Vol. 4: No. 1, June.

Islam M S and Moniruzzaman A.K.M. (2000), 'Domestic Saving Mobilization in Bangladesh: The Role of Scheduled Banks', *Islamic University Studies (PART-C)*, Vol. 3, No. 2, December.

Ostrom E, and Gardner R. (1993), Coping with Asymmetries in the Commons: Self-Governing Irrigation Systems Can Work. *Journal of Economic Perspectives* 7(4).

UNDP (2003), Human Development Report, deepening democracy in a fragmented world.

World Bank (2003_a), *The World Development Report*, Sustainable Development in a Dynamic World: Transforming Institutions, Growth, and Quality of Life, Washington D.C.

World Bank (2003_b), *The World Development Indicators*, C D Version.

17

INTRA-HOUSEHOLD RESOURCE ALLOCATION AND BARGANING POWER OF THE WOMEN USING MICRO-CREDIT IN BANGLADESH

Shahnaz Taranuum Abdullah & Munir Hassan***

BACKGROUND OF INTRA-HOUSEHOLD RESOURCE ALLOCATION

The fundamental issue in household economics is to decide how to allocate scarce household resources to different uses. When the household members have some goals and objectives, this problem reduces to the standard consumer decision problem. Here a consumer maximises his preferences over a set of attainable choice-options. Typically, the preferences are represented by a utility function, where the choice-options are forming the budget set.

If, however, the goods and objectives of the individual household members differ, the decision process within the household becomes relevant. The choice behaviour will not only depend on the goals and objectives of the household members but also on other determinants of the decision making process. One may think of the relative bargaining power of the individual household members or of the agreed procedure for taking decisions under disagreement, e.g. by

* Economics Department, University of Birmingham, United Kingdom.
** Associate Professor of Finance School of Business, Claflin University South Carolina, USA.

transferring the right to decide to the winner of a game of Black-Jack. In precarious situation -those where households have low wealth and limited choice options in labour, credit, and other key markets-the household dynamics of resource allocation decisions may be especially crucial to basic welfare outcomes of family members (Kusago, 2001).

So the basic question is 'How do decisions on household resource allocation come about?' Studies are showing that the pattern of allocation is changing depending on the person who is taking decisions. Recent intra-household theory has explored the conditions under which differences result in distinctive resource allocation outcomes (Carter & Katz, 1997; Lundberg & Pollack, 1993; Manser & Brown, 1980; Mc.Elroy & Horney, 1981; Woolley, 1988). Women can only exert individual preferences for resource allocation, if they have their own income and which they control. An increase in non-labour income for women result greater household spending on education, health and household service at about four times the rate that additional income for men increases similar expenditures (Thomas 1990, 1993). A number of studies around the world, especially in developing countries, have confirmed that shifts of income to women increases the children and family well being. Studies in Kerala, India by Kumar (1977); in Jamaica (Horton and Millar); in St. Lucia (Knudsen and Yates 1981); in Ghana (Tripp 1981); in Kenya (Carloni 1987); in Botswana (Carloni 1987); in Srilanka (Benson and Emmert 1977) and another multi village study in Guatemala (Blumberg 1986), strongly indicate a greater devotion of women's income than men's to everyday subsistence and nutrition[1]. A more recent study has shown the same trend in Bangladesh, where girls schooling, boy's schooling, total household expenditure and women's non land asset increased with women's income (Pitt and Khandker, 1995).

Women in Intra-household Resource Allocation Decision

In Bangladesh, in particular, women's access to earning opportunities is severely limited. The legal inheritance rights of the women are generally forfeited, their chances of becoming widows (because of age differentials between spouses at marriage) are a near certainty; their risk of divorce is moderate though emotionally salient; and their control by patriarchal structure is extreme (Dwyer et al 1988). But the society in Bangladesh is changing with different economic development criteria and policy implications. Over the last thirty years, there has been a steady upward trend in the participation of women in the labour market in developing countries as well as in Bangladesh; they are coming more and more into the development frontier. The participation of women in the labour force has been increased both in the formal and informal market.

At this present context, it is expected that women in Bangladesh will be more conscious about their decision-making role as they are becoming a source of earning. Since the women are taking the role of direct contributors in the family as the wage earners, the household expenditure pattern is changing according to their priorities. Income earning capacity of women influences the intra-household resource allocation, which, in turn, influences the gender relations in the household.

Impact of Micro-credit on Decision Making

Women in Bangladesh are becoming more involved in decision-making as they start being the active financial contributor in the family. Our study includes the women who are borrower of the MFIs'. The access to credit makes them more conscious about their preferences and their role in decision-making.

Table 1
Change in Decision Making

	Past *1994*	*Present* *2000-2001*
Male female joint-decision making for household expenditure	55.2%	46%
Female only Decision making	-	26%
Women involved decision making	-	72%

Source: IFRI data 1994 and author's own data derived from survey conducted (2000-2001)

Table 1 shows the comparison of the incidence of male-female joint decision making for the past (1994) and present (2001). Here we use the IFPRI data (1994) and the data from our field survey (2001). In case of joint decision making our study is showing a slightly lower percentage than the study IFPRI (1994). The present study is showing 26 per cent of the women are taking decisions without the consultation of their husband. 72 per cent of the women under the current study are involved in decision making either alone or with their husband[2]. This above table 1 creates the impression that the majority of the women under our study are involved in taking decisions in the household. Note, however, that our sample covers only the women who have access to credit.

This paper will examine the following two questions; Whether household decision-making is following the unitary model where the husband and wife have same preferences for household expenditure or whether they have different expenditure preferences.

Whether the income of the women from the micro-loan has any impact on the consumption expenditure of the household.

When the women are direct contributors in the household, whether there is any change in their husband's treatment towards them.

In this present study, we found that women decision making and men decision making significantly differ over the use of the loan. We also found out that though the income from access to credit enables the women to spend more on household expenditure but they are not receiving any better treatment from their husbands in the household unless if they invest their money in productive assets, where their husband has equal interest.

Part II will discuss the different models of intra-household resource allocation and in Part III we examine empirically whether the unitary model holds or fails to hold for our study. Part IV and Part V will discuss and summarises the results.

MODELLING OF HOUSEHOLD BEHAVIOUR: A REVIEW

Intra-household Resource Allocation in New Household Economics (NHE)

Intra-household decision making theory has started with Becker's seminal work on new household economics (NHE) extended the neo-classical model of individual consumer demand to households by assuming a single, well behaved utility function (Becker, 1973, 1974, 1981)[3]. Becker (1965) first introduced unitary household model where, in accordance of single set preferences, the household combines time, good purchased in the market and produced at home to produce commodities which generate maximising utility for total household. This model offers a number of important theoretical perspectives on the question of intra-household distribution. But if individual household members have different preferences, the assumption of a household welfare function requires that these differing preferences be aggregated. So the question is how to aggregate these preferences. The first solution is that a welfare function should reflect the consensus among the member (Samuelson 1956, Evenson et al 1979). It does not indicate how to reach this point of consensus. Another approach applies Sen's (1966) model of co-operatives to the household. Here family welfare is the weighted sum of the net utility of all members. Firstly, this requires cardinal utility functions, which allows the trade-off of the utility obtained by one member against the utility obtained by another. Furthermore, it is not clear how the weights are to determine in the absence of a dictator.

Yet another approach, which relies on the altruism of the decision-maker, is given by Becker (1974, 1981), and is known as the 'Rotten kid theorem'. Becker considers the case of a household with two members, a benefactor and a recipient. The recipient is selfish in that he or she derives utility solely from his or her own consumption. The benefactor, as an altruist, can increase the utility by transferring some of his or her own consumption to the recipient. Now suppose the recipient takes the action, which increases his own consumption but lowers the benefactor. The benefactor could respond by lowering transfers to the recipient, so much so that the recipient's new level of consumption is below his or her original level. Thus the preference of the altruistic and the preference of the household converge. But the problem of this theory is that the benefactor should be altruistic over all levels of the consumption of others. If consumption by others is either an inferior or a luxury good, the threat of reduced transfers may not be credible over all level of consumption.

The first point of departure of (NHE) from the orthodox economic theory is that it emphasises the household and not the individual in the centre of the analysis. The second point of departure is the assumption that the household is a unit of production as well as unit of consumption.

The NHE model has been criticised by number of scholars. Obviously, this type of criticism applies to representative agent model in general. The application of social choice theory or mechanism design would seem to be the appropriate answer from the perspective of economic theory. From the applied / empirical perspective, however, this approach fails to be convincing. The followings are the most important criticisms among the others; first, the household are assumed to be a single decision making unit ignoring the complex economic and social relations. If the household is a polygamous household, which is structurally different from monogamous household, common preference model may not fit there. Secondly, the NHE model can only operate on the assumption that the consumption unit and production unit is unified, and that all choices are made by the same decision making unit. Empirical evidence indicates that production and consumption are a great deal more heterogeneous and shifting than the NHE model allows. In addition the decisions about what and when to produce and what and when to consume either impossible to separate or empirically or are carried out by different groups of people (Evans 1991). Thirdly, Folbre (1986) argues that the joint utility function removes the possibility of exploring conditions of unequal exchanges and exploitation between family members, and in particular between men and women.

NHE approach often ignores the fact that the household choices can be motivated by anything other than prices and income. In fact research shows the societal norm and patriarchal culture may affect the maternal and paternal altruism (Chen et al, 1981, Henn 1983, Whitehead 1984)[4].

Presentation of the Unitary Household Models

This type of model can be obtain in different ways, as a 'common preference model' or an 'altruism model' or 'a benevolent dictators' model, based on whether all the family members share the same preferences or there is a single decision-maker who is taking decision.

Assumptions

Household consists of two individuals, *h* and *w*.

All members of the household share the same preferences.

Household members derive a common utility from the consumption of a vector of individual commodities and labour supplied $(x_0, x_h, x_w, l_h, l_w)$, influenced by a vector of household characteristicsg,

The household utility function is given by

$$U(x_0, x_h, x_w, l_h, l_w; g), \qquad ...(1)$$

Which is maximised subject to an income constraint?

$$p_0 \cdot x_0 + p_h \cdot x_h + p_w \cdot x_w = m_h \cdot l_h + m_w \cdot l_w + n_0 + n_h + n_w \; ...(2)$$

and non-negativity constraints

$$x_0, x_h, x_w \geq 0 \text{ and } 0 \leq l_h, l_w \leq l_{\max}$$

Where $l_{\max}$ denotes the maximal individual labour supply.

Total household income is composed of wage income and the non-wage incomes joint income n_t, husband's individual non-wage income n_h and wife's individual nonwage income n_w.

Under this model, income is pooled and maximisation leads to a series of demands goods and supplies of labour, which are the functions of prices $p = (p_0, p_h, p_w)$, wage rates $m=(m_h, m_w)$, total non-wage household income $n_t=n_0+n_h+n_w$, and household characteristics γ.

$$x_i = X_i(p, m, n; \gamma) \qquad j = 0, h, w \qquad \ldots(3)$$
$$l_i = L_i(p, m, n; \gamma)$$

Subject to the set of prices and pooled income, resources are allocated to the household, which maximises household utility.

Collective Models

In contrast to unitary models, which predict that household behaviour can be changed only by changes in prices and household incomes; collective models predict that a large range of policies can be used to affect household allocation outcomes. These include access to common property resources, credit, public works schemes, and legal and institutional rights (Subsuming, 1999). In this approach of the household, the analysis of decision making takes account of different characteristics, interests and resources, and therefore of different utility functions, on the part of household members.

In the traditional approach of micro-economic theory, households are considered elementary decision units. They are represented by a single utility function that is maximised under a budget constraint. According to Chiappori (1997) the most important distinction between the traditional approach and collective approach is that the traditional approach assumes that the single consumers have single -utility framework. The collective model recognises the existence of several decision making units and potential different preferences, which do not systematically aggregate into a unique household utility function.

In single-utility models, wages or non-labour incomes only affect behaviour through usual income and substitution effects, whereas much more complex influences can be taken into account within a collective framework. Collective decision making processes have outcomes that are Pareto-efficient; thus the central assumption is that households will never adopt a decision that is Pareto-dominated.

All collective models have two common features, first, they allow different decision makers to have different preferences, and second, they do not require a unique household welfare index as interpreted by a utility function (Chiappori 1992).

Where decision-making is concerned, collective model have two subclasses. One refers to co-operative game theory and the other to non co-operative game theory.

Co-operative game theory models represent the household decisions as the bargaining process applying the tools of co-operative game theory. The vast majority of bargaining models rely on a Nash solution (Nash 1953). The division of the gains from marriage, then, can be modelled as a function of the 'fall back' or 'threat point' position of each member: itself a function of extra environmental parameters (EEPs) such as laws concerning property and prohibitions on women working outside the home (McElroy 1990).

Non Co-operative game theory model relies on the assumption that individual's actions are conditional on the actions of others. The conditionally of action implies that the outcomes of non-co-operative models may fail to be Pareto efficient (Ulph 1988; Kanbur 1991; Carter and Katz 1997; Lundberg and Pollack 1993).

Bargaining Models

In economics of the household, approaches to the analysis of economic decision making that take account of different characteristics, interests and resources, and therefore of different utility functions, on the part of household members. Bargaining models are an alternative approach to the strict neoclassical view advanced by Becker which argue that household behaviour is motivated primarily by a collective concern for economic efficiency (Folbre, 1984). As in the collective model, the potential gains from making joint decisions are maximised and household production and consumption are Pareto efficient. Unlike the collective model, which only assumes that the outcome will be Pareto efficient, the co-operative bargaining model specifies which Pareto efficient point will be chosen.

THEORETICAL FRAMEWORK OF NASH BARGAINING PROBLEM

As before, consider two household members, h and w. Only now we assume that each household member has his or her individual preferences.

Their utility functions are

$$U_h\,(x_0, x_h, l_h) \;\; and \; U_w\,(x_0, x_w, l_w) \qquad ...(4)$$

Respectively. Here, x_h is a private good consumed by h (such as food, water, or health care), x_w is a private good consumed by w, l_h and l_w denote supply of labour. Furthermore, x_0 is a public good within the household, consumed by both household members in the same quantity, whether they co-operate or not (such as schooling of their children). Let p be the vector of the prices of all goods, m be the wage rates of h and w, and n_h and n_w be the respective individual non-wage incomes. n_0 is the joint non-wage income which is only obtained if both household members co-operate. If h and w do not co-operate, their individual utility functions are each maximised subject to their individual full income constraints.

We can write their indirect utility functions as

$$V_h\,(p_0, p_h, m_h\,, n_h; a_h) \;\; and \;\; V_w\,(p_0, p_w, m_w, n_w\,; a_w) \qquad ...(5)$$

The V's are interpreted as 'threat point', the utility obtained independent of co-operation, while the a's are referred to as extra-environmental parameters (EEPs)[5]. Suppose that these two individuals are considering co-operating in some activity. These are a number of reasons why this might be advantageous. For example, there may be economies of scale associated with the production of certain goods (household or non-household), or there may be some goods that can be produced and shared by couples but not by single individuals (e.g children, in some societies). Denote utility values when co-operating in a joint activity as u_h and u_w respectively, where u is defined over the household public good and individual consumption of goods and leisure. The utility values of the corresponding 'threat point' are v_h and v_w.

Both individuals gain from co-operation when for a combination of price, wages, non-wage incomes and EEPs

$$u_i - v_i > 0 \text{ for } i = h, w \qquad ...(6)$$

The outcome of this is a binding and enforceable agreement regarding the division of gains from co-operation. One approach uses the Nash utility gain product function, which takes the form

$$G = (u_h - v_h)(u_w - v_w) \qquad ...(7)$$

This is maximised subject to a joint full income constraint yielding demand functions (food, water, health care) of the following form:

$$x_i = x_i(p, m, n; a_h\, a_w), \text{ where } j = 0, h, w \qquad ...(8)$$

$$l_i = l_i(p, m, n; a_h\, a_w) \text{ where } i = h, w \qquad ...(9)$$

In the Nash bargaining model two individuals are considered instead of one altruistic person. The Nash model maintains that these two individuals take joint decisions as to maximise the product of their individual gains from marriage. The Nash demand function includes the husband and wife's income effect individually. Thus it is possible to test empirically how the wife's income has different effects on the household than the husband's income.

According to Mc. Elroy (1990) extra-environmental parameters are pure threat point shifters. In addition to own wages and non wages income, the EEPs include measures of employability (for example, dummies for various degrees of prohibition on market work by gender) and measures of wealth of one's family of origin. (Mc. Elroy, 1997)[6].

In the Nash bargain model the threat point plays a key role. The threat point is the maximum level of utility that spouses can get outside their marriage. An improvement in the threat point for either spouse results in household demands that more strongly reflect the preferences of that spouse. In the bargaining models of Manser and Brown (1980)[7] and Mc.Elroy and Horney (1981)[8] the outcome is determined by the feasible consumption set and a threat point that is interpreted as the utility of remaining single or getting divorced. The preference of husband and wife regarding the optimal allocation of resources among goods and services within the family need be the same and they are assumed to be independent.

For simplicity and to facilitate graphical illustration we consider a two-goods case-regarding food and investment in private assets. The individual indifference curves for husband and wives are shown in the Edgeworth box diagram (figure 1.1). The locus of the tangency points of husband's and wife's indifference curves, for given other prices, wage rates and income, trace the contract curve as shown in the figure 1.2. All points on the contract curve are Pareto efficient allocations. From the contract curve from the correspondent pairs of utility levels for husband and wife, the utility possibility curve (UPC) can be obtained which is plotted in figure 1.2.

The UPC1 forms the boundary of all feasible payoff pairs (u_h, u_w). Any point below the curve is feasible but not Pareto efficient. Let us denote the feasible payoff set as *S*. Note that points above UPC are unattainable. If the bargaining process ends without an agreement, then each individual obtains a disagreement payoff, which is also called the threat point payoff. The threat point $v = (v_h, v_w) = (V_h(\ ), V_w(\ ))$ is always below the UPC (as shown in the figure) because of the gains from marriage to both partners.

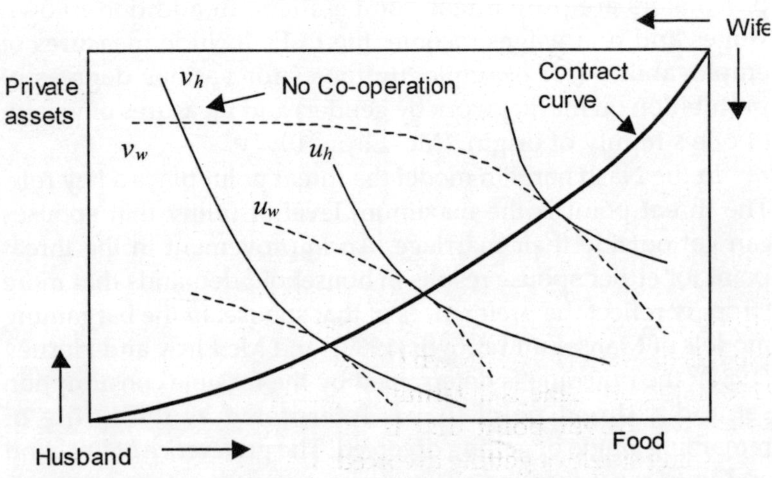

Figure 1.1 Edgeworth Diagram

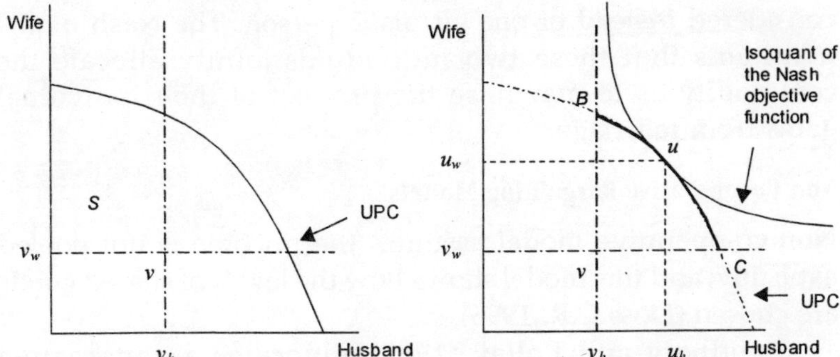

Figure 1.2: Utility possibility curve **Figure 1.3: Nash Bargaining Solution**

Figure 1.3 shows the Nash bargaining solution. Like before we assume a family consists of two members: a husband and a wife. Each obtains a utility value: u_h for the husband and u_w for the wife. If agreement is not reached, then the payoff represented by a threat point (v_h, v_w) indicates the utilities associated with a divorce or, alternatively a non co-operative outcome within the marriage. The Nash bargaining model provides the leading solution concept in bargaining models of marriage (Lundberg, Pollak, 1996)[9]. Graphically, the Pareto efficient payoffs are indicated as a solid line connecting the points *B* and *C* in figure 1.3. The Nash bargaining solution is the tangency point of the utility possibility curve. If the husband has a higher bargaining power than the wife, then solution point is closer to point *C* and it would be closer to point *B* if the wife's bargaining power were higher.

The utility received by husband or wife in the Nash bargaining solution depends upon the threat point; the higher one' s utility at the threat point, the higher one's utility in the Nash bargaining solution. Household demands depend not only on prices and total household income but also on determinants of the threat point (Lundberg and Polak, 1996).

This Nash bargaining model is not out of criticism. Assuming the Nash bargaining solution is overly restrictive and does not yield easily testable restrictions unless premarital utility function is known (Chiappori 1988, 1988).

In the Nash bargaining model two individuals are considered instead of one altruistic person. The Nash model maintains that these two individuals jointly allocate the commodity as to maximise the product of their individual gains from marriage.

Non Co-operative Bargaining Models

Non co-operative model assumes that income is not pooled explicitly, and this model shows how the levels of shared goods are chosen (Doss C.R, 1996).

Lundberg and Pollak (1997) advocates an alternative bargaining model named 'Separate-Spheres' based on two parent families.

A distinguishing feature of this bargaining model is that family demand behaviour depends not only on family resources but also on the resources controlled by each spouse individually. Individual control of resources matters because bargaining outcomes depend on threat point as well as on the feasible consumption set. The more resources an individual spouse controls, the more strongly that individual's preferences will be reflected in the intra-family distribution of resources. Estimation of these models requires much more detailed data that may include individual earnings and resources and transfers among household members.

TESTING THE MODELS AGAINST THE EMPIRICAL EVIDENCE

Testing the Common Preference and the Unified Model

In order to test the assumptions of the unified household model, Thomas (1993) uses data from Brazil to test whether the distribution of non-labour income within the household has any impact on expenditure. Thomas's results indicate non-labour income controlled by women is associated with larger increases of the household budget share being devoted to human capital and leisure. Thus the unified household model is rejected. A consequence, though not a surprising one, is that differential control of income translates into different patters of expenditure. It is widely perceived that men spend a higher share of their income on goods for their personal consumption than do women, alcohol, cigarettes, status consumer goods, and even 'female companionship'. In contrast, women are believed to be more likely to purchase goods for children and for general household consumption. Guyer (1980)[10] is particularly noted for this observation, although a number of other researchers have commented on the phenomenon as well. In this context we can conclude unified model has been rejected by number of studies where the common preference does not prevail. Unitary model of the household has been rejected in a variety of country settings in both developed and developing countries (Strauss and Thomas1995; Behrman 1997; Haddad et al 1997). One weakness of this model is that it considers all the incomes in the household are pooled. If preferences are not common to all household members, one household member must have the ability to monitor the others, which may create conflict of interests. Unitary models represent a special case of co-operative collective models where preferences are identical and, as a consequence, resources are pooled (Quisumbing,1999).

Factors Influencing Bargaining Model

Directly measuring one's bargaining power within the household is difficult if not impossible. The recent literature on intra-household resource allocation has focused on several factors that influence ones bargaining power and, thus, the ways in which resources are allocated within household. A body of recent micro-economic analysis has focused on command over economic resources, such as assets, unearned income, and transfer payments or welfare receipts (that is, factors that are 'exogenous-or external-to labour supply), as a major determinant of bargaining power.

Bargaining power determines the share of resources allocated to an individual within the household (Quisumbing et al, 1999). Quisumbing et al (1999) identifies four sets of determinants that affect bargaining power. These are (i) Control over resources such as assets. (ii) Influence, that can be used to influence the bargaining process;

(iii) mobilisation of interpersonal network; iv) Basic attitudinal attributes.

Economic resources are the major determinants of bargaining power, these include assets (e.g. Doss 1996; Thomas, Contreras, and Frankenberg 1997; Quisumbing,1994), unearned income (Schultz 1990; Thomas 1997), or transfer payments and welfare receipts (Lundberg, Pollack and Wales 1997; Rabaclava and Thomas 1997) The proxy for bargaining power are; 1. Public provision of resources to a particular member of the household and exogenous policy changes which affect the intra-household distribution of these resources (Lundberg, Pollak, and Wales 1997; Rubaclava and Thomas 1997); 2. Shares of income earned by women (Hoddinott and Haddad 1995); 3. Unearned income (Thomas 1990; Schultz 1990); Inherited asset (Quisumbing 1994; 5. Assets at marriage (Thomas, Frakenberg, and Contreras 1997) and 6. Current Asset (Doss 1996)[11].

Legal rights, skills, knowledge, the capacity to acquire information, education can also influence decision-making power. In some cases domestic violence can be used to extract resources from spouse or their families (Rao 1997; Bloch and Rao1996). Membership in organisation and social capital may also influence a person's power to affect household decisions. Basic attitudinal attributes that affect bargaining power include self-esteem, self-confidence, and emotional satisfaction. The group based micro-finance programs have been successfully includes empowerment approach as their major objective.

Quisumbing et al (1999) undertook a study to test whether the assets brought to marriage by each spouse have different effects on intra-household allocation outcomes. In this research the authors focus on two types of outcomes: household level income and individual level income. The survey has been undertaken on four countries e.g. Bangladesh, Indonesia, Ethiopia, South Africa.

Similarly, the extent of a person's social or economic fall back position influences the bargaining power. The members with more power often described in terms of 'voice' and 'exit potential' shape joint decisions. These terms voice means a family member's ability to bargain over the household resource allocation. Exit means the person's potential to exit the conjugal (familial) relationship (Katz, 1992)[12].

Hoddinott and Haddad (1995) using Ulph's (1988) non-co-operative model as a guide, they use two-stage least squares estimation with budget shares and women's predicted cash share of household income being treated as jointly endogenous. They find that doubling women's share of cash income within Ivorian households raises the budget share of food and lowers the budget shares of alcohol and cigarettes.

Test of Income Pooling and Collective Models

An additional perspective on income pooling is found in a study of informal credit programs in Bangladesh (Pitt and Khandker, 1994). This study finds that credit affects household education and consumption choices differently if women rather than men obtain it. As the study employs a fixed-effect methodology that treats the availability of credit much as an experiment, it is able to control for the fact that credit choices reflect household preferences. A few recent studies use extra-household environmental parameters (EEP's) to support collective models. Pitt Khandker (1994) their results are consistent with shifts in EEP's influencing intra-household distribution. They observe that communities where a credit program is in place have a higher demand for schooling than other communities. Although EEP'S may be one possible explanation for this difference, it could also be due to different expected returns mediated by economic impacts of credit or to pre-existing differences between communities for which they did not fully control.

One study undertook by Thomas Duncan (1997) shows that income in the hands of women is associated with a larger increase in the share of the household budget devoted to human capital (household services, health, and education) and leisure goods (recreation and ceremonies). In addition of that, this study also confirms that the proportion of the budget spent on food (consumed at home and away) declines more if the income is in the hands of the women, although food composition also changes, with nutrient intakes rising faster as women's income increases. It appears that, as income under the control of women rises, more is spent on health and nutrient related expenses. The evidence from this study Thomas Duncan (1997) indicates that child health outcome is consistent with this interpretation: maternal income has a significantly larger effect on the weight for height and height for age of children than parental income.

Influence of Heterogeneity

From the above discussion we can sum up that in most of the cases the unified household model has been rejected and there prevails preference heterogeneity among the men and women. Women and men have different systematic pattern of preferences, which shapes the household expenditure choices, based on who controls the income.

Kusago (2001) undertook a study on intra-household decision making in Malayisa which attempts to address two issues, preference differences from expenditure models and income control measures, by testing the role of preference heterogeneity and relative assets control in determining expenditure share decisions. According to the Kusago (2001) asset holding may be a good measure of the bargaining position of husbands and spouses over some types of decisions. The finding of this particular study has rejected the traditional single utility NHE model, advocating highly heterogeneous preferences at the household level and significant statistical evidence that women's preferences and power influence expenditure shares for some major items.

Lampietti et al (1999)[13] introduced a new test of common preferences models, where a hypothetical preference test has been applied to the case of medical expenses to combat malaria among households in Ethiopia. They found that woman gives higher preferences than men to purchasing malaria vaccines.

Smith and Chavas (1999)[14] explore the effect of preference of heterogeneity on agriculture production decision, household income and household members' well-being in the context of Burkina Faso. Their simulation exercises reveal, that both the level of preference of heterogeneity and the associated power divergence within the family are likely to influence the impact of price liberalisation on the household economy and household well-being.

Resource Control, Bargaining Power, and Household Allocation

Additional evidence on the gender-diffenentiated impacts of resource control on household level outcomes comes from recent micro-credit initiatives from Bangladesh. Two related studies examine the impacts of female and male borrowing from the Grameen Bank, BRAC and a government program called RD-12 on such outcomes as per capita household expenditure (income), girls' and boys' schooling and nutritional status (Khandker 1998; Pitt and Khandker 1998). These studies find that the household level impacts often differ substantially based on the whther the borrower is a woman or a man and that, in a number of instances, the marginal impacts of borrowing are greater for women than for men.

For example, in the case of all three micro-credit programs, the impact of female borrowing on per capita household expenditure (income) is about twice as large as the impact of male borrowing (table). As in the case of other form of resource control, female borrowing also appears to have a greater impact on child welfare than male borrowing.

Table 1.4
Impact of Female and Male Borrowing on Selected Household Outcomes (per cent change for a 10 per cent increase in borrowing)

	Grameen Bank		*BRAC*		*RC-12*	
	Male borro-wing	*Female borro-wing*	*Male borro-wing*	*Female borro-wing*	*Male borro-wing*	*Female borro-wing*
Household Indicators						
Per capita spending	0.18	0.43	0.19	0.39	0.23	0.40
Net Worth	0.15	0.14	0.20	0.09	0.22	0.02
Boy's schooling	0.07	0.61	-0.08	-0.03	0.29	0.79
Girls schooling	0.30	0.47	0.24	0.12	0.07	0.23

Source: Khandker 1998

For example, except in the case of BRAC, female borrowing has a greater positive impact on both girls' and boys' enrolment in school than male borrowing. At the same time, evidence indicates that male borrowing has a greater impact on household net worth than female borrowing. This suggests that while, at the margin, women seem to invest in the human capital of their children, men appear to invest more than women in physical capital.

The evidence presented above indicates that the distribution of resources within household-not just their total level-matters to intra-household allocations and investments. More specifically, the evidence shows that increasing female command of resources plays an important role in improving the relative status of women as well as in enhancing family and child welfare.

Frankenberg & Thomas (2001) undertook a study based on the measurement of power relation between the household members, namely, husband and wife in Indonesia. This particular study (Frankenberg & Thomas 2001) throws the lights on the intra-household power relations, aiming to identify whether common preference prevails among the household members or one member dominates the preference over the other. Frankenberg & Thomas (2001) make an effort to identify the indicators of relative power in the household. The authors also try to identify the some common expenditure decisions in the household where joint decision making is obvious. In this study (Frankenberg & Thomas 2001) has used three sets of questionnaire comprises of three different components. The first set of questionnaire focuses on how couples deal with money whereas the second set of questionnaire concerns how families make decisions about expenditure and use of time. The third set of questionnaire attempts to provide the insights into the relative status of husbands and wives within the household.

Another study has been undertaken in Mexico by Adato Michelle et al (2000), which is based on intra-household decision making patterns. In addition of intra-household decision making patterns, Adato Michelle et al (2000)[15] also throws the light on how parental preferences for child schooling changes on the child's gender. The results of this study Adato, Michelle et al (2000) found some interesting insights of intra-household decision making. According to the study Adato Michelle et al (2000) characteristics of husband and wife are the most consistent determinants of decision-making patters. This study confirms that the transfer payment to the women has increased the recognition of women's importance in the family and their degree of responsibility to ward the family relative to men.

Hellman (2000) studied on intra-household expenditure pattern in Bangladesh. This study has examined the effects of household asset ownership patterns on the morbidity status of male female pre-schoolers. In this particular study (Hellman, 2000) asset control by each spouse has been measured by three different dimensions, one, by the current asset holdings of parents, secondly, asset brought to marriage by each spouse, thirdly, family background factors of each parent that help to determine the their current asset holdings. The findings of the study Hellman (2000) indicates that resource control in the household has noticeable effects on child health, and that the effects differ according to the sex of the child. The results of the study (Hellman, 2000) clearly indicate that the unitary household model is not an appropriate description of household decision making, even in a setting such as rural Bangladesh. Using the different measures of parental assets, the study Hellman (2000) found that resources held by mothers have different effects on child health than those held by fathers; this leads to a rejection of the unitary model in favour of the collective household model. Asset brought to the marriage by each parent, a higher proportion brought by the wife reduces the morbidity of girl children (Hellman 2000). According to Hellman (2000) dowry (payments from the wife's to the husband's side at the time of marriage) most likely enhances the bargaining power of wives to make allocation decisions of marriage. The same evidence can be mentioned from other studies, namely, Russel et al (1999) show that dowry is a strong determinant of child weight-for-age in Pakistan. Rao (1997) and Rao and Bloch (1993) find in India that smaller dowries increase wife beating and reduce child caloric intake later in the marriage.

Modelling for the Present Study

Based on Nash bargaining models as discussed before we can show graphically the income from micro-credit has increased the woman's threat point and the bargaining power. We interpret our hypothetical household consisting of two individuals' husband and wife. Previously the husband was the sole earner in that household. Assume now the wife has started using micro-credit.

The above figure is showing the treat point of the wife is shifting from u_w to u^*_w as a result of the change in their income[16].

From the Nash bargaining model we know, wife's indirect utility function outside the marriage is

$$Z_w\,(p_o, p_{w,}\, m_{w,}\, n_w\,;\, \alpha_{w,})$$

Figure 1.4: Nash Bargaining Solution with Micro-Credit

Without Micro-Credit

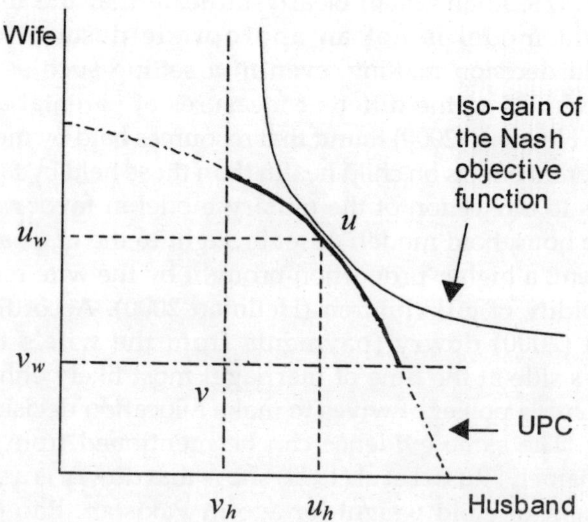

With Micro-Credit

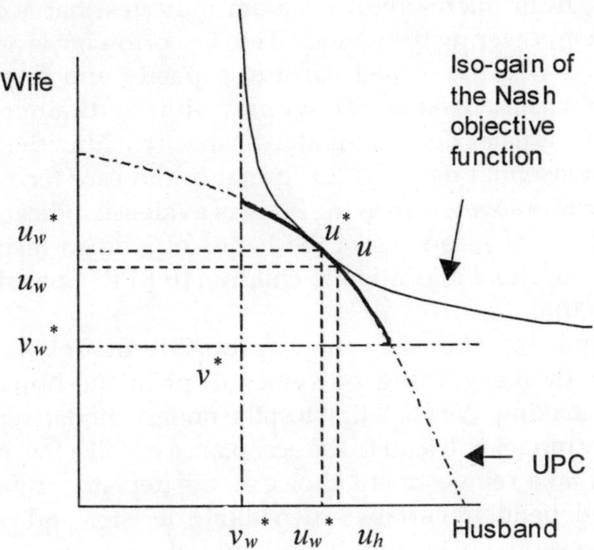

If we consider the income from the micro-credit is the a_w which will shift the wife's threat point from u_w to u_w^*.

The change of income will shift the UPC curve outwardly.

Assuming the husband's indirect utility is unchanged, Z_h $(p_o, p_h, m_h, n_h; \alpha_h)$.

In order to fit an appropriate empirical model for the present study the following important consideration can be noted.

First, in contrast to the view traditionally held by economist and policy makers that household members pool their resources and allocate them according to a unified set of preferences, there is mounting evidence that household resources are allocated in the face of competing preferences and unequal bargaining power among members. One implication of this is that the distribution of resources within a household, not only their total level, matters. Policies that alter the distribution of resources among different members of a household shift the balance of power across those members, with potentially important implications for gender equality and family welfare. For example, in Bangladesh the evidence from micro-credit program indicates that access to credit is empowering the women. Female borrowing is not only associated with increased earning capacity and improved command over assets for women, but with increased autonomy, greater decision-making capacity within the home, greater household demand for formal health care for women and girls. Moreover, a growing body of evidence indicates that greater level of resources in the hands of women results, in greater household allocation to children (IFRPRI Consultation draft, 2000).

Second, for choosing the appropriate model we shall consider the bargaining power concept in the household decision making. We shall first test the unitary model; rejection to unitary model will lead to the acceptance of collective model. We shall take reinvestment choice as the dependent variable of two independent variables men taking decision and women taking decision, for testing the null hypothesis.

Third, if we can reject the unitary household model the question is still comes which alternative bargaining model we can use for our model. It is very difficult to find out a suitable bargaining model. Our model will examine whether the wife's income influences the household pattern of expenditure or not. If it does we can argue wife's has different expenditure preference than her husband.

Fourth, we already have shown in our theoretical model using Nash model that micro-credit increase the threat point of the women. Chiaporri (1988) has argued that the Nash bargaining assumption is overly restrictive and does not yield easily testable restrictions, unless the premarital (indirect) utility function is known. But we cannot empirically test it, as we do not have any premarital data. One empirical solution is given by Montalto (1995)[17] to estimate the indirect utility function of the single person households and then to assume that these represent the threat points for similar persons in two-person household. We shall consider this as our future research. We simply consider the income from the micro-credit as the extra-household parameter, which can influence the indirect utility of the women outside the marriage.

Here, in our model we shall consider access to credit and the ownership of or control over assets as the determinants of the bargaining power of the women and men in the villages. Why among the other determinant we choose these two factors? 'The significance of these two factors, namely command over property (especially land) and access to employment (through credit), is strengthening a rural person's survival ability outside power as a bargaining determinant (Agarwal 1997).

Again, In order to determine the intra-household relationship pattern after accessing to credit we use husband's treatment as a dependent variable to see the impact of the income and asset control over their behaviour towards their wife.

METHODOLOGY AND EMPIRICAL ANALYSIS

Data Collection

The survey for this research was conducted during 2000 and 2001 on 200 individual borrowers who are participating in the credit programmes of BRAC and Grameen Bank. 100 borrowers of Grameen Bank were randomly selected from three villages in the Comilla district and the other 100 were BRAC members randomly selected from five villages in the Jaidebpur district. The names of the borrowers were obtained from the offices of BRAC and Grameen in the mentioned districts. Semi structured questionnaire were used to gather information from the borrowers. This method made it is possible to obtain accurate and sensitive information on decision taking behaviour of the borrowers. All the 200 borrowers were used in the analysis were women. The practical experience of direct interview sometimes has given some insights of the actual use of the loan and the impression of the women regarding their own well being and status.

Limitation of the Study

The following are the limitations that may prevent to get the reliable results.

1. Limitation of the questionnaire. The questionnaire that is used in this study is not sufficient to understand all the dimension of the bargaining power of the women. Additional research is needed in this field.
2. The present study is mostly based on refuting the concept of common preference model but did not provide enough idea of formulating an alternative bargaining model due to the limitations of the data

Testing the Models Against Empirical Evidence

Table 1.6
Tests of intra-household resource allocation model

Null Hypothesis	*Common preference model*	*Collective model*
Women's income does not affect Household expenditure	reject	consistent
Men and women decisions are the same for the use of the loan	reject	consistent

Source: The table is based on the analysis by Ross (1996)[18].

Under the common preference model, expenditure patterns should depend only on total household income-not on who earns it. We shall reject the null hypothesis if we find that income of women after using micro-loan has any effect on household expenditure.

Econometric specification and operational definitions of survey variables

For a test of the unitary model a dependent binary variable that states whether or not a decision has been taken to reinvest their profit from the loan.

If a unitary model held with common preference for household expenditure this variable should not be affected by a crucial variable on decision taking represented by two dummy variables against a base of joint decision taking.

Where D2 is variable representing women taking decisions on loan use, D1 represents men taking decisions on loan use and joint decision is a base.

The Control Variables are AGE which represents the age of the women borrower, which is a continuous variable. MAS represents the marital status of the women borrower which is a binary variable where married is taken as 1 and unmarried as 0. NOC is the number of children of the borrower.

To evaluate our second question that woman's income has different impact on household expenditure pattern, the following are crucial variables.

LOG MONTH is the log of monthly income of women, OWNHOUSE represents whether or not woman owns any house. It is also binary. (If owns house then 1 and if not 0. PROASSET represents whether or not woman has any productive asset. (If owns any productive asset like land then 1 and if not 0. OTHTERASSET whether or not woman has other assets, which can be used in lieu of cash-e.g. jewellery). It is also binary. (If owns asset then 1 and if not 0). ASSET represents whether or not woman has any savings in Banks. It is also binary. (If has any savings then 1 and if not 0).

We use income as control variables. We divide income variable into 3 different binary variables. Income from agriculture is AGRI. Income from trading is TRADING. Variable Y1 is the income from FARM , NURSERY , FISHING. Another control variable is education. Two education dummies are EDU1 education up to primary level. EDU2 is the education variable above primary level. No education is the base.

Results and Discussion

The results of the present study will be presented into 3 sections. In the first section we shall do the hypothesis testing for finding out whether the preference of men and women differs over a same expenditure decision. In order to test this we use two explanatory variables, men taking decision over the loan use and the women taking decision over the loan use. Here the dependent variable is reinvestment. This variable is a binary. Here the question was asked whether they use their profit for further reinvestment. If they say yes, we represents it as 1 and if they say no, we code it 0.

In the second section the evidences will be presented to

show the effect of women's income on expenditure share. We segregate our dependent variables according to the expenditure, i.e. food expenditure, clothing expenditure, and other expenditure which includes children's schooling.

In the third section will show the impact of income from micro-credit on different consumption pattern. Here, we divide the consumption into 3 different types, i;e food consumption (FOODCON), education consumption (EDUCON), consumption for medical (MEDICAL). Here the dependent variables are binary and we use logit regression model. We ask three different questions regarding this consumption. The questions were if they spend on food, education or medical from their income from micro-credit. If they say yes it is represented it as 1 and if they say no it is represented it 0.

In the last section will show the evidence whether the access to credit to women has changed their bargaining power with their husband. Here our dependent variable is husband treatment (HUSTREAT). This is a binary variable as well. The question was asked here to the women whether after accessing the micro-loan their husbands are treating them better than before. If they say yes, we represent it as 1 and if they say no we represent it 0.

SECTION 1: Hypothesis testing for women taking decision and men taking decision over the loan use

Our null hypothesis is that unitary household model will hold in Bangladesh where men and women have same preference for reinvestment.

From the above table we can see that men taking decision and women taking decision differ over the reinvestment decision. Men taking decision is positively and significantly related to reinvestment decision whereas women taking decision is negatively related to reinvestment and it is not significant. To sum up it indicates that if men are taking decision over the loan use they will prefer more reinvestment of the profit than that of the women. Why women are not interested for reinvestment? The reason could be two, one they may want to spend more on household consumption, second they want to keep the money for ownership of asset.

Table 1.7
Differences of Preferences Over the Loan Use

Dependent Variable: REINVEST
Method: ML-Binary Logit

Variable	*Coefficient*	*Std. Error*	*z-Statistic*	*Prob.*
C	-2.334439	1.369748	-1.704283	0.0883
D2_WOMEN_01	-0.197175	0.533785	-0.369391	0.7118
D1_MEN_01	1.437178	0.589430	2.438249	0.0148**
CHIL	0.741546	0.824509	0.899379	0.3685
AGE	0.080829	0.033240	2.431664	0.0150**
MAS	1.028892	0.784376	1.311733	0.1896
NOC	-0.101203	0.191449	-0.528615	0.5971
Mean dependent var	0.885000	S.D. dependent var		0.319823
S.E. of regression	0.302537	Akaike info criterion		0.679388
Sum squared resid	17.66504	Schwarz criterion		0.794829
Log likelihood	-60.93876	Hannan-Quinn criter.		0.726105
Restr. Log likelihood	-71.36860	Avg. log likelihood		-0.304694
LR statistic (6 df)	20.85968	McFadden R-squared		0.146140
Probability(LR stat)	0.001944			

** significant at 10% level

From the above table it is clear that women and men have different decision preference for the profit use.

SECTION 2: The following tables are regression results of the three expenditure items: food, clothing, schooling (other expenditure),

The above table presents the impact of log of monthly income on different monthly household expenditures. The first dependent variable (LOG (EXA) is the total expenditure after taking the micro-loan. We then divide our expenditure as food expenditure (LOG (FEXP), clothing expenditure (LOG (EXP), and other expenditures LOG (OTHEREXP), which includes expenditure on schooling of the children. Each of these categories is taken as the dependent variable for each model presented above.

Table 1.8
Impact of log monthly income on expenditure (OLS regression)

Dependent Variable:	*LOG(EXA)*		*LOG(FEXP)*		*LOG(CEXP)*		*LOG(OTHEREXP)*	
Variable	*Coefficient*	*t-Statistic*	*Coefficient*	*t-Statistic*	*Coefficient*	*t-Statistic*	*Coefficient*	*t-Statistic*
AGE	-0.00225	-0.40217	0.006714	0.878079	-0.0199	-2.09115*	0.008196	0.886481
CHIL	0.472737	2.295695*	0.275022	0.978249	0.042913	0.122648	-0.02353	-0.06264
NOC	0.074231	2.335289*	0.077025	1.774895**	-0.01534	-0.28401	0.169194	3.272871*
AGRI	-0.10773	-1.18596	0.07055	0.568884	-0.13984	-0.90602	-0.028	-0.19214
TRADING	0.059292	0.674484	0.288687	2.405431*	0.177769	1.190181	0.004011	0.02901
Y1	-0.079	-0.88684	-0.26578	-2.18549*	0.216387	1.42972	-0.20172	-1.38375
MAS	0.355163	2.480024*	0.73395	3.753894***	0.23065	0.947892	0.19028	0.84302
EDU1	0.064824	0.587059	0.0515	0.341616	-0.01945	-0.10364	-0.0792	-0.46013
EDU2	0.214038	1.503071	0.183337	0.943027	-0.11012	-0.45512	0.385803	1.708267*
LOG(MONTH)	0.099966	2.250748*	0.065365	1.077975	0.175426	2.324598*	0.175455	2.528039*
ASSET	0.226647	2.403954*	-0.05886	-0.45731	-0.18346	-1.14523	1.79534	1.199274
OTHERASS	-0.02549	-0.27756	0.038668	0.308386	-0.20461	-1.31116	0.031213	0.210618
OWNHOUSE	0.086293	0.891459	0.028213	0.213484	0.245142	1.490458	0.141838	0.948178
PROASSET	-0.09414	-0.93597	-0.01255	-0.0914	-0.19492	-1.14059	-0.2699	-1.69147**
C	6.297653	15.28626	5.66594	10.07352	4.193242	5.990325	4.462025	6.500143
R-squared		0.293674	0.226063		0.140896		0.275533	

Dependent Variable:	*LOG(EXA)*		*LOG(FEXP)*		*LOG(CEXP)*		*LOG(OTHEREXP)*	
Variable	*Coefficient*	*t-Statistic*	*Coefficient*	*t-Statistic*	*Coefficient*	*t-Statistic*	*Coefficient*	*t-Statistic*
Adjusted R-squared	0.232633	0.159179		0.066652		0.206064		
S.E. of regression	0.506582	0.691613		0.86074		0.764827		
Sum squared resid	41.57331	77.48917		120.0215		85.40428		
Log likelihood		-122.943	-178.05		-216.772		-177.412	
Durbin-Watson stat		1.849716	1.887926		1.379869		1.736859	
Mean dependent var		8.044861	7.625301		4.912651		6.584287	
S.D. dependent var		0.578293	0.754243		0.890944		0.858362	
Akaike info criterion		1.558677	2.181357		2.61889		2.390204	
Schwarz criterion		1.827843	2.450522		2.888055		2.677292	
F-statistic		4.811121	3.379946		1.89775		3.966248	
Prob(F-statistic)		0	0.000085		0.029988		0.000009	

* Significant at 5% level ** Significant at 10% level
*** Significant at 1% level

Here, the control variable, age of the women is not significant for total expenditure, share of food expenditure and other expenditure but only negatively significant for clothing expenditure. It means that as the women getting older they buy less clothing for theme-selves.

The second independent variable is whether the women have got any child (CHIL). It is a binary variable. It is not significant for any expenditure category.

The third variable is the number of child (NOC) of the women. It is positively significant with all dependent variables but not with clothing expenditure. It means that as the numbers of children are increasing, the women will spend more food and other expenditure, which is increasing significantly except the clothing expenditure. Clothing expenditure is not significant as it includes the expenditure on clothing of the borrower (women) only not for the children.

Here we use three sources of income for the women where they use their loan money as our control variables in this study. These are from agriculture (AGRI), from trading (TRADING) and from farm, nursery, fishing etc (Y1). Source of income, agriculture is not significant for any of the expenditure. Trading is positively significant for food expenditure and income from farming is negatively significant for food expenditure. It means that if the women use their loan money in trading, more likely that they will spend more on food expenditure. It is just reverse for income from farming etc, if the source of income is farming they will spend less on food consumption. It is quite obvious as they spend loan money on farming, fishing and poultry, they will buy less from outside and eat their own poultry, fish and milk.

Another control variable is marital status (MAS), which is positively significant for expenditure after taking the micro-loan and highly positively significant for food expenditure. This means that married women tend to spend more on food and total expenditure. This is not significant for clothing and other expenditure.

Another control variable is education of the women (EDU1), which is not significant for any expenditure category except other expenditure. Education above the primary level (EDU2) is positively significant with other expenditure. Other expenditure is the expenditure spend on the children's education and it is positively related to edu2 means as more women will be educated above the primary level they tend spend more on their children education as they will be more conscious about their children's education. Log of monthly income of the women is positively significant with total expenditure, with clothing expenditure and with other expenditure. This is not significant with log of monthly food expenditure though we found out that log monthly expenditure is positively related to food consumption (table-2). Consumption of food has been increased but not the expenditure on that, because the household may produce food on their own land and from their own farming, which may reduce the food expenditure but at the same time maintaining the increased consumption. Cash (ASSET) is positively significant with log of total expenditure but not with any other expenditure category. Keeping asset (OTHERASS) like jewellery and other semi- cash item is not significant for expenditure. Ownership of house also does not have any effect on expenditure. Ownership of productive asset is negatively significant with other expenditure. Here in this category we use ownership of shop as the productive asset. It indicates that if the women own a shop by using their loan money, for either theme-selves or for their husband, they will tend to spend less for their children education. It is may the reason in rural area people need another help to run a shop and the child could be used as the helping hand.

SECTION 3: In this section we shall discuss the impact of women 's income and the asset ownership on different consumption pattern.

The above table presents four logit regression models showing the effect of monthly income and asset control of the women on reinvestment of income and different consumption pattern. We include here food consumption, education consumption, and medical of the household. Here the all the dependent variables are binary. The women were asked

Table 1.9
Impact of log monthly income on reinvestment and consumption pattern: logit regression

Dependent Variable Independent Variable	*REINVEST*		*FOODCON*		*EDUCON*		*MEDICAL*	
	Coefficient	*z-Statistic*	*Coefficient*	*z-Statistic*	*Coefficient*	*z-Statistic*	*Coefficient*	*z-Statistic*
AGE	0.036477	0.625158	-0.04617	-1.58587	-0.04047	-1.44763	-0.03581	-1.46971
CHIL	1.615896	1.020046	0.676517	0.625856	0.660359	0.633232	-0.02156	-0.02328
NOC	-0.12394	-0.35223	0.290743	1.595865	0.301023	1.720005**	0.509928	3.315192***
AGRI	1.594734	1.493484	-0.25732	-0.54852	1.045709	2.155554*	0.123763	0.311993
TRADING	2.116341	1.886239*	0.674219	1.378146	0.911451	2.005704*	0.858608	2.215482
Y1	-1.05354	-1.13539	-0.74773	-1.44511	-0.30981	-0.66427	-0.06428	-0.16397
MAS	-2.16858	-1.41072	-1.03568	-1.35203	-2.1892	-2.22391*	-1.05257	-1.50409
EDU1	1.184307	1.336496	2.745769	4.656803	1.901872	3.483866***	1.228206	2.429773
EDU2	1.53213	1.185972	2.159541	2.989445**	1.215276	1.819003**	1.137056	1.767418**
LOG (MONTH)	0.928397	2.323088*	0.703585	2.831883*	0.531282	2.225548*	-0.01038	-0.05247
ASSET	-0.26105	-0.30702	-1.1411	-2.36934**	-0.95227	-2.10451*	-1.12922	-2.66312***
OTHERASS	1.386862	1.412877	0.328751	0.664814	0.192676	0.420548	-0.44682	-1.07742
OWNHOUSE	-0.71378	-0.7825	-0.88258	-1.70668**	-0.12837	-0.27223	0.333104	0.76693
PROASSET	1.482516	1.79391**	-0.22026	-0.42609	-0.32669	-0.65106	-0.0106	-0.02341
C	-6.55387	-1.805**	-4.03714	-1.84105**	-2.4294	-1.12789	0.253694	0.135954
Mean dependent var		0.932203		0.723164		0.689266	0.548023	
S.E. of regression		0.219772		0.400107		0.417239	0.471808	

Dependent Variable Independent Variable	*REINVEST*		*FOODCON*		*EDUCON*		*MEDICAL*	
	Coefficient	*z-Statistic*	*Coefficient*	*z-Statistic*	*Coefficient*	*z-Statistic*	*Coefficient*	*z-Statistic*
Sum squared resid		7.824562		25.9339		28.20236	36.06164	
Log likelihood		-29.3785		-78.582		-86.719	-103.968	
Restr. Log likelihood		-43.8786		-104.419		-109.685	-121.869	
LR statistic (14 df)		29.00016		51.67484		45.93128	35.80202	
Probability(LR stat)		0.01045		3.19E-06		2.88E-05	0.001117	
S.D. dependent var		0.25211		0.448704		0.464107	0.4991	
Akaike info criterion		0.501452		1.057424		1.149367	1.344276	
Schwarz criterion		0.770618		1.326589		1.418532	1.613441	
Hannan-Quinn criter.		0.610615		1.166587		1.25853	1.453439	
Avg. log likelihood		-0.16598		-0.44397		-0.48994	-0.58739	
McFadden R-squared		0.330459		0.247439		0.209379	0.146887	

* Significant at 5% level
** Significant at 10% level
*** Significant at 1% level

whether they spend their income on reinvestment for additional income or on food, education or medical expenditure. If they say yes, we assign 1 and if they say no, we assign 0. The control variable, age (AGE) of the women and having a child (CHIL) is not significant for any category of dependent variables. Number of child (NOC) is positively significant for education consumption and medical. It means that as the women have more children they will spend more for education and medical. If the income source is from agriculture, most likely the education consumption will be more, as the agriculture source of income is only significant for education consumption.

The source of income from trading is significant for reinvestment and education consumption. If the source of income is more farming, poultry and fishing (Y1) it is not significant for any type of consumption.

Marital status is negatively related to all the variables and only negatively significant for education consumption. It means that if the women are married then they will spend less on reinvestment and consumption specially, on education.

Primary education is highly positively significant for education consumption. Education of the women, higher than the primary level, is positively significant for food consumption and education consumption. It means if the women are educated up-to primary level they will more likely to spend more on their children's education and if the women are educated more than primary level they will spend more on food consumption along with the education for the children. Education above primary level is statistically significant for medical consumption. Log of monthly income of the women is statistically significant for reinvestment, food consumption, education consumption but not significant for medical. It could be due to the fact not every day people get sick so monthly income does not have any impact on medical consumption.

Holding of cash asset is negatively significant for food and education consumption. It means that if the women want to hold more cash they will likely to spend less on food and education consumption. Holding of jewellery or other semi-cash asset (other asset), is not significant for any variables. Ownership of house is negatively significant for food consumption. Productive asset is positively related to reinvestment and not significant for any independent variables.

SECTION-4: In this section we shall discuss the influence of women's income and asset holding on bargaining power.

Table 1.10
Impact of Asset Control on Husband Treatment:
Probit Model Dependent Variable: HUSTREAT

Variable	*Coefficient*	*z-Statistic*
AGE	-0.057462	-1.871447*
CHIL	0.044250	0.042655
NOC	0.407153	2.186966**
LOG (AMON)	0.273228	0.463291
LOG (BMON)	-0.059602	-0.114402
ASSET	-0.453407	-0.903252
OTHERASS	-0.112912	-0.202909
OWNHOUSE	-0.092508	-0.167289
PROASSET	1.278437	2.322522**
AGRI	0.921161	1.625503*
TRADING	1.105548	2.037670**
Y1	0.299185	0.603110
C	-0.719242	-0.194311
Log likelihood	-70.05450	
Restr. Log likelihood	-83.84736	
LR statistic (12 df)	27.58572	
Probability(LR stat)	0.006358	
S.D. dependent var	0.385083	
Akaike info criterion	0.933197	
Schwarz criterion1	1.65574	
Hannan-Quinn criter	1.027432	
Avg. log likelihood	-0.393565	
McFadden R-squared	0.164500	

* significant at 10 % level** significant at 5 % level

The above regression model shows the probit model where the husband's treatment is the dependent variable. The above table is indicating that women's asset control and monthly income have no significant effect on husband treatment except productive asset. Productive asset means ownership of shops.

It means that increasing asset ownership does not change the women's bargaining power over their husbands but only if they invest their money in ownership of shops they may exert some power. Why it is so? It is very obvious that if the women invest their money in shops that mostly their husband will run the shop and they will treat their wife well as the women are source of the capital.

The above table is showing that age of the women is significant and it is negatively related to husband's treatment, indicating that as the women get older they receive worse treatment from their husbands. Other two significant variables are sources of income, trading and agriculture. It means that as more women are using their loan money in trading and agriculture, they are receiving better treatment from their husbands. Again it is obvious that in agriculture they are investing their money in the land where their husbands are working and for trading most probably they are investing their money where their husbands are helping them. The above table is showing that monthly income after the micro-loan is positive (AMON) but not significant and income before taking the micro-loan is negative (BMON) but not significant as well.

SUMMARY OF FINDINGS

As the log of monthly income of the women is increasing total expenditure after taking the micro-loan, clothing expenditure, expenditure on children's education are also increasing.

Monthly income of the women does not increase food expenditure but it increases the overall food consumption, indicating higher supply of food from own land of the borrower or from farming, poultry where they are investing their loan money.

Holding cash asset is increasing expenditure after micro-loan.

Ownership of house and ownership of asset like jewellery have no effect on expenditure.

Holding of productive asset is only negatively significant with other expenditure, indicating as more women invest their loan money on ownership of shop, they will tend to spend less on their children's education as they need them for running the shop.

Holding of cash asset is negatively significant for food consumption, education consumption and for medical consumption.

Ownership of house is negatively significant for food consumption.

Holding of productive asset like a shop indicates higher proportion of reinvestment.

Asset ownership has no effect on husband's treatment except productive asset.

Older women get worse treatment from their husbands.

If the women invest their money in agriculture or trading they will receive better treatment from their husband.

CONCLUSIONS

This paper has demonstrated that men and women have non-identical preferences for the use of the loan. It also demonstrated that women's income is increasing the consumption expenditure as well as changing household consumption pattern. Our study fails to identify any improvement of the husband's treatment towards their wife as a result of their direct contribution in the household expenditure.

Our findings from the study can be summarised as follows, men decision making and women decision making is significantly different regarding reinvestment decision. If men are taking decision over the use of income from the loan they are most likely prefer reinvestment whereas women do not prefer reinvestment of their loan.

The women's monthly income from the loan uses is significantly changing the consumption expenditure as well as the consumption pattern of the household.

Haddinott and Haddad (1995) show that an increase in women's relative cash income is positively related to the expenditure shares of food and fuel and negatively related to alcohol and cigarettes. According to these authors household expenditure patterns are shaped by the relative power of different members over income. Our findings is consistent with this findings that women's income is increasing the food, clothing and educational consumption in the household.

Economic resources are the major determinant of bargain power (Quisumbing,1999) Here we took women's command over asset as the determinant of bargaining power. Our findings is showing that holding cash asset by the women is increasing the total money expenditure after taking the micro-loan but holding any other form of asset has no effect on expenditure. In case of holding productive asset like ownership of shop or cultivable land is decreasing expenditure on children's education.

To sum up our study found out that, women 's monthly income positively affects on both consumption expenditure and consumption pattern of the household. The husband and wife have different preference for reinvestment decision.

Our study has been undertaken in rural area in Bangladesh where women are highly dominated by their husbands. Our findings are certainly a positive breakthrough, which shows, that even in this strong patriarchal dominance and highly knitted Islamic culture women are still exerting their individual preference for household decision-making. Our finding about the intra-household relationship, where we try to find out the change of behaviour of the husbands towards their wife, reveals that husbands are treating their wives well, only if the wife acquire productive asset like cultivable land or ownership of shop where the husbands certainly have equal interest or if the wives are young and have more children. These findings are further conforming to the patriarchal culture of rural Bangladesh where men prefer younger wives and more children as a safeguard for smooth future. But again further research is recommended in this field due to the limitation of our data.

Finally, this study rejects the unitary household model and advocates that in household women have their own preferences for the household expenditure, which changes, as they become the direct income earner in the household. But their earning does not effect on the treatment they are getting from their husbands.

From this paper as a policy prescription we can conclude that women's income is certainly helping to increase the household expenditure for food and education but the women who have education more than primary education tend to spend more on their children's education expenditure. In respect of the consumption pattern our result is showing that, women who have education more than primary education level tend to spend more on education consumption, food consumption as well as medical consumption. Our findings are strongly advocating the necessity of the women's education who are in general more concern about the household consumption.

NOTES

1. Cited in Dwyer et al. (1998).
2. We could not get the same data of women individual decision making from IFPRI (1994) data.
3. Cited in Kusago et.al. (2001).
4. Cited in Evans Alison (1991).
5. EEPs affect the relative desirability of being single and may include access to common property resources and divorce laws.
6. For details see Hadded, L.J. Hoddinott, and H. Alderman, ets. 1997. Intrahousehold resource allocation in developing countries: Methods, models, and policy. Baltimore, Md., U.S.A.: Johns Hopkins University Press for the International Food Policy Research Institute p. 58.
7. Master, M., and M. Brown, 1980 Marriage and household decision-making: a bargaining analysis. International Economy Review 21 (1): 31-44.
8. McElroy, M.B., and M.J. Horney, 1981. Nash-bargained household decisions: Towards a generalization of the theory of demand, *International Economic Review* 22(2): 333-349.
9. For details see The Journal of Economic Perspectives, Vol. 10, issue 4, p. 139-158.
10. Guyer, J., (1981) Household and community in Africa, *African studies Review,* Vol. XXIV. no. 2/3.
11. Cited in Quisumbing A.R. et.al (1999).
12. Cited in Kusago et.al. (2001).

13. Lampietti et.al. (1999) Gender and Preferences for Malaria Prevention in Tigray, Ethiopia. Policy Research Report on Gender and Development Working Paper Series No. 3. Washington, DC: World Bank.
14. Smith Lisa C. and Chavas Jean-paul, Supply Responses of West Africa Agricultural Households: Implications of Intrahousehold Preference Heterogeneity. Food Consumption and Nutrition Division Discussion Paper 69, IFPRI, July 1999.
15. See for details, Adato Michelle et al (2000) The Impact of Proegresa on Women's Status and Intrahousehold Relations, *Final Report, IFPRI,* Washington, U.S.A. July 2000.
16. The income from micro-credit may enter into the wife's indirect utility function either as non wage come or extra-household parameter.
17. Montalto C.P. (1995) Measuring relative bargaining power using an economic model of cooperative Nash Bargaining, Department of Family Resource Management/Textiles and Clothing, Ohio State University, Ohio, U.S.A. Mimeo.
18. See for details Doss Cheryl R. (1996) Testing among Models of Intrahousehold Resource Allocation, *World Development* Vol. 24, No. 10, pp. 1597-1609.

REFERENCES

Adato Michelle et al (2000), The Impact of Proegresa on Women 's Status and Intrahousehold Relations, *Final Report, IFPRI,* Washington U.S.A. July 2000.

Bina Agarwal (1997), Bargaining" and Gender Relations: Within and Beyond the Household, *FCND Discussion Paper No. 27,* March 1997.

Becker, G. (1965), 'A Theory of the Allocation of Time', *Economic Journal Vol 75,* pp. 493-517.

Becker, G., (1973), A theory of marriage Part I. *Journal of Political Economy,* Vol.81, 813-826.

Becker, G., (1974), A theory of marriage Part II. *Journal of political economy,* Vol.82, 811-826.

Becker, G., (1981), *A treatise on the family.* Cambridge: Harvard University Press.

Carter, M., and E. Katz. (1997), Separate spheres and the conjugal contract: understanding the impact of gender-biased development. In *Intrahousehold Resource allocation in developing countries: Methods, models, and policy*, Baltimore, Md., U.S.A.: Johns Hopkins University Press for the International Food Policy Research Institute.

Dwyer Daisy and Judith B., (1988), *A home divided-Women and Income in the third World*. Stanford, California, U.S.A.

Duraisamy P. and M. Duraisamy, (2000), Nash Bargaining Approach to Household Behaviour: Theory and Evidence, Volume 48, No.4, *Indian Economic Journal*, pp. 35-40.

Doss Cheryl R. (1996), Testing among Models of Intrahousehold Resource Allocation, *World Development* Vol. 24, No.10. pp.1597-1609.

Evans Alison, (1991), *IDS Bulletin*, Vol.22 no.1, Institute of Development Studies, Sussex, U.K. pp 51-59.

Frankenberg E. and Thomas, D., (2001), Measuring power, *FCND Discussion Paper No.113*. IFPRI, Washington D.C. USA.

Filmer, D., E. M. King, and L.Pritchett (1998), Gender disparity in South Asia: Comparisons between and within countries. *Policy research working paper 1867*. Development Research group, Poverty and Human resources. Washington, DC: World Bank.

Guyer, J., (1981), Household and Community in Africa, *African studies Review*, Vol. XXIV. no. 2/3.

Hallman Kelly (2000), Mother-Father Resource Control, Marriage Payments, and Girl-Boy Health in Rural Bangladesh. *FCND Discussion Paper No. 93*, September 2000.

Kabeer Naila (1994) *Reversed Realities, Gender Hierarchies in Development Thought*, London, U.K.

Kusago, (2001), Preference, Heterogeneity, Power, and Intrahousehold Decision-Making in Rural Malaysia, *World Development* Vol. 29, No. 7. pp.1237-1256.

Haddad, L., J. Hoddinott, and H. Alderman, eds.(1997), *Intrahousehold resource allocation in developing countries: Methods, models, and policy*. Baltimore, Md., U.S.A.: Johns Hopkins University Press for the International Food Policy Research Institute.

Hoddinott, J., and L. Haddad (1995), Does Female income share influence household expenditures? Evidence from Côte d'Ivoire. *Oxford Bulletin of Economics and Statistics* 57: 77-96.

Lampietti et al (1999), *Gender and Preferences for Malaria Prevention in Tigray, Ethiopia. Policy Research Report on Gender and Development*, Working Paper Series No. 3, Washington, DC: World Bank.

Lundberg S. J., R. A. Pollak, (1993), Separate spheres bargaining and the marriage market. *Journal of Political Economy* 101 (6): 988-1010.

Lundberg, S. J., R. A. Pollak, and T. J. Wales (1997), Do husbands and wives pool their resources? Evidence from the United Kingdom Child Benefit. *Journal of Human Resources* 32 (3): 463-480.

Montalto C.P. (1995), Measuring relative bargaining power using an economic model of cooperative Nash Bargaining, *Department of Family Resource Management / Textiles and Clothing*, Ohio State University , Ohio , U.S.A. Mimeo.

Manser, M., and M. Brown (1980), Marriage and household decision-making: a bargaining analysis. *International Economic Review* 21 (1): 31-44.

McElroy, M. B., and M. J. Horney (1981) Nash-bargained household decisions: Towards a generalization of the theory of demand. *International Economic Review* 22 (2).

Nash, J. (1953), Two-person bargaining games. *Econometrica* 21: 128-140.

Pitt. M & Shahidur R Khandker, (1996), Household and Intrahousehold Impact of the Grameen Bank and Similar Targeted Credit Programs in Bangladesh, *World Bank Discussion Paper #320*, IBRD, Washington, D.C., USA.

Quisumbing A. and Brendicte de la Brire (2000), Women's Assets and Intrahoushold Allocation in Rural Bangladesh: Testing Measures of Bargaining Power *FCND Discussion Paper No.* 86, April 2000. IFPRI, Washington, D.C. USA.

Quisumbing A. and Maluccio (2000), Intra-household allocation and gender relations: New empirical Evidence from four Developing countries, *FCND Discussion Paper 84*, IFPRI, Washington, D.C. USA.

Rao, V. (1993) The rising price of husbands: A hedonic analysis of dowry increases in rural India. *Journal of Political Economy* 101 (4): 666-667.

Rao, V. (1997) Wife-beating in rural South India: A qualitative and econometric analysis. *Social Science and Medicine* 44 (8): 1169-1180.

Rao, V. (1998) Wedding celebrations as conspicuous consumption: Signalling social status in rural India. Paper presented at the 1998 North East Universities Development Consortium Conference, October, *Yale University*, Conn., U.S.A. Photocopied.

Samuelson Paul (1956), Social Indifference Curves, *Quarterly Journal of Economics*, Vol. 70, 1-22.

Smith Lisa C. and Chavas Jean-Paul (1999), Supply Responses of West Africa Agricultural Households: Implications of Intrahousehold Preference Heterogeneity,. *Food Consumption and Nutrition Division Discussion Paper 69*, IFPRI, July.

Sen (1966), Labour allocation in a cooperative enterprise, *Review of Economic Studies*, Vol.33, July; reprinted in Sen, 1984, 73-89.

Sen (1966), Peasants and dualism with or without surplus labour, *Journal of Political Economy*, Vol. 74, October; reprinted in Sen, 1984, 37-72.

Thomas, D. (1990), Intrahousehold resource allocation: An inferential approach. *Journal of Human Resources* Vol. 25 (4): 635-664.

Thomas, D. (1993), The distribution of income and expenditure within the household. *Annales de Economie et de Statistiques* 29 (January-March): 109-136.

Thomas, D., D. Contreras, and E. Frankenberg (1997), Child health and the distribution of household resources at marriage. University of California at Los Angeles and the RAND Corporation, Santa Monica, Calif., U.S.A. Photocopied. *www.IFPRI.org*.

18

ESTIMATING THE IMPACT OF GENDER INEQUALITY IN EDUCATION ON THE WELL-BEING OF WOMEN IN NIGERIA

*Gafar T. Ijaiya and I. O. Balogun**

INTRODUCTION

It is an established fact that all forms of inequalities (income, land, job and education) are detrimental to socio-economic development and well-being. Their severity seems to be more pronounced when viewed from the gender perspective, more so, if the distribution or allocation of those resources is biased against women (see, ADB 2002a, Evans 2001).

As Safilios–Rothschild (1991) puts it, "a society that has a powerful gender stratification system that tends to place men in decision making positions with women relegated to traditional training and economic activities with limited demand that do not provide them with adequate means of livelihood is an endangered society. For instance, if the gender inequality is such that leads to women's having less access to education and skills for productive employment, it will have a far-reaching effect in terms of poverty creation and perpetuation in the present as well as in the next generation" (see also Quisumbing and Maluccio 1999; Filmer 1999; Klasen 1999).

* Department of Economics, University of Ilorin, Ilorin, Nigeria.

This situation is more pronounced in less developed countries including Nigeria where a number of studies[1] indicate that under the auspices of tradition and religion the men discriminate against women thus depriving them access to education and skills for productive activities.

The aim of this paper therefore, is to corroborate this fact by examining the influence of changes in women education over the years on their well-being in Nigeria, using a time subscript and a difference-in- difference estimator.

In the next section, a conceptual overview of well-being and gender inequality in education is provided. Section three provides the data source and methodology used in determining the influence of gender inequality in education on well-being of women in Nigeria. Section four provides and discusses the results. Conclusion and recommendations are curtained in the last section.

CONCEPTUAL ISSUES: WELL-BEING AND GENDER INEQUALITY IN EDUCATION

Well-being: Definition and Determinants

Definition

According to Narayan, et.al (2000a, 2000b) well-being is synonymous with good quality of life which include material well-being often expressed as having enough bodily well-being which includes being strong, being in the right frame of mind and looking good; social well-being which includes caring for and settling children; having self-respect, peace, and good relations in the family and the community; having security, including civil peace, a safe and secure environment, personal and physical security, and confidence in the future; and having freedom of choice and action, including being able to help other people in the community.

Determinants of Well-being

According to Petri (1993) and the World Bank (1991), one of the key determinants of well-being in a given country is the presence of stable macroeconomic policies[2] and economic growth. For instance, when there exist sound fiscal and monetary policies in a country this will create a hospitable climate for public and private investment in both socio-economic activities which in turn promote productivity, increases income and the purchasing power of the people and their consumption-expenditure from which the nation's well-being improves.

The ability of individuals to have access to the basic needs of life e.g. food, assets, land, work, health, education, water and shelter also determine well-being. As stated by Lipton and Ravallion (1995) and Narayan, et.al (2000a) adequate food is a universal need for improved well-being. Access to adequate resources, especially land is another universal criterion of well-being. Ability to find a paid work, to obtain money, to buy clothes and to pay for health treatment and school expenses is another important determinant of well-being.

Closely related to the above is Sen's capabilities and entitlements doctrine. According to Sen (1985) as a determinant of well-being people's capabilities which refers to what people do and can do in their lives is also a determinant of well-being. It also includes things that can lead to a long and healthy life; to be knowledgeable; and having access to the resources needed for a decent standard of living, while entitlements tend to draw the attention of the people away from the mere possession of certain goods toward human rights and the command over the use of goods and services and the use of various economic, political and social opportunities within the legal system.

Picciotto (1992) highlighted the importance of people's participation on the development process that affects their lives. To him when people participate in the development process that affects their lives, there is the tendency for their well-being to improve since participation involves partaking, sharing and at times owning a particular project by the people. It is also referred to as either a process or a means towards an objective. As a process it denotes individuals involvement in the group's activities. As a goal driven concept, it encompasses the social interaction which characterizes a group as well as their contribution towards a designed end result.

Having access to state-provided infrastructural facilities is an essential criterion for well-being. As observed by Ward (1999), infrastructural services e.g. roads, water and electricity are significant because economic and social infrastructure is an essential overhead capital– a key element in national wealth. For instance, private firms will not get established, nor function effectively and efficiently where the infrastructure which provides the basic mechanism remains dysfunctional, disconnected, run down and inadequate. In the same view, public assets that generate directly real consumption service flows that benefit the people will be insignificant to the overall quality of life of the people most especially women.

The existence of good governance in any society is also a pre-condition for improved well-being. Sandstorm (1994) opined that good governance is reflected on the responsibility of the government in involving its citizens in the development decision that affect their lives and the government's responsibility to ensure accountability; openness and transparency for their actions so that resources can have maximum impact in benefiting the people.

As observed by Boeninger (1991), Brautigan (1991) Landell-Mills and Serageldin (1991) and Isham, et. al (1997) good governance allows for civil and economic liberties. Civil liberties such as the freedom of individual expression, a pluralistic and free media The ability of groups to organize and freedom of dissent and criticism are also essential elements of civil liberties since they facilitate greater citizen voice and enhance more effective government action on development. On the other hand, economic liberties would foster entrepreneurship, market activities and economic growth for the improvement of well-being to take place since there could be fewer regulations and fewer obstacles to individual economic opportunities.

Gender and Gender Inequality in Education

Gender Inequality

According to Cassell (2002) gender refers to a sense of being male or female or having the recognizable traits of one's sex.

The characteristics and behaviours that are generally associated with being a male are called masculine and those associated with being a female are called feminine. Masculine and feminine usually refers to a combination of physical traits such as bodily shape, voice and facial hair and acquired characteristics such as hairstyle, clothing, body and movements and display of emotions.

Olujobi (2001) refers to it as a division of humanity into two distinctive categories based on their sex. Sex being the obvious biological differences between men and women. To the sociologists, it is used to denote the roles played by women and men and deals not only with differences (how a society constructs feminine and masculine people) but also with how the society connotes power on each of the sexes.

On the other hand, inequality is often referred to as lack of equality; being unequal in amount, size, value or rank; lack of evenness, regularity or uniformity; lack of due proportion or uneven distribution of resources (World Book 2002).

Gender inequality is therefore a situation of uneven distribution of income, lack of access to productive inputs, such as credit and education, lack of command over property or control over earned income as well as gender biases in labour market and social exclusion between men and women. (Cagatay 1998; Harris-White and Saith 1997; Ravari 1998). It also connotes a situation where women do not have the same rights and enlightenments as men to human, social, economic and cultural development and where women do not have equal voice in civil and political life (Evans 2001).

Generally, gender inequality can be linked to the households and communities with very scarce resources. At the household level, the poor among them most especially women are forced to adopt short and long-term survival strategies which involve inequitable allocation of resources that treats preferentially members who are deemed to be the best endowed to help the household to survive. In most cases, the scarce resources are preferentially allocated to men and boys while the time-consuming tasks and responsibilities are more often allocated to women and girls who work more hours per day than men and boys. At the communities level there is a more powerful gender stratification system that places men in decision-making position with responsibility for the designation of funds for education and training and designation of profitable employment and training opportunities for men; and a system that relegates women to traditional training and economic activities with limited demand that does not provide them with adequate means to escape from poverty (Gentler and Alderman 1998; Safilios-Rothschilds 1991).

Education and Gender Inequality in Education

Generally, education is defined as a life-long process through which man's all round (moral, emotional, physical and intellectual) development is facilitated so that he can be useful to himself and the society into which he is born (Lawal 1989).

Given this definition our concern in this study is the western education which has become prominent in modern day development studies and whose attainment (irrespective of the level of attainment) is seen as very important to economic development and well-being since it enables the individual to perform new tasks, to receive and process new information, to communicate and therefore co-ordinate activities with one another, to evaluate and adjust to changed circumstances and to reduce subjective uncertainty and unnecessary anxiety (see Lau, et.al. 1991 and World Bank 1991).

Gender inequality in education therefore, can manifest through population issues: Because of the prevailing patriarchal values, cultural and religious norms poor women do find that a large number of children often constitute the only resources they can control. They can be assisted by them in the inequitable workload they do within the household. Children especially daughters are made to serve as relief from work for their mother and have therefore limited access to education and training that could help them escape from poverty in the future. In this way poverty is perpetuated from generation to generation and the gender gap continues to widen (Safilios–Rothschild 1991).

ADB (2002a) also observed that constraints arising from the socio-cultural norms such a forced marriages, early child bearing and rearing, gender biased teaching and educational materials, and girls responsibility for heavy domestic work at an early stage also continue to curtail women's access to education, thus making it difficult for them to acquire higher and relevant education.

According to Bamberger, et. al (2001), Cagatay (1997) and Kabeer (1997) one of the consequences of gender inequality in education is that it could led to a great deal of violence against women and gender injustice of the suppression of women and women's agencies, thus making it difficult for them to discuss the issues of power and changing power relations.

As observed by Safilios–Rothschild (1991), if the inequality is such that it leads to women having less access to education as well as skills for productive employment, it will have a far-reaching effect on them in terms of poverty creation and perpetuation of the present as well as the next generation. Stressing further, she said illiterate women with limited access to income can not take good care of their children with respect to health and nutrition; and women with a work over load and little or no access to regular income will use their daughter's labour for survival and thus deprive them of a chance to acquire education and training for escaping from the vicious circle of poverty in the future [see also Ghosh (1997), Jackson (1997) Klasen (2002)].

Klasen (2002) also observed that gender inequality in education may undermine a number of development goals. First, gender inequality in education and access to resources may prevent reductions in fertility and child mortality and the expansion of education of the next generation. Second, gender inequality in education may reduce economic growth. This is drawn from the importance of human capital to economic growth, which if it is low, investment rate will also be low because countries with lower human capital are said to always have smaller returns on investments.

DATA SOURCE AND METHODOLOGY

Data Source

A time series data for the period between 1985 to 2001 on the percentage of woman that are deprived access to education and female life expectancy at birth (years) were used. The percentage of women that are deprived access to education is used to capture the inequality in education among women, while the female life expectancy at birth is used as proxy for well-being.

The data were obtained from African Development Bank (2002b) Selected Statistics on African Countries for the year 2002 and African Development Bank (2002a) Gender, Poverty and Environmental Indicators on African Countries also for the year 2002.

The Model

In specifying the model emphasis is placed on whether gender inequality in education among women has any significant influence on the well-being of women in Nigeria.

Having established this link the first equation is therefore formulated as:

$$WB_t = f(GIE_t) \quad ...(1)$$

Following Barro and Sala (1995) and Grootaert, Kanbur and Oh (1995) methods of analysis that uses a time subscript ($_t$) and a first difference operator (Δ), we therefore model the relationship between the well-being of women and gender inequality in education among women [using a time subscript ($_t$) and a first difference operator (Δ)] as follows:

$$\Delta WB_t = f(\Delta GIE_t) \quad ...(2)$$

Equation (2) thus describes the changes in the well-being of women as a function of changes in gender inequality in education among women in Nigeria.

The introduction of the initial level of gender inequality in education among women in Nigeria i.e.(GIE_t) into equation (2) will give the following equation:

$$\Delta WB_t = f(GIE_t, \Delta GIE_t) \quad ...(3)$$

The transformation of equation (3) into a linear equation then becomes:

$$\Delta WB_t = \beta_0 + \beta_1 GIE_t + \beta_2 \Delta GIE_t + U \quad ...(4)$$

Where:

WB_t = the initial level of well-being of women in Nigeria.

ΔWB_t = changes in well-being of women in Nigeria.

GIE_t = the initial level of gender inequality in education among women measured by the percentage of woman that are deprived access to education in Nigeria.

ΔGIE_t = changes in gender inequality in education among women measured by the percentage of woman that are deprived access to education in Nigeria.

β_0 = the intercept

β_1 and β_2 = the parameter estimates that stands for the speed of convergence of gender inequality in education among women in Nigeria, with a positive value indicating a convergence of gender inequality in education among women to the equilibrium position, while a negative value indicates a divergence.

U = the error term

To estimate the model, a multiple regression analysis is used in order to reflect the explanatory nature of the variables. To verify the validity of the model, two major evaluation criteria are used: the a-priori expectation criteria which is based on the signs and magnitudes of the coefficients of the variables under investigation; and (ii) statistical criteria which is based on statistical theory, which in other words is referred to as the First Order Least Square (OLS) consisting of R-square (R^2), F-statistic and t-test. The R-square (R^2) is concerned with the overall explanatory power of the regression analysis, the F-statistic is used to test the overall significance of the regression analysis and the t-test is used to test the significant contribution of the independent variables on the dependent (Oyeniyi 1997).

Drawn from the model the a-priori expectations or the expected pattern of behavior between the dependant variable ΔWB_t and the independent variables GIE_t and ΔGIE_t are: $GIE_t < 0$, $\Delta GIE_t < 0$. Indicating that the initial level of the percentage of women deprived access to education and the negative changes in the percentage of women deprived access to education are expected to reduce the well-being of women.

RESULTS AND DISCUSSION

The results of the regression analysis are presented in Table 2.

Table 1
Regression Results of Well-being and Gender Inequality in Education among women in Nigeria

Explanatory Variable	*Co-efficient and t-values*
Intercepts (t)	54.2 (32.9)
GIE_t (t)	-0.37 (-7.83)
$DGIE_t$ (t)	-0.91 (-6.60)
R2	0.96
F	25.8

t-values in parenthesis

A look at the model shows that it is good, since it has an R^2 of 0.96 which in other words means that 96 per cent variation in the dependent variable (ΔWB_t) is explained by the independent variables (GIE_t and $ÄGIE_t$), while the error term take care of the remaining 4 per cent, which are variables in the study that can not be included in the model because of their qualitative features. At 5 per cent level of significance, the F-statistic shows that the model is useful in determining the influence of gender inequality in education among women on the well-being of women in Nigeria, as the computed F- statistic which is 25.8 is greater than the tabular F-statistic (2, 17) valued at 3.59.

The estimated parameters of the variables (initial level of women deprived access to education and the changes in the percentage of women deprived access to education) are both negatively related to well-being. An indication that both the initial level of the percentage of women deprived access to education and the negative changes witnessed over the years on the percentage of women deprived access to education have impacted negatively on their well-being. Statistically, this implies that at a point estimate of 100 per cent, a reduction in the percentage of women with access to education in Nigeria would have a cumulative effect of reducing their well-being by 91 per cent in the following year, given the significant role of education to poverty reduction and economic development (see Psacharopoulos and Winter 1992, and Subbaro and Raney 1993).

CONCLUSION AND RECOMMENDATIONS

Using a multiple regression analysis that includes the initial level of the percentage of women deprived access to education and changes in the percentage of women deprived access to education, this paper explored the relationship between gender inequality in education among women and the well-being of women in Nigeria.

From the analysis, our findings indicate that the initial level of gender inequality in education among women (proxied by the percentage of women deprived access to education) and the changes that have occurred over the years have impacted negatively on the well-being of the women. A situation that can be improved upon if certain policy measures are put in place. Prominent among them are massive enlightenment campaign that would raise awareness about the importance of educating women for economic development. In the forefront of this campaign should be the traditional rulers, community leaders, community-based organizations, non-government organizations, and the government through the use of the radio, the television, outdoor (street) broadcast and the use of town criers most especially in the villages or rural areas.

Women in Nigeria also need intense moral, financial and psychological support from their men folk that would remove the lesser sex syndrome on them. These supports if provided will no doubt remove the existing power relation where men always belief they are a superior sex.

Of great importance to enhancing women access to education are changes in socio-cultural norms that have deprived women better opportunities. These changes will be better enhanced if the behaviour of individuals and institutions (informal and formal) toward gender inequality is tilted towards the emancipation and empowerment of women.

Huge investment in the education of girls; increased enrolment of girls into school, most especially at the primary and secondary levels; introduction of more and re-habilitation of existing vocational training centers and making then gender sensitive; and the establishment of more adult education classes at less or no cost for poor women should be the concern of the government, non-government organizations and individuals.

Misappropriation of education funds and other equipment, policy inconsistency and corruption that have ruined the nation's educational sector must also be tackled. With stable education policies that address the issue of women education and the fight against corruption-the diversion of funds, facilities and resources for personal use by persons put in charge of all these would be put in check.

NOTES

1. See Ijaiya 2000; Narayan, et.al 2000a, 2000b.
2. The World Bank (1993) defined macroeconomic stability as a situation whereby inflation is kept under control, interest and external debts remain manageable and macroeconomic crisis that emerge are resolved quickly usually within a year or two.
3. The domestic duties include processing food crops, cooking food, fetching water and fire wood.

REFERENCES

African Development Bank (ADB) (2002a), *Gender, Poverty and Environmental Indicators on African Countries*. Abidjan: ADB.

African Development Bank (ADB) (2002b), *Selected Statistics on African Countries 2002*. Abidjan: ADB.

Bamberger M, Blackden, M. Fort L, and Manonkian V. (2001), Gender. *World Bank Poverty Reduction Strategy Programme Source Book.* Washington D.C.; The World Bank.

Barro, A and Sala I. M., (1995), *Economic Growth.* London: McGraw-Hill Inc.

Boeninger, E. (1991), Governance and Development: Issues and Constraints. *In Proceedings of the World Bank Annual Conference on Development Economics 1997.* Washington D.C.: The World Bank: 267-287.

Brautigan, D. (1991), Governance and Economy: A Review. *World Bank Policy Research Working Paper* No. 815.

Cagatay, N. (1997), Macroeconomic Policy and Poverty Reduction: The Gender Perspective Based on UNDP Research. *UNRISD, UNDP and CDS International Workshop* Kerala 24th-27th Nov.

Cagatay, N. (1998), Gender and Poverty. *UNDP Social Development and Poverty Elimination Division Working Paper* No. 5.

Cascell, E (2002), *Gender: Sexuality.* The World Book Inc. Chicago.

Evans, P. (2001), Sex and Gender: A World of Difference. *DFID Developments.* Issue No 13: 32-34.

Filmer, D. (1999), The Structure of Social Disparities in Education: Gender and Wealth. *World Bank Policy Research Report on Gender and Development* No. 5.

Gentler, P. and Alderman P. (1989), Family Resources and Gender Differences in Human Capital Investments. *In Proceedings of the Conference in the Family Gender Differences and Development held in the Economic Growth Center. Yale University in 1989.*

Ghosh, J. (1997) Assessing Poverty Alleviation Strategies for their Impact on Poor Women *UNRISD, UNDP and CDS International Workshop* Kerala 24th-27th Nov.

Grootaert, C; Kanbur, R and Oh, G. (1995), Dynamic of poverty-why some people escape and others don't: An African case study. *World Bank Policy Research Working Paper No.1499.*

Harris-White, B and Saith, R. (1997), An Analysis of the Gender Sensitive of Conventional Well-being Indicators. *UNRISD, UNDP and CDS International Workshop* Kerala 24th-27th Nov.

Ijaiya G.T. (2000), Feminization of Poverty in Nigeria: A Case Study of Households in Ilorin Metropolis. *African Journal of Business and Economic Research.* Vol. 1. No.1: 141-148.

Isham J., Kaufmann, D. and Pritchett, L. (1997), Civil Liberties, Democracy and the Performance of Government Projects. *World Bank Economic Review*. Vol. 30. No. 3:2-5.

Johnson, C. (1997), Working Intensity, Gender and Well-being. *UNRISD, UNDP and CDS International Workshop* Kerala 24th-27th Nov.

Kabeer N. (1997), What Colour is the Wind: Feminists Development Agencies and the Empowerment of Third World Women. *UNRISD, UNDP and CDS International Workshop* Kerala 24th-27th Nov.

Klasen S. (1999), Does Gender Inequality Reduce Growth and Development: Evidence from Cross-country Regressions. *World Bank Policy Research Report on Gender and Development* No. 7.

Klasen, S. (2002), Low Schooling for Girls, Slower Growth for All? Cross-Country Evidence on the Effect of Gender Inequality in Education on Economic Development. *The World Bank Economic Review*. Vol. 16 No. 3: 345-373.

Landell-Mill, P. and Seragelden, I (1991), Governance and the Development Process *IMF/World Bank Finance and Development* Vol. 28. No. 3.

Lau L, Jamison, D T and Lonat, F.F (1991), Education and Productivity in Developing Countries: An Aggregate Production Function Approach. *World Bank Policy Research Working Paper No. 612.*

Lawal, B. (1989), Nigeria's Education Crisis: A Marxist-Humanist Interpretation. *In Lawal B. and Olugbade K. (eds) Issues in Contemporary African Social and Political Thought. Vol. 1: 124-136.*

Lipton, M. and Ravallion, M. (1995), Poverty and Policy. *In Behrman, J. and Srinivason T.N. (eds.) Handbooks of Development Economics.* Vol. III: 2553–2657.

Narayan D., Peter R., Schaffc K, Rademacher A and Koch–Schulte S., (2000a), Voices of the Poor: Can Anyone Hear Us? Oxford University Press, New York.

Narayan, D., Chambers R., Shah M.K and Petesch P. (2000b), Voices of the Poor: Crying Out for Change New York : Oxford University Press.

Olujobi O.S. (2001), Sociological Analysis of Gender Discrimination. *Humanity: Jos Journal of General Studies*. Vol. 3: No. 2: 125-135.

Oyeniyi T.A. (1997), *Fundamental Principles of Econometrics*. Lagos: Cader Publication Ltd.

Petri, P.A. (1993), The Lessons of East Asia: Common Foundations of the East Asia Success. The World Bank. Washington D.C.

Picciotto, R. (1992), Participating Development: Myths and Dilemmas. *World Bank Policy Research Working Paper* No. 930.

Psacharopaulos, G. and Winter, C. (1992), Women's Employment and Pay in Latin America. *IMF/World Bank Finance and Development. Vol. 29. No. 4.*

Quisumbing, A. R. and Maluccio J. A. (1999), Intra-household Allocation and Gender Relations: New Empirical Evidence. *World Bank Policy Research Report on Gender and Development* No. 2.

Ravavi, S. (1998), Gendered Poverty and Change: An Issue Paper. *UNDP Research Institute for Social Development Discussion Paper* No. 94.

Safilios-Rothschild, C. (1991), Gender and Rural Poverty in Asia: Some Implications for Project Design. *The World Bank EDI Working Paper.*

Sandstorm, S. (1994), Poverty Reduction: Learning the Lessons of Experience. *IMF/World Bank Finance and Development*. Vol. 31. No. 3.

Sen, A. (1985), *Commodities and Capabilities*. North Holland, Amsterdam.

Subbarao, K. and Raney, L. (1993), Social Gains from Female Education: A Cross-National Study. *World Bank Discussion Paper* No. 194.

Ward, M. (1999), Perceptions of Poverty: The Historical Legacy. *IDS Bulletin*. Vol. 30. No. 2: 23-32.

World Bank (1990), Poverty. *World Development Report 1990*. Oxford University Press, New York.

World Bank (1991), The Challenge of Development. *World Development Report 1991*. Oxford University Press, New York.

World Bank (1993), *The East Asian Miracle: Economic Growth and Public Policy*. Oxford University Press. New York.

World Book (2002), *Gender*. The World Book Inc. Chicago.

19

EDUCATION AND HEALTH IN KERALA

*P. Arunachalam**

Education, health and housing are the three pillars of any civilized society. Educational advancement becomes a catalyst for economic development. Griliche (1964) has pointed out that a 10 per cent increase in farmer's education raised productivity by 3 to 5 per cent compared to only 1 to 2 per cent due to 10 per cent increase in land, fertilizer and machinery in U.S agriculture. According to Schultze (1961) investment in education is 3 to 5 times more attractive than investment in Physical capital. According to Hicks (1980) there is a strong correlation between literacy levels and life expectancy and that literacy may have an important influence on health and hygiene.

On 14th August 1947, Jawaharlal Nehru declared, "Long years ago we made a tryst with destiny and now the time comes when we shall redeem our pledge". The objective of this paper is to ascertain to what extent Kerala and to that matter India has succeeded in redeeming this pledge with respect to the three major sectors namely Education, Health and Housing. This paper indicates the loopholes in the development of these sectors and their probable implications on the development of the State Economy.

* Head Department of Applied Economics, Cochin University of Science and Technology, Kochi-22.

This paper is based on secondary data. The data sources for this paper are reports published by various agencies like the World Bank, UNESCO, Year Book (Government of India), Kerala Economic Review (Published by state Planning Board, Government of Kerala), the Indian Economic Survey 2004 and articles and research papers published by authors of repute. References are given wherever materials are taken from publications.

For the purpose of analysis this chapter is divided into two parts. Part 1 deals with education and Part 2 deals with health.

PART 1: EDUCATION

LITERACY AT THE NATIONAL LEVEL

The five decades after independence, the increase in literacy rate during the decade 1991-2001 has been the highest, i.e , from 52.2 to 64.8 per cent. For the first time the country witnessed a faster rate in female literacy rate from 39 to 54 per cent compared to that of males from 64 to 75 per cent Through this there was a narrowing of gender gap in literacy, which was 25 per cen tin 1991 to 22 per cent in 2001. There is also a converging trend in the rural- urban literacy gap. The rural-urban literacy gap decreased from 28.4 per cent in 1991 to 20.9 percent in 2001 (Indian Economic Survey 2004 p. 230).

ELEMENTARY EDUCATION

For realizing the goal of Universal elementary education, Constitutional (86th Amendment) Act 2002 was passed by the Parliament. The Act is a milestone in the country's march towards Universal elementary education.

A comprehensive programme called Sarva Shiksha Abhyan (SSA) was launched in November 2000 in collaboration with the States. The programme aims at improving the performance of the school system through a community owned approach and imparting quality elementary education to all children in the 6-14 age groups by 2010. Another programme called National Programme for Education of Girls at Elementary Level (NPEEGEL) was launched in 2003 for providing additional components for education of girls at elementary level under SSA.

The number of primary school stood at 6.64 lakhs and upper primary school at 2.19 lakhs in 2001-2002. The ratio of upper primary school to primary school was 1:3 in 2001-2002.

About 82.2 per cent of the children falling in the age group of 6-14 was enrolled in the schools in 2001-2002. But there is high rate of dropouts at the primary as well as upper primary level, the dropout rate being 39.03 per cent at the primary level and 54.6 per cent at the upper primary level during the reference period. Appendix-1 provides information regarding gross enrolment ratios for various years (in per cent).

SECONDARY EDUCATION

The secondary Education sector prepares the students the in the age group of 14-18 years for entry into higher education and for the world of work. The number of secondary and senior secondary schools during 2001 and 2002 stood at 1.33 lakh and they enrolled 30.5 million students.

HISTORY OF HIGHER EDUCATION

Modern Universities were started in India only in 1857. The first three Universities were Calcutta, Madras and Bombay. The first Education Commission (1882-83) was appointed by Lord Rippon on February 3, 1882 under the Chairmanship Sir William Hunter, Member, Viceroy's Executive Council. This commission is popularly known as Hunter Commission. The commission recommended,

1. Government should withdraw from management of secondary schools and take up the responsibility of primary education. District Boards and Municipal Boards should be established for the management of primary education.
2. Indigenous schools should be encouraged and priority should be given to the backward areas.
3. Grant-in-aid to encourage enterprise in managing secondary education.

4. Government should establish model schools.
5. Bifurcation of curriculum of secondary education into, "A" course leading to University and "B" course for commercial and literary pursuits, and
6. Grants-in-aid to colleges on the basis of staff and students strength.

INDIAN UNIVERSITY COMMISSION (1902)

Lord Curson appointed the Indian University Commission on January 27, 1902 under the chairmanship of Thomas Raleigh. The commission recommended:

1. Universities should be reorganized.
2. Uniformity in the nomenclature of the degrees in arts and science at the different Universities and examinations for the award of degrees.
3. Provisions for advanced courses of studies.
4. Systematic and strict supervision of affiliated colleges.
5. Reduction of members in Senate and Syndicate and proper representation of teachers in these bodies.

To give effect to the recommendations of the Commission Indian Universities Act was passed in March 21, 1904. The Act fixed the minimum and maximum number of members as 50 and 100 for senate. It also accorded legal sanction to syndicate. The area of jurisdiction of the universities was also fixed. Government was given right of approval to make amendments framed by senate

DR. MICHEL SADLER COMMISSION 1917-1919

The Sadler Commission was appointed to study the working of Calcutta University. But the commission studied the working of other Universities also and submitted recommendations with respect to the following aspects:

1. Starting of intermediate Colleges.
2. Separation of intermediate classes from universities and establishment of a separate Board free from the control of Education Department.

3. Fixing the duration of degree courses as three years.
4. Introduction of Honors Course.
5. Provision of more powers to teachers of universities.
6. Special Selection Committees for the appointments of Readers and Professors.
7. Establishment of Academic Councils and Boards of Studies.
8. Creation of different faculties, and
9. Appointment of full-time salaried Vice-Chancellors.

HARTAG COMMITTEE

This committee was appointed during 1928-29 and the committee submitted its report in 1929 containing the following recommendations.

1. Consolidation of Courses.
2. Standard and Service conditions of Teachers to be improved and
3. Removing stagnation and wastages.

SIR JOHN SERGENT COMMITTEE (1944)

The Committee submitted its report in 1944, which contained the following recommendations.

1. Establishment of University Grants Commission for coordinating the working of different Universities.
2. University Education should be restricted to selected students. (It may be recalled that the Hartag Committee has stated that the students are not fit for University education).
3. Compulsory physical education to students.
4. Establishments of technical schools and Technological Departments in Universities.

DR. THARA CHAND COMMITTEE (1948)

The committee submitted its report containing the following recommendations.

1. Admission to degree course only after secondary education.
2. The pay scales of teachers should be revised.
3. There should be refresher courses after every three years.

UNIVERSITY EDUCATION COMMISSION (1948-49) (DR.S. RADHAKRISHNAN COMMISSION)

The Commission made the following recommendations:

1. A large number of well equipped and well staffed intermediate colleges are to be established together with a good number of vocational institutions for students who do not go to Universalities.
2. The minimum number in arts and science faculties of a University be fixed at 3000 and 1500 respectively.
3. Library works and tutorials should supplement university classes.
4. The quality of teaching should be improved.
5. Starting facilities for agriculture and educational research.
6. Religious education to students.
7. Special examinations for recruitment.
8. Introduction of credit system at degree and P.G level.
9. University education should be placed in the concurrent list and financing of higher education should be the responsibility of the government.
10. Immediate establishment of University Grants Commissions.

SECONDARY EDUCATION COMMISSION 1952-53

Dr.Lakhsmana Swamy Mudaliyar was the Chairman of this Commission. The Committee recommended replacement of the two-year intermediate course by one-year pre university course. The Commission also recommended starting of three-year degree courses.

EDUCATION COMMISSION 1964 (KOTHARI COMMISSION)

Dr.D.S. Kothar commission was appointed in October 1964 and the Commission submitted its report on 29th June 1966 containing the following recommendations.

1. Radical improvement in the quality and standard of higher education.
2. Expansion of higher education to meet the manpower requirements of National development.
3. Improvement of university administration and organization.
4. Internal and continuous assessments seminars and workshops for improvement of teaching.
5. Autonomy for Universities and for Departments within the Universalities, as well as to selected colleges.

DR. P.V.GAJENDRAGADKAR COMMITTEE (JUNE 1969)

The Committee made the following recommendations with respect to the structure of Universities, functions and powers of statutory bodies, service conditions of staff etc.,

THE AMENDMENT OF THE CONSTITUTION

The 42nd amendment of the Constitution (1976) included education in the concurrent list and so education became the responsibility of both the Central and the State Governments

EDUCATION POLICY PERSPECTIVE (MINISTRY OF EDUCATION) AND NATIONAL POLICY ON EDUCATION 1986

Education Policy Perspective and National Policy on Education recommended better and more facilities to universities and colleges for their all around development, establishment of autonomous colleges and gradual replacement of affiliated colleges and redesigning of academic programmes to meet the demands of specialization. It also recommended formation of State Councils for Planning and Coordination (SCPC) of Programmes and projects, emphasis on transformation on teaching methods, financial support to high quality research, setting up of national research centers, encouragement of interdisciplinary research, de-linking of jobs and establishment of rural Universities.

THE RESOLUTION ON NATIONAL POLICY ON EDUCATION (1988) HIGHLIGHTED THE NEED TO

(i) Transform the educational system so as to relate it more closely to the life of the people

(ii) Make continuous efforts for expanding educational opportunities.

(iii) Make sustained efforts for raising the quality of education at all levels

(iv) Give special accord on the development of Science and Technology, and

(v) To provide and cultivate moral and social values.

The National Policy on Education was revised in 1992. The Standing Committee of the Parliament under the Chairmanship of ShriS.B.Chavan (the report of which was presented to Parliament in February 1999) highlighted the need for revamping School education and this was included in the National Curriculum programme for School Education published in November 2000.The 83rd amendment of the Constitution (1997) made right to free and compulsory education for children from six to 14 years of age a fundamental right. Enrolment rate at primary stage has reached 94.9 per cent during 1999-2000. Hundred per cent enrollment is expected to be realized by 2015.

The fund allocation for education under the different Five Year Plans is presented in Appendix-2. Appendix 3 and4 presents respectively information regarding India's position about adult and youth literacy vis-à-vis some Asian countries and literacy rate in India from 1951-2001 according to censes figures

POSITION OF EDUCATION IN KERALA

Today we are living in a knowledge-based society. In such a society education is a means to empower people to fight against poverty, hunger and superstitions fortified by ignorance. The power of education was well realized by the rulers of Travancore and Cochin princely states. It was this realization which prompted Rani Gouri Parvathi Bhai of Travancore to issue an edict in 1817 stating that" the state should defray the entire cost of education of its people in order that there might be no backwardness in the spread of enlightenment among them, that by diffusion of education, they might become better subjects and public servants and the reputation of the state might be advanced thereby. Because of the enlightened policies followed by the rulers of the princely states of Travancore and Cochin the period from the sixteenth to the eighteenth centuries was a period of growth in literacy in Kerala.

According to Cathleen Gough widespread literacy was an important feature of the pre-British society in Kerala. She holds the view that before the British rule, almost all Nair men and most Nair women were literate and more than 50 per cent of men in general and 25 per cent of women were literate in the early 18th century.

It was the Christian Missionaries who established modem type of schools in the state. The names of the London Missionary Society and the Christian Missionary Society are noteworthy in this respect. The institutions established by missionaries had two distinct features. First they spent largely from their own sources and secondly, they established schools mainly to serve the people in general especially the under privileged.

The Social Reform Movements that witnessed Kerala during the late 19th and early 20th centuries contributed to the spread of education in the state. The establishment of SNDP (Sree Narayana Dharma Paripalana) Yogam in 1903 and the pioneering work of their leaders such as Sree Narayana Guru, Kumaran Aasan and Dr. Palpu helped to spread education among the ezhavas/thiyyas. "We are the largest Hindu community in Kera1a... Without education no community has attained permanent civilized prosperity. In our community there must be no man or woman without primary education," declared Dr. Palpu.

The establishment of the Nair Service Society (NSS, 1914) and the activities undertaken by its leaders, especially Mannthu Padmanabhan made education available to economically poor Nairs and other sections of the society.

Then it was the turn of the Muslim Education Society (MES, 1964). Under the able leadership of Dr. Gaffoor the Society established educational institutions especially for the benefit of the Muslim community. Several other Christian denominations also started educational institutions for the benefit of their particular communities.

Unlike the missionaries, the communal societies started educational institutions mainly for the benefit of their own communities. Even then the services of the communal associations in the field of education was commendable and that placed Kerala in the vanguard of educational development.

The turn of the 20th century marked the democratization process in the state. Consequently each community intervened in the political process for communal gains. In fact, the first democratic government in Travancore was a coalition of Nairs, Christians and Ezhvas. Even when these communities competed with each other for power and privileges, they were found cooperating to share the spoils. The result was liberal grant-in-aid to private educational institutions.

The first democratic government that came into power in the state of Kerala under the leadership of Sri E.M.Sakaran_Namboodirppad (EMS) tried to regulate the education sector by introducing a comprehensive legislation. The Kerala Education Bill was passed for this purpose. The Bill envisaged

(a) Direct payment to teachers and other employees working in private schools.

(b) Withdrawal of financial assistance to educational institutions, which fail to comply with the provisions of the Bill.

(c) Appointment of teachers by the government.

(d) Production and distribution of text-books by the government.

(e) Take- over of erring institutions.

The Education Bill provided an opportunity for the communal associations to join together and fight against the government and that ultimately resulted in what is popularly called "the Vimochana Samara". Consequently the EMS ministry was dismissed by the Central Government in 1959.

The Ministry that followed the EMS ministry took a soft approach to the private management. Ultimately the government surrendered the right of appointment of teachers and other employees to the management and retained the responsibility of paying the salary of teachers and staff. This dichotomy paved the way for corruption in the appointment of teachers. Teaching posts became a commodity for auction.

By the middle of the 1960s a new experiment was started in the education sector in the state. A number of junior colleges and unaided institutions were started in the education sector. By the end of the 20th century pre-degree was separated from colleges and a number of higher secondary schools were started in the public and in the aided sectors. Even though the unaided sector was interested to start such institutions, permission was not granted. This has increased the financial burden of the state.

The economic reform initiated in the country has produced ripples in the education sector also. Education became a priced commodity. The idea of self-financing institutions at all levels has become a catchy slogan and guidelines for future policy. The New Education Policy is based on the theory that marketisation of education would enhance economic efficiency. This theory has resulted in closure of some of the so-called un-economic schools by the Antony government.

Though Kerala ranks first in terms of many social indicators and occupies an unenviable position in educational development (with more than 90 per cent literacy against the all India average of 52.2 per cent as per 1991 census), the quality of education is very poor in the state. This is evidenced from the poor performance of students from Kerala in competitive examinations.

Having provided a general introduction to education in Kerala let us discuss the specific areas, viz; primary, secondary, higher secondary and collegiate education sectors in Kerala.

The education system in Kera1a comprises of five stages. They are (a) pre-primary stage (b) Primary stage (c) secondary stage (d) higher secondary stage and (e) higher education stage. The pre-primary stage covers two years (LKG & UKG), primary stage four years, secondary stage six years and higher secondary stage two years. Pre-primary education is not compulsory in order to join the primary stage where the medium of instruction is the local language. For joining the English medium schools pre-primary education is a must. Two streams are available in the secondary stage. They are English medium and Malayalam medium. For English medium there are two streams: State scheme and the CBSE scheme. National level examinations are conducted for the CBSE and the syllabi for the scheme is prepared by the NCERT. The NCERT scheme is considered as superior to the State scheme. In the case of Higher Secondary also there are two schemes similar to that of the secondary system - the state and the CBSE. There is another scheme for secondary and higher secondary level of education which is popularly known as the vocational system of education. The National Council for Vocational Training (NCVT) conducts the examination of this stream. The higher education falls within the jurisdiction of the Universities. The universities prepare the syllabi for the various courses and they also conduct the examinations.

There are two streams in higher education. They are general education and professional education. National bodies regulate the professional education in the country. Medical education by All India Medical Council, technical education by the All India Council For Technical Education, legal education by the Bar Council of India and teacher education by National Council for Teacher Education. The University Grants Commission provides grants to universities and affiliated-Colleges for developmental activities and improving the standard of teaching and research. The University Grants Commission also provides special grants to Centers of Excellence.

From the above discussion it can be seen that the higher education system in India there is tremendous quantitative expansion in the number of institutions. The profile of education providers various in types, programmes, curricular offerings, mode of delivery and funding pattern. Under such conditions, variations in standard and quality are natural outcomes.

Arising out of the need for establishing standards in education especially in higher education in the context of the proliferation of colleges all over the country, the programme of action of the national policy on education I 1986 emphasized the need for a mechanism to be set up which will encourage self assessment in institutions and also assessment and accreditation by a council.

In view of the recommendations on the national policy on education 1986–the UGC constituted a committee under the chairmanship of Dr. Vasand Gowwariker, the then secretary Ministry of Science and Technology, Government of India. The committee submitted it s report in 1987 in March 1992 the UGC resolved to set up a National Accreditation Board in Higher Education. And the National Credit and Assessment Council (NAAC) was established in 1994 under sector 12 CCC UGC Act 1956.

The assessment and accreditation was started in 1997 with the 10 criteria of assessment, namely:

1. Course and objectives
2. Curriculum design and review
3. Teaching, Learning and evaluation
4. Research and publication
5. Consultancy services
6. Organization and Management
7. Infrastructural facilities
8. Support services
9. Student feedback and council ling
10. Generation and management of finance recourses.

Many initiatives have taken by the NAAC in establishing quality assurance and cells institutions and state quality cells and establishing linkages, entering into MOU's with State government and conducting institutional, regional and national workshops of accredited colleges as well as non accredited colleges. The NAAC is expected to maintain quality in higher education institutions in the country.

THE ADMINISTRATIVE SET-UP FOR EDUCATION

The Director of Public Instruction supervises education up to the Higher Secondary level. The Director of Collegiate Education supervises the functions of both private and government colleges. The Minister of Education determines the policies with respect to education; of course, with the concurrence of the cabinet. Assistant Education Officers (AEOs) supervise the working of primary education and the District Education Officers (DEOs) Secondary Level of Education at district levels. The Director of Public Instruction (DPI) conducts public examinations for 10 standard students. There are Deputy Directors of Collegiate Education to help the Director of Collegiate Education.

State intervention has made education less expensive and more accessible to all strata of the society in the state till the initiation of economic reform. But a sea change in the attitude of the government with respect to education is witnessed after the initiation of the economic reforms and that created problems for the lower income groups in getting access to higher as well as lower levels of education in spite of the fact that the government became so liberal in granting permission to start all types of educational institutions in the state. The government wants to make Kerala the destination for education, for people within and outside the country. But as the new institutions are started in the self-financing sector the accessibility of the lower income groups to education is restricted. Even though the government granted no objection certificates on the specific understanding that 50 per cent of the seats created in the new institutions is to be made available to candidates with merit, the recent Supreme Court and the subsequent High Court decisions regarding the rights of management with respect to admissions and fees vitiated the whole issue and promoted commercialization of education in the state.

SECONDARY EDUCATION

During 2000-01 there were 932 schools of which 416 were in the government sector, 508, in the aided sector 8, in the unaided sector with 3483 batches with an annual sanctioned intake of 174150 students.

K.K. George and. Ajith kumar in their study on "State's Secondary Education System" have highlighted the pre-eminent role of the private aided school sector in the secondary schooling stage in the state. They pointed out that the Private Aided School Sector shares 54 per cent of secondary school sector. The share in student enrolment and staff were 59 percent and 56 per cent respectively. Grants to private aided secondary schools were the largest single head of expenditure under secondary education, viz 56 per cent. The share of expenditure on government schools was only 34.4 per cent. By encouraging private initiative in educational field, the government could save on the capital expenditure and a portion of recurring expenditure. The study observed that grants-in-aid polices of the governments in the pre independence period had many positive features which are relevant to the present discussions on financing of education in the context of the state's escalating fiscal crisis. They could ensure community and local participation in educational development. Besides, these policies were conditional and were used as inducements for introducing government regulations on salary and service conditions of teachers, their minimum qualifications, the structure of fees, curriculum, textbooks inspection etc. It has been an established fact that the facilities available in most of the aided schools are better than those in government schools. In a recent study (2003) George et.al have pointed out that the per capita expenditure of the government in the education sector and especially in the higher education sector has been declining over the years and today it is one of the lowest in the country.

PROFESSIONAL EDUCATION

In Kerala, like anywhere else in India, the high achievers from schools almost invariably enroll for professional courses. A large number of engineering and other professional colleges have been established in the state recently. Different universities in the state also started more technical courses. Consequently, the Technical education infrastructure witnessed tremendous expansion during 1997-2003. At present there are 78 Engineering Colleges in the State of which 12 are government colleges, 18 Private aided colleges, 46 Self-financing colleges and one Regional Engineering College (Calicut). The annual intake of students in engineering colleges in 2003 stood at (21,773). Apart from the engineering colleges a number of law colleges, teachers' training colleges, polytechnics and business schools were started during the same period.

HIGHER EDUCATION

When Kerala was formed in 1956 there was only one University viz., the University of Travancore. After the formation of the State, the University was re-christioned as the University of Kerala and all the colleges working in Kerala including those affiliated to the Madras University were brought under the University of Kerala. Then there were only 28 colleges with 22000 students in their rolls. The number of colleges shot up to 181 and enrollments, 305000 by 1999. Of the 305000 enrolment in 1999 1.65 lack students belonged to the pre-degree level. Now the pre-degree sector is separated from the colleges and is placed under the Higher Secondary System.

At present there are seven Universities in Kerala viz. Kerala University, Calicut University, Cochin University of Science and Technology, Mahatma Gandhi University, Kannur University, Kerala Agricultural University and Sri Sankaracharya University of Sanskrit. The Sri Chitra Thirnnal Institute of Medical Sciences and Technology has the Status of a full-fledged University. In addition there is an Indian Institute of Management at Kozhikode with independent status. The last two institutions are under the control of the central

Government. The numbers of colleges under these Universities exceed 500. Over and above these there are a number of parallel colleges and institutions imparting training for the degrees of universities in Kerala, other Indian Universities and Universities in foreign countries. A regional center of the Indira Gandhi national Open University is also located at Kochi and it enrolls students for various courses.

The higher education institutions in the state are controlled at three different levels-the government/the Department of Collegiate Education, the Universities and the Private Managements. Sri T.N.Jayachandran who was once the Principal Secretary of Higher Education and who occupied the Vice-chancellorship of at least two universities in the state has stated that Kerala state has never had a formal education policy. According to him, the Education Minister enjoyed all the powers, and hardly there was any delegation. He adds, normally there is very little policy formulation at the secretariat level also. The minister gets ideas supported and abetted by Politicians and Government secretaries and they became part of the policy. This type of situation was responsible for creating problems in the arena of higher education. One of the major problems that the state faced was mismatch between demand and supply of courses. The mismatch was more pronounced in the area of technical and professional education. The technical and professional education had a very narrow base. .George and Ajith Kumar in their paper 'what is Wrong with kerala's Education System" vividly clarifies this. According to them the percentage of seats in engineering colleges per thousand of +2 students who hold a first class was only 23 as against 27.1 in the country. In this respect Kerala lagged behind many of the states in India. They add, only one out of seven applicants were admitted to engineering colleges, one out of ten in polytechnics and one out of 30 in medical colleges. Paramedical, teaching, hotel management and management, the situation is more worse. The position has changed as a result of the liberal policy adopted by Antony's government in sanctioning self-financing-professional colleges in the private sector.

The University is supposed to deal with academic and administrative matters with respect to all colleges coming under its jurisdiction. It is the authority to grant affiliation to new colleges and courses. But the government has usurped that authority, Says Jayachandran. He adds: the Syndicate, the chief executive body of the University is the hotbed of politics. The syndicate dominates even the Academic Council, the principal academic body of the University, and they normally carry the day with their excessive power and capacity to maneuver. The Vice-Chancellor, who shall have all powers necessary for the purpose of ensuring all the provisions of the Act, the Statutes, the Ordinances, the Rules and Bye-laws are faithfully observed and carried out, is reduced to the level of a mute and dumb witness of the (miss) deeds of the Syndicate.

It was a tragedy that Kerala did not utilize the facility of giving autonomous status to colleges, which were functioning efficiently. UGC was expected to ensure assistance up to Rs. 50 lakhs to such autonomous colleges under the 8th Plan. Our neighboring States used that facility and they went far ahead of Kerala in the field of higher education.

The curriculum existing in the higher education sector is obsolete and fossilized. It takes years to modify the same. If at all some modifications take place, that do not reflect either the need or the student's requirements. It only reflects the interest of the teachers and extra care is taken to protect them. There is no programme for skill development in most of the colleges and even in University departments. It is teaching rather than learning process that is practiced. Students have no choice to study subjects of their interest It is a straightjacket system. If a student specializing in economics wants to learn computer as part of his curriculum there is no provision. If he wants to learn mathematics, he can't do that. Colleges are just like factories producing degree holders. A major difference between a factory and a college is that factories produce standardized products of homogenous quality while colleges produce heterogeneous quality products some of which are not good for any use. The UGC has also contributed a lot to make the higher education system so bad.

The present government has shown some liberal attitude in sanctioning professional colleges. During the last two yeas the government has issued more than 500 No Objection Certificates (NOC) for starting different kinds of technical,. management, medical. Paramedical and teacher training and law colleges. We consider this a step in the right direction. This is the sign of realization on the part of the government that the former governments were committing tactical mistakes in the field of education by not permitting private sector to start new colleges.

One of the reasons for quality deterioration in higher education is lack of funds. The allocation for education under various Five Year Plans and unimaginative use of available funds.(see Appendix-2). It may be noted that higher education, in all countries, was heavily dependent on government funding. But the Liberalization, Privatization and Globalization (LPG) policy has put a break on government funding on education. During the 80's and 90's government was progressively reducing the allocation of funds to higher education. The percentage share of allocation to education, which stood at 6.5 of the budget during 1985-86 progressively declined, and stood at 4.6 of the budget in 1998-99. This reduction has adverse impacts on higher education in the State. Today teaching posts are kept vacant, library procurement curtailed, research discouraged.

Over the years the state was facing financial difficulties. There were many reasons for this. As we are not discussing this aspect, we don't want to give details on that aspect. Only thing that we want to convey is that the state is finding it extremely difficult to play the role of a provider. So it is time for the state to assume the role of a facilitator. The relevance of self- financing colleges is in this respect. With all the criticisms against self-financing colleges we support the idea, as it is a case of a Parato Improvement Situation.

We propose to conclude the discussion on education by adding three more points. One relates to research. The Universities, if they want to become centers of excellence, should promote research. We cannot imagine post-graduate teaching without research. So the fossilized and bureaucratic approach of the UGC in not considering research as part of work of teachers will produce irreparable damage in the higher education sector.

The second point relates to fund. Fund is not a problem. Where there is a will, there is a way. Only thing is that the university administration must have a positive attitude. They must believe that they are there to support the academic activities and not to obstruct the same. Many of the foreign Universities are attracting Indian students through the slogan "study abroad". If Indian Universities raise their standard they can reach out and attract foreign students under the campaign "Study in India". Even they can provide foreign degrees at a much lower cost by offering on-line programmes through collaborations with foreign Universities.

The third point is that the education sector as a whole in the state is characterized by the existence of a dual system. One segment offering high quality education catering to the affluent 5 per cent of the population and the second, consisting of low-quality institutions meant for the masses. The state never made any attempt in providing quality education. With government withdrawing gradually from the higher education scenario, the private players have shown *phenomenal* interest and commitment in providing professional education to thousands of youngsters.

Colleges ranging from good to average characterize the higher education scene in Kerala according to the national Assessment and Accreditation Council (NAAC). Which grades colleges on the basis of a seven-point assessment process. The educational institutions in Kerala put up a good performance said the Director of NAAC, V.S. Prasad. The NAAC has made the following recommendations.

1. Teaching should be given more weight age in colleges offering undergraduate programmes. The dissemination of information has to be given top priority.
2. Universalities in the State to concentrate more on research activities. Universities have been directed to

increase their internal revenue by securing research projects from funding agencies in India like the Department of Science and Technology and the Council for Scientific and Industrial Research.

3. Colleges in Kerala should equip students to meet the challenges in the era of information technology.
4. The introduction of more add-on courses in colleges was yet another recommendation. Colleges have been asked to introduce innovative teaching and learning methods.
5. The council urged some of the colleges to apply for autonomy fore experimenting with several aspects of teacher education. The council suggested that teachers be encouraged to update their knowledge regularly as part of the processes of improving the quality of education.

PRIVATIZATION OF EDUCATION

Privatization generally deals with Efficiency, Cost effectiveness, Increased productions and marketisation. The question is how far such arguments hold good in the case of education. The aim of education is the development of human resources. It cannot be treated at par with companies and agricultural products. As Nehru puts it "a university stands for humanism, for tolerance, for reason, for progress, for the adventure of ideas and for search for the truth". It is different from an agricultural or industrial good. Markets are important, but when it comes to human beings, what is more important is the principle of what economists call non-competing groups. Civilizations survive because transfers of income circumscribe markets. There are some groups who compete only in their own field and hence the refusal of some people to compete in the market place. Hence market cannot determine the price of service involving human beings. The sad state of affairs of self-financing institutions puts education at a disadvantages position. Self-financing colleges were started on the premise that the financial crisis faced by the education sector could be overcome by starting such colleges. In fact, such a policy had several inherent dangers. The demand for more self-financing colleges stemmed out of the widely prevalent notion that students were the sole beneficiaries of higher education.

The view that students should meet the full cost of education had been gaining ground since the 1990s. Such arguments made students consumers of the service industry called education. However, these views were not shared by the capitalist countries." Education increases the future earning of its beneficiaries, besides raising the knowledge and skill of a society. Thus, education contributes a lot to the labour productivity and competitiveness of the national economies.

The State Government had taken the stand that its role was limited to conducting entrance tests. It did not have any interest in regulating these self-financing colleges. There is always a mismatch between demand and supply, since education is the only sector, which lacks an education policy. The "policilessness" is the policy of many governments. In fact, the State Government had a role to play in ensuring social equity and occupational mobility. The Self-financing colleges did not make any effort to find out talents from wider circles. The government had commercialized the education sector. Education was considered as part of the social security measures. Nowadays, it was deemed as a profit-making venture. The state had many educational institutions that did not have any basic facilities for libraries. In many appointments are not made as per rules. Admission procedures are not transparent. Most of the teachers are under-qualified and appointed on hourly basis. And almost al institutions adopt different fee and donation structure. The state government had abdicated financing of professional colleges. In fact the government was concerned only with the question whether the managements were able to make profits from their institutions.

In spite of the defects in the system the NAAC has listed the following colleges namely CMS College, Kottayam, Farook College Kozhicode, Loyola College of Social Science

Trivandurm, Rajagiri College of Social sciences, Kalamassery, Sacred Heart College, Thevara, St.Berchman's College Changanacherry, St.Teresa's College, Ernakulam, union Christian College, Aluva, and Vimala College, Thrissur as Five Star Colleges. Mar Athnacious College, Kothmangalam was declared as "A" Grade college. In 2004 UGC has identified five colleges in Kerala namely University College, Trivandurm, Maharajas Colege, Ernakulam, Government Victoria College Palakkad, Prennen Government College, Thalassery, to grant Deemed University Status.

PART II: HEALTH

India is one of the signatories 'to Alma Ata Declaration in 1978.The Declaration aimed at "Health For All by 2000". But India will be quite far from realizing this dream even in 2010. One of the reasons for non-realization of the objective was consistent reduction in public fund allocation for the health sector. The allocation is only less than one per cent of the GDP, which is a mere one fifth of the total health spending in the country. According to the Economic Times Health Care 2001-02 Report, India's Health Care Industry grew at 13 per cent per annum over the last decade and is growing at 17 per cent annually at present. Earlier reports from Mckinsey pointed out that the health care industry was contributing to 5.2 per cent to India's GDP.

The Indian health care Industry is estimated to be around Rs. 1000 billion at present and expected to reach Rs. 2000 billion by 2012 with 17 per cent annual growth rate.

On an average in 1999 families expected to spend Rs. 10000 per annum towards medical expenses. In spite of this the India lags behind international standards on basic health care infrastructure and facilities. India has 94 beds per 10000 persons as compared to the WHO norm of 333 beds per 10000 persons. So also the density of doctors is low (only 43 doctors per 10000 person) and there is high incidence of diseases. According to World Health Report 2000 Indian's health expenditure is stood at 5.2 per cent of her GDP. A study of government public health expenditure shows that only 16 per cent is allocated to primary health care and 84 per cent to secondary and tertiary health care.

India has 5,03,900 doctors and 7,00,000 nurses and 162 medical colleges, 143 pharmacy colleges and 3,50,000 chemists. There are around 15100 hospitals with nine lakh beds. This indicates 1.5 beds per 1000 persons. China, Brazil and Thailand have an average of 4.3 beds per 1000 persons. WHO report states that India needs to add 8,00,00 hospital beds each year to meet the demands of the population. Of which 40000 beds must be added by the private sector

SOME ESTIMATES INDICATE THAT

(a) 1.2 million cancer cases will need to be treated in India by 2011.
(b) India had 5 million HIV positive population in 2002.
(c) About 18 out of every 1000 persons suffer from Neurological disorders.
(d) By 2010 India will have 47 million diabetic populations.

According to Sen., Education and Health can be seen to be valuable to the freedom of a person in at least five distinct ways.

They are

(i) Intrinsic importance: Education and health are valuable achievements in themselves.
(ii) Instrumental in personal roles. A person's education and health help him to do many things.
(iii) Instrumental in social roles: Education and health encourage demand for social need.
(iv) Instrumental in personal roles. Education and health broadens the horizon of people and generate benefits.
(v) Empowerment and distributive roles. With better health and education, disadvantageous groups can better resist oppression and inequality.

Also health should be viewed from two aspects: Health is wealth and also Health creates Wealth. The maxim that health is wealth highlights the increasing importance of health. The components of good health are (Biswanath 2001)

(1) Nutritious diet

(2) Hygienic condition of living

(3) Safe drinking water

(4) Information about good health care

(5) Existence of good health care facilities like hospitals and medical treatment facilities

(6) Financial ability to incur the medical expenses.

It is evident that among these requirements' most of them remain unfulfilled in the less developed countries.

India's achievement in the field of public health is not very impressive in spite of 55 years of planning. Public Health investment in India over the years has not only been relatively low but also continuously on the decline as a percentage of GDP. It has fallen to 0.9 per cent in 1999 from 1.3 per cent in 1990. Because of inadequate facilities less than 20 per cent of the population seeking outpatient department (OPD) services and less than 45 per cent undergoing in-patient treatment are availing public health services. The 2003 budget, which is inspired by the National Health Policy (NHP)-2002, seems to correct the bias to a great extent by allocating more funds for health sector initiatives. (Refer Appendix-5).

The measures pertaining to health sector have been designed keeping in mind three objectives:

(1) To contribute to enhanced national health

(2) To promote India as a global health destination; and

(3) To enable easier access to health facilities for the disadvantaged sections of the society.

The important measures in Health Sector include

(a) tax exemptions on income for financial institutions providing long term capital to private hospitals with over 100 beds under section 10(230) of the income-tax Act and

(b) in order to promote India as a health care destination and enable it to carve out bigger pie of the $ 3.5 trillion world healthcare market a string of tax incentives that include scrapping of customs duty on samples required for clinical trials, abolition of duty on equipments to boost R&D activity, waiver of excise duty and additional excise duty on many specified life saving drugs and life saving equipments are effected. Allowing companies to import duty free equipment up to 25 per cent of the previous year's export instead of one per cent is yet another incentive that will encourage bio-tech R&D.

HEALTH IN KERALA

Kerala has gone a long way in health care compared to the country as whole. This was largely due to the private initiative in the health care system. As in the field of education private sector made its presence in the health care system by starting well-established hospitals from early times. Good health is by definition, an integral part of social development. The World Health Organization (WHO) has defined the highest possible levels of health as "Physical, mental and social well-being and not merely the absence of disease or infirmity. It has also clarified that to have good health is a fundamental human right. Health was first recognized as a fundamental human right at the international conference on Primary health care at Alma Ata in Kazakistan of soviet Socialist Republic in 1978. The conference also fixed the year 2000 for attaining good health for all. April 6th is celebrated as World Health Day. As already mentioned Kerala has made remarkable achievements in health almost comparable to that of developed nations. Socio-economic factors like female literacy, social reforms, nutritional programmes, public distribution system and other forms of state intervention have contributed to this achievement in this field.

With its modest medical service, Kerala has been able to achieve good results in health care service The infant mortality rate in Kerala was only 12 per 1000 when it was 72 per 1000 at the national level. Maternal mortality rate in Kerala has remained between 1.5 and 2 for every 1000 deliveries whereas the average all-India ratio was 4.6 per 1000 deliveries. When birth rate per 1000 declined from 32.3 in 1970 to 18.2 in 1998 at the National Level it declined from 15.7 to 9 per 1000 in Kerala. Life expectancy at birth in Kerala was 46.17 years for males and 50 years for females in 1951. In 1998 it increased to 62.2 and 73.6 years respectively. Female literacy, women status, accessibility and availability of health services, equity, socio-political factors including social movements, public distribution system etc. have been prominent variables for health improvement in Kerala. Health improvement is influenced by three sets of factors (K.R.Nayar 1999)

(a) Health factors which include medical interventions

(b) Health promoting factors such as housing, water supply, sanitation and hygiene and

(c) Non-health factors, which include social and economic factors.

Kerala has unique achievements in immunization status. The vaccination coverage of infants against polio, BCG and measles was reported to be 100 or near 100 per cent in 1998-99. The state has succeeded in preventing the incidence of communicable diseases, leprosy, tuberculosis, filaria and malaria. Even though Kerala has made remarkable achievements in the above mentioned health indicators, diseases like cholera and malaria are making a recurrent comeback. On the other side, lack of regulation and government failure to enforce existing regulations are leading to several unethical and unfair practices in the health sector.

In spite of these achievements, during the past decade, Kerala witnessed several outbreaks of preventable diseases such as leptospirosis, meningitis, dengue fever and cholera. Despite the existence of a health care system in the public sector reaching almost every corner of the state, the official machinery is failing to prevent the outbreaks. It has often been pointed out that in the health department no one is responsible for the situation. Contaminated water supply, polluted environment, water logging, lack of cleanliness in public places and other areas continue. Effective remedial action is lacking in all these areas. The present scenario shows that the system of health care in Kerala is moving from a situation of success to one of crisis. Kerala presents a low-mortality-high-morbidity syndrome (P.G.K.Panikar, 1975). The State is today witnessing high incidence of cancer, heart disease, diabetics etc. The incidence of Japanese encephala and AIDS are also spreading. And unless measures are initiated on a war footing to check the spread of these diseases Kerala will face a crisis situation within the next ten years.

A disturbing trend is now seen in the health care system in India. Under the new economic policy the government started charging user fee from patients enjoying public health care system. The user fee is weaning away patients from public health care system.

The liberalization policies of the government have led to the mushrooming of private hospitals in the state. India's membership in the WTO and the acceptance of IPR and Patent rights affected the production of lifesaving medicines. Government hospitals charges have become beyond the reach of common man. Patients are charged on several counts such as nursing charges, treatment charges, service charges and professional charges apart from medicines. The net result has been the exclusion of the marginalized and vulnerable sections of the community from enjoying medical_care facilities. This is expected to produce irreparable damages in the health care system of the state. To minimize the damage on the health care system on account of the new policies under the economic reform health insurance becomes an absolute necessity. The time has therefore come to improve our understanding the role of health insurance in sustaining and distributing the benefits of health care services to the people.

Water is the most precious thing, which maintains life on earth. Good drinking water is the prerequisite for maintaining good health. When pure water was available in plenty drinking water was not a problem. But development of industries and cities created waste disposal problem. Streams and rivers and other sources of water became waste dumping places. The wastes produced by industries and cities led to various types of water pollution and supply of pure or uncontaminated drinking water has become a serious problem. The importance of pure drinking water can be seen form the high incidence of water born diseases in India and especially in the state of Kerala.. The proportion of population in the state who require access to protected water supply has been increasing. According to 1991 census, Kerala had 197 towns, which includes three corporations and 55-municipalities with "an urban population of 76.86 lakhs. Kerala's rural population in 1991 was 214.18 lakh. It is estimated that the urban population had increased to 86.651akh and rural population to 241.58lakh by 2000. Out of the estimated 60.51 lakh households, only 6.34lakh (10.47 per cent) were connected with house taps in 2000. In addition there were 1,36,000 stand posts; each stand post is expected to benefit a population of 250 as per Accelerated Rural Water Supply Norms. Steps have to be taken to increase and extend water supply schemes commensurate with the requirements of the rapidly growing population. Many towns are expanding at a fast rate and many new towns are coming up.

Though the proportion of population in the state with access to protected water supply has been increasing, a substantial portion of the population remains to be covered. As in October 2001 the rural population covered with protected water supply stood at 124 lakh. In addition 14 lakh rural population are partially benefited by spot sources. The urban population covered with safe water supply stood at 59 lakhs. With the accelerated effort made, the additional population covered with protected water supply was 50.94 lakhs during the ten-year period 1992-2001, out of which SC/ST population accounted for 8.27 lakh and 0.73 lakh respectively. Out of about 60 lakh households in Kerala 7.51 lakh were provided with house tap connections

The expenditure on water supply under plan and non-plan amounted to Rs. 110 crores in 1992-93, which sharply increased to about Rs. 260 crores in 1999-2000. But the protected water supply is not that protected. This is largely because the pipelines carrying drinking water are laid in an unhealthy manner. So drinking water often get contaminated. According to 1991 census, 51 per cent of the households in the state had sanitary latrines. The position was that 86 per cent of the households were rural household's of which 52 per cent (24.541akh) had latrine facilities. In urban areas 53 per cent of the total urban households have latrine facilities. Another factor that contributes to good health is sanitation and a good environment. Financial assistance from LIC of India, World Bank (after declaration of the decade 1981-90 as International Decade for Water Supply and sanitation) ADB bilateral assistance from foreign countries particularly the Netherlands, Played a major role in increasing water supply and sanitation facilities.

Dr. B. Ekbal, health activist and former Vice-Chancellor of the Kerala University, has stated that Government should spend more on the health care sector and not withdraw from it. In developed countries such as Canada and the U.K., the Government contributed about 75 per cent of the expenditure in the health sector. In the U.S., the Government 's share in expenditure in health sector was 44 per cent while in neighboring Bangladesh the figure was 43.8 per cent. However, in India the Government accounted for only 21.7 per cent of the expenditure in the health sector. Similarly, here the public expenditure in the health-care sector was only 0.6 per cent of the GDP while even according to the norm of the World Health Organization it should be five per cent. He said it was the provisions of the Indian Patent Law (1970) that enabled the country in achieving self-sufficiency in drug production and in making drugs available at a reasonable price. But if the country were to succumb to the regimes of TRIPS, all these gains would be lost.

LIFE STYLE DISEASES

The prevalence of lifestyle diseases like disabled mellitus and hypertension is much higher in Kerala than in other states, according to the Economic Review 2004. Recent surveys have revealed that about 8 per cent of the state's population is diabetic and it ranges from 6 per cent in rural area to 20 per cent in urban areas. One in three adults in Kerala also tend to be hypertension. Lack of physical activity, overweight and obesity create a favourable climate for diabetes and hypertension. The alarming increase in heart attacks and strokes in Kerala is partly owing to the high prevalence of hypertension. In four of the six categories of major non-communicable diseases–hypertension, diabetes, heart diseases, mental diseases-the prevalence rate in Kerala is much higher than the national rate. It is estimated that about 1 per cent of the Kerala population at any given time suffer from mental illness. Similarly, another 2 per cent to 3 per cent may be suffering from mental disorders, which may not be severe. Suicide is a manor problem in Kerala, which is estimated at 28.8 per 1 lakh people while the national average is 11.6 per 1 lakh people. In fact, 10.1 per cent of all suicides in India occur in Kerala while the state's population is only 3 per cent of the national population. Over the last one decade, the suicide rate in Kerala rose at a rate of 4.6 per cent.

Life style disease in Kerala

Table 1
Prevalence Rate of Major Disease

Sl. No.	*Name of Disease*	*Kerala*	*India*
1.	Epilepsy	81	120
2.	Hypertension	1433	
3.	Diabetes	980	221
4.	Heart Disease	914	385
5.	Mental Disease	283	132
6.	Cancer	39	43

Source: Human Development report of NCAER-2000.

Table 2
Prevalence Rate of Public Health Disease

Sl.No.	*Disease*	*Prevalence rate per 1000 population*	
		2002	*2003*
1.	Leprosy	0.66	0.05
2.	Filarial	1.28	N.A.
3.	Malaria	N.A.	0.08
4.	&.B.	0.70	0.67
5.	Acute Diarrhea Disease	16.96	15.43
6.	Pneumonia	0.60	0.90
7.	Enteric Fever	0.26	0.40
8.	Measles	0.07	0.15
9.	Respiratory Infection	221.42	247.89

Source: Directorate of Health Services.

INTEGRATED DISEASE SURVEILLANCE PROGRAMME

In the "Kerala Fast Forward Plan 2005" the State government proposed to set up an Integrated Disease Surveillance Programme in the health sector at the cost of Rs.12.38 crores. This includes reintroduction of the referred system and enunciation of policy on procurement of equipments in government hospitals.

NETWORK OF TRAUMA-CARE CENTERS

The Department of Health has drawn up a major project to set up a network of trauma-care centers connecting all districts so that emergency healthcare facilities are available within an hour's journey from any point on major State roads. The state, which has one of the highest accident rates in the country, also records more than 50 per cent of accident moralities within the first hour "Golden Hour" due to the inadequacy of trauma care facilities. The project envisages a structured network of trauma-care centers at primary, secondary and tertiary levels, each located within 80-100 km so that nearly 98 per cent trauma care coverage can be given to the entire population. The project is likely to be included in the next budget under the minimum needs programme. Primary trauma-care centers would be located at Primary Health Centers. Secondary trauma-care centers will be opened in select healthcare institutions in the districts and these would be linked to tertiary care centers located at different points by an efficient transport and communication system.

Features of the project:

1. Network of trauma-care centers
2. Four tertiary trauma-care centers at Kollam, Pathanamthitta, Palakkad and Manjeri, 22 secondary and 20 primary centers across taluks
3. Super specialties, Intensive Care Units (ICUs)
4. Training to medical and paramedical staff, Police, fire force personnel and voluntary organizations teachers, school children and parents on general road safety.

The implementation plan also suggests giving such training to divers when driving licenses are issued, periodic medical examination and vision testing. Kerala stands much above most of the poor countries with respect to access to education and health care facilities. Mean distance to the nearest facility in rural areas among the poorest 19 developing countries is presented in appendix-10.

REFERENCES

Jangira N.K (1994), "Learning Achievements of Primary School Children in Reading and Mathematics Research Based Interventions in Primary Education, New Delhi, NCERT, pp.59-84.

Litten, G.K, "The First Communist Ministry in Kerala-1957-59," K.P.Bagachi, Calculta 1982, taken from V.K.Ramachndran "On Kerala's Development," Indian Development Selected Regional Perspectives.

Dreze Jean and Amartya Sen. (1993), "Hunger and Public Action", Oxford university Press, Delhi.

Kathleen Gough (1996), Literacy in Kerala, in Goody (1968) taken from on Kerala's Development Achievements in Indian Development: Selected Regional Perspectives Ed.Dreze and Amartya Sen, Oxford University Press, New Delhi.

– – (1991), Association of Indian Universities.

Abdul Salim. A "The Cost of Higher Education in India, Anmol Publications Pvt., Ltd, new Delhi, p.2

V.K. Ramachandren," on Kerala's Development Achievements," Indian Development: Selected Regional Perspectives Ed. Dreze and Amartya Sen, Oxford university Press, New Delhi.

Ekbal.B (2001), Higher Education in Kerala towards a new Academic Agenda: national seminar on Globalization and Higher Education in India. 2-3 March Changanassery, Kerala.

Janghyala B.G. Tilak (2000), Higher Education and Economic Development in Kerala, State Level Workshop Series and national Conference Education in Kerala's Development: Towards a New Agenda October Kochi.

Biswanath Ray (2001), "Welfare, choice and Development: Essays in Honour of Amartya Sen, Kanishka publications, New Delhi.

Nayar.K.R (1999), " housing and Health another Kerala Conundrum, Kerala Development Experience (ed), M.A. Oommen, Institute of Social Sciences, Concept Publishing Company.

Panikar, P.G.K (1975), Fall in the mortality Rate in Kerala: An explanatory Hypothesis, EPW, No. 47.

– – Planning Commission, Government of India Seventh Five year Plan, Vol: 11, p. 292.

– – World Bank (1975), Housing; Sector Policy Paper Washington, p. 3.

– – (1999), Report of the Kerala Education commission Constituted by Kerala Sastra Sahitya parishad.

K. C, Sankaranarayanan and V. Karunakaran (1985), " Kerala Economy" Oxford and IBH publishing company.

George W. Schvyler (2002), "Globalization and Health: Venexuela and Cuba," Canadian journal of Development Studies, Vol: XXIII No. 4.

Economic Survey 2004

Facts For you (2004), November 1.

20

WOMEN'S HEALTH CARE BURDENS AND ILL-BEING IN SUB-SAHARAN AFRICA: EVIDENCE FROM A CROSS -COUNTRY ANALYSIS

*Gafar T. Ijaiya**

INTRODUCTION

In Sub-Saharan Africa, the notion that women are weaker sex has always put them at disadvantage positions in all aspect of socio-economic activities. Once aspect of their social life that have over the years being severely affected is their health status, which due to persistent discrimination have added to their health care burdens.

The health care burdens experienced by women in most Sub-Saharan African countries can be linked to their level income, level of dietary and sanitary practice that are too low. The lack of access to health care centres, treatments and drugs, the low level of education, and health specific knowledge, the imbalance of power between men and women within the household, the negative influence of socio-cultural norms, the low level of women participation in government and community activities, the lack of social capital, the negative influence of environmental and infrastructural factors associated with sanitation, road, transport, electricity supply

* Department of Economics, University of Ilorin, Ilorin Nigeria, E-mail: Gtijaiya@Yahoo.com.

and safe water, the influence of crisis (wars and conflicts) and economic depression are also identified as important factors that affects women health status (ADB 2003; Claeson, et. al 2001).

The consequences of these are the increase in the rate of maternal mortality rate and not too impressive rate of life expectancy at birth in some of the countries in the sub-region, which when compared with those in North Africa provide a pathetic situation for the sub-region. For instance, the maternal mortality rate in countries like Angola and Burundi are 1500 and 1300 per 100,000 respectively, while that of Libya and Tunisia are 75 and 70 per 100,000 respectively (ADB 2003).

The thrust of this paper therefore, is to examine the impact of women's health care burdens on their ill-being in Sub-Saharan Africa, using a cross-country data and multiple linear regression analysis.

The next section in this paper provides a conceptual and empirical overview or ill-being and women's health care burdens. Section three provides the data source and methodology used in determining of the influence of women's health care burdens on ill-being in Sub-Saharan Africa. Section four provides and discusses the results. Conclusion and recommendations are contained in the last section.

CONCEPTUAL AND EMPIRICAL OVERVIEW OF ILL-BEING AND HEALTH CARE BURDENS

Ill-Being: Definition, Causes and Consequences

Definition of Ill-being

According to Narayan, et.al (2000a) ill-being include lack of materials and wants such as food, housing and shelter, livelihood, assets and money; hunger, pain and discomfort; exhaustion and poverty in time, exclusion, rejection, isolation and loneliness; bad relations with others including bad relations within the family; insecurity, vulnerability, worry, fear and low self-confidence; and powerlessness, helplessness, frustration and anger. With all these, ill-being is however identical with poverty.

Relating ill-being to poverty, World Bank (1999) saw it as the lack of food, lack of shelter; being sick and not being able to go to school; not knowing how to read; not being able to speak properly; not having a job; fear for the future; losing a child to illness brought about by unclean water; powerlessness; lack of representative and freedom.

Similarly, Aku et. al (1997) saw ill-being form five dimensions of deprivation: (i) personal and physical deprivation experienced from health, nutritional, literacy and educational disability and lack of self confidence; (ii) economic deprivation drawn from lack of access to property, income, assets, factors of production and finance; (iii) social deprivation as a result of denial from full participation in social, political and economic activities; (iv) cultural deprivation in terms of lack of access to values, beliefs, knowledge, information and attitudes which deprives the people to control their own destines; and (v) political deprivation in terms of lack of political voice to partake in decision making that affects their lives.

Causes of Ill-being

Relating the causes of ill-being to poverty, Yahie (1993) observed that the causes of ill-being include among others things:(i) structural causes that are more permanent and depend on a host of exogenous factors such as limited resources, lack of skills, locational disadvantages and other factors that are inherent in the social and political set-up. The disabled, orphans, landless farmers, households headed by females fall into this category; and (ii) the transitional causes that are mainly due to structural adjustment reforms and changes in domestic economic policies that may results in price changes, increased unemployment and so on. Natural calamities such as drought and man-made disasters such as wars, environmental degradation and so on also induce transition ill-being.

As observed by Obadan (1997) the main causes of ill-being include: inadequate access to employment opportunities; inadequate physical assets, such as land and capital and minimal access by the people to credit even in a small scale; inadequate access to the means of supporting rural development in poor regions; inadequate access to markets where the people can sell goods and services; low endowment of human capital, productivity; inadequate access to assistance for those living at the margin and those victimized by transitory poverty and lack of participation. That is, failure to draw the people into the design of development programme that affect their lives.

According to Vanderschueran, et.al (1996) some analysts emphasizes on the macroeconomic causes of ill-being as resulting from globalization and liberalization of various economies which has exacerbated in Sub-Saharan Africa, where over the past 2 decades there has been limited growth of productive investment and employment. More specifically, Structural Adjustment Programme (SAP) implemented in many developing countries is emphasized as one of the main cause of ill-being. They explain the emergence of the new poor as a consequence of loss of jobs due to structural adjustment programme. At the micro level, they said the causes of ill-being is because most people lost their source of livelihood or because their purchasing power as declined. In other causes, ill-being is associated with a particular point in the people's family cycle: e.g. in the case of street children. For many, ill-being is the result of a sudden stock: the loss of the adult family income earner, the confiscation of street trader's stock because they work informally, the loss of their house demolished because it was in illegal land or damaged by natural or human disaster, the high cost of an illness in the family. Similarly, civil war and HIV/AIDS epidemic have generated considerable ill-being particular in some African countries (see also Armstrong 1991; World Bank 1993a, 1993b, 1994, 1995).

Consequences of Ill-being

Discussing the consequences of ill-being, Narayan, et.al (2000b) observed that because of ill-being, most households are crumbing under the weight of deprivation. While some households are able to remain intact, many others disintegrate as men, unable to adapt to their failure to earn adequate incomes under harsh economic circumstances, have difficulties accepting that women are becoming the main bread winners that necessitates a redistribution of income within the households. The results are often alcoholism and domestic violence in the part of men and a breakdown of the family structure. Women in contrast tend to swallow their pride and go out into the streets to do demeaning jobs, or in fact, do anything it take to put food on the table of their children and husbands.

As observed by Aku, et.al (1997) with ill-being spreading in a nation, there tend to be a general loss of confidence in the constituted authority, thereby generating disrespect and rendering government policies ineffective; there tend to be political apathy among contending forces; and there tend to be social disillusion with respect to what the societal objectives are and peoples' responsibilities towards the attainment of these objectives.

Using low life expectancy at birth as proxy for ill-being[1] a number of evidence from some African countries have indicated a drastic increase in ill-being and when compared with some East Asian countries it provides a pathetic situation. For instance, as indicated in Table 1 with the exception of Mauritius, Cape Verde, Comoros and Swaziland, the life expectancy at birth of countries like Botswana, Kenya, Lesotho and Namibia have dropped from 61, 56, 58, 58 years in 1990 to 42, 49, 52, 42 years in 1999 respectively. The key reasons for this are the on-going civil unrest, famine, HIV/AIDS pandemic and other reasons already stated above.

Health and Health Care

According to the World Health Organization (1978) cited in Awake (2001), health is not simply freedom from sickness or disease, but a state of complete physical, mental social well-being. Oxford English Dictionary (1989) defined it as soundness of the body; that condition in which its functions are duly and efficiently discharged. By extension, the general condition of the body with respect to the efficient or inefficient discharge

Table 1
Life Expectancy at Birth (years) in Sub-Saharan African (1990–1999)

Country	*1990*	*1991*	*1992*	*1993*	*1994*	*1995*	*1996*	*1997*	*1998*	*1999*
Angola	46	46	46	46	46	46	46	47	47	48
Benin	52	52	52	53	53	53	53	53	53	53
Botswana	61	58	55	52	50	47	46	44	43	42
Burkina Faso	45	44	44	44	44	44	44	45	45	45
Burundi	41	41	41	42	42	42	42	43	43	43
Cameroon	54	54	54	54	54	54	54	54	54	53
Cape Verde	66	67	67	67	68	68	69	69	69	70
Central Afr. Rep	47	47	46	45	45	44	44	44	44	44
Chard	45	46	46	46	46	47	47	47	48	48
Comoro	57	57	57	58	58	58	59	59	60	60
Congo	48	48	48	48	48	48	48	49	49	49
Congo Dem. Rep	51	51	51	51	50	50	51	51	51	52
Cote d Ivoire	48	48	48	47	47	46	46	47	47	47
Equatorial Guinea	47	48	48	49	49	50	50	50	51	51
Ethiopia	45	44	44	44	43	43	43	43	43	43
Gabon	52	52	52	52	52	52	52	52	52	52
Gambia	45	45	45	46	46	47	47	47	48	48
Ghana	58	58	58	59	59	60	60	60	61	61
Guinea	44	44	44	45	45	46	46	46	47	47
Guinea Bissau	43	43	44	44	44	44	44	44	44	44
Kenya	56	55	54	53	52	52	51	50	49	49
Lesotho	58	57	57	56	56	56	55	54	53	52
Liberia	38	40	42	43	45	47	48	50	51	53
Madagascar	55	55	56	56	57	57	57	58	58	59
Malawi	41	41	40	40	39	39	39	39	39	40
Mali	50	51	51	52	52	53	53	54	54	54
Mauritania	51	51	52	52	53	53	53	54	54	55
Mauritius	69	70	70	70	71	71	71	71	72	72
Mozambique	48	47	46	46	45	45	43	42	40	39
Namibia	58	57	56	54	53	52	50	47	45	42
Niger	46	46	47	47	48	48	48	49	49	50
Nigeria	49	49	49	49	49	50	50	50	50	50
Rwanda	23	26	30	33	37	40	40	40	40	40
Senegal	50	50	51	51	51	52	52	53	53	53
Sierra Leone	32	33	33	34	35	35	36	37	37	38
South Africa	59	57	57	56	55	54	53	51	50	48
Swaziland	57	58	58	59	59	60	60	61	61	62
Tanzania	49	49	48	48	48	47	47	47	47	47
Togo	49	49	49	49	49	48	49	49	49	49
Uganda	37	37	38	38	39	39	40	41	42	43
Zambia	43	43	42	41	40	40	40	40	41	41
Zimbabwe	51	50	48	47	45	44	43	42	42	41

Source: ADB (2001) Selected Statistics in African Country Abidjan: ADB.

of functions usually qualified as good, bad, weak and delicate (see also the New Book of Knowledge 1980).

On the other hand, health care is the care for the general health of a person, community and the nation, especially that which is provided by an organized health service or the way the body is kept sound and strong. This include diet, exercise, sleep, doctors help and avoiding danger. (Oxford English Dictionary 1989; New Book of Knowledge 1980).

Health Care Burdens

Women's health care burdens are manifestation of their inability to have access to health care services within the society they found themselves. As observed by Overholt and Saunder (1996) and Bitran and McInnes (1993) individual's health care burden depends on the individuals perception of need when he/she is sick which in turn depends on the individuals location (urban or rural), income and the level of education attainment; and the characteristics of all the providers which include the prices/costs of health care services provided, the location of the provider and the quality of the services provided (see also Bitran 1994).

ADB (2003) and Claeson, et.al (2001) reiterates that women's health care burdens have been compounded by the deterioration of public health care services and systems, deterioration in infrastructure (road network, electricity, sanitation facilities and water supply) and the decrease in public health spending and the privatization and commercialization of health care systems which has made health care expensive.

The burdens of health care services, which have deprived women access to health care services in Sub-Saharan Africa, have had severe consequences on their well-being by making them vulnerable to ill health and poverty. For instance, when compared with some of the countries in North Africa, the lack of sufficient health care services has over the years led to the increase in maternal mortality rate, increase in infant and under-5 mortality rates, increase the number of women living with HIV/AIDS, reduce life expectancy at birth and reduce the use of contraceptives for birth control.

As indicated in Table 2, Sub-Saharan Africa which comprises, Central Africa, East Africa, Southern Africa and West Africa has not have any remarkable improvement in it maternal, infant, and under-5 mortality rates and life expectancy at birth when compared with North Africa, the sub-region has had more cases of women living with HIV/AIDS than those of North Africa. Southern African countries alone had about 10 million women living with HIV/AIDS in 2001, 23 times more than those in North Africa.

Table 2
Indicators of Health Care Burdens in Sub-Saharan Africa and North Africa in 2001

Region	*Infant mortality per 1000*	*Under-5 mortality per 1000*	*Maternal mortality per 100000*	*Women living with HIV/AIDS*	*Life expectancy at birth (Years)*	*Contraceptive use % of women age 15-49*
Central Africa	88.5	175.6	858	3,174,500	49.4	10.4
East Africa	89.8	175.5	857	6.123,700	47.7	25.8
Southern Africa	87.7	146.7	580	10,780,000	44.3	42.2
West Africa	86.4	175.4	810	5,137,900	51.3	14.2
North Africa	49.0	91.2	246	451,000	66.3	47.0

Source: ADB 2003.

DATA SOURCE AND METHODOLOGY

Data Source

Cross country data for the year 2001 on ill-being proxied by life expectancy at birth and the determinants of health care burdens such as income of the people, numbers of health services personnel per 100,000 people, government expenditure on health care services, number of women in government, number of women that are illiterates, geographical location (urban and rural) and socio-political factors in Sub-Saharan Africa were used. The data were obtained from the African Development Bank Gender, Poverty and Environmental Indicators for African Countries for the year 2003.

The Model

In specifying the model emphasis is placed on whether women's health care burden have any significant impact on the ill-being of the women in Sub-Saharan Africa.

Having established this link, the model is therefore formulated as.

$$IB = f\,(WHCBs) \qquad \ldots(1)$$

With $WHCBs = f\,(IP, NHSP, GEXH, NWG, NWI, GEOL_R, SPFs)$ ...(2)

When equation (2) is substituted into question (1), the equation thus gives a multivariate relationship.

$$IB = f\,(IP,. NHSP, GEXH, NWG, NWI, GEOL_R, SPFs) \qquad \ldots(3)$$

With a multiple linear relationship as:

$$IB = a_0 + a_1\,IP + a_2\,NHSP + a_3\,GEXH + a_4\,NWG + a_5\,NWI + a_6\,GEOL_R + a_7\,SPFs + Z$$

Where:

IB = Ill-being proxied by life expectancy of birth (years).

IP = Income of the women proxied by the nations per capita income in US$

NHSP = number of health services personnel per 100,000 people.

GEXH = Government expenditure on the health sector in $US

NWG = number of women in government as a determinant of women influence on health care policies.

NWI = percentage number of women that are illiterate.

$GEOL_R$ = geographical location of the women (rural) proxied by distance to health care centres.

SPFs = socio-political factors with dummy 1 for favourable socio-political environment and dummy 0 for otherwise.

a_0 = the intercept

$a_{1...}$ a_7 = parameter estimates associated with the influence of the determinants of women's health care burdens and ill-being of the women in Sub-Saharan Africa.

Z = error term

To estimate the model a multiple linear regression analysis is used in order to reflect the explanatory nature of the variables. To verify the validity of the model, two major evaluation criteria were used (i) the a-priori expectation criteria which is based on the signs and magnitude of the co-efficient of the variables under investigation; and (ii) statistical criteria which is based on statistical theory, which in other words is referred to as the First Order Least Square Test, consisting of R-square (R^2), F-statistic and t-test. The R-square (R^2) is concerned with the overall explanatory power of the regression analysis, the F-statistic is used to test the overall significance of the regression analysis and the t-test is used to test the significant contribution of the independent variables (Oyeniyi 1997).

Drawing from the model, our a-priori expectations or expected behaviour of the independent variables on the dependent variable in the model are: IP <0; NHSP < 0; GEXH <0; NWG <0; NWI >0; $GEOL_R$ >0; SPFs > 0. Indicating that the less income the women have the more their ill-being, the less the number of health services personnel the more their ill-being, the less the expenditure of the government on the health sector the more their ill-being, the less the number of women in government the more their ill-being, while the more the number of women that are illiterates the more their ill-being, the more women we have in the rural areas the more their ill-being, the more unstable the socio-political environment the more their ill-being

RESULTS

Presentations, Interpretation and Discussion

The results of the multiple regression analysis conducted at 5% level of significance are presented in Table 3.

Table 3
Regression Results of Women's Health Care Burdens and Ill-being in Sub-Saharan Africa

Explanatory Variables	*Coefficient or Parameter estimates and t-values*
Intercept	50.65
(t)	(7.64)
IP	-3.44
(t)	(-1.35)
NHSP	-1.41
(t)	(-2.79)
GEXH	-2.52
(t)	(-1.49)
NWG	2.83
(t)	(1.64)
NWI	9.4
(t)	(1.14)
$GEOL_R$	1.22
(t)	(1.03)
SPFs	3.22
(t)	(1.87)
R^2	0.60
F	7.14

t-values in parenthesis

A look at the model shows that it is of good fit, since it has an R-square of 0.60, which in other words, means that 60 per cent variation in the dependent variable is explained by the explanatory variables, while the error term take care of the remaining 40 per cent which are variables in the study that can not be included in the model because of certain qualitative features.

At 5 per cent level of significance, the F-statistic shows that the model is useful in determining if the independent variables have any significant influence on the dependent variable, as the computed F-statistic which is 7.14 is greater than the tabulated F-statistic (8,46 degree of freedom) valued at 2.18.

In terms of the individual independent variables, the t-test shows that at 5 per cent of significance, only income of the women, the number of health services personnel, government expenditure on health care services, the number of women that are illiterate, geographical location (rural) and socio-political instability fulfilled our a-priori expectations, with income of the women, the number of health services personnel, government expenditure on health care services having an inverse relationship with ill-being, indicating that the less the income of the women; the less the number of health services personnel and the less the expenditure of the government on health care services the less the ill-being of the women. A situation that can be linked to the high rate of poverty in the sub-region, insufficient incentives for the training of medical personnel and the dwindling nature of government revenue (due to poor tax bases), high rate of corruption and the diversion of funds meant for the health sector to other sectors of the economy or to personal use.

That the signs of the number of women that are illiterate, geographical location (rural) and socio-political instability are positive as expected, is an indication that as these variables increases the ill-being of the women also increases. A situation that can be linked to strict religious and socio-cultural norms that deprived woman access to western education and only sees the role of woman as purely domestic, child-bearing and child- rearing; the prolonged political and ethnic conflicts witnessed in the sub-region, most especially in countries like Liberia, Sierra Leone, Rwanda, Angola, Democratic Republic of Congo, Somalia, Uganda and recently in Cote d' Ivoire. Conflicts that have led to the diversion of funds might for the provision of health care services to the prosecution of the war, and the total neglect of the rural areas where the bulk of the African women are found. Most of the rural areas are without essential social services like pipe borne water and health care services.

The above observations are in conformity with the views of ADB (2003), Overholt and Saunder (1996), Bitran and McInnes (1993) and Claeson, et.al (2001) that also attribute the inability of the people-most of them women and children-to have access to health care services to individual's location to where health care services are located, the individual's income and the level of educational attainment, the nature of the provider which include whether it is a public or private provider, the price/cost of health care services provided, the quality of the services provided and the state of the infrastructural facilities within the locality where the health care services are located.

CONCLUSION AND RECOMMENDATIONS

An empirical study of the impact of women's health care burdens on ill-being in Sub-Saharan Africa was carried out, using a cross-country data and a multiple regression analysis. The findings shows that the variables quantified as representing women's health care burdens (income of the women, number of health services personnel, government expenditure on health care services, number of women that are not educated, geographical location of most of the women-rural areas-, and socio-political instability) fulfilled all our a-priori expectations except the number of women in government which is insignificant. That these variables fulfilled our a-priori expectations is an indication that in Sub-Sahara Africa the more women found it difficult to have access to modern health care services the more their ill-being.

To ease the burdens of women to health care services would therefore require heavy investment in the provision of health care related infrastructural facilities, such as, education facilities, safe water and sanitation facilities in their homes and in the environment where they live, at least for the purpose of preventing diseases that would make them want to visit modern health care centers.

Increase in government spending on health care services is also essential, but what is more essential is the relevance of the services provided, its accessibility and affordability to the women. There is therefore the need for proper co-ordination between the government and other actors (such as, non-governmental organizations, community based-organizations and private sector providers) in the control and financing of essential health care services, at least at the primary health care level.

As a complement to the above is the empowerment of women through the provision of education, the provision of credit facilities, and political participation in governance, which would have long run effects in boosting their productive capacity and increasing their income generating efforts, which in effect could make them afford health care services when the fall ill. In line with this is the modification of the existing health financing arrangements that would ensure that women do not face large out-of-pocket payments when they fall ill and the introduction of schemes that provide income support to the women that are sick.

The effort at making health care services accessible, affordable, serviceable and of high organizational and technical quality should be a matter of national governance where accountability and transparency in the delivery of key inputs (drugs, vaccines, contraceptives, micro nutrients and trained staff) are made top priorities by the government. These are essential against the backdrop of the high rate of corruption and rent seeking experienced in the sub-region.

Combating tribal and civil conflicts that has besieged the sub-region is also essential given it effects on the displacement of the people most especially women and children, which in turn has compounded the problems of women in their quest for adequate health care services when they are ill. Related to this is the diversion of funds that should have been used for the provision of health care services, but instead are being used for the prosecution of wars, resolution of conflicts and for the provision of humanitarian assistance to displaced people at the refugee camps.

NOTES

1. See Ndekwu (1998)

REFERENCES

African Development Bank (ADB) (2001), Economic and Social Statistics on Africa. *African Development Report 2001*. New York: Oxford University Press.

African Development Bank (ADB) (2003), Gender, Poverty and Environmental Indicators on African Countries. Abidjan ADB.

Aku, P.S., Ibrahim, M.J. and Bulus, Y.D. (1997), Perspectives on Poverty Alleviation Strategies in Nigeria. *In Proceedings of the Nigerian Economic Society Annual Conference on Poverty Alleviation in Nigeria 1997. Ibadan:NES: 41-54.*

Armstrong, J. (1991), Socioeconomic Implication of AIDS in Developing Countries. *IMF/World Bank Finance and Development. Vol. 28. No.4: 14-17.*

Awake (2001), Good Health for All: Is it possible? New York: Watchtower.

Bitran, R.A. (1994), The Supply–Demand Model of Health Care Financing with an Application to Zaire. *World Bank Economic Development Institute Technical Materials.* Washington DC: The World Bank.

Bitran, R.A. and Mclnnes, D.K. (1993), The Demand for Health Care in Latin America: Lessons From the Dominican Republic and El-Salvador. *World Bank Economic Development Institute Seminar Paper* No. 46.

Claeson, M. Griffin C, Johnson T, McLachlan M, Soucat A, Wagstaff A. and Yazbeck, A. (2001), Health, Nutrition and Population. *World Bank Poverty Reduction Strategy Source Book.* Washington D.C.:The World Bank.

Narayan D, Platel R, Schafft K, Rademachor A, and Koch- Schutlte S, (2000a) Voices of the Poor: Can Any One Hear Us? New York: Oxford University Press.

Narayan, D., Chambers R., Shah M.K and Petesch P (2000b), Voices of the Poor: Crying Out for Change New York : Oxford University Press.

Ndekwe, E.C. (1998), Comparative Analysis of Living Conditions and Poverty in Africa. *In Proceedings of the Seventh Annual Conference of the Zonal Central Bank of Nigeria Research Units held in Makurdi between 8th to 12th June.* Abuja: CBN.

New Books of Knowledge (1980), Health. Canada: Grolier Incorporated.

Obadan.M (1997), Analytical Framework for Poverty Reduction : Issues for Economic Growth Versus other Strategies. *In Proceeding of the Nigerian Economic Society Annual Conference on Poverty Alleviation in Nigeria.1997. Ibadan NES: 1-18*

Oyeniyi T.A. (1997), Fundamental Principles of Econometrics. Lagos: Cader Publication Ltd.

Overhalt, C.A. and Saunder, M.K. (1996), (eds.) Policy Choices and Practical Problems in Health Economics: Cases From Latin America and the Caribbean. *World Bank Economic Development Institute Learning Resources Services.* Washington D.C: The World Bank.

Oxford English Dictionary (1989), Health Oxford: Clarendon Press.

Vanderschurean F, Wegelin. E and Wekwete K. (1996), Policy Programme Options for Urban Poverty Reduction. *Urban Management Policy Paper No.20.*

World Bank (1993a), The Macroeconomic Effects of AIDS. *World Bank Development Brief No. 17.*

World Bank (1993b), Investing in Health. *World Development Report 1993.* New York. Oxford University Press.

World Bank (1994), World Bank HIV/AIDS Activities Washington D.C. The World Bank.

World Bank (1995), AIDS and Development: Moving Beyond the Partial Paradigms. Washington .DC. The World Bank.

World Bank (1999), Understanding and Responding to Poverty. *http: 11 www World Bank Organization Poverty Mission/up/Ltm.*

Yahie A. (1993), The Design and Management of Poverty Alleviation Projects in Africa Evolving Guidelines Bared on Experience. *World Bank EDI Human Resources Division Washington D.C. the World Bank.*

PART-IV

POVERTY, CHILD LABOUR AND HUMAN DEVELOPMENT

21

WORLD FAILING POVERTY PLEDGES: TOWARD THE MILLENNIUM DEVELOPMENT GOALS

I

A new international report warns that most developing countries will drastically fall short of meeting agreed United Nations targets for tackling problems of poverty.[1] The joint study of the World Bank (International Bank for Reconstruction and Development-IBRD) and the International Monetary Fund (IMF) say the Millennium Development Goals (MDGs) are unlikely to be met on current trends. The MDGs include halving the proportion of the population in extreme poverty, ensuring primary education for all children and reductions in child and maternal deaths. In a specific sense, the millennium goals espouse the following eight specific objectives to be achieved by 2015, along with their subsequent accompanying accomplishments. The eight millennium goals, according to the United Nations agreed resolution adopted by 189 countries at the Millennium Summit in New York in September, 2000[2] are:

1. Eradicate extreme poverty and hunger. Halve, between 1990 and 2015, the proportion of the people whose income is less than one dollar a day.
2. Achieve universal primary education. Ensure that, by 2015, children everywhere, boys and girls alike, will be able to complete a full course of primary schooling.

3. Promote gender equality and empower women. Eliminate gender disparity in primary and secondary education, preferably by 2005, and in all levels of education no later than 2015.
4. Reduce child mortality. Reduce by two-thirds, between 1990 and 2015, the under 5 mortality rate.
5. Improve maternal health. Reduce by three-fourths, between 1990 and 2015, the maternal mortality ratio.
6. Combat HIV/AIDS, malaria, and other diseases. Halve halted by 2015, and begin to reverse, the spread of HIV/AIDS.
7. Ensure environmental sustainability. Integrate the principles of sustainable development into country policies and programs and reverse the loss of environmental resources. Halve by 2015, the proportion of people without sustainable access to safe drinking water; halve achieved by 2020, a significant improvement in the lives of at least 100 million slum dwellers.
8. Develop a global partnership for development. Develop further an open, rule-based, predictable, nondiscriminatory trading and financial system. Address the special needs of the least developed countries. Address the special needs of the landlocked countries and small island developing states.

II

With only less than 10 years left to achieve the MDGs, a greater sense of urgency is needed by all sides if the targets are to be met. Though many developing countries are making substantial progress towards achieving the MDGs as a result of improved policies, but better governance, and the productive use of development assistance may be deemed essential. Also, they could be done with the right mix of policy reforms and additional help from the developed countries. In a way, the developed countries need to show leadership by living up to the promises they made almost four years ago.

James Wolfensohn, president of the World Bank, called on governments of the developed countries to change their priorities and spend more on aid.[3] According to Wolfensohn, "the fundamental imbalance lies in the fact the developed world's disproportionate allocation of wealth as the numbers suggest that roughly, $900 billion on defense; $300 to $350 billion on agriculture and only $50 to $60 billion on aid, of which about half get these in cash."[4] Furthermore, he went on to assert that "we can make all the noise we want, but unless we deal with the fundamentals we will be playing at the fringes."[5] In this context, it is interesting to bring in the conclusion of the 16-member Commission on Africa, chaired by United Kingdom's Prime Minister Mr. Tony Blair. The Commission, after careful deliberations based on facts and figures, has recently arrived at the conclusion that African countries have fallen dramatically behind other developing countries with declining growth-rates, increasing poverty, and falling life expectancy. Meanwhile, declining aid from developed countries and closed markets for African goods have made things worse. The economic problems of sub-Saharan Africa are well known. It was Tony Blair himself, in October 2001, who called Africa's situation "a scar on the conscience of the world."[6] Since then, if anything, conditions have deteriorated. Africa is the only region of the developing world which is no better off than it was 25 years ago.[7] While rapid growth in China and now India is trying to lift millions out of poverty, Africa has stagnated, even going backward in terms of foreign trade and investment. The spread of the Aids epidemic across the continent, and the large number of conflicts, has also contributed to its economic stagnation, as has a reputation for corruption and poor governance.[8]

In recent years, many development experts have highlighted bad governments as the key problem which explains the low rate of African growth. For example, 40 years ago Nigeria was much richer than South Korea, a country with the same population. But Nigeria's oil wealth was squandered, while South Korea invested in its people and targeted key export industries in the West. Now South Korea, a leading exporter nation, has a per capita income 20 times higher than Nigeria's. And while both found it difficult to make the transition to full democracy, Korea did not suffer the wholesale looting of the national treasury, which Nigeria's military rulers inflicted upon it, leaving it generally judged to be one of the world's most corrupt countries.[9]

These days, the World Bank, the IMF and the U.S. tend to argue that rich countries should only lend to African countries that have shown themselves competent to use the money wisely. Some of the African members of the Blair Commission, especially South African finance minister, Trevor Manuel and Tanzania's president, Benjamin Mkapa are prime movers behind the New Partnership for Africa's Development (NEPAD), which has promised peer review and transparency in exchange for more investment[10] However, at the same time, though, many African countries accuse Western lenders of hypocrisy. They argue that if the West opened its market fully to African producers, especially of agricultural products like sugar, cotton, and beef, they would not need so much aid, and subsequently reject the argument that Foreign Direct Investment (FDI) will only come when they regulate their economies. Countries such as South Korea, they point out, kept a tight reign on investment for many years.[11] On the other hand, for 20 years Western finance ministers have been pressing poor countries to privatize their public services and open their markets to foreign trade. Africa is still poor. It is no good talking about helping Africa, while hanging on to these outdated discredited and discriminative policies. It is also true because of these Western policies that poorest countries in sub-Saharan Africa are paying back more in debt repayments than they are receiving in aid, thereby reducing their ability to focus more on health and educational programs. After all the paltry aid the sub-Saharan countries receive from the European Union (EU) countries is far less than EU spends on subsidies per cow than they do on per person in Africa.

Mr. Blair's Commission for Africa will not be the first time in recent years that Western governments have turned their attention to Africa. The United Nations and the World Bank have been targeting Africa in general and sub-Saharan Africa in particular, with aid programs for some time, and in recent times, especially related to Aids. And the United States has its own initiative for Africa,[12] including the Millennium Challenge Account and the Aids Fund. Mr. Blair is trying to model the Commission for Africa on the Wily Brandt report, which in the 1980s put development back on the political agenda with its recommendation that rich countries give 0.7 percent of their Gross Domestic Product (GDP) in foreign aid[13]–an objective that only few countries have reached.

Given the numerous commissions, and their failure to achieve change, Mr. Peter Hardstaff of the World Development Movement is right in stating that the Blair Commission is nothing but a diversionary tactic designed to draw attention away from 30 years of broken promises on Africa. Also, more skepticism arises from the timing of the report to be released. It is due in one year's time, when Britain will hold both presidency of the EU and the G8, with a summit schedule for the U.K. in June or July of 2005. Though leading UK, European politicians as well as United Nations officials in attendance, but a significant omission seems to be the absence of American representatives. Looking at this prospect Bob Geldof, one of the driving forces behind the Commission in the context of Africa's agony observed that "even the winds of globalization seems to have excluded Africa even further." Therefore, he is of the opinion that the developed world should move "from charity to justice."

III

Against this background, given the fact that just less than ten years left to achieve the MDGs demands a greater sense of urgency on the part of the both developed and the developing countries. To be realistic, as the recent World Bank study has revealed that to achieve the MDGs as envisaged, the developed countries can work towards meeting these goals by providing more and better aid hither to had not been provided. And, above all, allowing developing countries greater access to their markets by removing all kinds of barriers and subsidies to their agricultural sector.

Simultaneously, on the part of the developing countries, it is imperative that they should do more with right mix of policy reforms, better governance and productive and documented use of development assistance. These findings emerge from the World Bank study that focused on eighteen countries that account for approximately half of the world's poor and share one-third of global aid flows, are above all broadly represents the bulk of low-income countries with moderate to good macroeconomic policies. The eighteen countries that were part of the study are: Albania, Bangladesh, Benin, Bolivia, Burkina-Faso, Ethiopia, Honduras, India, Indonesia, The Kyrgz Republic, Madagascar, Mali, Mauritania, Mozambique, Pakistan, Tanzania, Uganda, and Vietnam. These countries basic approach has complemented the earlier works based on global and sectional approach to examine the cost of attaining all the MDGs (as stipulated by Devarajan, Swanson and Miller analysis, 2002).[14] In essence, this analysis concludes that countries with good policies have shown the positive effects of aid on these countries. Also, Burnside and Dollar, 2000[15] study refers to judgments about the adequacy of a country's policy, governance, and international framework in promoting poverty reduction through sustained and improved service delivery to the poor. No doubt, each of the above mentioned eighteen countries have made less than significant progress over the last decade, especially on the goals of reducing income poverty, promoting primary education, and increasing access to safe drinking water. But projects had varied-both across goals and across countries. All indicators point to the fact that at least progress has been made, in the case of child and maternity mortality and sanitation while Bangladesh, Indonesia, and Vietnam have made rapid progress towards some or all goals, Ethiopia, Madagascar and Pakistan have shown less improvement.[16]

Now the question boils down to the fact that if MDGs have to be realized, what amount of additional aid that can be not only needed, can also be used productively.

The international community has a number of options for addressing these challenges. We believe that the optimal strategy would be based on following five elements. They are:

1. Reconsidering the distributional criteria for expanded Official Development Assistance (ODA) funds to countries that are not normally counted among the poorest but that nonetheless have large numbers of absolute poor. This would mean a significant expansion of ODA to countries in South and East Asia. An important corollary would be a requirement that low-and middle-income countries with high concentrations of poverty used by ODA to address income inequalities and the causes of epidemic poverty.[17]
2. Carefully monitoring the macroeconomic situation and the effective use of ODA aid. A higher concentration of imported foods and services may be necessary in the short-term, limiting the portion of ODA used to finance domestically produced, non-tradable goods and services, it is not difficult to conceive of many necessary imported goods that could make an enormous difference in addressing critical shortages in many of the 18 countries (for example, pharmaceutical products, including the antiretroviral drugs used to treat HIV/Aids).
3. Setting up trust funds for the accumulation of ODA resources. Although most industrial countries are likely to have more budgetary room for an expanded ODA effort now than ever before, the developing countries' current limited ability to have more budgetary room for an expanded ODA flows may undermine the effectiveness of expanded aid.
4. Establishment of global trust funds. To rectify this structural and logistic constraint, it is imperative that the global community, in conjunction with the international institutions should develop a mechanism of establishing specialized trust funds. Such trust funds can be readily used for financing selected public

projects, in fact in a specific sense, they have already been in operation, such as the recently established global fund under the auspices of the United Nations to fight AIDS, tuberculosis, river blindness, malaria, among other deadly diseases. And,

5. To eliminate all trade barriers that keep exports from the developing countries out of industrial countries' markets. In this context, United Nations Secretary General, Kofi Annan, has called for trading nations to do more to help the poor benefit from international commerce. Opening the United Nations conference on June 16, 2004 trade and development in Sao Paulo, Brazil, he urged participants to create a "development based approach to trade." He further went on to state that "let us help developing countries take full advantage of trading opportunities." No doubt, the conference itself did not make any trade rules, which is the job of the World Trade Organization (WTO), nonetheless it set out to lay the foundation for not only a free trade but also a fair trade.

From all that is said and done, the main stumbling block standing between free access of the developing countries to agricultural products to the developed countries' markets, is the question of "subsidies" that are given to farmers in the developed countries to export their goods into the world market at an artificially low price, making it difficult for farmers from the developing countries to compete.

At the same time, on top of the subsidies, the industrialized countries are also accused of protecting their domestic markets for agricultural products through import duties. Brazilian president, Luiz Inacio Lula da Silva, on his part in the conference, spearheaded efforts to unite the developing world in trade talks, said that "the trade relations should be reformatted so as to give poor countries access to technology and investment." He further asserted that "globalization is not synonymous with development, it is not a substitute for development, but it can be used as an instrument for development." On a pessimistic note, Thailand's prime minister, Shinawatra, suggested to the delegates that "developing countries may focus on trading with each other rather than with the West, if rich countries fail to open their markets." He further went on to state that "my solution is that we try to reduce our dependence on developed countries' markets. In spite of their diverse approaches, the prediction is that the European countries and the United States will make a series of separate trade agreements to gain access to the markets of the developing countries without having to make serious concessions themselves, a subtle sign of higher forms of deception and hypocrisy.

In a way, as the Oxfam concludes, there seems to be a deliberate attempt used in international rules on trade to tighten the noose around the developing and poor nations and trapping them in poverty. Six of the world's ten most poorer countries are less prosperous than they were two decades ago. The Oxfam report further states that global trade rules are rigged to benefit rich nations instead of meeting the demands of the poor countries.

IV

In the final analysis, any significant attempt to help the progress of the developing countries towards the achievement MDGs definitely varies with country conditions. For example, the per capita incomes range from $750 to $9,000, and they differ also in terms of credit-worthiness and the adequacy of their policies. Lower income countries such as Guatemala, Morocco, Peru, and the Philippines, are similar to the wealthier low-income countries. Although, on the other hand, China and India which are lower-middle income countries. Their size, track record in sustaining growth and reducing poverty, and access to private capital flows make them distinctive. They have already achieved several of the MGDs and are on track to reach all of them by 2015. However, in 2003, about 200 million Chinese and about 150 million Indians lived on less than $2 a day. And it is also a time that more than 300 million lived on less than a dollar a day. Inequalities across regions and between rural and urban are also severe. To address these problems the governments of the developing countries should design a comprehensive reform of the intergovernmental fiscal system, in addition to sectional reforms to reform to improve service delivery. In tandem, substantial incremental spending will also be needed, the bulk of which will have to come from domestic sources. No doubt aid can play a role at the margin by helping to advance the necessary policy and institutional reforms needed for the developing countries to achieve MDGs more uniformly. So still there is room for optimism. For example, recently, admitting that there were flaws in the delivery system mechanism and constraints of funds, Prime Minister Manmohan Singh of India, said that "the MDGs of halving the proportion of people living below the poverty line by 2015 would be achieved going by available figures.[18] He further went to state that "as of now the available data suggests that India will be able to meet the target set in the MDGs for 2015."[19] With just less than 10 years left to achieve MDGs we hope this is the prevailing attitude of the developing countries, but unfortunately it is not. A greater sense of urgency is needed by all sides if the targets are to be met.

In a way, in his forward to the MDGs: a Compact Among Nations to End Human Poverty, the UNDP administrator, Mr. Mark Malloch Brown rightly pointed out that despite these original welcome commitments in principle to reducing poverty and advancing other areas of human development-the world is already falling short.[20] For example, the following charts just concentrating on the core of MDGs dealing with poverty, hunger, primary education, gender equality, child morality, access to water and access to sanitation, show an array of results in view of the current trends and the expected guess of the MDGs all point out the shortfall in achieving the MDGs by 2015.[21]

As the above charts clearly indicate, the world is already falling short of achieving the MDGs by 2015. Also, when progress is broken down by the individual goals of the MDGs, it is clear that more than 50 nations grew poorer over the past decade. Many are witnessing their life expectancy plummet

Progress towards the Millennium Development Goals

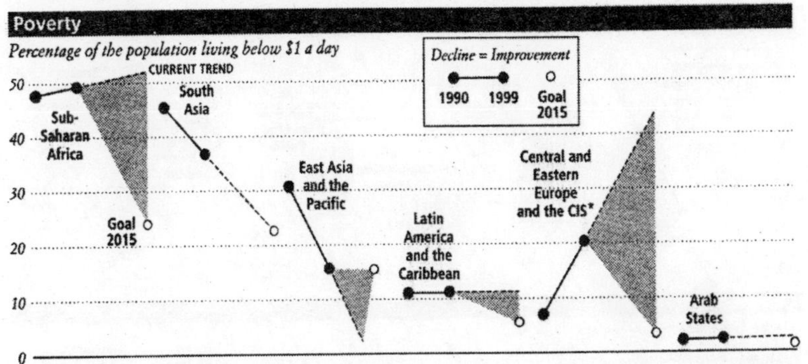

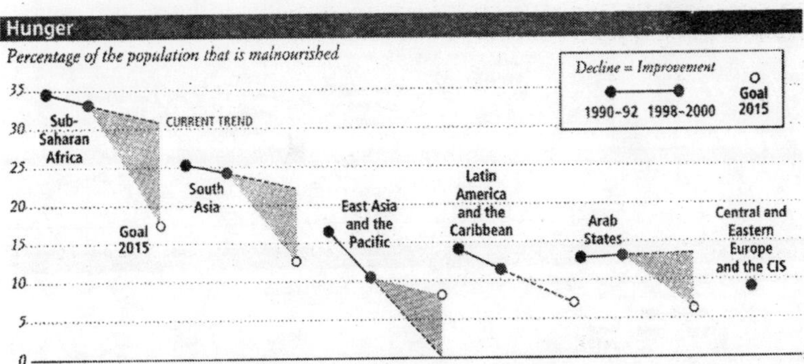

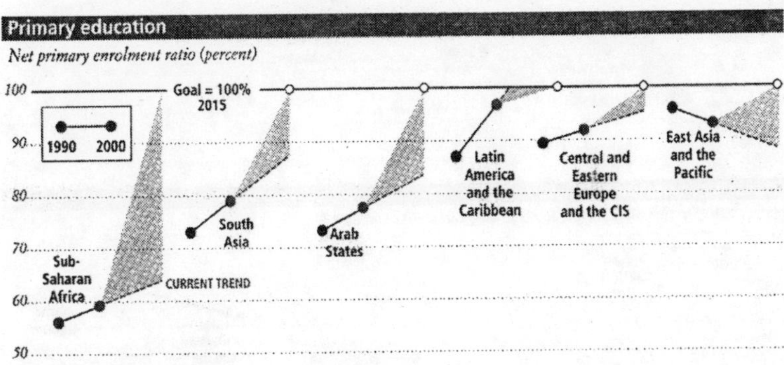

* refers to population living below $2 a day.

PRIORITY CHALLENGES IN MEETING THE GOALS

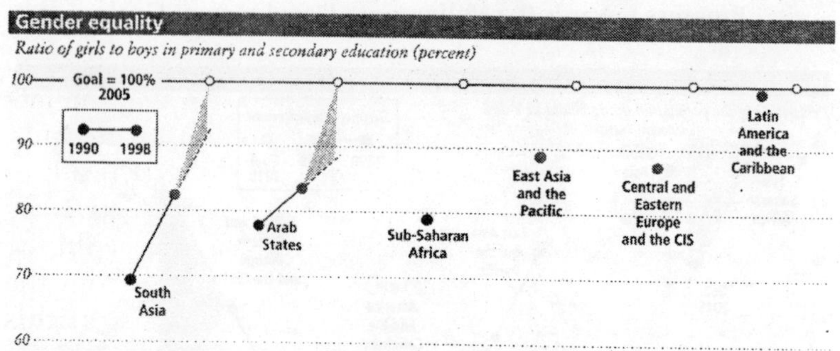
Gender equality
Ratio of girls to boys in primary and secondary education (percent)
100
90
80
70
60
Goal = 100% 2005
1990
1998
South Asia
Arab States
Sub-Saharan Africa
East Asia and the Pacific
Central and Eastern Europe and the CIS
Latin America and the Caribbean

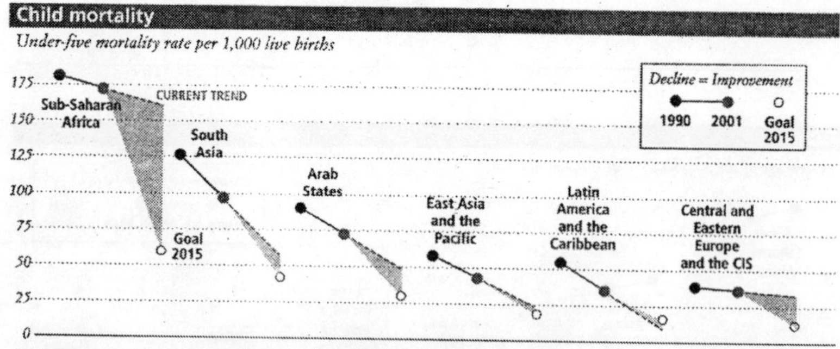
Child mortality
Under-five mortality rate per 1,000 live births
175
150
125
100
75
50
25
0
Sub-Saharan Africa
CURRENT TREND
Goal 2015
South Asia
Arab States
East Asia and the Pacific
Latin America and the Caribbean
Central and Eastern Europe and the CIS
Decline = Improvement
1990
2001
Goal 2015

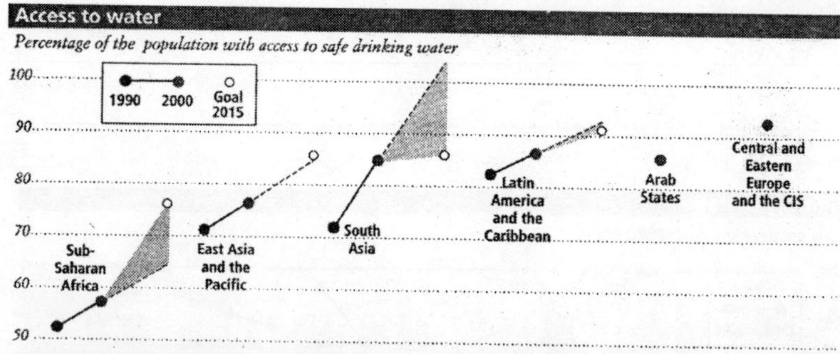
Access to water
Percentage of the population with access to safe drinking water
100
90
80
70
60
50
1990
2000
Goal 2015
Sub-Saharan Africa
East Asia and the Pacific
South Asia
Latin America and the Caribbean
Arab States
Central and Eastern Europe and the CIS

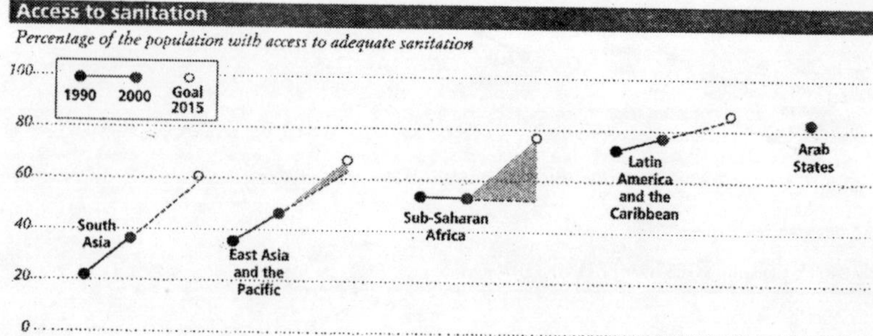
Access to sanitation
Percentage of the population with access to adequate sanitation
100
80
60
40
20
0
1990
2000
Goal 2015
South Asia
East Asia and the Pacific
Sub-Saharan Africa
Latin America and the Caribbean
Arab States

due to the widespread of HIV/AIDS virus. Some of the worst performers are in the areas of poverty, hunger, primary education, child mortality, access to water and access to sanitation. At this point, it is well worth to mention the fact that many developing countries are no doubt, making substantial progress towards achieving MdGs as a result of improved policies, better governance, and the productive use of development assistance. But they could do more with the right mix of policy reforms and additional help from the developed countries. The only thing needed most at this juncture is to scale up efforts to meet the MGDs by 2015. By acting now, particularly the developed countries, can hasten progress by providing more and better aid and by allowing greater access to their markets. Developing countries, on their part, will need to continue to improve their policies, with transparency and the way they are implemented. Anything short of this effort, certainly involves a serious risk that many countries will fall short of many of the MDGs.

V

In the final analysis, the achievement of MDGs by 2015 demands the following policies and actions on the part of the developed and the developing countries. They are: On the economic and financial side the developing countries should move aggressively in adopting sound xxx economic policies that support economic growth and stable capital flows. In addition, these countries should concentrate as never before on improving the private sector regulatory and institutional environment. Creating such an environment will definitely be supportive in establishing an enabling climate conducive to overall economic activity. On the part of overall governance, it is imperative the governments of the developing countries focus on improving public expenditure and revenue management by reforming the public administrative machinery, while at the same time improving transparency accountability and controlling of rampant corruption, which in a way is serving as a major stumbling block in the implementation of all public policies.

The developed countries on their part should support developing countries in their reform efforts by providing effective global public goods. In this context they can provide increasing amounts of aid, not only the amount of aid but also undertake enhanced debt relief.

As far as aid is concerned at current levels of about $50 billion annually, there is a large gap between the development ambition of the international community and the resources it provides. New commitments made since the Monterrey Conference in 2002, would raise ODA assistance by about $16 billion by 2006, which still falls far short of estimates of the sum needed to achieve the MDGs by 2015. What is needed to enable the developing countries to achieve the MDGs by 2015 the target date, the international community is calling for an increase in foreign aid to 0.7 percent (As of now only 5 countries have reached this level. They are Denmark, Luxembourg, The Netherlands, Norway and Sweden) of industrial countries Gross Domestic Product (GDP) from 0.24 percent of GDP at the present.

So in a way the international community can still easily achieve the MDGs by 2015, provided they take their pledges and commitments seriously and act on them. In this context, it is also important to summarize the recently released U.N. report on world poverty, written by former Harvard economist, Dr. Jeffrey Sachs, which not only once again reiterated the inevitable but also suggested some key recommendations in fighting poverty. They are: first, poor nations should plan to meet the U.N. goals; second, donors should target countries for a rapid development; third, rich countries should open their markets, and fourth, rich countries should increase their donations to about 0.44 percent of their GDPs and finally, there is need for more research to address the problems of the poor. The report finally concludes that if all the above recommendations are not taken seriously, there is no hope in realizing the MDGs by 2015.

NOTES

1. World Bank, World Bank IMF "Joint Report on World Poverty," April 15, 2003, Washington, D.C.
2. United Nations, Millennium Development Goals. Special Report # 17, pages 4-5, 2003, New York, NY.
3. World Bank, policy papers #23, page 10, September, 2004.
4. Ibid, p. 14.
5. Ibid, p. 14.
6. Parliamentary proceedings paper #1, October 2001.
7. United Nations. Statistical Summary of Developing Countries, p. 73, August 2003.
8. Ibid, p. 76.
9. World Watch Institute Germany, August 2004, p. 64.
10. BBC News/Business/Africa Commission's Uphill Task, April 23, 2004.
11. Ibid, p. 4.
12. President Bush Inaugural Speech, page 9, January 23, 2001.
13 Wiley Brandt Commission Report, Government of Germany, p. 37, 1984.
14. Devarajan, S.E. Swanson and M. Miller, 2002, Goals for Development, History, Prospect and Costs, p. 19 (Washington, D.C., World Bank).
15. Burnside, C. and D. Dollar, 2000, Aids Policies and Growth, American Economics and Review of___
16. Baird, M. and Sandhir Shedtj, "Getting There," how to accelerate progress towards Millennium Development Goals, International Monetary Fund" Finance and Development, December 2002, p. 14.
17. Heller, S. P. and Grupta, S. "Challenges in Expanding Aid Flows," Finance and Development, Striving Towards the Millennium Development Goals, IMF, January 2002, pp. 40-63.
18. Press Trust of India, December 23rd, 2004.
19. Ibid.
20. United Nations, Millennium Development Goals: A compact Among nations to End Human Poverty, UNDP Special Report #21, January 2003.
21. United Nations, UNDP World Research Paper #19, 2003, pp. 27-29.

REFERENCES

Birdsall, Nancy, and Michael Clemens. 203b. "What Rich Countries Can Do: The Global SocialContract.

Calderón, Fernando, and Christopher Pinc. (2003), ''Political Reforms and policies Enabling People's Empowerment and Advancing Human Development: The Challenges for Latin American Countries.''

David, Isidoro P. (2003), ''The International Statistical System and Statistical Capacity Building: Then and Now.''

Deaton, Angus. (2003), ''Data for Monitoring the Poverty MDG.''

Jolly, Richard. (2003), ''Global Goals: The UN Experience.''

Manor, James. (2003), ''Democtratisation with Inclusion: Political Reforms and People's Empowerment at the Grassroots.''

Pettifor, Ann, and Romilly Greenhill (2003), ''Debt Relief and the Millennium Development Goals.''

Reddy, Sanjay. (2003), ''Stagnation! Growth Failures, Coping Strategies and Human Development: Cross-Country Evidence and Policy Implications.''

Stewart, Frances. (2003), ''Conflict and the MDGs.''

Country Studies by the United Nations

Akder, Halis, (2003), ''Human Development Progress towards the Millennium Development Goals: Turkey.''

Backiny-Yetna, Prosper, Siaka Coulibaly and Marc Raffinot. (2003a), ''Country Case Study on Human Development Progress towards the MDGs at the Sub-National Level: Burkina Faso.''

— —.(2003b), ''Country Case Study on Human Development Progress towards the MDGs at the Sub-National Level: Mali.''

Bajpay, Nirupam. (2003), ''India: Towards the Millennium Development Goals.''

Bourgnignon, Francois and Morrisson. ''Inequality among World Citizens: 1820-1991,'' Delta Working Paper, Paris, 2002.

Collier, Pearl and Dollar, David. ''Aid Allocation and poverty reduction,'' World Bank policy research working paper no. 2041 (Washington, 1999).

Deaton, Angus. (2003), ''Data for monitoring the Poverty MDG.''

Deaton, Angus. ''Computing prices and poverty rates in India, 1999-

2000,'' Research Program in Development Studies, Princeton University, 2001.

Easterly, William. "The Elusive Quest for Growth: Economists Adventures and Misadventures in the Tropics." Cambridge, MA, MIT Press, 2001.

International Monetary Fund (IMF). "Streamlining IMF Structural Conditionally: Review of Initial Experience." http:/www.inf.org, 2001.

— —IMF Policy Discussion Paper 02/5 (Washington), ''Challenges in Expanding Development Assistance.''

Monsod, Solita, and Toby T. Monsod. (2003), ''Philippines Case Study on Human Development Progress towards the MDGs at the Sub-National Level.''

Sarmiento Gómez, Alfredo, Lucía Mina Rosero, Carlos Alonso Malaver and Sandra Álverez Toro. (2003), ''Human Development Progress towards the Millennium Development Goals in Colombia.''

World Bank. Task Force Report on World Bank Group Work in Low-Income Countries Under Stress. Washington, D.C., September 2004.

World Bank, (2001a), Globalization growth and poverty, Building an Inclusive World Economy. New York, Oxford University Press for World Bank.

World Bank. World Development Report 2000-2001: Attacking parity. New York, Oxford University Press for the World Bank.

— —, (2002), ''The Role and Effectiveness of Development Assistance,'' World Bank Research Paper (Washington): http://econ.worldbank.org.

Zubarevich, Natalia. (2003), ''Russian Case Study on Human Development Progress towards the MDGs at the Sub-National Level.''

Millennium Project Task Force Papers by the United Nations

Millennium Project Task Force 1. 2003. ''A Millennium Development Strategy for Achieving Poverty Alleviation and Economic Growth.''

Millennium Project Task Force 2. 2003a. ''Halving Global Hunger.''

— —. (2003b), ''Halving Global Hunger.'' Second draft.

Millennium Project Task Force 3. 2003. Achieving Universal Primary Education by 2015.

Millennium Project Task Force 4. 2003. "Child Health and Maternal Health."

Millennium Project Task Force 5. 2003a. "Combating HIV/AIDS in the Developing World."

— —. (2003b), "Combating Tuberculosis."

— —. (2003c), "Expanding Access to Essential medicines in the Developing World."

— —. (2003d), "Reducing the Burden of Malaria in the Developing World."

Millennium Project Task Force 6. 2003. "Environmental Sustanability."

Millennium Project Task Force 7. 2003. "Achieving the Millennium Development Goals in Water and Sanitation."

Millennium Project Task Force 8. 2003. "Improving the Lives of Slum Dwellers."

Millennium Project Task Force 9. 2003. "Trade and Finance and the Millennium Development Goals."

Millennium Project Task Force 10. 2003. "Science, Technology and Innovation: Challenges and Opportunities for Implementing the Millennium Development Goals."

22

POVERTY AND HUMAN DEVELOPMENT: A STATUS REPORT OF ANDHRA PRADESH

*T. Prabhakar Reddy**

CONCEPT OF MONITORING

There is substantial literature that generally refers to addressing poverty, which requires understanding its causes. As a matter of fact, once the cause of poverty is known the solution can be found out. Later, all the concerted efforts can be employed in a focused manner to eradicate the poverty. While the poverty reduction efforts are on, it is essential to develop some indicators for regular monitoring of the poverty reduction process. In fact, it helps in understanding the implementation arrangements, process, and suggesting necessary mid course corrections. Finally, it is useful in conducting the evaluation and knowing the impact of the programme/project.

Monitoring is a device that facilitates continuous learning and provides quality information for arriving at decisions. The poverty alleviation programmes aim at reducing the poverty

* *Poverty Economist,* Poverty and Social Analysis Monitoring Unit (PSAMU), a technical unit of State Poverty Eradication Mission, Government of Andhra Pradesh, Hyderabad.
# 5-10-192, III Floor, Hermitage Complex, HUDA Building, Hill Fort Road, Hyderabad 500 004, A.P.

levels of the household and improve the livelihood of poor people. Monitoring poverty and human development indicators entails checking that the objectives with which the programmes were designed are successfully achieved. Monitoring thus generates information for analysis, keeps watch on the changes that take place in the physical system, assesses the conditions of the components of the process and improves thinking that will help to develop a warning system. It also helps in verifying whether assumptions made and parameters adopted in formulation of the operational plan for the system are realized during the actual operation. It facilitates the identification of the constraints so that timely remedial measures are taken. Monitoring is thus a valuable tool for improving efficiency of the management system (R S Deshpande and K V Raju, ISEC, 2002).

Monitoring of poverty reduction efforts and achieving economic growth from time to time is required as it helps in understanding the performance of the economy and knowing the development trajectory. Therefore, monitoring has become indispensable for central and state government implemented programs. Indeed, A.P. is the leading state in implementing many direct transfer programs, which aim at reduction of poverty. Hence, the whole exercise of developing monitoring framework for poverty in Andhra Pradesh.

THE RATIONALE FOR DEVELOPING POVERTY MONITORING FRAMEWORK

There are five reasons for developing an overarching poverty monitoring framework in the state.

1. In pursuance of the Millennium Development Goals (MDGs), Tenth plan and Vision 2020 goals it is imperative to examine the status of state economy in achieving the said goals. Monitoring relative to goals will allow policy makers to identify indicators for which the state is off-track, and put in place corrective measures.
2. It is important to monitor poverty and human development indicators in view of many direct transfer

programs that are implemented in the state. Besides, effective targeting of transfers is a key issue in public policy to combat poverty. To ensure this, it is imperative to know the inclusion and exclusion errors in the transfer programs implemented by the state governments.

Apart from it, monitoring of data over time will give policy makers a sense of which direction indicators are moving in, and which indicators are improving faster. For instance, poverty rates in AP show a steady decline during recent years. However, urban poverty appears to have fallen particularly fast. It also helps the government to identify indicators where outcomes are not moving in the desired direction and make attempts to implement corrective actions.

3. Existing monitoring systems are not complete in the state and they lack holistic approach in evaluating the efforts deployed for eradicating the poverty. Besides, human development indicators are missing in the existing evaluation mechanisms. Therefore, an overarching monitoring framework is essential in tracking important indicators for knowing the trend of certain social and economic variables and suggesting for mid course corrections and finally looking into the overall working of the economy.
4. It is to know which groups/areas are particularly disadvantaged. Monitoring of data at appropriate levels of disaggregation will allow the government to identify groups and areas that are in need of special attention. For instance, in AP, malnutrition data suggests that SCs and STs are faring worse than the average population, girls are more likely to be undernourished than boys, and that children in rural areas are more disadvantaged than urban, on average. This suggests the need for further investigation and, possibly, targeted policies to redress the balance.
5. A poverty monitoring system can suggest how well

the state is faring relative to other states or national averages (comparators). While indicators *per se* may look impressive or record significant improvements, these cannot be evaluated in a vacuum. It is important to evaluate the performance against a benchmark. For instance, while AP has been performing above national averages for indicators like access to antenatal care among pregnant women, performance in education indicators like literacy are still somewhat behind the national average.

RELEVANCE TO ANDHRA PRADESH

AP has initiated a number of economic reforms with focused objectives of poverty reduction and improvement in quality of life. It is important to support the government with a well-organized database on poverty and human development. In fact, the poverty monitoring system for AP can help in (a) assessing how the broad policy regime-including reforms and poverty alleviation programmes-is affecting poverty and human development, and (b) enabling Government of AP to make more informed decisions concerning the poor.

A centralized poverty monitoring unit is particularly important in the context of AP, which has a wealth of information on development outcomes including administrative data. Following this, the purpose of the monitoring exercise is to take stock of available information and support the government in using their existing information in a more coordinated fashion. A centralized unit can not only lay out the facts but can eventually identify some key policy changes in attaining the state vision.

MDG, TENTH PLAN GOALS AND THE VISION 2020

Poverty reduction should occupy the central place in the economic and social development efforts of state and central governments, or the international community. It is, in fact, a potentially wise investment in so far as the development and poverty reduction is concerned. The 1995 World Social Summit placed poverty reduction squarely on the global development agenda. The development community including the governments, NGOs, individuals and others called for a halving of global poverty by the year 2015. It is in this context, the Millenium Development Goals have assumed significance as they are focusing on the poverty reduction and human development.

Following MDGs, the Planning Commission has set in the tenth plan goals that more or less incorporates much of the MDGs. Again the state of Andhra Pradesh has also spelt out its goals in Vision 2020, which are in accordance with the MDGs, and the tenth Plan Goals. They are as follows.

1. Eradicate poverty by 2020
2. By 2020, achieve total average fertility rate of 1.5 and population growth of 0.8 per cent a year.
3. Achieve total literacy by 2010
4. By 2020, reduce IMRs to 10 per 1000 live births and reduce Child Mortality rates to 20 per 1000
5. Reducing maternal mortality through the RCH programme
6. Prevent malnutrition
7. Eliminate child labour by 2020
8. Achieve life expectancy of 68.1 years for men and 70.6 years for women by 2020
9. By 2020, increase in tree and forest cover to 33 per cent.

CHOICE OF INDICATORS

Looking into the poverty debate and issues that appeared in the last two decades two things can be stated here. One is the need for monitoring of poverty and human development and the second is focus on non-consumption indicators of poverty. Since, the exercise of monitoring has assumed significance it is essential to develop a proper poverty monitoring system. The monitoring system should be quick and effective to introduce midcourse changes. Therefore, we need to mention three prerequisites of a good monitoring system.

1. The framework of monitoring should encompass a wide variety of indicators,
2. It should be ensured that these indicators are amenable for monitoring at a disaggregated level say, state, district and mandal level.
3. Availability of reliable data for these indicators regularly is equally important.

In view of perceived practical problems involved in monitoring certain indicators we need to suggest that there should be special surveys in understanding the levels of deprivation and social backwardness of groups. Furthermore, most of these indicators are interrelated and each one will have a direct influence on the other. Hence, keeping in view of causal relationship of these variables, the selection of indicators should take place.

The following section will explain the implications of each and every indicator that has been considered for monitoring of poverty and human development. In fact, the justification for considering certain indicators in the framework is explained below.

POVERTY

Proportion of People Below the Poverty Line[1]

The measure of poverty is essentially the income poverty concept based on per capita consumption expenditure. It speaks about the consumption level below a recommended balanced diet in terms of calories. It explains the situation of abject poverty where in the lack of minimum food in a day to sustain is given. According to official estimates based on 55th round (1999-2000) poverty in rural AP is recorded at 11 per cent whereas in urban areas it is 26.6 per cent. The overall poverty is recorded at 15.8 per cent, which is well below national average. Further, the head count estimates showed that the rural poverty is 15.9 while urban poverty is 38.8 and the overall poverty is 21.9 per cent.

Landlessness[2]

Land being the only income source of rural people we cannot expect that they can lead a better life devoid of it. Landlessness is a critical indicator through which one can understand the economic position of a family/household in a society. Possessing land provides them food security and a status in the society. Moreover, the land ownership is linked to most of the loan policies in the present day economy. Therefore, it is an indicator considered in understanding the lack of having an asset and its consequence. Despite the land reforms the landlessness is still high particularly among SCs and STs in Andhra Pradesh. Land structure in the state is still skewed and it is in favour of some caste groups.

Child labour

Many studies have shown that the child labour is a *sine qua non* of poverty and hunger. Lack of having proper income and supporting mechanisms the parents force them to go for labour and as a result they continue to groan under poverty when they are grown up. The incidence of child labour is high in Kurnool and Mahabubnagar districts in the state. In fact, the government of Andhra Pradesh has estimated that it is around 14 lakh children in the state in 2004. Nevertheless, the government has initiated campaigning against the child labour and the district collectors have taken a drive in reducing the child labour.

Slum Population

Slum population is an indicator of urban poverty and it is very high in places like Kothagudem, Chirala, Kadiri, Yemmiganur, Mancherial, Dharmavaram, Srikalahasti, and Narasaraopet. In Hyderabad city Qutubullapur is one area, which has shown high incidence of slum population.

Income, Wages and Prices

As we know, the income[3] of a person is an approximate indicator of development. Studying incomes of the population in a state regularly will reveal us the economic position, purchasing capacity and the quality of life of people of a region. However, it should be mentioned that the district level income estimation has some practical problems, as there is no estimate for the tertiary sector. Besides, the estimation of income for the primary and secondary sectors is not accurate.

An increase in the prices and a decrease in the real wages will have a direct impact on the living standard of poor as they affect the vulnerable sections adversely. Therefore, tracking of these indicators from time to time will enable the government in designing the proper policies for avoiding the adverse impact of price rise or a decline in the real wages. The formulation of policy may also include the compensation mechanisms for the poor.

A cursory look at the consumer price indices for agricultural labour and rural labour (CPIAL&RL) has shown that they have increased continuously from 2001-02 to 2003-04. According to RBI data CPIAL has increased from 311 to 332 for All-India and 328 to 346 for AP state. Similarly, CPIRL also increased from 313 to 334 for All-India and 328 to 346 for AP state. The above view is corroborated by the data of CPIIW too. During the year 2003-04 the CPIIW has shown an increase of 4.7 per cent and 3.7 per cent in the state and All-India respectively, when compared with that of the previous year.

According to Directorate of Economics and Statistics (DES) data wage differentials exist for males and females in the state. Average daily wage of women is 74 per cent of men's wages. While this is the average picture of the state inter district disparities are still large. To cite an example it is clear that the woman in Srikakulam district gets 50 per cent of wage[4] what a man earns in a day.

Going by increase in the prices and a decline in the wages it can be inferred that there is a likelihood of increase in the incidence of poverty in some places though it may be declining in other places. Therefore, any policy aiming at reduction of poverty should address the increase in consumer prices in rural areas either by increasing production and/or wages.

Employment

Employment status will clearly indicate the income position of a family or a household. If a person in a household possesses employment and receives income regularly then we can classify them as non-poor. Hence, it is essential to monitor the employment trends from time to time.

Employment growth (percentage per annum) in the state is significantly low (0.35) when compared with that of All-India (1.07). In fact, employment elasticity is also less than the All-India position reflecting the less responsiveness of employment generation to changes in gross state domestic product. It is a known fact that the employment has come down in the nineties and unemployment rose in many parts of the country. Rate of unemployment has increased from 6.69 to 8.03 per cent during 1993-94 to 1999-2000. In the absence of gainful employment the people in the economy will have a negative repercussion on their livelihoods and thereby resulting in the deterioration of living standards.

HEALTH

Health status is another key indicator of human development. It is discussed in terms of IMR, MMR, children fully immunized, child malnutrition, pre-natal and antenatal care for pregnant women etc.

Infant Mortality Rate (IMR)

In fact, IMR is an indicator, which shows the poor health services in protecting just born babies in the society. If the IMR per 1000 live births is high we can conclude that there is acute poverty and vice versa. The A.P. state government has fixed it at 10 per 1000 live births by 2020. Similarly, the child mortality rate has been fixed at 20 per 1000 children. National Family Health Survey-II data shown that the IMR is 69 and 73 for females and males respectively whereas child mortality rate is 28 (females) and 17 (males).

Therefore, child survival programmes should focus on specific groups of children with particularly high infant mortality rates, such as children who live in rural areas, children whose mothers are illiterate, children belonging to SCs, STs, and children from poor households. Further, efforts to expand the use of temporary contraceptive methods for delaying and spacing births would help reduce infant mortality as well as fertility. For this, the state government has decided to achieve 100 per cent immunization, 100 per cent usage of Oral Rehydration Therapy to prevent diarrhoeal dehydration.

Child Malnutrition

In fact, child malnutrition is the real problem in Andhra Pradesh and due to this child mortality is increasing every year. Under nutrition is much higher in rural areas than in urban areas and is particularly high among children from disadvantaged socio economic groups. According to NFHS-2 the prevalence of under nutrition (weight for age) is 35.1 for boys and 40.2 for girls. Nearly 72 per cent of children aged 6-35 months are anaemic, including a large majority of children in every subgroup of the population. Hence, the Integrated Child Development Scheme workers play an important role in filling that gap.

Life Expectancy at Birth and Sex Ratio-Children (0-6)

If life expectancy at birth is high it denotes the better living conditions for all and vice versa. Vision 2020 aims at achieving 68 and 70.8 years for men and women respectively. The sex ratio is 978 per 1000 males as per Census 2001.

Children Fully Immunized

Child immunization is an important component of child-survival programmes in India with efforts focusing on six serious but preventable diseases-tuberculosis, diphtheria, pertussis, tetanus, polio and measles. The objective of the Universal Immunization Programme (UIP) launched in 1985-86, was to extend immunization coverage against these diseases to at least 85 per cent of infants by 1990. According to NFHS-2 in Andhra Pradesh, 59 per cent of children age 12-23 months are fully vaccinated, another 37 per cent have received some but not all of the recommended vaccinations, and 5 per cent have not been vaccinated at all.

Couple Protection Rate and Institutional Delivery

The availability of health facilities to the poor will result in high couple protection rate and more number of institutional deliveries and *vice versa*. The contraceptive prevalence rate in the state was 47 in 1997 (the same as national average) compared to 12 per cent in 1971. In fact, between 1971 and 1997 fertility declined substantially in the state. According to NFHS-2 the couple protection rate is 63.2 in the state. Further, institutional deliveries are half of the deliveries taking place in the state i.e., 49.8 per cent.

PREGNANT WOMEN (15-49) RECEIVING ANTENATAL CARE

There is a goal that each pregnant woman should receive at least three antenatal check-ups plus two tetanus toxoid injections and a full course of iron and folic acid supplementation. But the reality is different. NFHS-2 revealed that the health services in A.P. are reaching many more women during pregnancy than during delivery or after childbirth. They have pointed out the important role of traditional birth attendants for the substantial proportion of births that occur at home. It is also revealed that 62.7 per cent of pregnant women have received antenatal check ups in the state.

Maternal Mortality Rate

Reducing maternal mortality through RCH, preventing pregnancies below 21 years, ensuring birth intervals of three years, restricting total number of births to two and others. In fact, this indicator is directly related positively to the poverty and other variables. In poverty stricken families there is high likelihood of maternal mortality and vice versa. The maternal mortality ratio (per 1000 live births) was 4.4 in 1990 and increased to 5.4 by 2000. Tenth plan target is that it should be reduced to 2 by 2007 and 1 by 2012.

Households Consuming Iodized Salt

Iodine is an important micronutrient and lack of iodine in the diet can lead to Iodine Deficiency Disorders (IDD). It can also cause miscarriages, brain disorders, cretinism and retarded psychomotor development. It is the single most important and preventable cause of mental retardation worldwide.

According to NFHS-2 only just over one-quarter of households i.e., 27 per cent use cooking salt that is iodized at the recommended level suggesting that iodine deficiency disorders are likely to be a serious problem. In fact, iodine deficiency can be avoided by using salt that has been fortified with iodine. In 1988, the Prevention of Food Adulteration Act was amended to fix the minimum iodine content of salt. Further, the Government of India (GOI) has advised all the states and union territories to issue notifications banning the sale of edible salt that is not iodized.

Total Fertility Rate (TFR)

TFR is a measure based on the ASFRs that gives the number of children a woman would bear during her reproductive years. Based on estimates for the three-year period before NFHS-2 the TFR was 2.25 births per woman. Furthermore, the TFR is slightly lower in urban areas than in rural areas mainly because the ASFR for the 15-19 age group is lower in urban areas. Based on estimates for the three year period preceding NFHS-1 and NFHS-2, the TFR fell from 2.59 to 2.25 (a decline of 13 per cent).

Prevalence of HIV, Diarrhea, ARI, Anaemia[5]

As we know the prevalence of HIV/AIDS is positively correlated to the poverty of a family/household. Among the HIV affected people majority are poor representing workers, lorry/truck drivers and commercial sex workers and others. In fact, economic compulsions are assumed to force them to take up such professions. As reported by APSACHS the prevalence of HIV[6] is 30.1 per cent in the state. Since the state of Andhra Pradesh is having high incidence of HIV positive cases, perhaps second in the country, the database is created and the problem is addressed in a focused manner. Diarrhoea is the second most important killer of children under age five worldwide following acute respiratory infection.

EDUCATION

Education is one indicator, which speaks about the absence of so many other things in a poor family. There is a positive correlation between the poor families and the lack of education. Further, lack of education is resulting in aggravating the social backwardness of the family by sending their children to work.

Literacy over 7 years, Children (6-14) enrolled in school

In fact, the literacy varies across boys and girls, the latter one having very less than that of former one. According to Census 2001 female literacy is 51 per cent whereas male literacy is 71 per cent. Of all the variables pertaining to education female literacy (within literacy) is one of the key indicators to monitor the human development. The reason is that often illiterate girls are susceptible to many problems such as child labour, child trafficking and child marriages. Hence, it is appropriate to monitor the levels of female literacy[7] in order to examine the human development. The enrollment ratio (6-10 years) is 112.65 for girls and 114.24 for boys during the year 2001-02. The state average is 113.48.

Dropout rates (6-14) and Primary School Completion

These are crucial indicators in understanding the efforts put in to reduce the child labour and the retention of the children in the school. Unless the children are sufficiently motivated to continue the schooling, the drop out rates would be higher. Besides, the parents of children should be compensated either through additional income or some incentives for the loss of income from child labour. The drop out rates for class one to five is 35.36 for boys and 33.64 for girls during 2001-02 as per Commissioner and Director of School Education, Government of Andhra Pradesh. The state average is 34.54 per cent.

Access to services (like kutcha home[8], safe drinking water, toilet and electricity facilities)

There is a gap between availability and access to services mentioned above in any developing society. In some cases, it is a question of non-availability of services. This particular indicator will provide us an understanding of who are the people devoid of these basic minimum civic amenities in rural as well as urban areas. As we know the non-food items are equally important in defining and estimating the poverty and well being of the people, the availability and access to these services will indicate the improvement of quality of life and human development of a particular region. Hence, the indicator is crucial in monitoring the poverty and human development.

EMPOWERMENT

In a world where political power is unequally distributed and often influences the distribution of economic power in such a way that it operates unfavorably to the poor. For instance, poor people frequently do not receive the benefits of public investment in education and health. They are often the victims of corruption and arbitrariness at various levels in the society. Further, poor people are active agents in their lives, but are often powerless to influence the social and economic factors that determine their well-being. Hence, the social and political empowerment of poor assumes significance.

Age at Marriage

In spite of several acts prohibiting the child marriages it is a continuing phenomenon in some of the districts in Andhra Pradesh. As a matter of fact, it is prevalent in STs and other economically backward sections. Although the government has prescribed age at marriage they do not scrupulously follow it. Indicators reflecting women's independence also point to an inequitous situation in the state. The median age at marriage is 17 in urban and 14.9 in rural areas for the women in the age group of 20 and 49 (NFHS-2).

Share of Women in Wage Employment

Women participation ratio in wage employment and the wage differentials have to be examined in so far as understanding the nature of poverty and its incidence. As a matter of fact, 56.2 per cent of women are engaged as agricultural labour whereas it is 29.6 per cent for men (Census 2001). On the other hand, average daily wages are rupees 36 and 49 for women and men respectively (DES, 2001-02). Many women are working in agriculture at low wage rate and it has shown lack of gender equity and balance.

Women Making Decisions about their Money & Health

It is a known fact that the women in a family have very less control on their health and money earned. When they are able to decide about their expenditure and health we can say that they are getting empowered. However, a process of empowerment of women is taking place in Andhra Pradesh through development of social capital. Many SHGs are formed and their capacities are strengthened. Decisions about their health, and expenditure pattern are being discussed frequently in their meetings.

Women experiencing Domestic Violence[9]

Many women are undergoing domestic violence due to their poor economic condition and for not being able to provide enough dowry or good food to the husband after the day's work and so on. It is, in fact, a common phenomenon in certain social groups, which are economically backward wherein husbands almost everyday beat up the wives. The domestic violence is continued unabated particularly in the rural areas, which is also corroborated by standard of living index in NFHS data. When we enquired the reasons it found to be the economic reasons. The point we would like to mention is that the poverty of a family becoming a cause to the domestic violence. Therefore, if the women are empowered socially and economically then the problem can be addressed to a great extent. NFHS-2 data has shown that among women (since age 15) who report beatings more than 9 out of 10 (91 per cent) have been beaten by their husbands and one out of eight have been beaten by their in-laws. In fact, 23 per cent of women in AP have experienced violence, and 21 per cent have been beaten or physically mistreated by their husbands.

Women Elected Representatives in Panchayats[10]

Poverty outcomes are also greatly affected by social norms, values and customary practices that within the family, the community or the market, lead to exclusion of women or the socially disadvantaged. Therefore, facilitating the empowerment of women by making state and social institutions more responsive to them is also key to reducing poverty. Hence, it is critical to have an indicator of women's participation in panchayats (*number of women elected representatives in panchayats* as against the Legislative Assembly or the Parliament), which is a local self-government, and the initiator of development in the village. Apart from the above indicator we have also considered indicators such as the age at marriage, share of women in wage employment, women making decisions about their own health and women experiencing domestic violence for knowing women's empowerment.

Other Indicators of District-Level Imbalances

Per capita GDDP: Basically, *gross district domestic product*[11] will give us an idea of a district as far as the level of development is concerned. While going by each district with the help of this indicator we can know the inter-district imbalances. Per capita GDDP of AP is Rs. 11,293 during the year 2000-01 which is below the national average. Further, within AP Medak topped the list by securing Rs. 16,680 whereas Vizianagaram stood in the last with Rs. 7691. On the other hand, Karimnagar, Anantapur, Krishna, Guntur and East Godavari have shown a deceleration in the growth of per capita GDDP during 1998-99 to 2000-01. In fact, these districts have performed well till 1998-99 but within two years they began lagging behind needs further probing.

Yield per hectare of Principal crops: The district-wise yield per hectare of principal crops can be obtained here which can throw light on the inter-district disparities. In fact, the indicator mentioned above depends to a greater extent on the irrigation availability in each district apart from the influence of other variables like mechanization, HYV seeds and so on. When we consider the above indicator for analyzing the inter-district imbalances it is equally important to consider the irrigation potential[12] of each district.

Urbanization: Urbanization is an outcome of several variables like industrialization, the level of development and migration from a region etc. Firstly, when the industries are concentrated in a locality it will lead to the development of a township and later on a city. Secondly, if the existing town is the hub of activities (due to the development) it will further attract the people especially the entrepreneurial class from nearby rural areas who will invest their surpluses in various avocations, which in turn generate more number of activities, and thereby resulting in urbanization. Thirdly, landless people as well as marginal farmers with half or one acre of land will go to towns and cities in search of employment and income resulting in slum population.

Of all the reasons stated above for the urbanization to take place, either the first or the third will have a greater impact. Again within these two, migration is contributing to the urbanization to a great extent in so far as the poor moving to the towns and cities is concerned.

Therefore, urbanization need not be always an indicator of development; sometimes it may represent the incidence of poverty of the region. For instance, the urbanization in Telangana region is due to the migration of poor from rural to urban areas on the one hand, and the entrepreneur-farmer investing his/her resources in the trade and commerce on the other. Urbanization is another way of looking at the regional imbalances in a state in so far as the public investment in creating the irrigation potential, roads and communications and so on.

CONCLUSIONS

The foregoing analysis has clearly brought out that the poverty has come down during nineties. However, due to decreasing employment opportunities (including employment elasticity), increasing prices, wage differentials and the pressure for delivery of services due to migration has resulted in the low quality of life particularly in human development. Going by increase in the prices and a decline in the wages it can be concluded that there is a likelihood of increase in the incidence of poverty in some places though it may be declining in other places. Therefore, any policy aiming at reduction of poverty should address the increase in consumer prices in rural areas either by increasing production and/or wages.

The National Human Development Report has also stated that the rank of AP in All-India has come down from 8 to 10 reflecting an alarming situation in the state. Nevertheless, the state government is, presently, striving to improve the position of human development through increased allocations for health and education.

NOTES

(The views expressed here are author's personal and do not represent the organization with which he is working).

1. Consider the list of indicators for the source of data, periodicity and the level of disaggregation etc.
2. Agricultural census used to provide data and information for landlessness, but since 1991 it is ceased.
3. Per capita income of a person, in spite of limitations, is an approximate indicator of development. In the absence of district level per capita income we will consider state level income. However, we are trying to estimate the district level incomes.
4. We have checked with the Statistical Abstract of 2003, published by DES in which there is no data on wages of agricultural labour. They provide wage data pertaining to labour at different coal fields.
5. The prevalence and the incidence of Diarrhea, ARI, Anaemia is very high among the very poor and poor households and it is directly related to the poverty situation. It has been observed many times in our field visits to the rural areas and in fact, there is substantial evidence on it.
6. Recent press reports suggest that the department of health and family welfare is collecting information on AIDS for each district annually. Therefore, we can conduct district level analysis too.

7. For this, the data are available with the Census every 10 years. Though primarily we are dependent on the Census, NSS and NFHS for the data, Directorate of School Education (DSE) provides the data annually and up to the district level.
8. NFHS is providing the data at a state level whereas the Census is giving up to district level. Further, the level of disaggregation is up to rural, urban, SC, ST and others in the case of NFHS whereas the Census provides State, district, SC, ST and others data. However, there is an exception that the data on Kutcha homes is provided by NSS, MICS up to state level, with rural, urban, SC, ST and others.
9. The data on domestic violence are provided by NFHS for every 5-6 years at the state level. For knowing how women are getting empowered in view of the domestic violence there is a need to conduct some special surveys that can throw light on the issue and disaggregation of data becomes available at the district level.
10. Often political power decides the distribution of economic power and hence, the unequal power structure is unfavorable to the rural poor. Besides, politically empowered people can access to resources (CPRs) and take part in the anti-poverty programmes. Therefore, it is critical to examine the political and social empowerment of women in particular and the marginalized in general. Hence, the indicator is number of women elected representatives in panchayats. Data for this indicator are provided by State Election Commission for every 5 years. Further, the level of disaggregation can be up to mandal and even to village. For analysis purpose, we can confine to mandal only.
11. When we divide the GDDP with the district population we can obtain the per capita income of a person in each district. This would be more meaningful to have a rough estimate of income levels of a district.
12. DES has provided the data on irrigation potential, from various sources, of each district annually.

REFERENCES

Planning Commission (2003), *National Human Development Report,* Planning Commission, Government of India, New Delhi

International Institute for Population Sciences, May (2000), *National Family Health Survey (NFHS-2) India, 1998-99: Andhra Pradesh.* Mumbai:IIPS

Statistical abstracts (2004), of *Directorate of Economics and Statistics,* Govt. of A.P., Hyderabad.

R. S. Deshpande and K V Raju, "Towards Setting Up A Framework For Monitoring Poverty And Human Development Indicators", *Proceedings of the workshop on "Poverty and Human Development Monitoring System"* held in Bangalore during February 2-3, 2001.

Government of A.P., Planning Department: *Economic Survey, 2004-2005.*

Government of India, *Census of India, Andhra Pradesh, 2001.*

Government of India, *Reserve Bank of India, Bulletins 2004,* Mumbai.

23

POVERTY AND GIRL CHILD LABOUR: A STUDY IN BRICK KILNS

*Siddhartha Sarkar**

INTRODUCTION

The issue relating to child labour is a global phenomenon. In India the incidence of child labour is in almost all sector. It has been estimated that children working in India in between 60 and 115 million the highest number in the world, which is 25 per cent of the working children of the world. In developing countries the number working children between the age of 5 and 14 is projected about 250 million, at least 120 million of them work full time (World Bank 1999). The majority of the children working in rural areas engage in agricultural activities while urban children lead to work in service and manufacturing. Although official statistics suggest that more boys work than girls the main difference is that boys tend to work in more visible types of employment while girls perform a low paid household jobs. While this difference is taken into consideration, boys and girls work in similar proportions. Whatever be the proportions existing in India, child labour contributing significantly to Indian economy is worth investigating. Presently children are being

* Department of Commerce, Dinhata College, Dinhata, Cooch Behar, West Bengal.

moved away from their families to work in hazardous and exploitative activities in the informal sectors like match, firework, brick kiln, glassware, carpet, shoe making etc. On account of more working hour in adverse conditions, most of child labour face chronic health hazards such as cuts, loss of body parts, burns, skin diseases, sight or hearing loss and acute respiratory illness. There are two groups of factors, which determine the decision to become active in the informal sector, more specifically, the structural as well as opportunity factors. The structural factors consist of financial pressure, socio-psychological pressure and institutional constraints. The opportunity factors consist of individual background, skills, education, living condition or non-individual components, environment, values, standards etc. (Sarkar 2004). Estimates of child labour range from 11.28 million to what constitutes the 'nowhere' children that some non-governmental organizations claim to be the alternative estimation of potential child labour over 100 million (Chaudhuri 1996). This is even more so in the context of the girl child who has the added disadvantage of non-recognition of most of her work carried out as an unpaid, household member. This has to be kept in mind while presenting the official estimates of girl child labour across the country (Visaria 1999). According to 1991 Census, nearly 5 million girls are working either as main or marginal workers. Of the 76 million girls in the population among the age group 5-14 years, there will be many more silent workers. Among the main workers, there are more than 3 million girls and nearly 5 million boys at the all India level. Another 1.6 million girls are categorised as marginal workers, while only half a million boys fall in this category. The child work participation rate in India [i.e. child workers (main plus marginal) as a proportion of the total population in the age group 5-14 years] is 7 for males and 6 for females. Variation in the female child work participation rate (FCWPR) is more than that of the male children across the states. From very insignificant levels in Kerala and Punjab, the proportion of working female children ranges up to 14 per cent in Andhra Pradesh. Other states where the FCWPR is reported to be high are Mizoram, Madhya Pradesh, Karnataka, Maharashtra and Rajasthan (Table 1).

Table 1
State-wise Child Work Participation Rates
Child work participation rate

State	*Person*	*Male*	*Female*
Andhra Pradesh	12	11	14
Arunachal Pradesh	6	5	7
Assam	6	7	4
Bihar	4	5	3
Goa	2	2	2
Gujarat	7	6	8
Haryana	3	4	2
Himachal Pradesh	5	4	6
Karnataka	11	11	11
Kerala	1	1	1
Madhya Pradesh	10	9	11
Maharashtra	8	7	10
Manipur	5	4	5
Meghalaya	9	10	8
Mizoram	11	10	12
Nagaland	6	5	7
Orissa	6	7	6
Punjab	4	6	1
Rajasthan	8	6	10
Sikkim	5	5	5
Tamil Nadu	6	5	7
Tripura	2	3	2
Uttar Pradesh	4	5	3
West Bengal	5	7	3
India	6	7	6

Source: Computed from *Census of India*, 1991

The female to male ratio among total child workers reveals the number of girls working for every 1000 male child workers. In the areas where the sex ratios among child workers surpass 1000, this reflects the discriminatory treatment meted out to girls and their excessive use in labour activities as opposed to boys in the region. Girls are mostly marginal workers, while more boys figure as main workers. The states where girls predominate as main workers over boys are Arunachal Pradesh, Manipur, Himachal Pradesh, Goa, Nagaland, Maharashtra, Mizoram, Sikkim, Andhra Pradesh and Tamil Nadu. Among the marginal workers, girls exceed boys in all states except for Kerala and Nagaland (Table 2).

Table 2
State-wise Sex Ratios among Total Population, Main and Marginal Workers Sex ratios among

State	*Total population (5-14 years)*	*Main workers*	*Marginal workers*
Andhra Pradesh	948	1040	3300
Arunachal Pradesh	933	1328	2958
Assam	964	336	3095
Bihar	880	335	3554
Goa	968	1201	1966
Gujarat	925	586	7960
Haryana	860	300	4120
Himachal Pradesh	966	1273	1892
Karnataka	981	830	3338
Kerala	983	751	985
Madhya Pradesh	926	758	3066
Maharashtra	941	1156	2746
Manipur	966	1281	1736
Meghalaya	983	702	1674
Mizoram	986	1125	1090
Nagaland	955	1165	962
Orissa	987	494	3799
Punjab	883	80	5453
Rajasthan	888	827	4413
Sikkim	980	1058	1516
Tamil Nadu	955		6100
Tripura	960	1033	2521
Uttar Pradesh	858	512	2777
West Bengal	963	269	1710
		323	
India	918	638	3281

Source: Calculated from *Census of India*, 1991

The burden of work on girls is higher in the districts where the participation of girls in work exceeds that of the boys. Hence it is these districts that are identified in this analysis.

Of the 440 districts belonging to 24 states, 218 districts have a higher number of girls working than boys in the age group 5-14 years, either as main or marginal workers (Table 3). A larger number of girl children are working in all districts of Himachal Pradesh, Arunachal Pradesh, Manipur, Mizoram and Goa. Other states where almost all the districts record a higher participation of girls are Andhra Pradesh, Rajasthan, Maharashtra, Sikkim, Nagaland and Tamil Nadu. More than half the number of districts in the states of Gujarat, Karnataka and Madhya Pradesh also display comparatively higher work participation levels of girl children.

Table 4
Sex Ratio Among Child Workers and Number of Districts with Higher Number of Girls Working

State	*Sex ratio among child workers (SRCW)*	*No. of districts with SRCW>1000*	*Total no. of districts*
Andhra Pradesh	1127	19	23
Arunachal Pradesh	1391	11	11
Assam	563	4	23
Bihar	522	6	42
Goa	1343	2	2
Gujarat	1129	13	19
Haryana	536	3	16
Himachal Pradesh	1521	12	12
Karnataka	1039	13	20
Kerala	792	3	14
Madhya Pradesh	1075	27	45
Maharashtra	1426	29	30
Manipur	1344	8	8
Meghalaya	776	-	5
Mizoram	1107	3	3
Nagaland	1159	6	7
Orissa	866	6	13
Punjab	160	-	12
Rajasthan	1443	24	27
Sikkim	1081	3	4
Tamil Nadu	1205	18	21
Tripura	697	-	3
Uttar Pradesh	465	7	63
West Bengal	456	1	17
India	879	218	440

Source: Calculated from *Census of India*, 1991.

Poverty is one of the most fundamental issues, and urgently needs to be addressed. Moving people out of poverty forms a basis of much international development policy. The way poverty is conceptualised has changed in recent years. When people considering as 'poor' describe their own situation, they consider that their well-being is not enough, for example, they feel a lack of access to sufficient levels of food, water, clothing, shelter, sanitation, healthcare, and education. The change in conceptualisation of poverty has lead to new ways of addressing moving people out of poverty. Although there is still an emphasis on income generation through increasing the opportunities for the poor women and girl child to participate in markets, there has been a broadening of strategies to enable the empowerment of poor women. Empowerment aims to address the inequalities, including gender inequalities, which prevent people from influencing policies and interventions, which affect their lives. Statistical exercises based on different sets of data have established that child labour is positively related, among other factors, to poverty, education, agriculture, and the overall work participation ratio. Girls are also preferred in specific sectors to undertake piece rate, home-based, contractual work as in the case of beedi making, bricks making, making matches, fireworks, agarbatti making, bangle making and so on, or in the case of tasks involving sorting, packaging, labelling, etc. (Chandrasekhar 1997). Increasing the security of poor people by addressing the factors, which create their vulnerability, has become a part of international development thinking. How is informal activity seen in the new approaches to poverty alleviation? Illness reduces the ability of poor people to improve their livelihoods and increases their vulnerability, not only preventing adults from working effectively but also negatively effecting children's learning by keeping them from school. The informality-poverty nexus has distinct gender characteristics. Within households, where there are adult men and women, the gendered division of labour generally allocates to women the responsibility for household tasks provision related to their spheres of influence in the household. They are often supported in this work by girls and sometimes boys, who can be kept out of school thereby damaging their own future livelihood choices. Women's access to decision-making within the household and community is restricted, limiting their ability to influence processes and resource allocation. Poor men and women do not necessarily become poor in the same ways, for example, a man might loose his job, and a woman, who has always depended on her husband for financial support, may become a widow, forcing her to start looking for a paying job later in her life, which she might be ill equipped to do so. Men and women have different ways of adopting strategies for addressing their poverty, men are more easily able to migrate while women stay put managing the household and creating home-based enterprise they can run from own house. Therefore, the informalisation strategies that are intended to assist people to move out of poverty must take these gender aspects into account. The cultural explanation is not necessarily distinct from the poverty explanation. It has often been argued that child work was essential to the survival of the children and their families. It is indeed obvious that, by and large, poverty is an important reason why children work. If they were not working, the survival of the entire family could be at stake. Child labour as a matter of fact can be beneficial to the child, not only in terms of the preparation for the tasks of adulthood, but also in terms of the direct improvement of their health condition. Since labour adds to the family income, it will add to the nutritional intake of the young worker, and the morbidity levels of the working child may even be lower than the levels prevailing among comparable counterparts. With these considerations in mind, it is not uncommon to divide child labour into four categories, from intolerable to hazardous to neutral and ending up with varieties of child work, which may even, have a positive impact on the future adult. Acute poverty is usually advanced as a reason for sending children to work. This is obviously an explanation that requires neither substantiation nor verification. It is common sense to accept that the poorer the family, the poorer the district, the poorer the country, the higher would be the incidence of child labour. A closer observation, however, suggests that this is the case in a restricted sense only. The first problem with this explanation is that poverty is difficult to define and that poverty in any case refers not just to economic poverty. There are certain thresholds below which people will find it difficult to survive. These thresholds are defined by nutrition, sanitation, health and shelter. At the level of deprivation, below these minimum thresholds, there is not much of an option between work and non-work. Deprivation often comes as a shock effect: the dead or severe illness of the adult breadwinner has often been documented to be a direct cause underlying child labour. Poverty defined as human deprivation goes to the root of the child labour problem. Child labour is a source of income of poor families. Studies show that a child's income accounted for between 34 and 37 percent of the total household income. Therefore a child labour's income is important to the livelihood of the vulnerable family. There are several reasons for growing tendency of child labour in India. However poverty, possibly, may be considered as major reason, which contributes to harmful child labour in India. The percentage of population of India living in the poverty is high. Poverty has an obvious relationship with child labour and studies reveal a positive correlation between child labour and poverty. For poor, there are a few sources of bank loans and other credit sources, here enters local money lenders, parents exchange their children to local money lenders with an agreed money. As the earnings of bonded child labourers are less than the interest on loans, these bonded children are forced to work until interest on loan accumulates. A bonded child can only be released after his parents make a lump sum payment, which is extremely difficult for the poor. Although poverty is cited as the major cause of child labour, but it is not merely determinant, inadequate number of schools expenses of schooling and even attitudes of parents also contribute to child labour. Some parents feel that children should work in order to develop skills in job market instead of taking advantages of formal education. The other reasons are high average rate of illiteracy (52.11 per cent, 1991 census) among the parents which push their children to engage in child labour force in lieu of providing them education and other facilities, insufficiency of protective legislation and regulations and lack of strong child labour unions in India. In short socio-economic conditions in India contribute to greater incidence of child labour. For the sake of future of all children, it is an immediate necessary to ensure sustainable economic growth and development especially in country like India where child labour is on the rise. It relates to many factors that cannot be quantified or streamlined into econometric exercises. Deprivation relates to exclusion, to vulnerability and to ignorance as much as to physical weakness and lack of property assets. Children living under such conditions, especially when a shock event has torn normal family life apart, will work in order to survive. By working, they find an individual answer to calamities for which society does not take responsibility. Poverty, as it as traditionally defined, usually combines a number of factors such as the existence of many children per households, with low literacy levels and with a horizon of low-paid and unskilled jobs, open to child labour (Lieten 2002).

OBJECTIVE AND METHODOLOGY

The objective of the study is to delve into the girl child labour process in brick kilns, employment and working conditions, socio-economic security and how they coalesce paid work with other responsibilities. In the present endavour emphasis is given more on socio-economic characteristics of girl child labour associations in the kilns based on the primary data collection. This study is based on observations, interviews and a sample of 65 girl child workers from a total of five brick kilns in North Bengal region. The stratified random sampling method has been adopted while collecting sample workers.

FINDINGS

The brick kiln is mainly a small-scale manufacturing unit where manual labour and hard work is predominant. There are 50,000 brick kilns all over India employing average 100 workers–male workers counted only who are on the muster rolls of the employers (Gupta 2003). Workers of brick kilns comprise of vulnerable section of the society mostly women and children. In rural settings poor families often send their children to work in the informal sectors in order to increasing household income and ensuring family survival.

The manufacturing process of bricks consists of moulding, carrying unbaked dried bricks, baking and stacking. The female labour is preferred for moulding and often carrying bricks, while the male workers carry out other activities. Girl child labour is especially engaged in moulding. The bricks workers are employed by the principal employer or by the contractor. The wage rate for bricks making largely varies from one kiln to another. The principal employers or manufacturers after making discussion with the concerned trade union settle the wage rate. So, there is every possibility of revision of wage rate. In brick kilns, female and girl child workers are mostly preferred because of the limitation of alternative job opportunities for them and moreover, they can be easily exploited by the contractors in paying a lower wage rate. The wage rate for the girl child workers irrespective of nature of work varies from an average of Rs.60 to Rs.75 per 1,000 bricks and working hour ranges between 8 to10. It is observed from the study that among the girl child, the illiterates constituted 27.7 per cent. 46.2 per cent of them had school going experience. The bricks workers may be recruited by the principal employer or contractor. The survey discloses that only 4.6 per cent of the total children were employed by the principal employers or manufactures, while most of the girl child labour were recruited by the contractors. The demand for contract employment was on the rise because of limited opportunity to work as direct factory labour. The economic compulsion was the main reasons of the children behind taking up bricks making as their livelihood. It is interestingly to note that most of the girl child labourers enter the labour force for meeting own educational expenses. The survey shows the responses about work experiences of the girl child workers in bricks making. The respondents were asked to recall the age at which they began working. 29.2 per cent of the workers reported that they had been working for less than a year, while 64.6 per cent of the workers had an experience of 2-3 years. The majority of child workers joined the labour force at the age of 9-11 years old.

The respondents were badly affected by fumes of the kiln. It is found that some health related problems like skin diseases, asthma increased with age and number of years work. 23.1 percent of the girl workers had no major health problems except the problems like headache, shoulder pain, leg pain etc. All the rest had faced acute health problems due to inhalation of dust of baked clay. The girl child workers had to do simultaneously their own household task. They had to combine wage work with their domestic responsibilities. It is found that in addition to bricks making, the workers had to do help their mother in sundry household task. The girl workers had nearly full responsibilities on the activities like washing utensils and water collection. The contribution of child workers to their families was in no way negligible. It is observed that in the economic sphere the status of most of the workers was similar as that of other members in their family. 53.8 per cent of the workers contributed more than Rs 400 per month to their family. Most of the girl workers contributed in the range of Rs 500 to Rs 700 per month and majority were found to spend a part of their earnings for their education.

CONCLUDING REMARKS

Therefore girl child labour is a significant problem in India. The prevalence of it is shown by the child work participation rates, which are higher in India than in other developing countries. The policies that reduce girl child labour have strong support on purely economic grounds. While children are sent to work at very young age for extended period they do not develop the skills necessary to earn higher wages later in life and a society loses needed human capital.

Several approaches in order to deducing girl child labour have been suggested. However our suggestions are:

- Increasing primary school enrollments tend to decrease

girl child labour.

- Raising parental awareness of loss of human capital associated with girl child labour.
- By brute enforcing laws and regulations governing girl child labour.
- Providing support services to girl child labour.
- Targeting women self help group as a part of the getting rid of girl child labour.
- Launching rural energy entrepreneurship programme that improve the earning of the poor people may help to reduce girl child in long run.

REFERENCES

Chandrasekhar, C.P. (1997), "The Economic Consequences of the Abolition of Child Labour: An Indian Case Study". *The Journal of Peasant Studies.* Vol. 24 No. 3 pp. 137-79.

Chaudhuri, D.P. (1996), Dynamic Profile of Child Labour in India 1951-1991. ILO. New Delhi.

Gupta, J. (2003), "Informal Labour in Brick Kilns: Need for Regulation". *Economic and Political Weekly.* Vol.XXXVIII No. 31 pp. 3282-3292.

Lieten, G.K. (2002), "Child Labour and Poverty: The Poverty of Analysis". *The Indian Journal of Labour Economics.* Vol. 45, No. 3 pp. 451-464.

Sarkar, S. (2004), "Theorising in Informal Sector: Concept and Context". *Social Action.* Vol. 54 No.4 pp. 356-373.

Visaria, P. (1999), "Levels and Patterns of Female Employment, 1911-1994". In T. S. Papola and A. N. Sharma [eds] book *Gender and Employment in India.* Vikas Publising House, New Delhi.

World Bank (1999), Entering 21st Century. World Development Report 1999/2000. Washington DC.

24

ERADICATION OF WORST FORMS OF CHILD LABOR IN HAZARDOUS WORKING ENVIRONMENT: A CASE OF *BIDI* FACTORIES IN BANGLADESH*

M. Zulfiquar Ali Islam & A.H.M. Zehadul Karim***

INTRODUCTION AND STUDY BACKGROUND

The International Program on the Elimination of Child Labour (IPEC) of the International Labour Organization (ILO) was launched in 1992 with a desire to prevent and eliminate child labour throughout the world. Since its emergence, the IPEC has been sponsoring collaborative efforts with its members to materialize their desired goals. Yet the participation of under-aged children in multifarious work-activities is a widespread phenomenon around the world.

Although, child labour is legally restricted in many countries of the world yet, the International Labour Organization estimated that there were about 40 million children labour force below 15 years of age who were engaged in paid employment in 1985, and in spite of repeated penalties declared by many nations, the number still remained at 34 million until 1988. A recent ILO survey indicated that 73

** Associate Professor, Department of Sociology, University of Rajshahi, Rajshahi 6205, Bangladesh.

*** Professor, Department of Anthropology, University of Rajshahi, Rajshahi 6205, Bangladesh.

million world's children are employed equivalent to 13 per cent of those aged between 10 to 14 years which is another alarming example of this issue (see ILO 1996). It is also evident that the exploitation of children at their various hazardous workplaces is extraordinarily ubiquitous in the developing countries (see Karim 2005; Karim, Islam and Farooq 2004; Islam 2005, 2004a, 2004b, 2003a, 2003b, 2002, 2001; Karim and Islam 2001; Mishra 2000; Burra 1998; Nieuwenhuys 1994).

The IPEC started functioning in Bangladesh since 1994 when the Government signed an MOU on National IPEC programme with the ILO. Since then, the Government has been striving to address the child labour issue in the country by implementing various action programmes organized by his own effort and through the NGO, and the trade unions. Thus, it has been reported that 11000 children were reached through various interventions carried out by these programmes over the last six years (see ILO 2001). Yet, a very recent estimation indicated that a total of 6.3 million children under 14 years of age work in Bangladesh; and among them, 12 per cent of the child labour force are aged between 5 and 9 years, the remaining 88 per cent fall between 10 and 14 years of age (GPRB and UNICEF 1999). Data from the same source have identified 301 occupations for the child labour and among them, 27 have been classified as hazardous for the children (see GPRB and UNICEF 1999). And accordingly for that reason, the USDOL Worst Forms of Child Labour Project desired to withdraw estimated 30,000 children from various hazardous occupations and to prevent another 15,000 younger siblings of these children from taking their positions in the prospective labour market (see ILO 2001).

CHILD LABOUR: THE CONCEPTUAL CLARIFICATION

The concept of child labour conjures up a particular image. We see that children in many Third World countries are chained to a rigorous work for their own survival where they perform a variety of works in widely divergent socio-economic conditions. A decade ago, UNICEF determined that child labour is exploitative if it involves children working at an early age and if it exerts excessive physical, social or psychological stress (see UNICEF 1997).

Age limit for the child labour is a formal reflection of society's judgment about he childrens' responsibilities in work. In almost all the countries, their age limit is determined by formally restricting the children to work. The legal minimum age for all the work in Egypt is 12; in the Philippines, it is 14; and in Hong Kong, it has been fixed to 15 (see Bequele and Boyden 1988). Many countries make a distinction between light and hazardous work by earmarking minimum age of 12 for the former and ages between 16 and 18 for the hazardous work (see Bequele and Boyden 1988). The ILO Minimum Age Convention (1973 convention No. 38) also adopts this view by limiting the children to accept the hazardous jobs not before the age of 18.

In Bangladesh, the minimum age for completing a primary education is 10; and it requires another three years to complete the middle schooling. Since middle schooling is a minimum requirement for a job in class four positions, it is expected that one must either complete the middle schooling or primary education and for that reason, age 15 may be identified for restricting child labour in Bangladesh. And from legal point of view, following the ILO convention, we should not allow any one to accept hazardous job before age 17.

METHODOLOGY AND DATA SOURCES

The present paper assembles the findings of two independent studies (see Islam 2001; Karim 2001) that were conducted in Bheramara, Daulatpur, Kushtia Sadar, Kumarkhali and Mirpur Upazilas of Kushtia District in Bangladesh. The district of Kushtia is the most prominent for *bidi* production. In these research, we have identified eight *bidi* factories and their surrounding catchment areas as our study locales. We surveyed a total of 1914 *bidi* child workers households. A total of 2296 children from these households are impelled to work in the hazardous environment of different *bidi* factories of Kushtia.

The studies were principally based on structured survey questionnaire. The interviews allowed us to generate a detailed database on the family-level information of the working children in the study areas. Apart from this survey, we have also interviewed the owners, their management people and the trade union leaders of the respective factories. In addition to that, a total of 26 FGDs were conducted to know the attitudes and reactions of the working children's parents and their community people.

SOCIO-DEMOGRAPHIC PROFILE OF THE WORKING CHILDREN IN THE *BIDI* FACTORIES

This part of the research provides the socio-demographic data on the *bidi*-working children based on the survey in Bheramara, Daulatpur, Kushtia Sadar, Kumarkhali and Mirpur Upazilas of Kushtia. An attempt has been made here to assess the child labour situation in the selected *bidi* factories of those Upazilas.

The data on sex indicate that out of the total 2296 children in the three selected *bidi* factories of Bheramara, Daulatpur, Kushtia Sadar, Kumarkhali and Mirpur Upazilas. Among them, 1701 (74.09 per cent) are the boys and the remaining 595 (25.91 per cent) are all girls. Like other professional organizations in the country, male participation in the *bidi* factories is also quite higher than that of the girls. The average per households child labour is 1.20 (Table 1). A preponderant majority (n=1107; 48.21 per cent) of them are the members of the age limit from 5 to 12 (Table 2). They worked various *bidi* producing activities in Akiz Bidi Factory (n=354; 15.42 per cent, Monomohan Bidi Factory (n=340; 14.81 per cent), Nasir Bidi Factory (n=426; 18.55 per cent), N. Zaman Industries Ltd. (n=254; 11.06 per cent), Banani *Bidi* Factory (n=328;14.29 per cent), Kalam *Bidi* Factory (n=66; 2.87 per cent), Sonali *Bidi* Factory (n=475; n=20.69) and Monsur *Bidi* Factory (n=53; 2.31%) (Table 3).

The working children in the *bidi* factories are engaged in rolling, filling and packing works in the *bidi* factories. We obtained definite data for comparison on specific work-

Table 1
Number of Child Labourers' Households by Upazila

Upazila (sub-district)	*Child Labourer Male n*	*%*	*Female n*	*%*	*Total*	*Households n*	*%*	*Child Labourer/ Household*
Bheramara	719	65.84	373	34.16	1092	864	45.14	1.26
Daulatpur	930	80.94	219	19.06	1149	1001	52.30	1.15
Kushtia Sadar	43	95.56	2	4.45	45	40	2.09	1.13
Kumarkhali	8	88.89	1	11.11	9	8	0.42	1.13
Mirpur	1	100	-		1	1	0.05	1.00
Total	1701	74.09	595	25.91	2296	1914	100	1.20

Table 2
Number of Child Labourers by Age Group

Age Group	*Total Child Laborers*				
	Male		*Female*		
	n	*%*	*n*	*%*	*Total*
≥5 - ≤12	732	66.12	375	33.88	1107
≥13 - ≤14	451	77.49	131	22.51	582
≥15 - <17	518	85.34	89	14.66	607
Total	1701	74.09	595	25.91	2296

Table 3
Number of Child Labourers by *Bidi* Factories

Name of Factories	*Male*		*Female*		*Total*
	n	*%*	*n*	*%*	
Akiz Bidi Factory	330	93.22	24	6.78	354
Monomohan Bidi Factory	198	58.24	142	41.76	340
Nasir Bidi Factory	351	82.39	75	17.61	426
N. Zaman Industries Ltd.	189	74.41	65	25.59	254
Banani *Bidi* Factory	245	74.70	83	25.30	328
Kalam *Bidi* Factory	20	30.30	46	69.70	66
Sonali *Bidi* Factory	318	66.95	157	33.05	475
Monsur *Bidi* Factory	50	94.34	3	5.66	53
Total	1701	74.09	595	25.91	2296

activities; and it was been found that 409 (17.81%) are engaged in rolling, 1918 (83.54%) are doing the filling work and 1861 (81.05%) children are engaged packing work in the *bidi* factories (Table 4). It is further evident from our data that out of a total 2296 children, 1918 (83.54%) are the worst group of child labourers (Table 5). A total of 794 (34.58%) children thus have been identified as the vulnerable group to worst forms of child labour in Kushtia. Among them, 416 (52.39%) are the young siblings of less than 5 years old and the remaining 378 (47.61%) children are coming from different age categories.

As indicated above, the children are engaged in three differential types of work-activities, *i.e.*, rolling, filling, and packing; and they have been grouped together in Table 4. The variation of sex and age differential in these activities has also been shown there in Table 4 in details. It is evident from the table that the children belonging to the age of 5 to 12 are mostly engaged in rolling, filling, and packing works. Out of 2296 children, 1107 (48.21%) are the working children who are specifically coming from this category.

In order to ascertain the position of worst forms of child labour in the eight factories of different Upazilas, we have calculated their accurate number. It was found that combing the three different work- activities, there are 1918 (83.54%) children who could very well be identified as the worst forms of child labour in Kushtia District (for details see Table 5.) A clear identification of the vulnerable groups to worst forms of child labour has been another important aspect of this research. These children become vulnerable as because, they often accompany their parents during works and thus they become the victim of circumstances.

It is usually expected that a person should not work more than 8 hours a day. But our children on an average are found to work 8.32 hours or per day. And their average daily income is Taka (Bangladesh Currency, Taka 1 = US $ 60 in 2001) 32.16. The data in this item further suggest that the average monthly working days for these children are 20.34 (for details see Table 7).

Table 4
Child Labourers in Bidi Industries with Their Different Work-activities

Age Group	*Rolling*			*Filling*			*Packing*			*Total Child Labour*
	Male	*Female*	*Total*	*Male*	*Female*	*Total*	*Male*	*Female*	*Total*	
>5 - <12	197.79	22592.21	244	71981.98	15818.02	877	69382.40	14817.60	841	1107
>13 - <14	1110.78	9189.22	102	44791.04	448.96	491	43991.46	418.54	480	582
>15 - <17	57.94	5892.06	63	51794.00	336.00	550	50994.26	315.74	540	607
Total	358.56	37491.44	409	168387.75	23512.25	1918	164188.18	22011.82	1861	2296

Note: Multiple responses are computed. The decimal figures indicate percentage.

Table 5
Total Worst Forms of Child Labour in Kushtia

Age Group	*Rolling+Filling+Packing*			*Filling+Packing*			*Filling Only*			*Grand Total*
	Male	*Female*	*Total*	*Male*	*Female*	*Total*	*Male*	*Female*	*Total*	
>5 - <12	538.46	861.54	13	68883.09	10416.91	828	2672.22	1027.28	36	877
>13 - <14	866.67	433.33	12	43192.09	377.91	468	872.73	327.27	11	491
>15 - <17	466.67	233.33	6	50594.57	295.43	534	880.00	220.00	10	550
Total	1754.84	1445.16	31	162488.74	20611.26	1830	4273.68	1526.32	57	1918

Note: The decimal figures indicate percentage.

Table 6
Vulnerable Groups to Worst Forms of Child Labour by District

	Younger Siblings					*Child Workers in Rolling Only*					*Vulnerable Group*				
	Male		*Female*			*Male*		*Female*			*Male*		*Female*		
Age Group	*n*	*%*	*n*	*%*	*Total*	*n*	*%*	*n*	*%*	*Total*	*n*	*%*	*n*	*%*	*Total*
>0 - <4	213	49.32	203	50.68	416	-		-		-	213	49.32	203	50.68	416
>5 - <12	-	-		-		14	6.06	217	93.94	231	14	6.06	217	93.94	231
>13 - <14	-	-	-			3	3.33	87	96.67	90	3	3.33	87	96.67	90
>15 - <17	-	-	-			1	1.75	56	98.25	57	1	1.75	56	98.25	57
Total	213	49.32	203	50.68	416	18	4.76	360	95.24	378	231	29.09	563	70.91	794

Table 7
Average Daily Income from *Bidi*, Working Hours, Working Days of Child *Bidi* Workers

	Sex	*Age Group*			
		≥5-≤12	*≥13-≤14*	*≥15-<17*	*Total*
Average Daily Income from *Bidi* (Taka)	Male	37.00	40.10	49.93	41.70
	Female	8.08	9.47	17.16	10.00
	Total	25.99	32.37	43.18	32.16
Average Share of Total *Bidi* Income (%)	Male	43.87	57.99	56.56	51.64
	Female	22.38	23.41	28.17	23.64
	Total	35.69	49.26	50.72	43.21
Average Working Hours/Day	Male	8.99	9.79	9.80	9.46
	Female	5.35	5.90	6.29	5.64
	Total	7.62	8.83	9.08	8.32
Average Working Days/Month	Male	20.15	19.96	20.22	20.11
	Female	21.23	21.00	19.44	20.86
	Total	20.56	20.22	20.06	20.34
	Male	Female			
Average Hourly Income from *Bidi* (Taka)	4.41	1.77			
Average Monthly Income from *Bidi* (Taka)	838.59	208.60			

It is our contention that through asking several questions we shall be able to find out the real effect that a family may have as soon as its children are withdrawn from the *bidi* works. At the investigation, it came up that the most important problem that will arise due to this was their acute subsistence problem. Among the respondents, more than two-third of them expressed about their economic crisis for which they will not be able to survive.

THE OPINIONS AND VIEWS OF THE PARENTS AND THEIR COMMUNITY PEOPLE

The Focus Group Discussions (FGDs) were conducted systematically in a very informal manner to know the reaction of the child workers' parents and their community people at the local level, which included persons of different sex and ages. The women and the children also participated in the FGDs very spontaneously.

It has already been mentioned earlier that a total of 26 FGDs were conducted in our study areas. These FGDs involved the villagers from these areas who are found to work in Akiz Bidi Factory, Monomohan Bidi Factory, Nasir Bidi Factory, N. Zaman Industries Ltd., Banani *Bidi* Factory, Kalam *Bidi* Factory, Sonali *Bidi* Factory, Monsur *Bidi* Factory and the other factories and industries of the above mentioned Upazilas. At least 50 to 75 people of different ages were participated in most of the FGDs. We have already indicated that the women who also participated in our discussion very spontaneously and the children of the locality gathered there with an inquisitive thrust to observe the happenings.

Almost all the persons form this opinion that they do not want their children working in the *bidi* factory. Yet, they have to allow their children to work for *bidis*. The general consensus that emerges from the discussion is that poverty compels them to send their children to seek employment in such hazardous activities. They have the feeling that since tobacco is growing abundantly in Kushtia, the only business, which could attract the people, is establishing *bidi* factory. Working in the *bidi* factory earns them cash money to subsist their families. And it is quite likely that the poor and needy persons would be excited for earning this cash money but, our discussion also gives the indication that some middle and average farmers often accept this job only to multiply their income.

While asking to judge their awareness about the unhealthy effect of working in the *bidi* factories, as 50 to 60 percent people on an average in the FGDs opined that they are well aware of it. But what can be done? They want alternative jobs for their families. In one of the FGDs in Bahadurpur the participants viewed that poultry raising could be an effective alternative income generating activities for their people.

Regarding their attitudes about education, the great majority of the people are of the opinion that they are ready to go for it. They expressed their willingness to send their children to schools. They have the realization that uneducated children do not have any future goal nor do they have any affection from the villagers. To cite an example for FGDs in Sonarkuthi, the respondents say that in their village the children who are going to school are very much reluctant to play and interact with those who are working for the *bidi*s.

The participants are also very much aware that tobacco filling is injurious to health. They have multifarious problems of health. Many of them have chronic cough, some say that they always feel feverish. The villagers want a healthy living and for that reason, they want to withdraw their children from this unhealthy work situation.

However, the villagers say that if they withdraw their children from the *bidi* factories, their families will have to find out some alternative jobs for the adults. In study areas, people are eager to work for the garments factories, some say that are trained in sewing as many workers have experiences of working in the garments factories in Dhaka. A few person say that women could be trained to learn sewing. A sizeable number of the respondents say that they rear cows and goat for they were provided loan to buy cattle. Some of the respondents feel that they can buy high yielding variety seeds to produce grains for their families. A few of them went to sell the grains in local markets and thus earn some money for their livelihood. Among the other alternative strategies, many respondents in the FGDs went to start some kind of petty business if they get a short-term loan at a very low rate of interest.

As our prospective project wants to know the opinions that whether the villagers will support any education programme introduced for the upliftment of the rural people. The villagers are ready to cooperate with any one who will come up with a vision to educate the children of their locality.

CONCLUDING VIEWS AND RECOMMENDATIONS

At the closing, we can draw some useful analytical conclusions here in this section. While conceptualizing the inner goal of this project, we bore this in mind that the research is targeted to receive the views of different groups people at the field level, which may allow our potential partners to take decisions for their future planning.

Among the participants at the community level, a great majority of the people (approximately 70 to 80 per cent) have somehow, realized that working for the *bidi* has a very bad effect on their children. They are willing to provide positive support in regard to eliminating the child labour. They rather felt it very comfortably that their children should go to schools. Yet, many of the parents had to send their children to work for the *bidi* factories. The main reason is the economic hardship.

Our data further indicate that the people in the villages are aware of the unhealthy effect of working in the *bidi*. We asked them whether they are willing to withdraw their children from the *bidi* factories. They agreed to this with a condition that they should be provided with some kind of other facilities. We wanted to know very specifically as to under what situations the parents are willing to withdraw their children from the *bidi* works. Most of the respondents said that if their families get economic support to generate their income, they will certainly think about it. They have multifarious options in regard to this. For example, a consensus has emerged from a FGD in village Jamalpur of Bahadurpur Union of Bheramara that the people would like to start poultry raising to earn their subsistence. They also require some kind of technical knowledge for this, which they may learn very easily.

Some of the villagers say that they could start a fishery project on a cooperative basis to increase their economic position. Many of the villagers thought that they could work in the garments factory. And for this purpose, they requested to establish some garment industries in their locality.

A group of villages opined that dairy farm could be established in their areas and the villagers can go for cattle raising. The women participants said that they could do some sewing work staying at home and thus taking care of their families. They need both machine and some kind of technical knowledge for this purpose. Some of the villagers gave options that they will send their children to schools if the children get some part-time works for their family subsistence.

In view of the high priority given to the agricultural sector, the villagers want a large concentration on it. Meanwhile, considerable progress has been made in popularizing high yielding variety seeds for rice cultivation. The general response of the people goes for getting supply of the irrigation equipments at a very cheap subsidized rate.

RECOMMENDATIONS FOR INTERVENTION POLICIES

Based on the foregoing discussion, we may go for providing some concrete suggestions here for the future planners of this project. In that case, we would suggest the following strategies made on the views of the parents of child laborers, and their community people, factory owners and their managerial personnel, trade union leaders.

(i) First of all, we have to make the people aware of the unhealthy hazardous environment in the *bidi* factories. We have to explain to them the real bad effect of it for their children. For this purpose, we may employ the school teachers, local elites and senior respected villagers to mobilize the community people. A regular counseling system consisting of this group of people very often should speak to the people on a regular basis.

(ii) Certain social and cultural factors act as impediments to the implementation of the project, but they are not always insurmountable. As we are perhaps aware that in Bangladesh villages (which is also true for our study area), the rural elites play a significant role in the implementation of any programmes in their locality. The factory owners and the managerial class often make good linkages with them in the villages. A realistic analysis of the rural power structure explaining their nature and strength would solve this problem very well.

(iii) The project may take some special fascinating programmes for the children so that they get attracted to go to the schools. The school-going children may be provided with the books and supplies at a very cheaper or nominal price.

(iv) The families who withdraw their children from the *bidi* activities may be provided with some kind of economic support to generate their family income.

(v) The rural community place a very high value on vocational training, and for that reason, projects for building technical training schools for children will get appreciable support from the villagers. The establishment of such vocational training institutes can only be ensured for those who really do not want to continue their higher-class studies and instead, seek employment at an early stage.

(vi) A short term loan with a very small interest rate may be given to the villagers with a condition that they utilize them properly and, also at the same time, they agree to repay them on a regular basis.

(vii) The local elites, leaders, wealthier persons, *bidi* factory owners and other responsible persons may take responsibilities for educating the poor children and enrolling the child laborers withdrawn from *bidi* activities in school. They may be the viable channels for preventing the vulnerable younger children from enrolling in *bidi* activities and eliminating *bidi* child labor by enrolling them in school and provide them with all financial support for education up to at least primary level.

(viii) We would further say that the legal provision to restrict child labour in any sector should be enacted and a proper implementation of it should be ensured.

IN-TEXT CITATIONS

BBS (Bangladesh Bureau of Statistics), (1989), *Small Area Atlas of Bangladesh*. Dhaka: BBS.

BBS (Bangladesh Bureau of Statistics), (1991), *Bangladesh Population Census*. Dhaka: BBS.

Burra, N. (1998), *Born to Work: Child Labour in India*. New Delhi: Oxford University Press.

GPRB (Government of the People's Republic of Bangladesh) and UNICEF (1991), *Census of Bangladesh*. Dhaka: GPRB.

(1999), Minutes of the National Symposium on the Situation Assessment and Analysis of Children and Women in Bangladesh held in Dhaka in September.

ILO (International Labour Organization), (1996), Child Labour in Malaysia. Kuala Lumpur: Forum for Labour Studies.

(2001), Terms of Reference for the Action Research Project of *Preventing and Eliminating the Worst Forms of Child Labour in Selected Formal and Informal Sectors,* First Phase: BGD/00/P50/ USA. Funded by United States Department of Labor (USDOL). ILO Area Office, Dhaka.

Islam, M Zulfiquar Ali, (2005), *Baseline Surveys on Child Labour Situation in Match Industries of Dhaka and Chittagong Districts*. Dhaka: International Labour Organization (ILO), February.

(2004a), "Worst Forms of Child Match Laborers in the Hazardous Workplace Environment of Bangladesh: A Study on Intervention Policies", a paper presented in the *session of Health, Environment and Development: Struggle and Survival under the commission on Human Rights and Development of the IUAES (International Union of Anthropological and Ethnological Sciences) Inter Congress Mega Urbanisation, Multi-ethnic Society, Human Rights and Development. It is organized by the* University of Calcutta, Kolkata, West Bengal, India. Its national collaborators were Anthropological Survey of India, Centre for Alternative Research in Development (CARID), Government of West Bengal, Indira Gandhi Rashtriya Manav Sangrahalaya, Indian Museum, Dr. Ambedkar Foundation, and Population Foundation of India. The UNESCO, Paris, and Wenner-Gren Foundation for Anthropological Research, New York were its international collaborators. The *Inter Congress* was *held at the* University of Calcutta, 35, Ballygunge Circular Road, Kolkata 700019, India *during 12-15 December.*

(2004b), Female Child Labourers in the Match Industries of Bangladesh. In Kushtia District. In K.T. Hossain, M.H. Imam and S.E. Habib (eds.), *Women, Gender and Discrimination*. Rajshahi: Higher Education Link (HEL) Programme between Sociology Department of the University of Rajshahi and Sociology Department of the University of Manchester funded by Department for International Development (DFID) and managed by British Council, March.

(2003a), Prevention and Elimination of Child Labor in Bangladesh: A Case of Child *Bidi* Workers. In Kushtia District. In K.T. Hossain, M.H. Imam and S.E. Habib (eds.), *Women, Health and Poverty*. Rajshahi: Higher Education Link (HEL) Programme between Sociology Department of the University of Rajshahi and Sociology Department of the University of Manchester funded by Department for International Development (DFID) and managed by The British Council, March.

(2003b), "Worst Forms of Child Laborers and Their Vulnerable Siblings in Bangladesh: A Study on the Interventions for Elimination and Prevention", *Journal of the Institute of Bangladesh Studies*, Vol. XXVI.

(2002), "Worst Forms of Child Laborers in Hazardous Environment in Bangladesh: A Case of Match Industries in Dhaka City", a paper presented in the *CUS 30th Anniversary Conference on Towards Livable Cities* organized by the Centre for Urban Studies, University of Dhaka at the Bangladesh Institute of Administration and Management (BIAM) to be held on 01-02 November.

(2001), "Report on Child Labour Situation in *Bidi* Factories in Kushtia District" prepared under the project of *Preventing and Eliminating the Worst Forms of Child Labour in Selected Formal and Informal Sectors,* First Phase: BGD/00/P50/USA. An ILO (International Labour Organization) Action Research Report for the USDOL Worst Forms of Child Labour, ILO Area Office, Dhaka from 05 April 2001 to the 14 June.

Karim, A H·M Zehadul, (2005), *Baseline Surveys on Child Labour Situation in Leather Tannery Industries in Dhaka Districts*. Dhaka: International Labour Organization (ILO), January.

(2001), "Report on Child Labour Situation in *Bidi* Factories in Kushtia District" prepared under the project of *Preventing and Eliminating the Worst Forms of Child Labour in Selected Formal and Informal Sectors,* First Phase: BGD/00/P50/USA. An ILO (International Labour Organization) Action Research Report for the USDOL Worst Forms of Child Labour, ILO Area Office, Dhaka from 05 April 2001 to the 14 June.

Karim, A H M Zehadul, and M Zulfiquar Ali Islam, (2001), "A Situational Analysis of Child Labour in the *Bidi* Industries in Kushtia District", an action research paper presented in the *ILO/IPEC National Workshop on Child Labour Situation in Some Selected Sectors and Development of Action Program Proposals* at the BRAC

Centre for Development and Management (BCDM), Rajendrapur, Gazipur, 08-09 June.

Karim, A H M Zehadul, M Zulfiquar Ali Islam and M Omar Farooq, (2004), *Baseline Surveys on Child Labour Situation in Bidi Industries in Kushtia, Tangail and Rangpur Districts.* Dhaka: International Labour Organization (ILO), December.

Mishra, L. (2000), *Child Labour in India.* New Delhi: Oxford University Press.

Nieuwenhuys, O. (1994), *Children's Lifestyle: Gender, Welfare and Labour in the Developing World.* New York: Routledge.

UNICEF, (1996), State of the World Children, New York: Oxford University Press.

(1987), Analysis of the Situation of Children in Bangladesh. Dhaka: UNICEF.

25

SOCIO-ECONOMIC DISPARITY IN NORTH EASTERN REGIONS OF INDIA: PROSPECTIVE CHALLENGES AND OPPORTUNITIES

*D. Rudra Prakash Pradhan**

INTRODUCTION

India is one of the largest countries in the world having 3287 thousand sq km of surface area and more than 1048 millions of population (WDR, 2004). It extends over 3200 km from north to south and 2400 km from east to west, containing a variety of climates, soils and flora. It is a land of contrasts having floods and droughts, deserts and evergreen forests, mountains and plains in close proximity (Singh, 1993). Over the past decades, India has made good progress in increasing her incomes and improving its standards of living. After the 1991 balance of payment crisis, economic growth picked up, income poverty continued to decline and many socio-economic indicators continued to improve. The growth rate of GDP has reached a high of 7.8 per cent in the 1990s compared to a mere 5.5 per cent in the preceding decade (GOI, 2002-03). Per capita income of constant price (1993-94) has increased from Rs. 3744 in 1951-52 to Rs. 10207 in 1999-2000 (NAS, 2000). The production of food grains has increased from a low of 55 million tons in 1950-51 to 209 million tons in the turn of the century (CMIE, 2002).

The performance of merchandise exports has been somewhat erratic, as it stimulus from a low of Rs. 730 crore in 1951-52 to a high of Rs. 209018 crore in 1999-2000 (GOI, 2002-03). There is also substantial improvement in foreign exchange reserves, which has been increased from a low of Rs. 864 crore in 1951-52 to a high of Rs. 264036 crore in 2001-02 (RBI, 2003). Nevertheless, the successes in the above economic fronts are severely outweighed by marked failures in the field of social sector. Even after more then five decades of planned economic development, more then a quarter of our population of remains under abject poverty (26.1 per cent; GOI, 2002-03). Coupled with this, around 44.2 per cent population does not get $ 1 income a day and 12 per cent do not have privilege of using safe drinking water. Above all, India occupies 124th position among 173 nations in the world as far as the achievement in the field of human development is concerned (HDR, 2002).

What is striking fact is that unlike any other country in the world, India remains a country with stark contrasts and noteworthy disparities. In the recent period, a number of studies (Nagaraj et al., 1999; Rao et al., 1999; Ahluwalia, 2000; Shand and Bhide, 2000; Bhattacharya and Sakthivel, 2004) have observed that regional disparities in India has widened economically with special reference to state domestic product. Similarly in the social sector, there is also large-scale disparity across the states/regions (Deshpande et al., 2002; Pradhan, 2004). Some states and regions perform so well in the field of social sector development that they are comparable even with the leading industrialized nations of the world. On the contrary, there are also some regions/states that still exist in our country, which remain below the average of the poorest nations of the world (Shivkumar, 1997). Kerala, a southern state of India, has surpassed the neighboring country China in general and also all its provinces in almost all the indicators of human development (Dreze and Sen, 1999). On the other hand, state like Bihar, Uttar Pradesh, Rajasthan, Madhya Pradesh, Orissa and Assam lag far behind Kerala (Deshpande et al., 2002) and are also well below a number of less developed countries including some countries of the Sub-Saharan Africa (Nayak, 2002).

In short, India's improvement in economic growth and social sector development is not at all uniform across the states/regions. Some states performed far better and comparable to leading nations in the world and some states are under performed and comparable to less developed countries in the world. As a result, India pushed down their relative position vis-à-vis other states and sharpened inter-state disparities (Joseph, 2004). Regional disparity in India is now a matter of serious concern. It is well known that in a large economy having different regions with different resource bases and endowments would have a dissimilar growth path over time (Bhattacharya and Sakthivel, 2004).

The convergence theorem (Barro, 1991), however, postulates that when growth rate of an economy accelerates, initially some regions with better resources would grow faster than others. But subsequently, by the law of diminishing return, first growth rates would converge because of differential marginal productivity of capital (higher in poorer regions and lower in richer regions) and this, in turn, would bridge the gaps in the level of income across regions. The related empirical evidence is, moreover, very controversial now. It has also been observed that when an economy is liberated, especially after controls on investment are lifted, regions with better infrastructure attract more investment (especially foreign capital through market mechanisms) and thus, in turn, leads to regional inequality, at least in the early phase of reforms. The regional disparity in China after economic reforms is a classic example of this. This is also partially true in India, where the growing regional disparity in the post reforms period is now a matter of serious concern. In India, the poor states have not only performed poorly but also their failure in stem population growth and an existence of poor income, poor availability of infrastructure and probably poor governance has left them again in an worsen position (Bhattacharya and Sakthivel, 2004).

The above discussion relates to regional disparity goes against balanced regional economic development of our country, which is one of the prime objectives in Indian planning. Moreover, an attainment of balance regional development both at the inter-state and intra-state level is very important for a pluralistic and multiethnic society like India (Agarwala and Hazarika, 2002). But in spite of planning, regional disparity is still remained a serious problem in our economy. The goal of balanced regional development is, moreover, conflicting in nature in the short run because of heavy investments in social capital and thus, infrastructure in poor regions may only bring them to the national development. But it may be possible at the cost of those people and regions, which may enhance their production with little investment in social capital and infrastructure. In a situation of scarce resources, little income and poorer people, the region will further decline its national output. This is a matter of serious concern for both planners and policy makers.

In the light of above backdrop, present paper makes an attempt to examine the patterns of socio-economic development that the NER and its constituent states have, thus far, achieved. It aims to examine the nature and extent of inter-regional disparities in the socio-economic sector of NER in the last two decades and their implications thereof. The rest of the paper is organized into six different sections including the earlier introduction. Section II discusses the socio-economic profile of NER. Section III reveals the analytical framework. Section IV highlights the spatial patterns of socio-economic development in NER. Section V notices the challenges and opportunities that exist in NER. Section VI finally comes out with probable recommendations for NER.

ECONOMIC PROFILE OF NORTH EASTERN REGION

North Eastern Region (NER) of India is known for its vast natural resources and a cauldron of different people and cultures. NER comprises seven 'sister' states, namely, Arunachal Pradesh, Assam, Manipur, Meghalaya, Mizoram, Nagaland and Tripura (Agarwala, 1996; Srivastava, 1998; Basak, 2002). Geographically, the seven north eastern states together occupy an area of 255.083 lakh sq km and comprise about 8.06% of India's total land area (Table 1). The whole area is categorically divided into three geographical divisions-the Shillong Plateau, the North Eastern Hill Basin and the Brahmaputra Valley. About 65 per cent of this land area in the NER is under forest, making it one of the greenest areas in our country, besides the Andaman and Nicobar Islands (Dutta, 2002). NER, therefore, is considered as one of the most biodiversity regions in the world.

NER is generally bounded by hills and with the mighty Brahmaputra River slashing a central path between its north and south. Assam comprising the heart of NER, whereas Arunachal Pradesh lies to its north, bordering China, Tibet and Bhutan. On the other hand, Bangladesh and Myanmar lie to its south west and east. The torrential Brahmaputra deposits are its rich alluvial silt along with the banks of plains in Assam. Tropical rain forest, rich in flora and fauna, spreads their arms across Arunachal Pradesh to Assam. It is a land, where tea is an industry, handicrafts as a major occupation and martial arts as a favoured sport. The Macmahon line separates the north east India from Tibet. This region is connected with rest of India only through a narrow corridor in North Bengal, having an approximate width of 33 km on eastern side and 21 km on western side. This narrow corridor is popularly known as 'Siliguri neck' or 'Chicken's neck'.

The National Commission of Agriculture (GOI, 1976) has identified the states of Arunachal Pradesh, Meghalaya, Mizoram, Nagaland and Tripura are entirely in hill areas. The plains of this region are mainly made up of separate landmasses-the Brahmaputra Valley and the Barak Valley in Assam and the Tripura plains in South. In Manipur, the valley is small, comprising only about 10 per cent of the total state area. Though NER reflects ecological and cultural contrasts between hills and plains, there are also significant elements of continuity. Available medieval and modern records further indicate the interdependence and interaction between hills and plains. The climate as well as temperature varies from tropical plains to mountains and hills. The region is well known for its high rainfall along with very high humidity. The topography

Table 1

Geographic and Demographic Aspects of North Eastern States

Items	*NER1*	*NER2*	*NER3*	*NER4*	*NER5*	*NER6*	*NER7*	*NER*	*India*
Area (in Sq Km)	78523	10492	22327	22429	16579	21087	83743	255180	3166290
Percent all-India	2.48	0.33	0.70	0.71	0.52	0.67	2.64	8.06	--
Forest coverage (in %)	27.41	57.7	78.64	42.23	21.60	75.11	63.0	65.0	--
Population (in million)	26.6	3.19	2.39	2.31	1.99	0.9	1.09	38.5	102.7
Per cent all-India	2.59	0.31	0.23	0.22	0.19	0.09	0.11	3.70	--
Per cent of urbanization	11.1	15.3	27.5	18.6	17.2	46.1	12.8	21.23	27.8
Population growth[1]	18.85	15.74	30.02	29.84	64.41	29.18	26.21	30.61	21.34
Density of population[2]	340	304	107	103	120	42	13	151	324
Tribal population (in %)	12.82	30.95	34.41	85.53	87.70	94.75	63.66	58.5	8.01

Note: NER1: Assam; NER2: Tripura; NER3: Manipur; NER4: Meghalaya; NER5: Nagaland; NER6: Mizoram; NER7: Arunachal Pradesh; NER: North Eastern Region;[1]: Percentage of population growth in between 1991-2001; and[2]: Density of population is measured per sq km.

Source: Economic Survey, Government of India; Census of India, Government of India; and Centre for Monitoring Indian Economy, Mumbai.

of these hills is generally rugged and vast areas are inaccessible. The total annual rainfall, commences from March to mid October, varies significantly across the regions. In Khasi and Jaintia Hills, annual intensity of rainfall reaches the maximum of about 1080 centimeters, around Cherrapunjee and Mawsynram (having highest rainfall in the world).

The total population of NER, as per 2001, is 38.5 millions and it constitutes about 3.75 per cent of the country's total population. The percentage growth rate of population is relatively decline in all the states of NER except Nagaland, where growth has been increasing from 56.08 per cent in 1981-91 to 64.41 per cent in 1991-2001. About 88 per cent of its total population live in rural areas and comparably higher to national average (75 per cent). Assam is most densely populated state in this region, having population of 26.6 million and the density of 340 per sq km. In contrast, Arunachal Pradesh is the least populous state in NER, having the density of 13 per sq km (Table 1).

The literacy percentage of NER, as per 2001, is quite high in NER, ranging from a low of 54.74 per cent in Arunachal Pradesh to a high of 88.49 per cent in Mizoram, as against country's average of 65.38 per cent. Most importantly, female literacy in all the NER states, except Arunachal Pradesh (44.2 per cent), is substantially higher than the national average of 54.2 per cent (Mohan, 2003). The Human Development Index (HDI[1]), in respect of Manipur and Mizoram in particular, as also for Nagaland and Tripura, has placed higher then national average in 1991. The Gender Development Index (GDI[2]) has also placed higher than national average in respect of these four states (NHDR, 2001). So far as economic development is concerned, NER has a low rank (Joseph, 2004). However in the case of health attainment and educational development, the performance of NER is quite high (Mohan, 2003). The incidence of poverty in NER has exposed in a downward trend. However, the percentage of population below the poverty line has placed higher than that of national average (26.1 per cent; GOI, 1999-2000). Most interestingly, poverty ratio of Mizoram (19.5%) is substantially lower in NER and also lower to country's average in the year 1999-2000. The sex ratio, as per 2001, of NER is 937, as against national figure of 933. The sex ratio is relatively high in Manipur (978) and relatively low in Nagaland (909) (Table 2).

Table 2
Social Indicators of North Eastern Regions of India, 2001

Items	*NER1*	*NER2*	*NER3*	*NER4*	*NER5*	*NER6*	*NER7*	*NER*	*India*
HDI	0.386	NA	NA	NA	NA	NA	NA	0.386	0.472
Literacy Rate	64.28	73.66	68.87	63.31	67.11	88.49	54.74	65.72	65.38
Life Expectancy	56.7	NA	NA	NA	NA	NA	NA	56.7	61.10
IMR	78	NA	NA	NA	NA	NA	NA	68	71
Sex Ratio	932	950	978	975	909	938	901	937	933
Poverty Ratio	40.3	NA	NA	NA	NA	NA	NA	34.72	26.10
IDI	104.4	92.85	83.5	77.6	89.89	84.49	71.89	86.37$	100

Note: HDI: Human Development Index; IMR: Infant Mortality Rate; IDI: Infrastructural Development Index; Na: Not available; and other notations are already defined earlier.

Source: Economic Survey, Government of India; Census of India, Government of India; National Human Development Report, Planning Commission of India; and Centre for Monitoring Indian Economy, Mumbai.

The region is predominantly tribal in composition. Except Assam (about 13 per cent), all other states are well above 30 per cent (See Table 1). The overall tribal population is account for 58.5 per cent in NER. However, the percentage is higher in Arunachal Pradesh, Meghalaya, Mizoram and Nagaland. The tribal population is mostly predominant in primary activities with inadequate infrastructural facilities and lack of secondary and tertiary activities. Besides, the complexity in number of tribes including sub-tribes, having distinct language, dialect, customs and institution, and being in different stages of socio-economic development is a challenge to our development pianners (Neog, 1997).

The average growth of SDP in NER is estimated as 6.0 per cent during 1996-97 to 2000-01. Although this is slightly higher than that of 5.7 per cent for the country as a whole, it masks marked fluctuations in growth rates over time in different states as well as the sharp disparities in growth rates across the states. The average per capita SDP of NER, except Nagaland, which is relatively higher among north eastern states, is substantially below to all India average (Rs. 9643) over the period 1995-96 to 2000-01 (Mohan, 2003). The per capita SDP, in contrast to NER, is also relatively high in Megahalaya and Arunachal Pradesh and substantially low in Assam, Tripura and Manipur (Table 3). In the sectoral contribution, the share of primary and tertiary sector is

Table 3
Per capita Net State Domestic Product at Constant Price (1993-94)

	1993-94	*94-95*	*95-96*	*96-97*	*97-98*	*98-99*	*99-00*	*00-01*
Assam	5715	5737	5760	5793	5796	5664	5978	6157
Tripura	5534	5364	5707	6239	6828	7396	7967	8372
Manipur	5833	5565	5612	6331	6770	7076	8147	7955
Meghalaya	6720	6705	7221	7225	7413	7935	8333	8460
Nagaland	9129	9410	9646	9880	10287	9188	8726	NA
Mizoram	NA	NA	NA	NA	NA	NA	NA	NA
Arunachal Pradesh	8612	8407	9424	8635	8693	8829	8580	9013
NER	6923	6865	7228	7350	7631	7681	7955	7991
India	7394	7745	7943	8416	8615	8936	9285	9508

Note: The figure of Mizoram is not available for the base year 1993-94.
Source: EPW Research Foundation, Mumbai.

relatively higher in all the states NER. It may be seen that, except few instances, the share of the primary sector to SDP has dwindled drastically over the years. On the other hand, the share of secondary and tertiary sector has been increasing in all most all the states of NER (Table 4).

The economy of NER is mainly rural and agrarian in nature (Nayak, 1997; Srivastava, 1998). In the industrial base, the scenario is not at all encouraging. The existence of industries as well as the shares of fixed capital, invested capital, net value-added and the number of workers in the industrial sector of NER, in contrast to all-India position, have declined over the period from 1995-96 to 1999-2000 (Mohan, 2003). In short, agriculture seems to be backbone of NER. About 80 per cent of the population dependent upon agriculture and agriculture employs nearly 68 per cent of total workforce of NER. The region offers scope for cultivation of a wide variety of agricultural crops due to its diversities in topography, altitude and climatic conditions. The extent of cultivable land in NER, however, varies from state to state. Land is the most critical resource in most of the north eastern states and its availability and management for agricultural activities are pre-requisite for raising the region's overall agricultural production and productivity. Moreover, the agricultural system of NER is predominantly traditional in nature (Ramakrishnan, 1993; Agarwala, 1996; Ganguly, 1997).

Table 4
Sectoral Distribution of (Per cent) Net State Domestic Product at Constant Price (1993-94)

	1993-94			*1996-97*			*1999-2000*		
States	*A*	*I*	*S*	*A*	*I*	*S*	*A*	*I*	*S*
Assam	42.07	19.34	38.59	39.89	19.02	41.09	39.38	21.48	39.14
Tripura	37.4	8.8	53.79	34.07	11.01	54.92	29.4	15.74	54.86
Manipur	37.87	15.73	46.4	32.76	18.66	48.58	29.01	21.56	49.43
Meghalaya	28.63	15.27	56.1	30.28	15.77	53.95	28.28	18.18	53.54
Nagaland	25.85	12.24	61.91	24.33	18.69	56.97	32.68	11.11	56.21
Mizoram	NA	NA	NA	NA	NA	NA	NA	NA	NA
Arunachal Pradesh	48.06	22.73	29.2	44.25	22.78	32.97	37.27	20.16	42.57
NER	36.65	15.69	47.67	34.26	17.66	48.08	32.67	18.04	49.29
India	32.75	23.94	43.31	30.62	24.68	44.7	25.2	21.83	52.97

Note: The figure of Mizoram is not available.
Source: EPW Research Foundation, Mumbai.

The high yielding verities programme has been successful in the irrigated valleys but has not touched other hill zones. The coverage of HYV area has been in increasing trend. But due to slow pace of infrastructure (Mahajan, 1996) and non-availability (timely) of essential agricultural inputs, the programme is improperly managed (Nayak, 1997). Fertilizer consumption in NER is relatively very low in comparison to national average. This is mostly due to defective fertilizer distribution system, lack of supply, inadequate transport, storage and credit facilities, raising cost of fertilizers and the occurrence of primitive techniques of production (Agarwala, 1996). Moreover, the green revolution, which involved seed technology, was not suitable in the hill areas, where horticulture development rather than crop production can usher in economic development (Mohan, 2003).

The overall geographical land per person of the NER is 0.81 hectares, which is much higher than the all India average of 0.39 per person. Among the NER states, the ratio is highest in Arunachal Pradesh (9.69 Hectares/Person) and lowest in Assam (0.35 Hectares/Person). About 80 per cent of the farmers in the NER belong to the small (<1.44 ha) and marginal (<0.40 ha) category. With the increase in population, average size of holdings is gradually reducing over the years. However, the average size of land holding for the NER (1.60 ha) is higher than the all India (1.57 ha) average. Among the states, average size of land holding is highest in Nagaland (6.92 ha) and lowest in Tripura (0.97 ha) [Table 5]. As a result, mechanization of agriculture and adoption of modern farming practices is not feasible in these small plot size and subsequently, subsistence farming is predominant in NER and thus, there is no more commercial surplus.

The cultivable area, as a percentage to geographical area, in NER (24.69 per cent) is less than that of national average (59.22 per cent). The percentage is highest in Meghalaya (47.88 per cent) and lowest in Arunachal Pradesh (3.50 per cent). The percentage utilization of cultivable area in NER (62.04 per cent) is also less than to national average (73.05 per cent) and mono cropping is the predominant method of cultivation. In the absence of multi-cropping, agricultural surplus is questionable. The utilization is lowest in Meghalaya (19.18 per cent) and highest in Tripura (89.35 per cent). Among the NER, Assam takes the highest position both in terms of available cultivable area and net sown area (Table 5). The performance of agriculture in NER is, however, uneven in nature (Agarwala,

Table 5
Average Size of Farm Holding and Percentage of Cultivated Area

	X_1	X_2	X_3	X_4	X_5	X_6	X_7	X_8
Assam	0.41	1.39	2.70	5.23	74.17	1.31	43.18	82.08
Tripura	0.40	1.53	2.69	5.14	121.57	0.97	29.56	89.35
Manipur	0.55	1.37	2.56	5.01	12.16	1.24	7.35	85.37
Meghalaya	0.54	1.38	2.54	5.48	13.0	1.81	47.88	19.18
Nagaland	0.69	1.43	2.92	6.34	16.85	6.92	37.76	33.71
Mizoram	0.62	1.57	2.78	4.0	0.0	1.34	21.11	24.49
Arunachal Pradesh	0.6	1.5	2.81	5.76	18.43	3.62	3.5	63.14
NER	0.43	1.41	2.70	5.56	25.2	1.6	24.69	62.04
India	0.40	1.44	2.76	5.9	17.3	1.57	59.22	73.05

Note: X_1: Marginal farm holding; X_2: Small farm holding; X_3: Semi-medium holding; X_4: Medium holding; X_5: Large holding; X_6: Average holding size; X_7: Cultivated area as percentage of total geographical area; X_8: Total net sown area as a percentage of total cultivated area; Figures of farm holding are in hectares; Data from X_1 to X_6 relates to the year 1990-91; and data relates to X_7 and X_8 relates to the year 1995-96.

Source: Centre for Monitoring Indian Economy, Mumbai.

1996; Nayak, 1997). In the period of 1986-87 to 1991-92, the compound annual growth rate (CAGR) of cultivated area in NER is 1.13 per cent and the growth of food grains production and its yield are 5.80 per cent and 4.62 per cent respectively. This is also higher than the national average of growth of area (-0.85 %), food grains production (3.26 per cent) and yield (4.15 per cent). But significantly in the period of 1991-92 to1996-97, the performance of NER is relatively lower then that of national average in all these three aspects (Table 6).

All in all, the performance of agriculture is not at all satisfactory in NER This is partly because of low usage of HYV seeds, fertilizers and other agricultural inputs. Besides, the uses of primitive techniques are also substantially responsible for the low performance of north east agriculture. Moreover, the use of modern inputs is simultaneously not feasible in the hill areas. Sometimes factors like lack of purchasing power, indifference, risk and uncertainty, ignorance, etc. also adversely affect the use of modern inputs (Neog, 1997).

Table 6
Progress of Agriculture (Food grains) in North Eastern Region of India

Items		*NER1*	*NER2*	*NER3*	*NER4*	*NER5*	*NER6*	*NER7*	*NER*	*India*
	Area	2579.8	286.0	173.0	138.8	147.0	52.7	175.0	3552.3	127197
1986-87	Production	2588	374.0	258.0	131.3	93.0	52.8	187.0	3684.1	143419
	Yield	1003	1308	1491	946	633	1002	1069	1037	1128
	Area	2749.9	272.5	164.3	133.5	182.4	66.0	188.7	3757.3	121871.2
1991-92	Production	3379.2	486.7	350.1	155.3	203.6	90.2	219.8	4664.9	168373.2
	Yield	1229	1786	2131	1163	1116	1367	1165	1300	1382
	Area	2728.7	272.7	172.5	133.1	199.5	77.5	186.8	3757.3	124509.5
1996-97	Production	3532.1	556.1	390.7	151.9	211.9	133.8	219.6	4664.9	199321.2
	Yield	1294	2039	2265	1141	1062	1726	1176	1300	1601
	Area	1.29	-0.96	-1.03	-0.78	4.41	4.60	1.52	1.13	-0.85
CARG 1	Production	5.48	5.41	6.30	3.41	16.97	11.30	3.28	5.80	3.26
	Yield	4.15	6.43	7.40	4.22	12.01	6.41	1.73	4.62	4.15
	Area	-0.15	0.01	0.98	-0.06	1.81	3.26	-0.20	0.07	0.43
CARG 2	Production	0.89	2.70	2.22	-0.44	0.80	8.21	-0.02	1.24	3.43
	Yield	1.04	2.69	1.23	-0.38	-0.99	4.77	0.19	1.17	2.99

Note: CARG 1: Compound annual growth rate for the period of 1986-87 to 1991-92; CARG2: Compound annual growth rate for the period of 1991-92 to 1996-97; and other notations are defined earlier.

Source: Centre for Monitoring Indian Economy, Mumbai.

The adverse impact of institutional changes has also severely affected the socio-economic environment and bio-diversity of NER. Most of such changes have been taking place in varying degrees in different states of NER. As a result, it goes against sustainable development and substantially affects the socio-economic conditions of the people (Ganguly, 1997). Furthermore, an existence of large-scale variation in socio-economic infrastructure across the states of NER affects the overall economic performance. This has also been investigated separately in the next section.

ANALYTICAL FRAMEWORK

The term development reflects an improvement in all sectors of the economy and is used to describe the process of economic and social transformation (Thirlwall, 1986). In the matters of development, some regions enjoy complete dominance over the others and some show moderate to a high degree of proximity among themselves. The identification of regional level of development is, however, a multi-dimensional process and requires an investigation in various socio-economic indicators like agriculture, industry, transport, communication, education, health, banking and many others.

Since the combination of all such indicators is more or less responsible for development, one should measure the overall level of development for each region. Moreover, the disparities of each region can be measured by projecting the above major group of indicators. In order to establish the same, an attempt has been made to formulate an overall composite index. The term composite index simply represents as a conversion of multi number of indicators to a single index of overall development. It is a very relevant tool for analyzing the regional disparities on the basis of chosen indicators of development.

There are several methods like Equal Weightage Indexing method, Deprivation method, taxonomic method and Principal Component Analysis (PCA) method are available to construct a composite index. However the present study applies PCA, as it helps in measuring economic development differential at various principal component levels as well as the aggregate level of development. The method of PCA is a special case of the more general method of factor analysis. The aim of PCA is to construct, out of set of variables, X_i's (I= 1, 2, ..., n), a new set of variables (P_i) called principal components, which are linear combination of the X's (Koutsoyiannis, 1978; Dadibhavi, 1986; Mallikarjun, 2002; Bhakar and Bhargava, 2002). Expressing it mathematically,

$$P_1 = a_{11}X_1 + \dots\dots\dots\dots + a_{1n} X_n$$

$$P_2 = a_{21}X_1 + \dots\dots\dots\dots + a_{2n} X_n$$

$$P_m = a_{m1} X_1 + \dots\dots\dots\dots + a_{mn} X_n$$

This can, further, be represented as in matrix form, which is as follows:

$$p_i = \sum_{i=1}^{m} \sum_{j=1}^{n} a_{ij} Z_{ij} \quad \text{...(1)}$$

Where, a_{ij}'s are called loadings of the factors (principal component) and are chosen in such a way that the constructed principal components satisfy two conditions. First, principal components are uncorrelated in nature. Second, first principal component P_1 absorbs and accounts for the maximum possible proportion of the total variation in the set X's, the second principal component absorbs the maximum of the remaining variation in the X's (after allowing for the variation accounted for by the first principal component) and so on. In this procedure, the data matrix is transformed to a new set of uncorrelated variables, which account as much of the variation as possible in descending order.

In PCA, as many principal components are formed as there are variables but only a first few of them are important, as they explain maximum proportion of the total variance in the original data. It may be that the first two or three of these variables (principal components) that accounts for substantial variation say 80 per cent to 90 per cent and the contribution of the remaining variables are relatively very small. In such circumstance, it becomes essential to derive the remaining principal components (Raza and Mahmood, 1998). The method of PCA can be applied by using the original values of the X_j's or the standardized variables Z_j, which is defined as $Z_{j} = X_{ij}/s_x$. Accordingly, the above representation can be represented as:

$$P_i = \frac{\sum_{i=1}^{9} \sum_{j=1}^{7} a_{ij} X_{ij}}{\sigma_{x_i}} \qquad ...(2)$$

Where, P_i = Principal components of ith items; i = 1, 2, ……., 9 items; j = 1, 2, …. 7 states; a_{ij} = Loadings of ith items in jth states; σ_{xi} = Standard deviation of ith items.

As per the previous literature (Agarwala, 1996; Ganguly, 1997; Srivastava, 1998), the study of socio-economic status of north eastern states mostly bounded by geographical variations, especially in terms of altitude, rainfall, soil characteristics, etc. The differences in socio-cultural practices of different tribal communities and their method of production practices also further affect the socio-economic status of NER. Besides, the non-availability of data in contrast to certain parameters makes the situation more worsen (Srivastava, 1998). Keeping in mind of above such problems, the present paper considers 15 selected indicators. These are as follows: Percentage of gross cropped area to total reported area, Percentage of gross irrigated area to gross cropped area, Per hectare consumption of chemical fertilizer (in kg), Percentage of villages electrified, Road length per 100 sq km, Railway route length per 100 sq km, Number of post office per lakh population, Number of bank branches per lakh population, Per capita bank credit, Per capita bank credit to agriculture, Per capita bank credit to industry, Number of primary health centers per lakh population, Number of hospital and dispensary beds per lakh population, Number of primary schools per lakh population and Number of middle/higher schools per lakh population.

It is to be noted here that the present paper deals with six different years for studying the socio-economic disparity of

NER. As a result, some of the variables, which may have substantial impact on socio-economic disparity in this region, have not been taken care simply because of its non-availability. The data used under this study are secondary in nature and have been collected from various sources like Centre for Monitoring Indian Economy, Mumbai; Economic Survey, Government of India; Economic and Political Weekly (EPW) Research Foundation, Mumbai and National Account Statistics, Government of India.

SPATIAL PATTERNS OF SOCIO-ECONOMIC DEVELOPMENT

To assess the overall level and topology of socio-economic development of seven sister states of north eastern states, fifteen different indicators for the five bench mark years, viz., 1980, 1985, 1990, 1995 and 2000 have been selected. The performance of such indicators in each state and NER as a whole, in contrast to national average, is not at all encouraging over the years except certain cases (Mohan, 2003). Moreover, socio-economic indicators reflect that there exists inter-regional disparity among the north east states (CMIE, 2002). Since our objective here is to examine the combined influence of each socio-economic indicator, we restrict our discussion to overall composite index.

It is substantially true that all the variables, which have been taken for the present analysis, seem to be mutually co-associated (either positively or negatively) with each other for all the five different years. However in the present analysis, we have subsequently chosen nine socio-economic indicators for constructing overall composite index in order to avoid negative weightage. These are: gross cropped area (in percentage), gross irrigated area (in percentage), consumption of chemical fertilizer (in kg), village electrification (in percentage), road length (per sq km), per capita bank credit (in rupees), bank credit to agriculture (in rupees), bank credit to industry (in rupees), and primary schools (in number).

The underlying concept here is to reduce a large number of variables into a smaller number of orthogonal factors/ components and explain the variation in the data matrix in terms of a relative few factors. These are independent linear combinations of the constituent variables and are called principal components and usually explain the maximum of total variation and represent as first principal component factor. The technique justifies its application, as it does explicitly take into account the problem of multicolinearlity among the original indicators by orthogolisation of whole set of variables and gives mathematical weights for constructing a composite index by a linear aggregation. The present study employed here only first principal component simply because it happens to be the linear combination of variates, ensuring the maximum sum of squares of the correlation co-efficient with variables.

Ensuring comparability of socio-economic infrastructure facilities for the five different periods under the study, coefficients obtained for the year 1980 data are used for construction of composite index of socio-economic infrastructure for the rest four years. The composite indices are presented in Table 7. The figures reflect that there exist regional disparities in socio-economic infrastructure across the states of north east India. The availability of socio-economic infrastructure is highest in Assam in all the years except 1990 and this is followed by Tripura and Nagaland. However, these facilities are lacking in the states of Mizoram, Arunachal Pradesh and Meghalaya.

Table 7
Infrastructure Development Index of North Eastern Regions of India

	1980	*1985*	*1990*	*1995*	*2000*
Assam	12.29	12.54	12.52	12.67	17.73
Tripura	9.02	9.492	13.91	12.36	17.00
Manipur	8.32	8.180	8.869	11.69	16.57
Meghalaya	7.75	8.429	8.657	13.56	14.11
Nagaland	9.91	12.53	11.75	13.05	15.43
Mizoram	3.62	6.653	7.640	10.70	12.30
Arunachal Pradesh	4.94	5.192	8.945	8.219	12.27
NER	7.98	9.108	10.47	11.76	15.06

Source: Calculated by author.

In the year 1980, the overall composite index value of north eastern region is 7.98 and corresponding to this average, Assam, Tripura and Nagaland are in above position and Manipur, Mizoram, Arunachal Pradesh and Meghalaya are in lower position. The situation is also very similar in the subsequent years. However, it is true that the overall performance of all the states of north eastern region is more or less improving over the years. Except few instances (Tripura in 1995 and Arunachal Pradesh in 1995), the trends of all the states as well as NER are relatively in upward direction. This reflects that, probably, there is subsequent emphasis has been given by the government in the form of investment in socio-economic infrastructure facilities in the states of north east India.

Interestingly, the performance of Mizoram is relatively better among all the states of NER, as its trend of overall composite index has been increasing over the years. This is probably due to the existence of low poverty ratio and high percentage of literacy in the state. Besides these peculiarities, regional disparities still exist in the north eastern states of India and over the years, the disparities seem to be relatively significant. A pair wise mean test has been conducted here to judge its statistical reliability. The results of this test have been reported in Table 8. In all the cases, the disparities are statistically significant either at the probability level of 1 per cent or 5 per cent except in the years between 1990 and 1995, where the significance level is at 10 per cent probability (See Table 8).

It is substantially true that an existence of regional disparity in socio-economic infrastructure retains economic growth in a great extent. To be specific, in the agricultural sector, it leads to increase productivity differential across the states. This is because of its complementary role towards agriculture. The above phenomenon is also well experienced in north eastern region of India, where the disparity is not only exist across the states and over the years but also statistically significant. No doubt that the performance of north east infrastructure is improving over the years, however comparing to other region of India, the performance is substantially poor. This could be justified through the help of infrastructural development index, which has been designed by Centre for Monitoring Indian Economy, Mumbai (CMIE, 2002). Most interestingly, the ranking in terms of rural infrastructure in NER are also high, contrary to the general impression (Mohan, 2003). Above all, there is a great need of policy implications for north eastern states for the further improvement in its socio-economic infrastructure.

Table 8
Paired Sample Test (t-test)

Pair of Year	*t-value*	*Significance level (Two tailed test)*
$Y_1 - Y_2$	-2.534	<0.039
$Y_1 - Y_3$	-3.769	<0.007
$Y_1 - Y_4$	-5.374	<0.001
$Y_1 - Y_5$	-16.395	<0.000
$Y_2 - Y_3$	-2.037	<0.081
$Y_2 - Y_4$	-4.165	<0.002
$Y_2 - Y_5$	-10.181	<0.000
$Y_3 - Y_4$	-1.840	<0.105
$Y_3 - Y_5$	-8.998	<0.000
$Y_4 - Y_5$	-5.641	<0.001

Note: Y_1: 1980; Y_2: 1985; Y_3: 1990; Y_4: 1995; and Y_5: 2000.
Source: Calculated by author.

CHALLENGES AND OPPORTUNITIES

The development of NER has remained agenda for both central government as well as perspective states government. Accordingly, North Eastern Council (NEC) has been set up in 1972, which plays a major role in this direction. As a regional planning body, it has taken up a series of projects for the balanced development of NER. Providing further focus to development initiatives in NER, government has established the Department of North Eastern Region (DONER) and subsequently, launched several programmes like Hill Area Development Programme (HADP) and Border Area Development Programme (BADP).

Furthermore, government has recently announced new industrial policy for the NER (December 1997), which encompassed a comprehensive incentive package for stimulating industrial development, and creation of a non-lapsable Central Resources Pool (1998-99) for ensuring speedy development of infrastructure in NER. There is also Prime Minister's Special Package of over Rs. 10000 crore for the socio-economic development of NER (January 2000). All in all, the region has not been lacking in policy attention and programmes.

In response to socio-economic development of NER, the region has following fortifies:

- Relatively high literacy rates and high human development, as compared to rest of the country.
- High skill levels in certain areas, especially in textiles.
- An abundant natural resource endowment. Especially, the forests of NER are rich in oil-based plants. There are huge prospects for oil based industries like agar wood oil, turpentine oil, cinnamon leaf oil, citronil oil, lemon grass oil and so on. These oils are particularly useful for cosmetics, varnishes, rubber, etc.
- There are at least 120 known medical plants are available in NER. Well-planned exploitation of these resources, through environmentally sustainable basis, can be used for the promotion of medical plant based drugs and pharmaceutical industries.
- Potential for the development of tourism industry and having potentiality for exports and regional cooperation.
- The agro-climate of NER has unique diversities and has a great potential for propagating horticulture crops including vegetables, fruits and flowers.
- NER is blessed with variety of silk worms, mulberry, muga, tussar and eri. The silk fabrics of NER are already well known and fetch relatively high prices. A better marketing of these products certainly widespread in India and abroad.

- It is a gateway to the ASEAN, which is one of the fastest growing potential markets today and has proximities to the SAARC countries for growing international trade through SAPTA.
- Discussions are already underway for the enhancement of regional cooperation in the BIMST-EC. The cooperation has identified six sectors- trade and investment, energy, fisheries, tourism, technology and communication and transport for cooperation. Among them, first four sectors have a comparative advantage to NER (Mohan, 2003).

In short, NER has locational advantage and endowed with rich natural resources like oil and natural gas, agro and forest-based products and scenic surroundings, which provides a backdrop to its development as a base for foreign investors.

RECOMMENDATIONS

In response to the above discussions, the paper comes out with following suggestions:

- There is a great need of improving socio-economic infrastructure, in terms of both quantity and quality, in NER. Special importance should be given to the states like Mizoram, Meghalaya, Manipur and Arunachal Pradesh.
- There is necessitate of popularizing the issue and importance of socio-economic infrastructure facilities and this needs creating awareness among the people of NER.
- There is need of stressing research and development activities in NER, which can forecasts and suggests the issue of socio-economic infrastructure as per the needs of each state.
- Establish interlinking among sectoral activities along with antipoverty programmes and other rural developmental programmes.
- Introduce appropriate technology in NER with respect to each states requirement. This requires the need based

research and training approaches, ensuring quick transfer of technology to each state and different farmer's land.

- Eradicate socio-economic problems of NER, which is essentially related with large number of ethnic groups.
- Avoid community ownership of land and small size of operational holding. This certainly troubles the use of socio-economic infrastructure in the agriculture.
- There must be necessary political will for effecting genuine decentralization of power and investment of resources for the equitable development of the socio-economic sector.
- There is strongly need of proactive public policy to induce more investment in backward NER, either through public investment or through fiscal incentives. An effort is also made to encourage private investment in the above area.
- Minimize the effect of adverse ecological balance due to deforestation. This may be recovered by putting stress on non-farm activities in the region, especially by establishing eco-friendly industries like electronics, watch making, etc. Appropriate training should also be imparted to the local people, to equip them with necessary skills, to get them employed in such industries.

To conclude, with the issues and problems associated with NER, there is great need of balance distribution of socio-economic infrastructure in the region. It helps in mechanizing agriculture, which seems to be backbone of north east, and also attracts other developmental activities in the region. This necessitates government should come out with a well-defined state policy on socio-economic infrastructure. Central government also needs to be intervened to find a lasting solution. Besides, all the development agencies, which exist in NER, should suitably reorient and amend their approach and pattern of assistance and provides support for overcoming the problems of socio-economic infrastructure. This will ensure balanced and rapid regional development in NER. All in all, a new formidable approach is essentially needed in NER so that the resources available in the region are utilized properly for the fullest possible along with the resources that come into the region from outside.

NOTE

1. HDI: Human Development Index, which usually captures through economic, educational and health attainments.
2. GDI: Gender Disparity Index, which captures the proportion of female attainments to that of males for a common set of variables.
3. ASEAN: Association of South East Asian Nation.
4. SAARC: South Asian Association of Regional Cooperation.
5. SAPTA: South Asian Preferential Trading Agreement.
6. BIMST-EC: Bangladesh, India, Myanmar, Sri Lank, Thailand-Economic Cooperation.

REFERENCES

Agarwala, A. K. (1996), "Agricultural System and Behaviour in North Eastern States", in V. S. Mahajan (ed) Agriculture, Rural Development and Panchayati Raj, pp. 811-822, New Delhi: Deep and Deep Publications.

Agarwala, A. K. and P. L. Hazarika (2002), "Regional Disparities in Economic Development of Assam: A District Level Study". *Indian Journal of Regional Science,* Vol. 34, No. 2, pp. 121-136.

Ahluwalia, M. S. 2000 "Economic Performance of States in Post-reforms Period". *Economic and political Weekly,* Vol. 35, No. 19, pp. 1637-1648.

Barro, R. J. (1991), "Economic Growth in a Cross Section of Countries". *Quarterly Journal of Economics,* Vol. 106, No. 2, pp. 407-433.

Basak, C. M. (2002), "Urban Housing Development Strategies of the North Eastern Region of India". *Indian Journal of Regional Science,* Vol. 35, No. 1, pp. 48-52.

Bhakar, R. R. and P. Bhargava (2002), "Disparities in Infrastructural Development in Rajasthan". *Indian Journal of Regional Science,* Vol. 35, No. 1, pp. 57-66.

Bhattacharya, B. B. and S. Sakthivel (2004), "Regional Growth and Disparity in India: Comparison of Pre-and Post-Reforms Decades". *Economic and Political Weekly,* Vol. 39, No. 10, pp. 1071-1077.

CMIE (2002), Centre for Monitoring Indian Economy, Mumbai.

Dadibhavi, R. V. (1986), "Regional Disparities in Agricultural Infrastructure Development: A Study of Karnataka". Indian Journal of Economics, Vol. 67, No. 264, pp. 75-87.

Deshpande, R. S., L. Venkatachalam and A. Narayanamoorthy (2002), "Policies for Access, Equity and Equality: Physical Resources and Human Resources", in Sustainable Agriculture Water Resources Development and Earth Care Policies, pp. 140-168, New Delhi: Bhoovigyan Vikas Foundation.

Dreze, J and A. Sen (1999), Indian Development-Selected Regional Perspectives, New Delhi: Oxford University Press.

Dutta, P. C. (2002), "Development of Social Forestry in Assam of North Eastern Region". *Indian Journal of Regional Science,* Vol. 34, No. 2, pp. 52-62.

Ganguly, J. B. (1997), "Structural Changes in Jhum-based Economy and Growing Inequalities in North-Eastern Tribal Society", in M. C. Behera and N. C. Roy (ed) Trends in Agrarian Structure in the Hills of North-East India, pp. 87-98, New Delhi: Commonwealth Publications.

GOI (1976), Report of the National Commission on Agriculture, Part-XIII, Ministry of Agriculture, New Delhi: Government of India.

GOI (2002-03), Economic Survey, Ministry of Finance, New Delhi: Government of India.

Joseph, M. (2004), "Performance of the Northern States: A Comparative Analysis". Economic and Political Weekly, Vol. 39, No. 6, pp. 564-579.

Koutsoyiannis, A. (1978), Theory of Econometrics-An Introductory Exposition of Economic Method, New Delhi: MacMillan Press.

Mahajan, V. S. (1996), "Poverty Alleviation in North-East- Basic Groundwork Should be Prepared First", in V. S. Mahajan (ed) Agriculture, Rural Development and Panchayati Raj, pp. 807-810, New Delhi: Deep and Deep Publications.

Mallikarjun, M. (2002), "Intra Regional Disparities in Economic Development". *Indian Journal of Regional Science,* Vol. 34, No. 1, pp. 1-11.

Mohan, R. (2003), "Economic Development of the North East Region: Some Reflections". *Reserve Bank of India Bulletin,* Vol. 12, December, pp. 925-937.

Nagaraj, R., A. Aristomene and M. A. Veganzones (1998), "Long-run Growth Trends and Convergence across Indian States", OECD Technical papers, No. 131, pp. 1-58.

NAS (2000), National Accounts Statistics, CSO, New Delhi: Government of India.

Nayak, B. D. (1997), "The Trends of Agrarian Structure and Its Impact on Agriculture in North-Eastern Hill Region of India", in M. C. Behera and N. C. Roy (ed) Trends in Agrarian Structure in the Hills of North-East India, pp. 25-31, New Delhi: Commonwealth Publications.

Nayak, N. C. (2002), "Human Development in India in Post-reforms Period: Issues and Challenges", in Azali et al. (ed) *Asia Pacific Economics and Business Conference Proceedings,* Vol. 1, pp. 335-344, Serdang: Universiti Putra Malaysia Press.

Neog, A. K. (1997), "Transforming Hill Agriculture in Tribal Areas of North East India", in M. C. Behera and N. C. Roy (ed) Trends in Agrarian Structure in the Hills of North-East India, pp. 99-108, New Delhi: Commonwealth Publications.

NHDR (2001), National Human Development Report, Planning Commission, New Delhi: Government of India.

Pradhan, R. P. (2004), "Human Development in India: A Present Scenario". Management Trends, Vol. 1, No. 1, pp. 26-35.

RBI (2003), Reserve Bank of India Bulletin, Mumbai: Government of India.

Ramakrishnan, P. S. (1993), Shifting Agriculture and Sustainable Development: An Interdisciplinary Study from North Eastern India, New Delhi: Wiley Eastern Publications.

Rao, M. G., R. T. Shand and K. P. Kalirajan (1999), "Convergence of Incomes across Indian States- A Divergent View". *Economic and Political Weekly,* Vol. 34, No. 13, March 27- April 2.

Raza, M and A. Mahmood (1998), Statistical Methods in Geographical Studies, 4th Edition, New Delhi: Rajesh Publications.

Shand, R. and S. Bhide (2000), "Sources of Economic Growth- Regional Dimensions of Reforms". *Economic and Political Weekly,* Vol. 35, No. 41, pp. 3747-3757.

Shivakumar, A. K. (1997), "Poverty and Human Development: The Indian Experience". Human Development Report, UNDP, New York: Oxford University Press.

Singh, H. P. (1993), "Regional Development and Planning in India: A Review", in R. S. Tripathi and R. P. Tiwari (ed) Regional Disparities and Development in India, pp. 1-33. New Delhi: Ashish Publications.

Srivastava, S. C. (1998), "Development and Disparity: Agriculture in North East India", *Indian Journal of Economics,* Vol. 79, No. 313, pp. 195-217.

Thirlwall, A. P. 1986, Growth and Development with Special Reference to Developing Economies, New Delhi: MacMillan Press.

HDR 2002, Human Development Report, UNDP, New York: Oxford University Press.

WDR 2004, World Development Report, UNDP, New York: Oxford University Press.